A Gift From
Pastor & Mrs. Silva

MERRY CHRISTMAS!

Dedication

To my wife Denise, who for thirty-six years has been by my side and fully supported me during my military career.

To our sons, Josh and JohnMichael, who, from their birth through childhood, selflessly served their country by sharing their father during my time in service.

To our grandson, Cooper, to whom falls the honor of continuing the family name that is rich with a long line of veterans.

Table of Contents

Acknowledgements

Special thanks to all the men and women who have served our country and the spouses and children who have been by their sides, including those in our family and those who have been a part of the Navigators connection group at Lancaster Baptist Church. A special thanks also to missionaries to the US military, who minister to those in uniform and their families.

Without the painstaking research performed by my wife, Denise, this devotional would not have been possible. I am grateful, not only for the many hours she put into checking dates, finding pertinent topics, and sending me the "seed" thoughts that became the subject matter for many of these devotionals, but also for her countless prayers that this would become a reality and blessing to all who read it. I owe her a debt of gratitude.

Thank you also to Mike and Sue Hauenstein, who, more than thirty years ago, shared with us the good news of salvation and led us to a saving knowledge of the Lord Jesus Christ.

Finally, thank you to Dr. Paul Chappell, who has been our pastor for over twenty-three years. His love, leadership, teaching, and mentorship in our lives has been monumental and we are eternally grateful.

A Note from the Author

Dear Friend,

The use of military field manuals in the western world dates back as early as the fourth century when Flavius Vegetius Renatus, a Roman military expert, wrote a treatise entitled *De Re Militari (The Military Institutions of the Romans).* From the time of Charlemagne, it was not uncommon for medieval battle commanders to have a copy of Vegetius' work on their person when on campaign.

The phrase *boots on the ground,* from which the title of this devotional is derived, comes from a news interview in 1980 when US Army General Volney Frank Warner discussed the military's ability to rapidly deploy troops to respond to a contingency. A scriptural parallel is seen in Matthew 9:38 as the Lord Jesus Christ told us to pray for more laborers to enter the harvest fields. One might say He was asking for more "boots on the ground."

The Christian life is not intended for those who want to be in the rear with the gear. It calls for a response; it necessitates boots on the ground as we soldier on through the daily challenges of living and witnessing for Christ. The devotions in this book are designed to be something of a field manual for the Christian soldier, encouraging and equipping you to "fight the good fight of faith" (1 Timothy 6:12).

As a veteran of the United States Air Force who served my country for twenty-five years, I am sensitive to the unique challenges military couples face and have written this book with you in mind. In particular, I'm excited to think of this being a resource for shared spiritual connection when one spouse is deployed.

For those readers who are not in the military, I pray this book is an encouragement to you as well, and I ask you to pray for those in active duty. They endure hardships that a civilian cannot possibly understand. Additionally, pray for the family members of those in uniform who are often left to take up the slack of running the home and raising the children while their loved one is deployed. Finally, pray for our veterans. Our nation has not always offered the thanks that is owed to these treasured heroes.

Regarding the cover art for this book, my wife suggested the various articles depicted. The Bible is my personal study Bible. I wear the boots and the helmet during World War II reenactment events. The dog tags are a replica of the ones worn by my great uncle, Norris Byron Wells, Jr., who was killed in action on 28 August 1944 in Southern France during the Battle of Montelimar. (See the devotion given on 26 November for an amazing story of his last days and legacy.) The first-aid pouch is a replica of the type carried by World War II paratroopers.

Each daily reading in *Boots on the Ground* is written to point every reader—military, veteran, or civilian—to Christ and to His Word. Each reading begins with a verse or passage from the Bible and then provides a story from military history and a devotional truth based on the Scripture passage. At the bottom of each page, you will find references for your longer-form Bible reading. You can follow these references to read through the entire Bible or simply the New Testament in a year.

In the back of the book, the publisher has included some tools for effective Christian growth as well as a few additional Bible reading schedules. Also in the back is a Scripture index listing on which page each verse or reference in the book is mentioned.

Throughout these pages, you will come across devotions that emphasize our need for eternal salvation, which can only come through Jesus Christ. If you do not yet know Christ as your personal Saviour, I would especially like to point you to page 385, which presents God's wonderful plan of salvation, as well as to the devotions given on 29 and 30 June, in which my wife Denise and I share our personal testimonies of coming to faith in Christ.

Whether you are a new Christian or have known the Lord for decades, it is my prayer that each devotion in *Boots on the Ground* will point you to God's Word, strengthen your walk with Christ, and encourage you in your spiritual battle.

Sincerely in Christ,
MSgt Randy Wells, USAF, Ret.

JANUARY

Peace Treaty

1 January 1698

For he is our peace, who hath made both one, and hath broken down the middle wall of partition between us;—**Ephesians 2:14**

During the 1620s, France and England each laid claim to portions of the northeastern area of North America. France controlled the St. Lawrence River Valley, which encompassed Ontario and Quebec, while England controlled the northeastern seaboard. Between these two areas lay a vast region inhabited by the Abenaki Indians. Following the great migration of Puritans to the New England coast, the French and English continued their relationship with the Abenakis through trading, standing as their allies against rival tribes, and seeking their aid in conflicts with one another. However, this in no way guaranteed a peaceful coexistence between the Abenakis and the Europeans. Since the Abenakis had closer ties to the French than the English, it was common for Abenaki warriors to attack English settlements along the Massachusetts frontier.

A particularly brutal incident occurred in July 1694 when Abenaki warriors attacked the town of Groton, Massachusetts, killing twenty colonists and capturing twelve. Over the next three years, this would be a familiar theme between Massachusetts's colonists and the Abenaki Indians. Relations changed, however, on 1 January 1698, when the colonists and Abenakis signed a peace treaty.

Those of us who know Christ as our personal Saviour have an even greater peace than the peace between two nations. Through the atonement of the Lord Jesus Christ, we find our peace with God. Romans 5:1–2 tells us, "Therefore being justified by faith, we have peace with God through our Lord Jesus Christ: By whom also we have access by faith into this grace wherein we stand, and rejoice in hope of the glory of God."

Praise the Lord today for the peace Christ has provided us with God. And look for an opportunity to share this message of peace with someone who does not yet have "peace with God through our Lord Jesus Christ."

Gaining Victory through Revival

2 January 1492

Wilt thou not revive us again: that thy people may rejoice in thee?—**Psalm 85:6**

School children remember the year 1492 as the date "Columbus sailed the ocean blue" and discovered the New World. But the year began with another significant event—the ending of the Granada War on 2 January. The end of this war was also the end of the 780-year Spanish Reconquista.

In AD 711, a Muslim group, the Umayyad Caliphate, took over the Iberian Peninsula, driving out the Visigoths, who had converted to Nicene Christianity in the late sixth century. For the next three hundred years, Muslim Moors ruled what is now called Southern Spain.

Once the Crusades began in the eleventh century, however, the idea of a Catholic reconquest, referred to today as the Spanish Reconquista, took hold in much of Western Europe. In fact, the spread of Roman Catholicism was seen as necessary to further the progression of Western civilization.

In 1482, the Granada War began and eventually overwhelmed the Moors and conquered Grenada. After the war, Grenada's Muslims were forced to either convert to Roman Catholicism, become slaves, or face exile.

The idea that true conversion could come through physical threat or that salvation comes through a church rather than through Christ is not only false according to the Bible, but it was also cruel according to history. Nevertheless, there is a personal application we can consider through the idea of the Spanish Reconquista—restoration of what has been lost.

As born-again Christians, we can't lose our salvation, but we can lose our joy and fervency for the Lord (Psalm 51:12). The Christian journey holds daily spiritual battles, and sometimes we lose to the attacks of Satan and the flesh. Our tendency is to give up or become complacent. But, God invites us to humbly confess these defeats and sin to Him and ask Him to revive our spiritual lives. Through the revival God brings to our hearts, He restores our joy and gives us the strength to live in the victory Christ has provided.

New Regime

3 January 1868

For this is the will of God, even your sanctification,—**1 Thessalonians 4:3**

In 1600, a medieval Samurai warrior named Tokugawa Ieyasu ended hundreds of years of Samurai warfare with the establishment of the Tokugawa Shogunate. Similar to the ancient Greek oligarchy, the Shogunate was a centralized "feudal" system in which more than two hundred clans, or han, maintained fiscal and military autonomy while their lords served as part of Tokugawa's authoritarian government. From Tokugawa's rule and for the next 250 years, the Shogunate presided over a dynasty that focused on reestablishing order in social, political, and international affairs. To that end, this dynasty prohibited trade with Western nations and excluded Christian missionaries. Following US Navy Commodore Matthew Perry's arrival in 1854, Japan opened up trade with America and the Shogunate's days were numbered.

On 3 January 1868, Japanese Emperor Meiji orchestrated a coup d'état when the incumbent Shogun resigned. Known as the Meiji Restoration, the event transformed Japan into a modern state by establishing new technology and transportation, as well as restructuring and strengthening their military.

The Meiji Restoration reminds us of the salvation and sanctification processes in a Christian's life. Salvation is that single moment of choice to trust fully in Christ's sacrifice on the cross as payment for our sin. At this moment, the Holy Spirit takes up residence in our lives and begins a transformation process from within. This process is called "sanctification."

The Meiji Restoration started the process of transformation, but it took time to modernize the country. Similarly, the Holy Spirit takes up residence when we accept Christ, but the work that He begins in us takes a lifetime. Sanctification begins at salvation, but we must make the daily choice to submit to and follow the Holy Spirit's leading in our lives.

Change of Plans

4 January 1913

Trust in the LORD with all thine heart; and lean not unto thine own understanding. In all thy ways acknowledge him, and he shall direct thy paths.—**Proverbs 3:5–6**

Field Marshal Alfred von Schlieffen is best remembered as the mastermind behind the strategy which Germany used during the early hours of World War I. The German High Command recognized that the best method to hold off the mounting Russian mobilization in the East was a rapid "knockout blow" in the West. Field Marshal Schlieffen advocated attacking France via Belgium and Holland and then shifting German forces back to the Eastern Front to blunt the Russian advance. On paper, the plan looked like a success, but, in practice, technological innovations such as the machine gun stymied the German advance and resulted in the war settling into a stalemate of trench warfare.

Schlieffen never saw his plan carried out as he died on 4 January 1913. Twenty-six years later, as Adolf Hitler and his top brass planned their spring offensive into Western Europe in 1940, Germany dusted off Schlieffen's plan. A German general, however, convinced Hitler to try a different plan . . . the Manstein Plan. This adjusted strategy proved decisive as German tanks and troops pushed through the rugged Ardennes Forest, eventually capturing Paris in June. Had the Germans followed the Schlieffen Plan, the French might have been better prepared since they had been at the receiving end of that plan once before.

It has been said, "Man proposes, but God disposes." Man's plans are never a successful guarantee. When we place our plans ahead of God's revealed Word, we are bound for failure. This is why we must trust in the Lord and follow His Word. He promises that when we do, He will direct our paths.

Our plans often need to change to align with unforeseen challenges. But God never changes, and when we trust in Him, we can be confident in His guidance in our lives.

Patience Brings Triumph

5 January 62 BC

Wait on the LORD: be of good courage, and he shall strengthen thine heart: wait, I say, on the LORD.—**Psalm 27:14**

The Roman consulship was an elected office in which two men served jointly for a one-year term. During battle, the consuls rotated overall command of the famed Roman legions every other day. A consulship was a highly respected position of power during the Republican era.

Lucius Sergius Catiline hailed from an aristocratic Roman family, and from an early age, aspired to be a Roman consul. Ambitious Catiline worked hard to establish himself as a force in the Republic, impressively performing the normal political and military duties required for consul.

Unfortunately, Catiline's attempts to gain the consulship were frustrated twice by political rivals. Rather than exercise patience to try again, he decided to seize the consulship by force. Though the record is sketchy, Catiline seems to have been involved in several plots, including one to assassinate both sitting consuls in 65 BC. When these plots failed, he managed to gather a coalition of disgruntled Roman army veterans who were unhappy with General Sulla. When word reached Consul Marcus Tullius Cicero, Catiline and his army fled Rome. The Roman Senate quickly dispatched its finest legions to destroy Catiline. On 5 January 62 BC, Catiline gave a speech to his men right before engaging the Roman legions. Catiline and his troops perished during this battle. Had Catiline simply waited, he might have gained the consulship without bloodshed.

Many times, Christians get ahead of God and frustrate His plans to bless them. When a trial comes, we try to fix it ourselves instead of seeking God's plan within the trial. Realizing that trials are there for a God-ordained purpose is part of the growing process for every Christian. As Romans 5:3–5 says, "And not only so, but we glory in tribulations also: knowing that tribulation worketh patience; And patience, experience; and experience, hope: And hope maketh not ashamed; because the love of God is shed abroad in our hearts by the Holy Ghost which is given unto us."

Choose Your Allies Wisely

6 January 1950

Make no friendship with an angry man; and with a furious man thou shalt not go: Lest thou learn his ways, and get a snare to thy soul.—**Proverbs 22:24–25**

In 1949, the Chinese Nationalist movement under Chiang Kai-shek was toppled by Communist leader Mao Tse-tung. On 6 January 1950, the United Kingdom officially accorded diplomatic recognition to the People's Republic of China. Many questioned Britain's decision to abandon her support for the Nationalist Chinese Government, a government with whom it was allied with during World War II. Winston Churchill summed up the reasons best when he said in November 1949, "The reason for having diplomatic relations [with Communist China] is not to confer a compliment, but to secure a convenience." Without a favorable diplomatic platform, the United Kingdom feared its opportunity to influence events in the Far East would be jeopardized. Apparently, having influence was more important than taking a stand against Communism.

The Bible speaks much on associations, alliances, and friendships. King Solomon foolishly allied himself with the Pharaoh of Egypt and married his daughter. Israel's King Menahem gave his country's tax money to the wicked king of Assyria for military support. King Jehoshaphat joined forces with King Ahab, one of the worst kings of Israel. The Bible uses examples of how the foolish choice of an ally brought about disaster, but it also speaks of victories because of a good ally, as in the case of Jonathan and his armor bearer. And Ecclesiastes 4:9 tells us that "two are better than one; because they have a good reward for their labour."

Today, more than any other time in history, Christians must guard their choice of allies. We should work to ally ourselves with those who will make us stronger spiritually and influence us for good. If we ally ourselves with the wrong influences, we will bear the consequences for our alliances, and we may even then become a wrong influence to others.

Be a friend to anyone, and share the gospel with everyone. But, choose your alliances and influences wisely.

Genesis 16–17 // Matthew 5:27–48

Using the Available

7 January 1709

And the LORD said unto him, What is that in thine hand? And he said, A rod.
—Exodus 4:2

At the outset of the eighteenth century, Sweden was a major European superpower due to the military reforms of Swedish King Gustavus Adolphus (1594–1632). At the turn of the century, Sweden's neighbors formed a coalition against her to reduce her power. Peter the Great of Russia, Augustus II of Poland, and Frederick IV of Denmark attacked Sweden's allies in April 1700. For the next twenty-one years, Sweden fought against the Russians, Poles, and Danes in what became known as the Great Northern War.

The Swedes were renowned for their fierce battle tactics. Arranged in four lines, Swedish battalions would hurl themselves upon enemy defenses. At a distance of seventy paces, the first two lines of troops would suddenly stoop over, allowing the soldiers behind to fire a blasting volley. The charge would resume with the men in the front firing their weapons at point blank range. A general melee would then ensue as the Swedes attempted to finish off their enemies in hand-to-hand combat.

But on 7 January 1709, the Swedes suffered a major loss (four hundred killed and six hundred wounded) when they tried to besiege a Ukrainian outpost at Veprik. The Russian defenders poured water over the tops of their earthworks transforming them into walls of ice, so the Swedes were unable to scale the fortress and became sitting ducks for Russian muskets.

If the Russians had tried to use the same fighting strategies as the Swedes, they would have failed. Instead, they used what was already in their hands to gain the victory. Many Christians struggle with doing God's will for their lives because they compare their abilities, talents, education, finances, or opportunities to others. God will use anyone who is willing and available, regardless of abilities or disabilities. So rather than wasting time comparing and making excuses, we should look for unique ways to serve God with the abilities and opportunities He has placed before us.

Genesis 18–19 // Matthew 6:1–18

Revealed Glory

8 January 1806

And when Joseph had taken the body, he wrapped it in a clean linen cloth, and laid it in his own new tomb, which he had hewn out in the rock: and he rolled a great stone to the door of the sepulchre, and departed.—**Matthew 27:59–60**

On 8 January 1806, an unprecedented funeral was held in England. Down the Thames River, nobility and foreign dignitaries accompanied a casket in a royal funeral barge that was topped with an elaborate black canopy, adorned with black ostrich feathers. This maritime procession stretched from Greenwich to Whitehall in London. The following day, a warship-shaped hearse took the casket through the streets of London to St. Paul's Cathedral with admirals, ship captains, and thousands of soldiers accompanying the hearse. In both parades, thousands of grieving citizens paid tribute to the fallen. The funeral service lasted four hours.

While an outpouring of this magnitude is typically reserved for royalty, the man lying in the casket was the warrior Admiral Horatio Nelson, who had achieved a spectacular victory over a superior force and thus delivered England from the shadow of oppression. His stunning victory over Napoleon at the Battle of Trafalgar secured his place as England's most famous seafarer. During that decisive battle, Nelson had been struck down and died. He met his death at his greatest triumph.

The contrast between Admiral Nelson's lavish funeral and the simple acts of Joseph of Arimathea at Jesus Christ's funeral is astounding. Matthew's gospel humbly records that Jesus' burial had no fanfare, no gathered mourners, and certainly none of the pomp associated with Nelson's death. He, who "endured such contradiction of sinners against himself" (Hebrews 12:3), was wrapped in linen and placed in a cave after His death. While the world increasingly looks for ways to squelch the influence of Christ, there is soon coming a day when He will split the eastern sky and return as He promised. When that day occurs, all that has been highly esteemed among men will pale in comparison to His revealed glory.

A Deceptive Outlook

9 January 1493

There is a way which seemeth right unto a man, but the end thereof are the ways of death.—**Proverbs 14:12**

One of the most familiar tales of global exploration is that of Italian explorer, Christopher Columbus. In 1492, Columbus received permission and provision from the dual monarchy of Castile and Aragon to explore the Atlantic. During his first of four voyages, Columbus reached what he perceived was India, which in essence was the modern-day Bahamas.

Three months later, on 9 January 1493, while Columbus sailed to Hispaniola, he spotted three "mermaids" and described them as "not half as beautiful as they are painted." Mermaids are mythical half-female, half-aquatic creatures that have supposedly existed in seafaring cultures since the time of the ancient Greeks. In reality, Columbus observed three manatees, not mermaids. Manatees are slow-moving, aquatic mammals with human-like eyes, bulbous faces and paddle-like tails.

Columbus was convinced he had seen mermaids during his voyage, when, in fact, he was merely observing an animal of which Europeans had no prior knowledge. Often, our hearts deceive us into believing something that is not true. For example, many are convinced that their good works will gain them entrance into Heaven when this life ends. Others believe that "God helps those who help themselves." Neither of these outlooks are found in God's Word, and both find their basis in the ignorance of biblical truth.

Jeremiah 17:9 says, "The heart is deceitful above all things, and desperately wicked: who can know it?" We should never trust our hearts as a source of wisdom or direction. We must be careful that we do not equate our feelings with truth, but that we base our beliefs on what the Bible says. Eternity is too long to be mistaken about getting to Heaven, and time on Earth is too short to believe in the deceptions of our hearts.

No Going Back

10 January 49 BC

And Jesus said unto him, No man, having put his hand to the plough, and looking back, is fit for the kingdom of God.—**Luke 9:62**

The term "crossing the Rubicon" has become an aphorism for making a determined decision with no thought of turning back. In 59 BC, Julius Caesar had manipulated his way to the position of Roman consul. After serving a year in that position, he invaded Gaul and, over the next seven years, effectively subdued the native Celtic and Germanic tribes.

Ceasar's popularity with the Roman people set him at odds with the Roman Senate, who eventually called upon him to resign his command and disband his legions. Pompey, a rival of Caesar, was entrusted with enforcing the edict. Caesar was faced with a huge decision: either acquiesce to the Senate or move southward, crossing the Rubicon River, to confront Pompey and plunge the Roman Republic into a civil war. An ancient Roman law forbade any general from crossing the Rubicon River and entering Italy proper with a standing army; to do so was considered treason.

On 10 January 49 BC, Julius Caesar brought his troops to the banks of the Rubicon and turned to his men, crying, "Still we can retreat! But once let us pass this little bridge, and nothing is left but to fight it out with arms!" With that, Caesar crossed the Rubicon followed by his loyal, trusting men.

Someone once said, "Every disciple of Christ is saved, but not everyone saved is a disciple." Surrendering all to Christ equates to spiritually crossing the Rubicon. Just as Caesar's men had to count the cost of following their leader, a Christian must be willing to count the cost of following Christ. Caesar's men trusted him not knowing the outcome, yet we as Christians sometimes struggle to trust our leader even though we know He wins in the end. Our surrender to His plan and strategy for spiritual warfare should be no harder than following a human leader into battle. When we make the final decision to follow Christ with no thought of turning back, we will ultimately see the victories despite the opposition.

Sin's Reparations

11 January 1923

For we know that the law is spiritual: but I am carnal, sold under sin.
—**Romans 7:14**

Reparation refers to the compensation imposed upon a vanquished country to be paid to the victors following the cessation of hostilities. After World War I, the Treaty of Versailles forced Germany to pay 132 billion gold marks to cover civilian damage caused during the war. The primary benefactors of these payments were France and Belgium, due to the number of battles fought within those two countries. When Germany reneged on making payments, French and Belgian troops occupied the industrial Ruhr region of Germany on 11 January 1923. The Ruhr occupation, which would last almost three years, caused outrage in Germany. The Weimar government of Germany encouraged trade unions still working in the Ruhr to organize strikes to halt industrial production. Then, when Germany was unable to pay its workers, the last resort was to print extra bank notes, a policy that fueled the hyperinflation of 1923. All of these events traced back to the reparations imposed on Germany.

The apostle Paul concluded "that the law is spiritual: but I am carnal, sold under sin" (Romans 7:14). Until a person receives Christ as their Saviour, they are like a defeated nation that must continually pay reparations to the victor. Satan is a cruel taskmaster and demands continuing payments.

Once we trust Christ as our Saviour, however, the Bible declares that we are "freed from sin" (Romans 6:7). Even so, many Christians believe the lies of Satan by yielding to their flesh and lusts, living as if the reparations and weight of sin are still present. Romans 6:1–2 speaks of this: "What shall we say then? Shall we continue in sin, that grace may abound? God forbid. How shall we, that are dead to sin, live any longer therein?" Do not live a defeated life. Remember that Christ has freed you from sin, and live in the victory He has provided.

Unwelcome Persecution

12 January 1493

Yea, and all that will live godly in Christ Jesus shall suffer persecution.
—2 Timothy 3:12

In 63 BC, Roman Consul Pompey the Great laid siege to the city of Jerusalem. The ancient Jewish historian Josephus reported that a large number of Jews were taken to Sicily to serve as slaves. Under the reign of Holy Roman Emperor Frederick II, the Jews received the same rights and privileges as other citizens, as well as Frederick's special protection against the Crusaders.

During the late fourteenth century and early fifteenth century, Sicily had been an independent kingdom, although linked to the kingdom of Aragon. When Ferdinand and Isabella united Aragon and Castile in 1479, Sicily fell under direct Spanish rule. A few years after Ferdinand and Isabella had taken over, they declared their plan to expel all Jews from their kingdom, which included the island of Sicily. By 1492, there were some thirty thousand Jews living in more than fifty different places on Sicily. But on 12 January 1493, the expulsion of the Jews from Sicily took effect. This was not the first time, nor would it be the last time, that the world has viewed antisemitism.

Persecution is not new to the people of God. Christians have experienced persecution since the first century. In fact, the Bible tells us we should *expect* persecution: "Yea, and all that will live godly in Christ Jesus shall suffer persecution."

While never enjoyable, our reaction to persecution should mirror that of the Lord Jesus, "Who, when he was reviled, reviled not again; when he suffered, he threatened not; but committed himself to him that judgeth righteously" (1 Peter 2:23). No matter the persecution or tribulation, we have the promise that nothing will separate us from God's love (Romans 8:35–39), and we can rest in the assurance that this world is not our home.

Setbacks

13 January 1842

For a just man falleth seven times, and riseth up again: but the wicked shall fall into mischief.—**Proverbs 24:16**

The British army holds the distinction of being involved in more diverse locations than any other army in the world. In fact, there was a time when "the sun did not set on the British Empire," because its territories spanned the globe. Nevertheless, among the various British army regiments that have served over the centuries, one bears the unenviable reputation of having been defeated more often than any other regiment in the history of British service—the former 44th Regiment of Foot.

Originated in 1741 by James Long, the 44th Foot demonstrated long and faithful service to king and country. Along the way, however, the 44th experienced its share of defeats. During the Jacobite Rebellion in 1745, the 44th lost nearly all of its officers fighting the Scottish forces of Bonnie Prince Charlie at the Battle of Prestonpans. After killing most of the British officers, Scottish highlanders easily subdued the confused and leaderless British troops. Ten years later, during the French and Indian War, the 44th again lost heavily at the Battle of Monongahela. On 13 January 1842, during the First Anglo-Afghan War, a group of Afghan raiders known as Ghilzais ambushed the 44th as they were retreating from Kabul. Only one man escaped death or capture to make it back to India, Dr. William Brydon.

The Apostle Paul understood what it was like to experience setbacks and defeat. In 2 Corinthians 11:23–28, he gives the church at Corinth his "résumé" of what it meant to truly suffer for Christ. However, Paul never let those difficulties keep him from serving Christ faithfully.

It is embarrassing to consider how little it takes to cause some Christians to fall out of the race. Despite our setbacks, ultimately, we have the victory in Christ. "But thanks be to God, which giveth us the victory through our Lord Jesus Christ. Therefore, my beloved brethren, be ye stedfast, unmoveable, always abounding in the work of the Lord, forasmuch as ye know that your labour is not in vain in the Lord" (1 Corinthians 15:57–58).

A Secure Throne

14 January 1724

He shall be great, and shall be called the Son of the Highest: and the Lord God shall give unto him the throne of his father David:—**Luke 1:32**

King Philip V was famous for a variety of reasons, not the least of which was his notorious grandfather, King Louis XIV. Although born a Frenchman, Philip became the first member of the French Bourbons to rule Spain. When Spain's King Charles II died without a male heir in 1700, his will named his half-sister's grandson, Philip V, his successor. Philip's ascension to the Spanish throne was contested by Austrian Archduke Charles, causing the War of the Spanish Succession. The war ended with the Treaty of Utrecht, which forbad any joining of the Spanish and French crowns.

On 14 January 1724, Philip V abdicated his throne to his oldest son, Louis I, because he hoped to circumvent the treaty and succeed to the French throne, effectively placing Western Europe under the French Bourbons. Seven months later, Louis I died of smallpox, requiring Philip to return to the Spanish throne.

No human throne is secure. History is filled with fallen dynasties and kingdoms. In 2 Samuel 7:8–16, God articulated the Davidic covenant and promised King David perpetuity through his line. This eternal throne will be established at the Second Coming of Jesus Christ, and His kingdom will be forever. "And the seventh angel sounded; and there were great voices in heaven, saying, The kingdoms of this world are become the kingdoms of our Lord, and of his Christ; and he shall reign for ever and ever" (Revelation 11:15).

While it may sometimes seem that evil rules in our world, we have the promise of Christ's return and eternal rule of this world. "And I heard a loud voice saying in heaven, Now is come salvation, and strength, and the kingdom of our God, and the power of his Christ: for the accuser of our brethren is cast down, which accused them before our God day and night" (Revelation 12:10).

Sweet Tooth

15 January 1919

Hast thou found honey? eat so much as is sufficient for thee, lest thou be filled therewith, and vomit it.—**Proverbs 25:16**

The beloved children's book, *Charlie and the Chocolate Factory*, tells the tale of five children who get the chance to tour a magnificent candy factory. In one memorable anecdote, one of the children falls into a chocolate river. For some, this may not sound like a tragedy, considering how many people love chocolate, but for the character in Roald Dahl's book, it was a nightmare.

On 15 January 1919, an event occurred in Boston, Massachusetts that, but for the fact that it really happened, could have come from the pages of Dahl's timeless classic. Known as the Great Molasses Flood of 1919, this bizarre accident ranks as one of Boston's worst disasters in history. Shortly after noon in Boston's North End, a dilapidated, leaking tank containing more than two million gallons of fermenting, sticky molasses exploded. The force of the explosion sent metal rivets through the air like shrapnel, cutting the steel girders of an elevated railway. Surrounding buildings collapsed and knocked others off their foundations. An eight-foot-high wave of molasses swept away freight cars and caved in buildings' doors and windows. The sticky mess covered the neighborhood and spread out two to three feet thick across downtown, burying and drowning anything in its path. US Navy sailors from the USS *Nantucket* arrived on the scene in droves but were mired in the sticky muck, which stained the waters of Boston Harbor brown for many days. In all, twenty-one people and dozens of horses died in the flood, and the clean up took weeks. To this day, local residents claim that on a hot summer's day, one can still smell the molasses.

Too much of an otherwise good thing is not good. This is where the biblical principle of moderation is important. As humans, we tend to take things to excess, so Scripture warns us to just enjoy what is sufficient. Philippians 4:5 says that this principle should be evident in a Christian's life: "Let your moderation be known unto all men. The Lord is at hand."

Waiting on the Reward

16 January 2001

Therefore, my beloved brethren, be ye stedfast, unmoveable, always abounding in the work of the Lord, forasmuch as ye know that your labour is not in vain in the Lord.—**1 Corinthians 15:58**

Theodore "Teddy" Roosevelt is best known for serving as America's twenty-sixth President. Thrust into the office when President William McKinley was assassinated, Roosevelt's colorful career as a writer, rancher, deputy sheriff, and all-around adventurer guaranteed he would have the grit to lead America for the eight years he served.

Prior to the presidency, Roosevelt was also a soldier. When the Spanish-American War erupted in 1898, Roosevelt resigned from government service and helped to form a volunteer cavalry regiment. Known as the "Rough Riders," Roosevelt led his band of Native Americans, college athletes, cowboys, and ranchers in a charge up San Juan Hill on 1 July 1898.

Afterward, Roosevelt was recommended for the Congressional Medal of Honor for his heroism. But due to political infighting, the recommendation was rejected. On 16 January 2001, President Bill Clinton held a ceremony in the White House and presented the Medal of Honor to Roosevelt's great-grandson. After 103 years, Roosevelt's deeds were formally recognized.

As Christians, we may never receive the world's recognition or accolades for what we have done for the cause of Christ. Recognition, however, should never be our motive. Our reward will come at the Judgment Seat of Christ. The rewards of fighting the spiritual battles of this life will be heard in the words from our Commander-in-Chief, "Well done, thou good and faithful servant" (Matthew 25:21).

With this in mind, we should remember the encouragements of Scripture: "And let us not be weary in well doing: for in due season we shall reap, if we faint not" (Galatians 6:9). "Be patient therefore, brethren, unto the coming of the Lord. Behold, the husbandman waiteth for the precious fruit of the earth, and hath long patience for it, until he receive the early and latter rain" (James 5:7).

Snared

17 January 1950

For man also knoweth not his time: as the fishes that are taken in an evil net, and as the birds that are caught in the snare; so are the sons of men snared in an evil time, when it falleth suddenly upon them.—**Ecclesiastes 9:12**

Armored cars have been around since the late nineteenth century. Initially used to protect those inside from bullets and shrapnel, it was not until the early 1900s that armored cars were specifically used for transporting money, jewels, and other valuables.

On 17 January 1950, eleven men stole over $2 million from the Brinks Armored Car depot in Boston, Massachusetts. The mastermind of the heist was Tony "Fats" Pino, who recruited ten other thieves to assist him. Dressed like Brinks employees, the robbers managed to get away with $2.7 million, the largest robbery in American history up to that time. In what seemed like the fool-proof scheme, the robbers thought they had executed the perfect crime. Six years later, however, one of the robbers made a deal with the FBI leading to the arrest of his accomplices . . . only days before the statute of limitations for the heist expired.

Sin is deceptive in that we think that just because we do not immediately reap the consequences, God has somehow forgotten about it. The Bible is clear in Numbers 32:23, "Be sure your sin will find you out." Sin often looks pleasurable and inconsequential. Hebrews 11:25 speaks of Moses "Choosing rather to suffer affliction with the people of God, than to enjoy the pleasures of sin for a season." Moses lived in Egypt, the biblical picture of the world. Just as we live in the world, we must choose to live for Christ instead of giving into the temptations of our flesh.

Thinking we got away with sin or that sin won't hurt us is one of Satan's most-used deceptions. Whether sin keeps us from a close relationship with God or causes division with our loved ones, its consequences are never pretty. James 1:14–15 warns us, "But every man is tempted, when he is drawn away of his own lust, and enticed. Then when lust hath conceived, it bringeth forth sin: and sin, when it is finished, bringeth forth death."

Flying against the Flow

18 January 1957

Enter ye in at the strait gate: for wide is the gate, and broad is the way, that leadeth to destruction, and many there be which go in thereat:—**Matthew 7:13**

During the height of the Cold War, three B-52 Stratofortress bombers assigned to the 93rd Bomb Wing departed Castle Air Force Base in California as part of Operation Powerflite. The historic operation was a demonstration to the world that the United States Air Force could deliver nuclear weapons anywhere in the world. To prove this, each of the three B-52s flew 24,325 miles non-stop around the world, which took forty-five hours and nineteen minutes. As the weary airmen stepped off their respective aircraft on 18 January 1957, General Curtis LeMay pinned decorations on each man. For aerial gunner Airman 1st Class Eugene Preiss, Operation Powerflite was indeed unique. He became the first person to fly around the world backward.

This world constantly beckons us to conform to its way of doing things, to stay with the pack. Those who go against the grain are ridiculed and scorned. Romans 12:2 challenges us, "And be not conformed to this world: but be ye transformed by the renewing of your mind, that ye may prove what is that good, and acceptable, and perfect, will of God."

But the people who have changed this world have been the people the world could not change. As we work and live, may we never lose sight of the fact that we are a called out group of people whom God wants to use to spread the gospel. "But ye are a chosen generation, a royal priesthood, an holy nation, a peculiar people; that ye should shew forth the praises of him who hath called you out of darkness into his marvellous light" (1 Peter 2:9).

Will we be ridiculed for our stand? Yes. Will we be persecuted for our convictions? Yes. But the Lord desires us to be the light in a darkened world. He calls us to be "blameless and harmless, the sons of God, without rebuke, in the midst of a crooked and perverse nation, among whom ye shine as lights in the world" (Philippians 2:15).

Diligent Days

19 January 1807

The soul of the sluggard desireth, and hath nothing: but the soul of the diligent shall be made fat.—**Proverbs 13:4**

Known as the "Grey Fox," Robert Edward Lee was born 19 January 1807 in Stratford Hall, Virginia. The son of Revolutionary War officer Henry "Light Horse Harry" Lee, young Robert E. Lee was destined to follow in his father's footsteps and became a soldier. Lee graduated from West Point at the top of his class and served in the US Army for thirty-two years. As a leader, Lee was known for his organizational skills and organized each day according to three cardinal rules.

First, Lee strove to always accomplish a day's work within the day allotted, even if that day's workload included pushing paper. One of his staff officers remarked, "He was not satisfied unless at the close of his office hours every matter requiring prompt attention had been disposed of." Second, Lee believed in turning in by 2200 hours and rising early. Lee was often in his saddle before dawn so he could steal a march on the enemy. Third, Lee knew the importance of taking time for rest and reflection. Whenever possible, he set aside thirty minutes in the afternoon to ride his horse into the countryside just to clear his head.

As a God of order, God desires that a Christian "let all things be done decently and in order." While it was probably not always convenient for Lee to apply a structured regimen to his life, it nevertheless paid off.

How are your days structured? Psalm 90:12 says, "So teach us to number our days, that we may apply our hearts unto wisdom." Time is one of the most precious gifts that God has given us, and wasted time cannot be retrieved. To ensure that we are not wasting the time on Earth that God has given us, we must plan and schedule our days. An even better example than General Lee is Jesus Christ who maintained a laser focus on His mission in coming to Earth: "My meat is to do the will of him that sent me, and to finish his work" (John 4:34). Diligent, scheduled days do not turn into regretful ones.

No Canceling This Appointment

20 January 1937

And as it is appointed unto men once to die, but after this the judgment: **—Hebrews 9:27**

Appointments . . . we all have them. Many times, we find ourselves either accidentally breaking them or trying to find a way to reschedule them due to our busy lifestyles. Invariably, however, appointments are a fact of life.

Given the myriad details with which a presidential inaugural committee must deal, mistakes are inevitable. One such mistake was that Franklin D. Roosevelt received an invitation to his own inauguration set for 20 January 1937—an appointment he dared not miss! Through the White House social bureau, he humorously sent word that the necessity of official business would regrettably keep him away from the inauguration. Relenting, however, he sent a further note in his own handwriting:

> I have rearranged my engagements and think I may be able to go. Will know definitely January 19th.
> Sincerely,
> F. D. R.

While man may escape or reschedule many appointments in this life, his appointment with death cannot be changed. Hebrews 9:27 states, "And as it is appointed unto men once to die, but after this the judgment." Every one who is born into this world has an inevitable death date. The question is, will you be ready for this appointment? The only way to answer this question in the absolute affirmative is to place your faith in Jesus Christ as your personal Saviour. The Bible tells us that our good works cannot save us (Ephesians 2:8–9). Yet it also promises us, "For whosoever shall call upon the name of the Lord shall be saved" (Romans 10:13). If you have trusted Christ as your Saviour, you have no need to fear your appointment with death, for this appointment is also an invitation to the presence of Christ: "We are confident, I say, and willing rather to be absent from the body, and to be present with the Lord" (2 Corinthians 5:8).

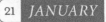

Starving for the Word

21 January 1781

Blessed is the nation whose God is the Lord; and the people whom he hath chosen for his own inheritance.—**Psalm 33:12**

Privation is one of the sad collateral effects caused by war. During World War II, many thousands suffered the pangs of hunger as food was scarce. In the Thirty Years War (1618–1648), entire villages in Germany were laid waste due to the spread of disease and crop failure.

But during the Revolutionary War (1775–1783), there was a different kind of privation felt amongst the American colonists. The war with Britain had cut off the supply of Bibles to the United States resulting in a congressional mandate to import twenty thousand Bibles from "Scotland, Holland, or elsewhere." On 21 January 1781, Philadelphia printer Robert Aitken (1734–1802) implored Congress to officially sanction a publication of the Bible, which he was preparing out of his own pocket. Congress agreed and passed a resolution the following September making "Aitken's Bible" the first English language Bible published in North America.

When comparing US congressional priorities today to those of the late 1700s, we see a marked difference. What a revival we would see if today's leaders felt as strongly about the importance of getting the Word of God to its citizenry, as did those first members of Congress. Change in our country has to start with Christians hungering for the Word of God.

In Matthew 5:6 Jesus promised, "Blessed are they which do hunger and thirst after righteousness: for they shall be filled." When was the last time you hungered for God's Word more than food? In John 6:35, Jesus said, "I am the bread of life: he that cometh to me shall never hunger; and he that believeth on me shall never thirst."

To live in a time in history when God's Word is readily available in our own language, but then not to read or study it, is great foolishness. Don't be a spiritually-starving Christian simply out of neglect. Just as food is to our bodies, so God's Word is the sustenance for our spiritual lives.

Get the Seed Out

22 January 1879

Is the seed yet in the barn?—**Haggai 2:19**

On 22 January 1879, the British Army suffered one of the worst defeats of its colonial history. The Battle of Isandlwana marked the first major confrontation between the British Empire and the Zulu Kingdom. Following their invasion into South African Zululand, the British encountered a force of some 20,000 Zulu warriors armed with cowhide shields and spears. While British troop strength only numbered around 1,800, their state-of-the-art weapons and professional training would more than offset the numerical advantage of their primitive adversary . . . or so they thought.

As thousands of Zulus approached the British encampment at Isandlwana, Colonel Anthony Durnford's arrogance doomed his men. Because he underestimated the tenacity of the Zulus, Durnford failed to form his men into the characteristic British "square," a defensive perimeter that allowed riflemen to engage an enemy from virtually any direction. Additionally, Durnford committed one of the greatest logistical *faux pas* in military history by storing their ammunition in a central depot sealed in heavy wooden boxes, fastened by copper bands, and held down by screws in the lids. None of Durnford's troops had screwdrivers to open the boxes. Survivors' accounts tell of the confusion of desperate men trying to break open the heavy containers with their bayonets, scoop up bullets, and frantically run off to their distant lines to resume firing. The British might well have withstood the Zulu onslaught had they had access to the plentiful ammunition. As it was, fewer than a dozen British escaped the slaughter.

In Jesus' parable of the seed and the sower (Matthew 13:3–23), He compares the seed to the Word of God. Like bullets locked up during battle, seed left in the barn does nothing. As Christians, we have access to this seed. We require no special tools to get to it. We simply need to obey the Holy Spirit to get the seed out of the barn and into the hearts of those who don't know Christ. Who can you share the gospel with today?

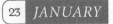

Double-Minded Aviator

23 January 1941

And Elijah came unto all the people, and said, How long halt ye between two opinions? if the LORD be God, follow him: but if Baal, then follow him. And the people answered him not a word.—**1 Kings 18:21**

When Hitler invaded Poland in September 1939, few Americans thought it necessary that the United States get directly involved, but most wanted the US to send support to Britain and France. Some Americans, however, were content to do nothing at all. One of the principal spokesmen for this group was noteworthy aviator Charles Lindbergh. Lindbergh was a key member in the America First Committee, an organization that brought together pacifists, pro-fascists, communists, isolationists, and anyone else opposed to American participation in the war. On 23 January 1941, Lindbergh was the star witness against the Lend-Lease Act before the House Foreign Affairs Committee and recommended that the US negotiate a non-aggression pact with Germany rather than send tangible aid to France and Britain.

While Lindbergh claimed to be American, his defense of Nazi Germany went against American ideals of freedom and democracy. His opposition to providing needed assistance to the Allies suggested that he might possibly be in sympathy with the Nazis or was terribly misreading the reality of the situation.

Many Christians do something similar in that they profess allegiance to Christ but live with one foot in the world and one for Christ. James 1:8 says, "A double minded man is unstable in all his ways." A few chapters later, James also mentions, "Ye adulterers and adulteresses, know ye not that the friendship of the world is enmity with God? whosoever therefore will be a friend of the world is the enemy of God" (James 4:4). Straddling the fence of the world and Christianity is not going to allow our journey with God to advance. Although we may say we love God, having a foot in the world yields opposition to the faith and doctrines of the Word of God. Don't be double-minded; choose a side. Jesus deserves your whole devotion.

Exodus 7–8 // Matthew 15:1–20

Sullivan's Sacrifice

24 January 1883

For God so loved the world, that he gave his only begotten Son, that whosoever believeth in him should not perish, but have everlasting life.—**John 3:16**

Thomas Sullivan was born on 24 January 1883 in Harpers Ferry, Dubuque County, Iowa. The son of Irish immigrants, Thomas married Aletta Abel and the couple had five sons: George, Francis, Joseph, Madison and Albert. All five sons enlisted in the US Navy to fight in World War II and insisted they all be stationed on the same ship—the USS *Juneau.* During the Guadalcanal Campaign, the *Juneau* was struck twice by Japanese torpedoes and sank. Awaiting news of his sons, Thomas was getting ready for work on the morning of 12 January 1943 when three men in uniform knocked at his door.

"I have some news for you about your boys," one of the officers said.

"Which one?" asked Thomas.

"I'm sorry," the officer replied. "All five."

Thomas and Aletta's boys gave the ultimate sacrifice for their nation. Referring to the tragedy, Vice President Henry A. Wallace stated that the brothers' deaths represented "one of the most extraordinary tragedies which has ever been met by any family in the United States."

It would be difficult to imagine the anguish and grief that must have enveloped Thomas Sullivan as he heard the news of his sons' fate. No doubt, Mr. Sullivan loved his sons dearly. He could not have helped mourning the fact that many of the people who would enjoy the freedom for which they gave their lives would not even know their five names.

God gave His Son over two thousand years ago to die for the sins of all people . . . many of which do not even know His name and thus have not experienced His salvation. While the sacrifice of the Sullivan family is noteworthy, it pales in comparison to the sacrifice of the sinless Son of God who "hath given himself for us an offering and a sacrifice to God for a sweet smelling savour" (Ephesians 5:2). Let's thank Him for His sacrifice and tell others how they can experience His salvation.

Exodus 9–11 // Matthew 15:21–39

Diamond in the Rough

25 January 1905

But we have this treasure in earthen vessels, that the excellency of the power may be of God, and not of us.—**2 Corinthians 4:7**

On 25 January 1905, Captain Frederick Wells, superintendent of the Premier Mine in South Africa, was eighteen feet below the surface when he spotted a flash of what he believed to be broken glass embedded in the mine wall. Thinking it was a joke, Wells retrieved the crystal from the wall with his knife. He presented the find to the mine's owner, Sir Thomas Cullinan. Upon closer examination, the piece of crystal was in fact a 3,106-carat diamond weighing 1.33 pounds. Cullinan sold the diamond to the Transvaal Colony government for 150,000 British pounds. Prime Minister Louis Botha decided to present the diamond to King Edward VII as a birthday gift.

Because of the diamond's worth, British detectives were placed on a steamboat that was rumored to carry it, and a parcel was ceremoniously secured in the captain's safe. This, however, was a diversionary tactic; the stone on the steamboat was a fake. The actual Cullinan diamond was entrusted to the postal service and shipped to London in a plain box. The registered package safely arrived in London via plain parcel post.

It's hard to believe that something with this value was entrusted to something as common as the postal service. Yet, God has entrusted something of much greater value in us—Himself. When we trust Christ as our Saviour, He gives us eternal life and indwells us. In Colossians 1:27, Paul described it this way: "To whom God would make known what is the riches of the glory of this mystery among the Gentiles; which is Christ in you, the hope of glory." The value of Christ in us cannot be determined in terms of money. We are a common "postal service" entrusted with the presence of Christ and the glorious message of the gospel. "For God, who commanded the light to shine out of darkness, hath shined in our hearts, to give the light of the knowledge of the glory of God in the face of Jesus Christ" (2 Corinthians 4:6).

A Pardoned Outlaw

26 January 1875

Who is a God like unto thee, that pardoneth iniquity, and passeth by the transgression of the remnant of his heritage? he retaineth not his anger for ever, because he delighteth in mercy.—**Micah 7:18**

The names Frank and Jesse James are forever immortalized as two of the post-Civil War's most notorious outlaws. Both served in the controversial Confederate company known as Quantrill's Raiders, but their violent ways continued after the war when they began robbing railroads and banks. On 26 January 1875, men from the Pinkerton Detective Agency firebombed the Jameses' homestead in an attempt to flush Frank and Jesse from the house. As it turned out, neither brother was home that night. Instead, the attack maimed their mother and killed their nine-year-old half-brother. After the attack, Frank and Jesse ramped up their activities and began targeting men from the Pinkerton firm.

In 1882, a member of the James gang assassinated Jesse. His brother Frank surrendered shortly thereafter and was tried for his crimes in Gallatin, Missouri. Amazingly, no jury would convict the outlaw as many were sympathetic southerners who saw the James brothers as nineteenth-century Robin Hoods. Frank James was acquitted of all charges. He walked out of the Huntsville courthouse a free man. It had been the trial of the century, and he remained a free citizen until his death in 1915.

Frank James certainly deserved punishment for his crimes, yet he was acquitted and declared not guilty. None of us deserve Heaven. The Psalmist declared: "For thy name's sake, O LORD, pardon mine iniquity; for it is great" (Psalm 25:11). Like David admits in this psalm, our sin is great. In fact, "There is none righteous, no, not one" (Romans 3:10). Nevertheless, God in His mercy offers a pardon for all. "But God, who is rich in mercy, for his great love wherewith he loved us, Even when we were dead in sins, hath quickened us together with Christ, (by grace ye are saved;)" (Ephesians 2:4–5). When we trust Christ as our Saviour, we are eternally pardoned.

Reunion Day

27 January 1981

Beloved, now are we the sons of God, and it doth not yet appear what we shall be: but we know that, when he shall appear, we shall be like him; for we shall see him as he is.—**1 John 3:2**

On this day in 1981, President Ronald Reagan and his wife Nancy, welcomed home the fifty-two American hostages who had been held captive in Iran for 444 days. These hostages were humiliated before crowds, not permitted to speak or read, and rarely allowed a change of clothes. Throughout the Iran hostage crisis, there was a frightening uncertainty about their fate, never knowing whether they would be tortured, murdered, or freed. That all changed when Reagan delivered his inaugural address in 1981. Within a few hours, the hostages were released and began to make their way home to American soil. Some have speculated that it was Reagan's tough stand on foreign policy that persuaded the Iranians to release the hostages.

The reception the hostages received in Washington DC was welcoming. Thousands of citizens waving yellow ribbons and balloons cheered the former hostages through the streets of Washington as a motorcade led by Vice President George H. W. Bush bore the freed Americans to a private reception by President and Mrs. Reagan in the Blue Room of the White House.

As spectacular as it was, the reception given by the President and First Lady to those fifty-two captives pales in comparison to the reception awaiting those who have been freed from the burden of sin. Revelation 22:1–5 describes where we will spend eternity: "And he shewed me a pure river of water of life, clear as crystal, proceeding out of the throne of God and of the Lamb. In the midst of the street of it, and on either side of the river, was there the tree of life . . . And there shall be no more curse: but the throne of God and of the Lamb shall be in it; and his servants shall serve him: And they shall see his face." What a wonderful day that will be when God Himself welcomes us Home!

Marching as to War

28 January 1834

I press toward the mark for the prize of the high calling of God in Christ Jesus.
—Philippians 3:14

During the Battle of Antietam in 1862, Confederate General A. P. Hill marched his troops seventeen miles in eight hours. During World War II, Colonel Robert Sink marched his 506th Parachute Infantry Regiment 137 miles from Camp Toccoa to Fort Benning. Hannibal marched his army some 1,600 miles over treacherous terrain in 218 BC. Marching is something a veteran never forgets. Whether in basic training or battle, marching is part of military life.

On 28 January 1834, Sabine Baring-Gould was born in Exeter, England, to wealthy parents. By 1865, Gould was overseeing a grammar school in Yorkshire. Each year, the village celebrated Whit Monday, which is observed the day after Pentecost Sunday. As part of the festivities, schoolchildren walk to surrounding villages to pray blessings on fellow students and citizens. To motivate his students as they marched from village to village, Gould penned a song for them to sing. We know it today as "Onward, Christian Soldiers."

Onward, Christian soldiers, marching as to war
With the cross of Jesus going on before.
Christ, the royal Master, leads against the foe;
Forward into battle see His banners go!

The words of the hymn make it clear that the focus is on spiritual battle. The Apostle Paul said, "I press toward the mark for the prize of the high calling of God in Christ Jesus." If these words would have been used in military terms, Paul would be encouraging us to march after spiritual victory "like a mighty army." Spiritual warfare is real, and Christians must be prepared to fight against the attacks of Satan. This is why Ephesians 6:11 admonishes us, "Put on the whole armour of God, that ye may be able to stand against the wiles of the devil."

A Loving Husband

29 January 1843

Husbands, love your wives, even as Christ also loved the church, and gave himself for it;.—**Ephesians 5:25**

William McKinley was born 29 January 1843, in Niles, Ohio. As a young man, he briefly attended Allegheny College before taking a position as a schoolteacher. When the Civil War broke out in 1861, McKinley enlisted in the Union Army, eventually rising to the rank of brevet major of volunteers. Following the war, McKinley returned to his native Ohio and studied law. He opened his own law practice in Canton and married Ida Saxton.

Tragedy struck early in the couple's marriage as Ida lost her mother and two daughters within months of one another. She lost her health which she never recovered, becoming a chronic invalid for the rest of her life. Despite his busy schedule, which included being elected President of the United States in 1896, McKinley lovingly cared for his wife throughout his political career, winning praise from the public for his loving devotion to her. Sadly, McKinley was assassinated on 14 September 1901. Without the assistance of her husband, Ida's health further deteriorated. She died less than six years later and was laid to rest next to her husband and their two daughters. William McKinley never allowed his political career to eclipse the love he had for his wife. Truly, it could be said that President McKinley gave of himself to his wife.

The Lord Jesus Christ is the greatest example of unconditional love and calls upon every husband to love his wife the way He loved the church. The love Christ had for the church is a sacrificial love. "For even the Son of man came not to be ministered unto, but to minister, and to give his life a ransom for many" (Mark 10:45). Without thought for Himself, Jesus came to serve, and ultimately, to die for the whole world. As husbands, we are to give of ourselves to our wives as Christ gave of Himself. Her needs should come before our own, and we should serve her as Christ served those around Him. One of the greatest commands of Jesus is to love as He loved.

On the Right Side

30 January 1984

Then Moses stood in the gate of the camp, and said, Who is on the LORD's side? let him come unto me. And all the sons of Levi gathered themselves together unto him.—**Exodus 32:26**

During World War I and World War II, German soldiers wore belt buckles with the words "*Gott mit uns*" emblazoned across the front piece. Translated into English, these three German words mean "God with us." During both world wars, there were soldiers in the German Army who truly believed God was on their side as they fought in those epic conflicts.

On 30 January 1984, President Ronald Reagan delivered a speech to the National Religious Broadcasters Convention in Washington. During his speech, Reagan stated, "We must be cautious in claiming God is on our side. I think the real question we must answer is, are we on His side?"

Rather than trying to get God to "rubber stamp" our agenda, we must ensure we are aligned with His perfect will. God's will is that all men be saved: "Who will have all men to be saved, and to come unto the knowledge of the truth" (1 Timothy 2:4). However, it is also His will for Christians to surrender to the process of sanctification.

Sanctification means "to make holy, set apart as sacred." John 17:17 says, "Sanctify them through thy truth: thy word is truth." In order to follow God's will for holy living, we must follow the truth of His Word. Too often we justify our fleshly actions and choices with a haphazard, "I prayed about it" or "I believe God wants me to." Sometimes these phrases are used as Christian excuses to follow our flesh.

When we go into spiritual battle, we must ensure we have the Lord's power and blessing behind us. If our lives are fraught with sin, we cannot be in the Lord's will, and our battle will be lost. Psalm 66:18 says, "If I regard iniquity in my heart, the Lord will not hear me." Daily maintaining a close relationship with the Lord and surrendering to His will and His Word will keep you on the winning side.

Desertion of Duty

31 January 1945

For Demas hath forsaken me, having loved this present world, and is departed unto Thessalonica; Crescens to Galatia, Titus unto Dalmatia.—**2 Timothy 4:10**

Private Edward Donald "Eddie" Slovik was assigned to the US 28th Infantry Division in August 1944, during World War II. Slovik threatened to desert if forced into combat, but his authorities ignored the threat. The next day he did desert, only to return a day later to sign a confession of desertion. By signing the confession, Slovik affirmed that he would run away again if forced to fight. One of his officers tried to persuade him to recant, warning that the consequences could be grave. Obstinately, Slovik refused to take back the confession and was confined to the stockade.

Because the 28th Division had seen numerous cases of self-inflicted wounds or desertions at this stage of the war, a unit legal officer offered Slovik a deal: enter combat immediately and avoid court-martial. Slovik refused, was tried for desertion, and convicted in less than two hours. The verdict was death by firing squad. Slovik appealed the verdict, but to no avail. Slovik was to be made an example. One last appeal was made to Supreme Allied Commander General Dwight D. Eisenhower, but Eisenhower upheld the sentence, personally signing the execution order. At 1000 hours, 31 January 1945, Private Slovik was shot to death by a twelve-man firing squad.

The Christian life is compared to many things in Scripture, but one comparison that resonates with anyone who has served in the military is warfare. The Apostle Paul admonishes in 2 Timothy 2:3, "Thou therefore endure hardness, as a good soldier of Jesus Christ." Deserters bring shame to themselves, their families, and their country. When a Christian deserts the faith, he brings shame to God, other Christians, and the cause of Christ. May we not be like Demas or Private Slovik, forsaking those who are counting on us. All of God's soldiers are needed to win the battle for lost souls until the final trumpet sounds and victory is declared.

FEBRUARY

Stay Salty

1 February 1865

Salt is good: but if the salt have lost his saltness, wherewith will ye season it? Have salt in yourselves, and have peace one with another.—**Mark 9:50**

During the American Civil War, the making of salt from sea water became a major industry in Florida due to the Union barricade that restricted the delivery of European salt. The Confederacy relied upon salt for a variety of reasons, much of which concerned the preservation of meat, fish, butter, and other perishables. The greatest concentration of salt works was located along the St. Andrews Bay coastline where sea water was plentiful, fuel was abundant, and delivery to Southern troops was relatively easy because of the network of wagon trails already in place. This activity did not escape the notice of federal sailors. From 1862 to 1865, the Union attempted to destroy the salt works of Florida. On 1 February 1865, the USS *Midnight* landed at St. Andrews Bay and destroyed the salt works, which ended this vital Confederate industry.

The Lord Jesus told His followers in Matthew 5:13, "Ye are the salt of the earth: but if the salt have lost his savour, wherewith shall it be salted? it is thenceforth good for nothing, but to be cast out, and to be trodden under foot of men." Because food is dehydrated by salt, bacteria cannot contaminate the food. But when salt loses its savor, it loses its power to preserve from contamination.

When salt loses its "saltiness," it becomes worthless. For this reason, Satan seeks ways to remove a Christian's saltiness. He wants to entice us to do things that would destroy our integrity and commitment to Christ, thus destroying our influence for Christ. By removing the preserving components, our lives become contaminated with the world's influence, affecting all others around us. In order to stay away from the contamination of the world, a Christian must use the Word of God "to keep himself unspotted from the world" (James 1:27).

Wait for the Gold

2 February 1812

And let us not be weary in well doing: for in due season we shall reap, if we faint not.—**Galatians 6:9**

During the early nineteenth century, Russia's Alaskan colonists began looking toward the coast of northern California for a more stable settlement. California's longer growing season and abundant sea otter population off the coast of San Francisco proved alluring to Russian settlers. A large company of Russians and Aleuts sailed for California, landing off the coast of Santa Rosa and establishing Fort Ross on 2 February 1812. Unfortunately, things did not work out for the Fort Ross settlers as they had hoped. The sea otters had been hunted to near extinction, and the cool foggy summers made it tough to grow fruit and grains. The settlers decided to off-load the fort and move elsewhere.

After overtures to sell the fort to the British and Mexicans fell through, the Russians found a buyer in John Sutter. Sutter reportedly purchased the fort in 1841 for $30,000 and constructed a saw mill on the property. Seven years later, one of his employees discovered gold near Sutter's Mill, igniting the California Gold Rush.

Could the Russian settlers have discovered gold if they had stayed in the area? One can only surmise. But those settlers aren't the only ones who have given up too soon. Sometimes Christians lose interest in following the Lord because the Christian life doesn't immediately bring all the benefits they hoped it would. This is what happened to some of the earliest followers of Jesus: "From that time many of his disciples went back, and walked no more with him" (John 6:66). When the sayings of Jesus became too hard to hear, these disciples gave up.

Are there unfulfilled expectations that are making you want to give up? Instead of looking at the disappointments, look to the future blessings that God promises to all those who stay faithful to Him. "Moreover it is required in stewards, that a man be found faithful" (1 Corinthians 4:2). Wait for the gold.

Exodus 29–30 // Matthew 21:23–46

A Divisive Message

3 February 1917

Now I beseech you, brethren, mark them which cause divisions and offences contrary to the doctrine which ye have learned; and avoid them. **—Romans 16:17**

Contrary to popular belief, America's entry into World War I was not due to the sinking of the RMS *Lusitania*. Although more than 120 Americans perished as a result of Germany's unprovoked attack on that civilian ocean liner, President Wilson withheld a declaration of war in accordance with his isolationist stance, and Germany called a halt to its policy of unrestricted targeting of passenger liners two months later. For the time being, America remained neutral.

In January 1917, however, a telegram from a German diplomat to Mexico was intercepted and relayed to Wilson. The Zimmerman telegram stated Germany would give Arizona, New Mexico, and Texas to Mexico in exchange for its help in defeating the United States. Along with the telegram, Germany also began unrestricted submarine warfare again breaking the Sussex Pledge of 1916.

On 3 February 1917, President Woodrow Wilson spoke before Congress and announced that due to Germany's behavior toward the United States, he was breaking off all diplomatic relations. A little over two months later, America officially declared war on Germany.

Those who quietly go about stirring divisions between friends or within churches hinder both fellowship and unity. This is one reason that Paul cautioned the believers in Rome to beware of those who would seek to divide them, either through false teachings or through ungodly behavior. There may come a point when we have to choose to break ties with those we once thought were like-minded in order to maintain unity in the body of Christ. When someone tries to be divisive within the church of God, the Bible speaks of marking them so that others may be discerning of their divisive ways.

Finish Your Course

4 February 1789

Better is the end of a thing than the beginning thereof: and the patient in spirit is better than the proud in spirit.—**Ecclesiastes 7:8**

On 4 February 1789, George Washington, commander of the Continental Army during the Revolutionary War, was unanimously elected as America's first President. Washington had selflessly led his army through various hardships and campaigns against British redcoats from 1776–1783. His hair grew gray and he nearly went blind shouldering the burden of command. When the time came for him to resign his commission, he told Congress, "Having now finished the work assigned me, I retire from the great theatre of action."

Washington's farewell address to Congress reminds us of the Apostle Paul, who said to Timothy in 2 Timothy 4:7–8, "I have fought a good fight, I have finished my course, I have kept the faith: Henceforth there is laid up for me a crown of righteousness, which the Lord, the righteous judge, shall give me at that day: and not to me only, but unto all them also that love his appearing." George Washington was a man who finished what he set out to do. Through criticism, health challenges, and hardships, he remained committed to the cause.

As Christians, may we learn from Washington's example of how an ordinary person exhibited extraordinary character during a trying time in his life. God never promised that the Christian life would be easy and void of trouble. But He does promise strength to continue in the face of hardships and an eternal reward for faithfulness. "My brethren, count it all joy when ye fall into divers temptations; Knowing this, that the trying of your faith worketh patience. But let patience have her perfect work, that ye may be perfect and entire, wanting nothing. . . . Blessed is the man that endureth temptation: for when he is tried, he shall receive the crown of life, which the Lord hath promised to them that love him" (James 1:2–4, 12). Hardships will come, but as Washington learned, finishing the task despite the hardships brings a lasting reward.

Unconcerned

5 February 1958

What man of you, having an hundred sheep, if he lose one of them, doth not leave the ninety and nine in the wilderness, and go after that which is lost, until he find it?—**Luke 15:4**

In a 2001 news conference, Air Force weapons advisor Dr. Billy Mullins made the startling statement, "We still think it's irretrievably lost. We don't know where to look for it." Incredibly, Dr. Mullins was speaking of a 7,600-pound hydrogen bomb.

On 5 February 1958, a US Air Force B-47 bomber, carrying a live hydrogen bomb, collided with an F-86 fighter jet over the state of Georgia. The mid-air collision destroyed the F-86 and severely damaged the bomber. Because of its cargo, the Air Force bomber could not make an emergency landing, so it was ordered to drop its nuclear payload into the Atlantic Ocean somewhere off the eastern coast of Georgia, near a little resort town called Tybee. While no radiation or any ill effects have ever been traced to the lost bomb, the Air Force has occasionally returned to look for it, yet without success. Experts estimate that the bomb lies buried beneath eight to forty feet of water and five to fifteen feet of mud and sand. In 2005 the Air Force Nuclear Weapons and Counter-proliferation Agency advised the Air Force to stop looking for the bomb and leave it in place.

One would think that the residents of Tybee would have relocated after hearing that a nuclear bomb was a considerable distance from their shores, but such is not the case. Instead, Tybee has thrived as a resort spot, and advertising makes no mention of the lost nuclear bomb.

Our world is filled with people lost in their sin, without the hope of eternal life. Yet, like the citizens of Tybee, many Christians give little thought to the lost. The Lord Jesus Christ told three parables in Luke 15 illustrating His concern for all who are lost, and in Luke 19:10 He declared, "For the Son of man is come to seek and to save that which was lost." Before we are quick to judge the Air Force for giving up on their search of the bomb, let's be sure that we are dynamically searching for the lost.

A Friend in Need Is a Friend Indeed

6 February 1778

A man that hath friends must shew himself friendly: and there is a friend that sticketh closer than a brother.—**Proverbs 18:24**

As determined as Washington's Continental Army may have been, historians believe that had France not joined forces with the colonists, America may never have won her independence from Great Britain. On 6 February 1778, France and the young American nation signed the Treaty of Alliance, on the condition that France gain the British West Indies upon American independence.

During the Battle of Yorktown in 1781, the French naval fleet barricaded British General Cornwallis and kept reinforcements and supplies from arriving. This move proved critical to the final defeat of the British. France came at just the right time when our fledgling nation needed a friend.

Over the course of human history, friendships and alliances have been important. To have a good friend—one who strengthens, challenges, and encourages—makes a person truly rich. We see several such friendships in the Bible, including that of David and Jonathan.

Jonathan, a prince of Israel and the supposed heir to Israel's throne, did not befriend David because of what David could do for him. Rather, he became David's friend when David most needed one, even going as far as to warn David against Jonathan's jealous father, King Saul: "Jonathan told David, saying, Saul my father seeketh to kill thee: now therefore, I pray thee, take heed to thyself until the morning, and abide in a secret place, and hide thyself" (1 Samuel 19:2). Jonathan knew that David was God's chosen king of Israel, but instead of getting jealous, he focused on encouraging and helping David on numerous occasions. "And Jonathan Saul's son arose, and went to David into the wood, and strengthened his hand in God" (1 Samuel 23:16). When David finally ascended to the throne, he repaid Jonathan's friendship by caring for Jonathan's crippled son Mephibosheth. If you want to have friends, be a friend yourself with no thought of what you can gain from it.

Death Has Died

7 February 1979

The last enemy that shall be destroyed is death.—**1 Corinthians 15:26**

During World War II, Nazi physician Dr. Josef Mengele—who performed bizarre medical experiments on living humans at the notorious Auschwitz death camp—personified death. He was known for wearing white gloves while he supervised the "selection" of incoming Jewish prisoners to Auschwitz. Those he did not choose for his horrific experiments were immediately taken to the gas chambers and murdered. Those who endured his cruel experiments would likely have preferred death to the torture suffered at his hands. Mengele would earn the title "Angel of Death" from Holocaust victims. Like many Nazi war criminals after the war, Mengele managed to evade capture and initially escaped to Argentina. When Nazi hunters began closing in on Mengele, he fled to Brazil. On 7 February 1979, Mengele suffered a fatal stroke and drowned while swimming at a local beach in Bertioga, Brazil.

No doubt, thousands of people were terrified at the prospect of encountering Mengele—the very embodiment of sadistic horror, cruelty, and death. Even today, people shiver in revulsion at his picture knowing the atrocities this doctor performed. A doctor should be a symbol of life and hope, but Mengele became a symbol of death.

Thankfully, we have the promise that the Lord Jesus Christ defeated death when He rose from the tomb. Hebrews 2:14–15 says, "Forasmuch then as the children are partakers of flesh and blood, he also himself likewise took part of the same; that through death he might destroy him that had the power of death, that is, the devil; And deliver them who through fear of death were all their lifetime subject to bondage."

For the Christian, death has no sting and is nothing to be feared. "O death, where is thy sting? O grave, where is thy victory? The sting of death is sin; and the strength of sin is the law. But thanks be to God, which giveth us the victory through our Lord Jesus Christ" (1 Corinthians 15:55–57).

A Foolish Blunder

8 February 1250

The wise shall inherit glory: but shame shall be the promotion of fools. **—Proverbs 3:35**

During the Seventh French Crusade, King Louis IX led his army up the Nile River towards the Egyptian-held town of El Mansura. For two months, Louis looked for a way to cross the river and finally located a spot four miles away that would be safe for their cavalry to use. Once across, the French knights would attack the Egyptian camp and destroy the Egyptian army.

The crossing of the ford in the river required immense discipline as no rider was to leave his position in the column, nor charge ahead until the entire force had crossed. Louis' brother and lead knight, Robert of Artois, chose to disregard the king's orders. After crossing the river with a third of the French forces, he spotted three hundred Arab horsemen and gave chase without waiting for the other French divisions to cross the river. On 8 February 1250, Robert led his division into the town of El Mansura. Once they reached the narrow streets of El Mansura, the Muslims attacked Robert's small detachment, and the main Egyptian army moved into the town and cut off the Crusaders' retreat. Few escaped. Robert and over three hundred knights were killed. Through the foolishness of one man, Louis lost his brother and a third of his cavalry in a single stroke.

The book of Proverbs is filled with the consequences of the foolish. While none of us would want to be accused of being foolish, we often act foolish by going against our King's commands. God wants all Christians to live wisely, applying and seeking knowledge in a discerning and biblical way. Wisdom comes to those who obey the commands of the King and listen to the counsel of His Word. Proverbs 28:26 warns and promises, "He that trusteth in his own heart is a fool: but whoso walketh wisely, he shall be delivered."

A Real Action Hero

9 February 1964

God is our refuge and strength, a very present help in trouble. Therefore will not we fear, though the earth be removed, and though the mountains be carried into the midst of the sea; Though the waters thereof roar and be troubled, though the mountains shake with the swelling thereof. Selah.—**Psalm 46:1–3**

On 9 February 1964, the Hasbro Toy Company introduced the world to the G. I. Joe action figure. Hasbro reportedly coined the term *action figure* to avoid asking boys to play with a "doll." Manufactured as an alternative to Barbie, G. I. Joe was a huge success for Hasbro. Millions of young American boys, including this author, spent hours playing with their G. I. Joes during the late 1960s and early 1970s.

Standing around twelve inches tall, G. I. Joe had moveable joints, artificial hair, and the characteristic scar under his right eye. Initially, G. I. Joes were marketed as a World War II-themed soldier, complete with combat boots, olive-drab uniform, dog tags, and a field manual. During the early '70s, Hasbro expanded the action figure's role as an adventurer, explorer, and all-around do-gooder. Themed accessories coincided with G. I. Joe's adventures, and a pint-sized wooden footlocker was available to stow the various weapons, accessories, and uniform changes required by G. I. Joe. When playing with G. I. Joe, one could rest assured that he would triumph over any obstacle placed in his way, unless of course a piece of him broke or was lost in the bottom of the toy box.

We have a true hero who will always be there, will never break, and will never be lost. His name is Jesus Christ, and He is a "very present help in trouble." What a comfort it is to know that Jesus is right there with us at all times. He protects us while we sleep: "I will both lay me down in peace, and sleep: for thou, LORD, only makest me dwell in safety" (Psalm 4:8). He holds us when we need strength and comfort: "Nevertheless I am continually with thee: thou hast holden me by my right hand" (Psalm 73:23). And He promises to never leave us: "for he hath said, I will never leave thee, nor forsake thee" (Hebrews 13:5).

The Great Exchange

10 February 1962

For he hath made him to be sin for us, who knew no sin; that we might be made the righteousness of God in him.—**2 Corinthians 5:21**

At the height of the Cold War, an incident involving a US pilot created a unique opportunity for two men to exchange places. In May 1960, U-2 pilot Francis Gary Powers was shot down by a Soviet surface-to-air missile over Sverdlovsk, Russia. Unable to activate the aircraft's auto-destruct mechanism, Powers parachuted to the ground and into the hands of the Russian secret police force, the KGB. He was subsequently convicted of espionage and sentenced to ten years in a Soviet prison. On Saturday, 10 February 1962, twenty-one months after his capture, Powers was exchanged in a "spy swap" for Soviet KGB Colonel Rudolf Ivanovich Abel. The two men were brought to opposite ends of the Glienicke Bridge in Germany, and at exactly 0852 hours, both men walked to the other side of the bridge and into the waiting arms of their nations' handlers.

Nations who exchange prisoners go to great lengths to make the exchange even or favorable to their own sides. But more than two thousand years ago, God performed an exchange that was incredibly lopsided in *our* favor. He exchanged the perfect, sinless righteousness of His Son for the sinfulness of man. Isaiah 64:6 describes our good deeds as filthy rags: "But we are all as an unclean thing, and all our righteousnesses are as filthy rags; and we all do fade as a leaf; and our iniquities, like the wind, have taken us away." Yet God the Father made God the Son "to be sin for us, who knew no sin; that we might be made the righteousness of God in him."

What amazing unconditional love that our God shows by exchanging our filthy sinful garments for robes of righteousness! "After this I beheld, and, lo, a great multitude, which no man could number, of all nations, and kindreds, and people, and tongues, stood before the throne, and before the Lamb, clothed with white robes, and palms in their hands; And cried with a loud voice, saying, Salvation to our God which sitteth upon the throne, and unto the Lamb" (Revelation 7:9–10).

Overwhelmed

11 February 1573

But as it is written, Eye hath not seen, nor ear heard, neither have entered into the heart of man, the things which God hath prepared for them that love him.
—1 Corinthians 2:9

Sir Francis Drake is a name synonymous with seafaring adventure. On 11 February 1573, while on a mission to seize Spanish gold and silver on the Isthmus of Panama, Drake paused to climb a tall tree at the request of the natives with him. After almost reaching the top, he stepped out onto a large platform and looked around. Behind him, lay the Caribbean Sea, from where he had just traveled. Before him, lay the vast Pacific Ocean, a sight which no Englishman had seen before. Drake was so overwhelmed at the sight, he immediately fell to his knees and prayed that God would "give him leave and life to [sail] once in an English Ship in that sea." Over six years later, God granted his request when he sailed the Pacific Ocean during his quest to circumnavigate the world. Ultimately, Drake completed his circumnavigation of the world in September of 1580, becoming the second man to do so.

As we think of Drake's excitement and awe of the Pacific Ocean, let us also dwell on the awe that we will feel when we catch our first glimpse of Heaven. "Nevertheless we, according to his promise, look for new heavens and a new earth, wherein dwelleth righteousness" (2 Peter 3:13).

Jesus spoke of Heaven in John 14. "In my Father's house are many mansions: if it were not so, I would have told you. I go to prepare a place for you" (John 14:2). The Apostle Paul tells us that the glories of Heaven are such that no man can even comprehend the splendor and joy that awaits those who have received the Lord Jesus Christ as Saviour. Christians have so much to look forward to in Heaven. As Drake was excited for the adventure of sailing the Pacific Ocean, we also should be looking for the day when we will be with Christ eternally. "Looking for that blessed hope, and the glorious appearing of the great God and our Saviour Jesus Christ" (Titus 2:13).

The King of Gluttony

12 February 1771

And put a knife to thy throat, if thou be a man given to appetite. **—Proverbs 23:2**

Known as "the king who ate himself to death," King Adolf Fredrik of Sweden was anything but an assertive monarch. Following his government's anemic attempts to reconquer the Baltic provinces, Fredrik was placed on the Swedish throne in 1751 for the purpose of reclaiming the absolute monarchy held by previous kings. He failed in this and was essentially only a constitutional figurehead. Unlike other European monarchs of his day, Fredrik never campaigned or led men into battle. Rather, he spent his idle time making decorative snuffboxes.

Adolf Fredrik died of a stroke in Stockholm on 12 February 1771, after consuming a meal of lobster, caviar, sauerkraut, kippers, and champagne. He chose to top off this sumptuous feast with fourteen servings of sweet rolls served in bowls of warm milk.

The Bible is clear on the dangers of excess and gluttony. It seems that, among other applications, the Apostle Paul's assertion in 1 Corinthians 9:27 surely referred to personal discipline as well: "But I keep under my body, and bring it into subjection: lest that by any means, when I have preached to others, I myself should be a castaway." Obesity due to overindulgence has become a real problem in America. Proverbs 25:16 states: "Hast thou found honey? eat so much as is sufficient for thee, lest thou be filled therewith, and vomit it." This verse speaks of moderation: a good thing becomes a bad thing when it is not moderated.

Not only must we be aware of gluttony physically, but we must also be careful that gluttony for worldly pleasures does not ruin our spiritual appetite. We may need to take a break from things we enjoy doing in order to keep our spiritual lives healthy. "All things are lawful unto me, but all things are not expedient: all things are lawful for me, but I will not be brought under the power of any" (1 Corinthians 6:12).

Co-Regents with Christ

13 February 1689

Blessed and holy is he that hath part in the first resurrection: on such the second death hath no power, but they shall be priests of God and of Christ, and shall reign with him a thousand years.—**Revelation 20:6**

After ascending the throne upon the death of his brother Charles II, English King James II reinstalled Roman Catholicism as the nation's primary religion. His reign was tumultuous to say the least as he squabbled back and forth with English Parliamentarians over how England would be governed. When it was announced that James had fathered a Catholic heir, leading nobles solicited Protestant William III of Orange to land an invasion force from the Dutch Republic in order to take the throne from James II. Known as the Glorious Revolution, William landed unopposed in November 1688, resulting in James II fleeing to France. On 13 February 1689, William and his wife Mary Stuart were crowned King William III and Queen Mary II, England's co-regents.

Although Mary was actually the daughter of James II, she had been raised Anglican by her uncle Charles II. When William of Orange landed in England, he joined in marriage to Mary, thus granting her the status of co-regent. During the reign of William and Mary, Parliament passed the English Bill of Rights, which prevented future Catholic rulers on the English throne and limited the power of the monarchy.

Similar to the union of William and Mary, Revelation mentions the Christian's co-regency with Jesus Christ during His Millennial Reign. Those who have united themselves with the Bridegroom, the Lord Jesus Christ, will experience the joy of reigning with Him. Imagine the glory and splendor that we will experience in reigning with our King. "I will greatly rejoice in the LORD, my soul shall be joyful in my God; for he hath clothed me with the garments of salvation, he hath covered me with the robe of righteousness, as a bridegroom decketh himself with ornaments, and as a bride adorneth herself with her jewels" (Isaiah 61:10).

Buried in the Depths

14 February 1942

. . . and thou wilt cast all their sins into the depths of the sea.—**Micah 7:19**

On Valentine's Day 1942, the light cruiser USS *Juneau* was commissioned under the command of Captain Lyman Swenson. The *Juneau* became famous when she was sunk during the Battle of Guadalcanal, taking the lives of the five Sullivan brothers. Never before in the history of World War II had five siblings served together on the same ship. The deaths of the Sullivan boys caused the US War Department to enact the "Sole Survivor Policy," which is designed to protect members of a family from combat duty if they have already lost a family member in military service.

In March 2018, an underwater exploration team, funded by Microsoft co-founder Paul Allen, discovered the *Juneau* approximately three miles below the ocean's surface off the coast of the Solomon Islands in the South Pacific. Allen's ship is the only privately-owned vessel in the world equipped to explore as deep as 19,000 feet. His expeditions have also discovered the final resting place of other World War II ships, including the USS *Lexington* and the USS *Indianapolis*. Many families have found a sense of closure in knowing the whereabouts of their loved ones lost at sea.

While Mr. Allen's philanthropic efforts are no doubt appreciated, no amount of money or deep sea technology will enable anyone to locate our sin. When the Lord Jesus Christ paid our sin debt, He "buried" them.

God not only forgives and covers our sins, but He also casts them into the sea and remembers our sins no more. Micah 7:18–19 says, "Who is a God like unto thee, that pardoneth iniquity, and passeth by the transgression of the remnant of his heritage? he retaineth not his anger for ever, because he delighteth in mercy. He will turn again, he will have compassion upon us; he will subdue our iniquities; and thou wilt cast all their sins into the depths of the sea."

Praise God for His full forgiveness. He not only pardons our sin, but He completely removes it. We can face today knowing that we are fully forgiven.

God Knows the Way

15 February 1760

Hold up my goings in thy paths, that my footsteps slip not.—**Psalm 17:5**

During the period of maritime history known as the "age of sail," ships were classified, much like today, according to how many guns were aboard, method of propulsion, and other physical properties. In 1664, England's King Charles II supervised the launching of the HMS *Royal Katherine*. King Charles hoped his new eighty-four-gun ship would serve England's needs in fighting the Dutch in the Second Anglo-Dutch War. Not only did she fare well during the Dutch war, but the *Royal Katherine* also performed exceptionally during a series of wars fought in the seventeenth and eighteenth centuries. In 1706, she was renamed *Ramillies* in homage to England's victory during the Battle of Ramillies.

On 15 February 1760, after ninety-six years of almost continual service, the *Ramillies* sank because the ship's master had mistaken their location as they neared the Devon shore. The previous day, a violent storm had pushed the *Ramillies* eastwards until a promontory called Bolt Tail came into view. Thinking he was at Rame Head and heading back to Plymouth, the ship's master advised the captain to hoist the sails and run toward Plymouth Sound. Once the sails were up, the high winds pressed the canvas to the point that the main mast crashed into the deck, followed by the mizzenmast. Without any control of direction, the *Ramillies* ripped past Bolt Tail and smashed her stern right into a large cave at the bottom of the cliffs. As the vessel broke apart, more than seven hundred people drowned.

Often, we think we know better than God regarding the direction our lives should take, and, like the *Ramillies*, we find ourselves without direction. Rather than trying to figure out a solution on our own, we should turn to God and seek His direction. Proverbs 3:5–6 encourages us to trust Him and lean on His guiding hand: "Trust in the Lord with all thine heart; and lean not unto thine own understanding. In all thy ways acknowledge him, and he shall direct thy paths."

God Is Our Fortress

16 February 1270

And I will make thee unto this people a fenced brasen wall: and they shall fight against thee, but they shall not prevail against thee: for I am with thee to save thee and to deliver thee, saith the Lord.—**Jeremiah 15:20**

Founded during the twelfth century in Jerusalem, the Teutonic Order was a fraternal Catholic order that became a military order. In 1237, an autonomous branch of the Teutonic Order called the Livonian Order was formed. At the start of the thirteenth century, the Livonian Order took it upon themselves to convert the indigenous peoples of Lithuania to Catholicism. When this proved fruitless, they decided to force them to convert.

On 16 February 1270, the Livonian Order marched toward the village of Karuse to battle the Lithuanians. Both armies met on the frozen Baltic Sea. The Livonian Order, comprised of knights on horseback and foot soldiers, squared off against the entire Lithuanian army. The Lithuanians placed a screen of troops out in front in order to block the Livionians from seeing them arrange their sleighs as an improvised barricade. Once the knights attacked, the Lithuanians retreated behind their sleighs. The Livonian cavalry ran headlong into the barricade. As horses and knights got stuck between the sleighs, the Lithuanians easily picked them off with spears and won a decisive victory.

When it seems things are falling apart all around us and God has forgotten us, we can be comforted in the fact that He has promised to deliver us. "The Lord is my rock, and my fortress, and my deliverer; my God, my strength, in whom I will trust; my buckler, and the horn of my salvation, and my high tower" (Psalm 18:2). No matter the strength and attacks of Satan, we can have deliverance and victory if we depend upon the Lord and fight with His armor and His resources. Always remember the promise of 1 John 4:4, "Greater is he that is in you, than he that is in the world."

Priceless Peace

17 February 1568

Therefore being justified by faith, we have peace with God through our Lord Jesus Christ:—**Romans 5:1**

Since its inception in 1299 under the rule of Osman I, the Ottoman Empire controlled a large portion of Eastern Europe, the Middle East, and the Levant for a period of about four hundred years. With Constantinople as its capital, the Ottoman Empire was at the fulcrum of interactions between the East and West. Under Sultan Suleiman the Magnificent, the empire reached its zenith, as the Ottomans subdued and annexed portions of Habsburg-controlled Hungary following nearly two hundred years of war.

On 17 February 1568, representatives of the Holy Roman Emperor Maximilian II agreed to end their long-time struggle against the Ottomans and signed a treaty with Ottoman Sultan Selim II. Maximilian agreed to not only end hostilities, but to also pay the Ottomans an annual tribute of 30,000 ducats (about $4.5 million today) and grant them authority in Transylvania, Moldavia, and Wallachia (modern-day Romania). Had Maximilian refused Selim's demands, it is doubtful there would have been any lasting peace.

Peace with God is a free gift through the person and work of the Lord Jesus Christ. God does not demand for us to pay for it as so many peace treaties throughout history have demanded.

Furthermore, once we have peace *with* God through Jesus, He gives us the gift of the peace *of* God in our hearts through difficulties. When the disciples were with Jesus in the storm on Galilee, they panicked while Jesus slept. Finally, out of fear and desperation, they roused Jesus from sleep. He immediately brought peace to the storm. "And he arose, and rebuked the wind, and said unto the sea, Peace, be still. And the wind ceased, and there was a great calm" (Mark 4:39). When we face the storms of life, Jesus brings peace in the midst of the storm. He may not always calm the storm, but He will calm us through His peace.

The Unseen Killer

18 February 1519

Wherefore, as by one man sin entered into the world, and death by sin; and so death passed upon all men, for that all have sinned:—**Romans 5:12**

On 18 February 1519, Spanish conquistador Hernán Cortés embarked upon an expedition of conquest in what is now modern Mexico. Following an arduous journey aboard ship, the Cortés party landed in Cozumel. Following a brief interlude with the native population, Cortés chose to lead his men into the interior with the ultimate goal of amassing fortune both for himself and his regent, King Charles V. That decision resulted in the clash of two dissimilar cultures, which occasioned the annihilation of an entire people group—the Aztecs. Brutal fighting between the Spanish conquistadors and Aztec warriors escalated, but victory was not found for either side until an unseen killer was introduced.

One of Cortés' soldiers had contracted smallpox. By the early sixteenth century, smallpox had become fairly well established in Europe and most Europeans had built up an immunity against it. For the indigenous Mesoamerican population, however, it was deadly because the Aztecs had not built up a resistance. More than a quarter of the entire Aztec population died of the smallpox virus. The Aztecs were a powerful tribe that might have held off the Spanish invaders if not for this unseen killer.

Like smallpox, sin is a silent, unseen killer that debilitates and ultimately brings death. As with smallpox, sin needs a cure. Thankfully, God sent a "cure" for sin when He sent Jesus to die for our sin.

Jesus not only died for sin, but He also resurrected from the dead, which means He has power over sin and death. "Who hath saved us, and called us with an holy calling, not according to our works, but according to his own purpose and grace, which was given us in Christ Jesus before the world began, But is now made manifest by the appearing of our Saviour Jesus Christ, who hath abolished death, and hath brought life and immortality to light through the gospel" (2 Timothy 1:9–10).

Deliverance

19 February 1861

But God be thanked, that ye were the servants of sin, but ye have obeyed from the heart that form of doctrine which was delivered you. Being then made free from sin, ye became the servants of righteousness.—**Romans 6:17–18**

Although serfdom was a medieval form of social structure, it continued to be the predominant relationship that existed between peasants and nobility in Tsarist Russia even after the birth of the modern age. For hundreds of years, the Imperial Russian Empire saw nothing wrong with this social structure. When Tsar Alexander I became ruler in 1801, he sought to end serfdom, but unfortunately, he died from typhus in 1825 before bringing it to an end. His successor, Nicholas I, also disliked the practice, but fearing the Russian nobility, he did nothing to stop it. His son Alexander II, however, put an end once and for all to the blight of Russian serfdom. On 19 February 1861, Alexander II issued his famous Emancipation Manifesto, which finally abolished serfdom in Russia. Ironically, at that time, America was a year into her civil war in which the issue of slavery was front and center. Serfdom is not the same as slavery, but it does have similarities.

In Bible days, the Israelites experienced slavery in Egypt which lasted for 430 years. The Bible describes their plight in Exodus 1:13–14: "And the Egyptians made the children of Israel to serve with rigour: And they made their lives bitter with hard bondage, in morter, and in brick, and in all manner of service in the field: all their service, wherein they made them serve, was with rigour." Eventually, God sent deliverance through Moses.

In many ways, Israel's deliverance from Egypt is a picture of our deliverance from sin. Thankfully, because of Christ, we do not have to wait 430 years to be delivered from sin's bondage, nor must we wait for a leader to issue an emancipation manifesto. We can be free from sin's bondage when we turn to Christ in faith and call out to Him as our Saviour. Not only does Christ free us from the penalty of sin, but He also frees us from its power. As His children, we are free to say "no" to sin and live for Him.

Faithful until Death

20 February 1974

Moreover it is required in stewards, that a man be found faithful.
—1 Corinthians 4:2

On 20 February 1974, a young traveler named Norio Suzuki ventured to Lubang Island in the Philippines in an attempt to persuade Japanese officer Hiroo Onoda to surrender. After Onoda refused, Suzuki returned to Japan and contacted the government, which found Onoda's superior, Major Yoshimi Taniguchi. Taniguchi flew to Lubang and approached Onoda's hideout to deliver the surrender order in person. You see, Lieutenant Onoda had never been officially notified that World War II had ended almost twenty-nine years earlier, so he continued his resistance, hiding in the Philippine mountains. He did not give in until his former commanding officer was located and sent to him personally. When he emerged from the cave he had made his residence, he turned over his sword, his functioning rifle, five hundred rounds of ammunition, and several hand grenades, as well as the dagger his mother had given him in 1944 to kill himself if he was captured. Onoda never quit. In fact, had he not been informed by his superior officer of the war's end, there is no doubt he would have remained faithful until death. Lieutenant Onoda is not remembered as a great military leader. Students of military history will probably not encounter him in their studies at West Point or Annapolis. Nevertheless, Onoda epitomizes what it means to be faithful.

The spiritual war around us will rage until we are called Home by our Commanding Officer, the Lord Jesus Christ. Until that day comes, we are to remain faithful until death.

In Revelation 2:10, Christ encourages and comforts the church in Smyrna which endured great persecution: "Fear none of those things which thou shalt suffer: behold, the devil shall cast some of you into prison, that ye may be tried; and ye shall have tribulation ten days: be thou faithful unto death, and I will give thee a crown of life." Christian, be faithful.

An Unconventional Conquest

21 February 1918

(For the weapons of our warfare are not carnal, but mighty through God to the pulling down of strong holds;)—**2 Corinthians 10:4**

On 21 February 1918, a combined force of Australian, British, and New Zealand forces captured the city of Jericho during the Palestine Campaign of World War I. Although most of the attention in this war centers on the epic battles waged on the Western Front, a great deal of fighting occurred in the Middle East.

In an effort to secure his exposed right flank, British General Edmund Allenby ordered a force to capture territory east of Jerusalem, which stretched to the Dead Sea. The opposing force consisted of well-entrenched Turkish troops based on hilltops.

Under the cover of darkness, the New Zealand Mounted Rifles Brigade and the Third Australian Light Horse Regiment reached the floor of the Jordan Valley and turned northwards toward the ancient city of Jericho. Around 0800, a lone mounted infantry troop of Third Light Horse entered Jericho and discovered the Turkish garrison had withdrawn. For all intents and purposes, the British Army captured Jericho without firing a single shot.

Thousands of years before this event, Old Testament Israelites under the leadership of Joshua also captured Jericho, without having to fight. God had expressly forbidden the Israelites from using weapons of any kind. Instead, they walked the city's circumference one time for six consecutive days. On the seventh day, they circled Jericho seven times, and then the people shouted while the priests blew their shofars bringing the walls down.

God's ways are not man's ways. Often in life, we think our human reasoning is sufficient to tackle problems that come our way, when God simply desires we trust Him. "For my thoughts are not your thoughts, neither are your ways my ways, saith the LORD. For as the heavens are higher than the earth, so are my ways higher than your ways, and my thoughts than your thoughts" (Isaiah 55:8–9).

The Benefit of the Doubt

22 February 1783

Charity suffereth long, and is kind . . . Beareth all things, believeth all things, hopeth all things, endureth all things.—**1 Corinthians 13:4, 7**

John Jay is best remembered as being America's first Chief Justice of the Supreme Court. As a man skilled in the legal proceedings, one would expect Jay to dispense justice both professionally and without prejudice. Indeed there is no historical indications that he failed to do either. But as much as John Jay acted righteously in fulfilling the requirement as top judge of the land, he also was merciful.

On 22 February 1783, Jay wrote a personal letter to his former friend Silas Deane. Deane, a delegate to the Continental Congress, had been charged by Congress for financial impropriety. In his letter to Deane, Jay never sidestepped the issue of Deane's legal predicament, but rather offered to expedite matters to reach a just conclusion. Rather than castigating his former colleague, Jay did something most of us are unwilling to do—he gave Deane the benefit of the doubt. In the closing lines of his letter to Deane, Jay wrote,

> I still indulge an idea, that your head may have been more to blame than your heart; and that in some melancholy desponding hour, the disorder of your nerves infected your opinions and your pen. God grant that this may prove to have been the case, and that I may yet again have reason to resume my former opinion.

As humans, we are too often quick to judge others. First Corinthians 13, however, the great chapter on love, tells us that when we love someone, we hope for the best in them rather than assuming the worst.

How different our relationships would be if we offered others the benefit of the doubt rather than our assumptions. It is possible to be both just and merciful. Rather than focusing on someone's negative traits, why not treat them with kindness and respect?

Spiritual Exercise

23 February 1848

I love them that love me; and those that seek me early shall find me.
—Proverbs 8:17

John Quincy Adams was the son of John and Abigail Adams. Aside from being a lawyer, John Quincy Adams was a diplomat who helped negotiate the Treaty of Ghent which ended the War of 1812. In 1824, he won the presidency, but served only one term. He died on 23 February 1848, at the age of eighty. It has been said that he was the most fit president in American history because of his regimented exercise of walking more than three miles a day and regularly swimming in the Potomac River. While physical fitness no doubt contributed to his long life, Adams made a point of spending time cultivating his "spiritual fitness" as well. He once said, "My custom is to read four or five chapters of the Bible every morning immediately after rising. It seems to me the most suitable manner of beginning the day. It is an invaluable and inexhaustible mine of knowledge and virtue."

The Bible tells us that "bodily exercise profiteth little: but godliness is profitable unto all things, having promise of the life that now is, and of that which is to come" (1 Timothy 4:8). The Apostle Paul does say that physical exercise will profit us, but his message is clear: godliness should be exercised more in our lives. Certainly John Quincy Adams valued physical fitness, but he also valued spiritual fitness by starting each day with time in God's Word. This should also be a Christian's regimen: physical exercise to keep physically healthy and spiritual exercise to keep spiritually healthy.

To remain a healthy Christian, here are some exercises to do. Remain in God's Word and in prayer every day. Stay in church and in service to others. Encourage those around you. Instead of complaining or questioning trials, ask how God wants to grow your faith through the trials. When you have the desire to quit, keep pushing yourself; remember, muscles get stronger when the resistance is greater. Don't be a lethargic Christian who knows what is right but does little. Rather, obey the admonition of James 1:22, "But be ye doers of the word, and not hearers only."

Guaranteed Persecution

24 February 300

My brethren, count it all joy when ye fall into divers temptations;—**James 1:2**

On 24 February 300, Roman Emperor Diocletian issued an edict that started one of the greatest periods of Christian persecution in history. Following his rise to power in AD 284, Diocletian changed the government to an absolute monarchy. This became known as the Dominate, meaning the emperor was the sole source of all power: he was above all Roman laws and over every inhabitant of Rome, regardless of rank. His hatred toward Christianity compelled him to attempt to wipe out any followers of Jesus Christ. He hunted down Christians; he burned the Scriptures; he destroyed churches. Yet, he could not wipe out Christianity. In 313, Constantine issued the Edict of Milan, which ended some of the persecution and restored property and privileges to Christian leaders.

The Christian life is not one of ease and certainly not without difficulties. In fact, the Bible guarantees persecution to those who will strive to live godly in Christ Jesus: "Yea, and all that will live godly in Christ Jesus shall suffer persecution" (2 Timothy 3:12). When we choose to live the way the Bible tells us to live, Satan and the world will not like it. Throughout most of history, biblical Christians have lived as outsiders, suffering for their faith.

In America, we have not seen the depths of persecution that the first-century Christians experienced, but as our nation continues to remove herself from the biblical foundations used to create our nation, we must be ready for persecution. Our views will not be popular and our privileges may be taken away, but we can rest assured that God will give us the grace and strength we need to endure the persecution if and when it comes. "There hath no temptation taken you but such as is common to man: but God is faithful, who will not suffer you to be tempted above that ye are able; but will with the temptation also make a way to escape, that ye may be able to bear it" (1 Corinthians 10:13).

A Banished Army

25 February 1947

For he that is entered into his rest, he also hath ceased from his own works, as God did from his.—**Hebrews 4:10**

On 25 February 1947, a group of generals in Berlin signed what was known as Law No. 46. This law read, "The Prussian State, which from early days had been the bearer of militarism and reaction in Germany, has [officially] ceased to exist."

For nearly four hundred years, Prussia was the prominent German state. Men like Frederick the Great, Kaiser Wilhelm, and Otto von Bismarck hailed from this militaristic land of splendid uniforms and *pickelhaube* (spiked) helmets. While many nations have an army, Prussia was said to be an army with a nation because the "Great Elector" Frederick William of Brandenburg made Prussia the strongest of the northern German states. Even when the German states united in 1871, Prussian leadership remained at the head of government and military. Prussian troops excelled in close order drill and were renowned for their maneuverability on the battlefield, giving rise to the modern battle strategy known as *blitzkrieg*. But in the winter of 1947, Prussia ceased to exist. No longer would there be soldiers in the Prussian army called upon to fight.

Very soon, soldiers of Christ will be caught up in what we call the Rapture. "Then we which are alive and remain shall be caught up together with them in the clouds, to meet the Lord in the air: and so shall we ever be with the Lord" (1 Thessalonians 4:17). The phrase *caught up* is from the Greek word *rapturo*, which is where we get the English word *rapture*.

When God calls us home to Heaven, Christians will no longer be called upon to fight. We will be unified with Christ, and He will fight the final battle of mankind with His Words. "These shall make war with the Lamb, and the Lamb shall overcome them: for he is Lord of lords, and King of kings: and they that are with him are called, and chosen, and faithful" (Revelation 17:14).

The Battle That Never Was

26 February 1775

If it be possible, as much as lieth in you, live peaceably with all men. —**Romans 12:18**

In what could be called the "battle that never was," the Battle of Salem ranks as one of the strangest in history. In late February 1775, the British discovered that some cannons were stored in an armory in Salem, Massachusetts. British Colonel Alexander Leslie was ordered to march troops there and confiscate the guns. On 26 February, Leslie marched 240 Redcoats from Boston to the North Bridge in Salem. Word of this leaked to colonial militia and dozens of colonists gathered on the other side of the bridge to protest the British arrival.

Although Colonel Leslie's force far outnumbered the militiamen and were better trained and better armed, Leslie could not bring himself to start a fight, and so he offered to negotiate. Pastor Thomas Barnard of the First Church of Salem, a militia captain, agreed to discuss matters. Colonel Leslie told Pastor Barnard that his specific orders were to march to Salem and conduct a search for hidden cannons. Therefore, he proposed that if the colonists permitted him to cross the bridge and make a token search, he would thereby have satisfied his orders and could return to Boston. This seemed reasonable so the colonists agreed. Leslie and his troops crossed the bridge, walked 825 feet into Salem, turned around, and promptly returned to Boston. As a result, the beginning of the American Revolution was delayed by fifty-two days.

Confrontation with others is unavoidable, but how we respond to it is not. Colonel Leslie could have fired upon the militiamen and no doubt completed his mission, yet he chose a peaceful solution. Our reaction to others can be a positive or negative reflection on Christ. Matthew 5:9 says, "Blessed are the peacemakers: for they shall be called the children of God." When we live peaceably with others and help to be a peacemaker for others, those around us see Christ in us.

Taking Sides

27 February 1545

They went out from us, but they were not of us; for if they had been of us, they would no doubt have continued with us: but they went out, that they might be made manifest that they were not all of us.—**1 John 2:19**

During the reign of King Henry VIII, he sought to soothe relations with Scotland by arranging a marriage between his son Prince Edward of Wales and the infant Mary Queen of Scots. Scottish nobles rejected Henry's overtures, causing him to declare war on Scotland. This was nothing new for the Scots, as they had been periodically at war with England since the thirteenth century. On 27 February 1545, the English army encamped on Ancrum Moor, near the border town of Jedburgh. The English forces were comprised of around 5,000 men, of which 700 were Scottish borderers, who had sworn allegiance to England. Scottish forces numbered around 2,500.

The battle began when the English spotted a small Scottish cavalry unit moving northwest from Peniel Heugh Hill and turned back to pursue them. What the English could not know, however, was that the Scots were luring them into a trap. As the English cavalry crossed the top of the hill and galloped down the far side, they were blinded both by the setting sun and by the wind blowing their own gunpowder smoke back into their faces. The Scots seized the opportunity to attack. Most importantly, the 700 Scottish borderers who had supposedly sworn allegiance to the English tore off their red crosses signifying English allegiance and dispatched the English trying to retreat. It was a decisive Scottish victory.

According to 1 John 5:12, there are only two groups of people in this world—those who have the Son of God and those who do not. "He that hath the Son hath life; and he that hath not the Son of God hath not life."

Being a Christian means taking sides: it means choosing to stand with Christ. While it may have appeared the English could rely on those 700 borderers, they revealed their true nature when their countrymen were attacked. Be careful about trusting those who may have the wrong allegiance.

Faulty Peacemaker

28 February 1844

For they have healed the hurt of the daughter of my people slightly, saying, Peace, peace; when there is no peace.—**Jeremiah 8:11**

The Industrial Revolution revealed the engineering genius of many of the world's noteworthy inventors, scientists, and physicians. John Ericsson, a Swedish engineer, possessed an extraordinary talent for working with steam-powered vehicles. In 1842, Ericsson supervised the building and launching of the US Navy's first steam screw warship named the USS *Princeton*. This ship boasted the world's largest naval gun, a ten-ton behemoth called "Peacemaker."

On 28 February 1844, President John Tyler, along with his cabinet and several dignitaries, sailed on the *Princeton* down the Potomac River. During the cruise, Captain Robert Stockton showcased the power of the Peacemaker gun by firing at ice floes in the river. Spectators marveled at the immense destructive power of the fifteen-inch bored cannon. After reaching Mount Vernon, Stockton ordered a cease-fire, and the guests went below deck. Not all the spectators, however, were satisfied with the firing show, and several went back up for another display. At the urging of the Secretary of the Navy, Stockton ordered the gun to be fired again. When the lanyard was pulled, the explosion breached the side of the gun, sending lethal shrapnel into the crowd. President Tyler, who had been standing at the foot of the gangway, barely escaped injury. When the smoke cleared, there were six dead and twenty injured. I can think of no greater misnomer than calling this gun "Peacemaker." The name didn't change the destruction it caused.

As in the prophet Jeremiah's day, there are people today who will inaccurately tell you that all is well—at peace—when in reality, all is not well. Worldwide peace will only come when the Lord Jesus Christ returns to this Earth to establish His kingdom. But you and I can know the peace of God in our hearts today through committing our cares to Him in prayer (Philippians 4:6–7).

Dedicated Soldier

29 February 1840

Wherefore gird up the loins of your mind, be sober, and hope to the end for the grace that is to be brought unto you at the revelation of Jesus Christ;—**1 Peter 1:13**

Of the 183,000 African-American soldiers who fought in the Civil War, twenty-one received the Congressional Medal of Honor. William Harvey Carney, born 29 February 1840, became the first African-American to receive our nation's highest honor. Born a slave in Norfolk, Virginia, Carney escaped to Massachusetts via the Underground Railroad and volunteered to serve with the famous 54th Massachusetts Regiment, an all-black regiment immortalized in the 1989 film *Glory*. During the assault on Fort Wagner in Charleston, South Carolina, Carney grabbed the American flag after the flag bearer was shot down. He then led the way to the parapet to plant the colors. During this Union push, Carney was shot in the face, yet he refused to allow the flag to touch the ground and held it while his troops charged the Confederate line. Unfortunately, the generals sounded a retreat and Carney, wounded twice more, struggled back across the battlefield to return the flag to Union lines. Before turning over the colors, Carney modestly said, "Boys, I only did my duty; the old flag never touched the ground!" Nearly forty years later, Carney was awarded the Congressional Medal of Honor for his heroism under fire.

William Harvey Carney serves as an inspiration to us all when it comes to dedication. Despite being shot three times, Carney was dedicated to getting the American flag back to his lines before the enemy could take it. How dedicated are we to the cause of Christ? Someone once said, "The test of a man's character is what it takes to stop you." The Apostle Paul was determined that nothing would stop him in his dedication to Christ. As he faced upcoming persecution, he boldly declared, "But none of these things move me, neither count I my life dear unto myself, so that I might finish my course with joy, and the ministry, which I have received of the Lord Jesus, to testify the gospel of the grace of God" (Acts 20:24).

MARCH

Who Looks to You?

1 March 2013

And the things that thou hast heard of me among many witnesses, the same commit thou to faithful men, who shall be able to teach others also.—**2 Timothy 2:2**

On 1 March 2013, the final volume of Aristotle's work *Nicomachean Ethics* was published by Harvard University after being translated from its original Greek by Professor of Philosophy C. D. C. Reeve.

Aristotle, who lived in the fourth century, is perhaps best known for being the world's first great philosopher. For twenty years, Aristotle was a part of Plato's circle in Athens, Greece, until differences developed which ultimately caused a rift in their relationship. Aristotle then left Athens and moved to Pella, the capital city of Macedonia. Shortly after moving, he was asked to teach a group of young noblemen in the court of King Philip II of Macedon.

This ancient version of a preparatory school taught various subjects such as mathematics, exercise, horsemanship, and philosophy. As was common during that time in history, a full-time tutor spent more time with his charges than the boys' parents did. Consequently, Aristotle had an incredible influence on the young minds entrusted to his care. Many of his pupils became great generals and leaders, but Aristotle's most famous pupil was the heir to the Macedonian throne—Alexander the Great. One day, Alexander would conquer all of the known world and be regarded as history's greatest general. Much of who Alexander the Great was as a leader could be traced to the influence of Aristotle.

Everyone has influence on someone. John Donne said, "No man is an island entire of itself; every man is a piece of the continent, a part of the main." In the Bible, we see the godly influence that Paul was on the young pastor Timothy. As Paul trained Timothy and then admonished Timothy to transfer truth to "faithful men, who shall be able to teach others also," we should be aware of our influence and purposefully invest in teaching others. Influence is a gift. So make sure your influence is a positive one that builds others and points them to Christ.

Indecisive

2 March 1904

And Elijah came unto all the people, and said, How long halt ye between two opinions? if the LORD be God, follow him: but if Baal, then follow him. And the people answered him not a word.—**1 Kings 18:21**

Theodor Seuss Giesel was born in Springfield, Massachusetts, on 2 March 1904. In 1936, a storm arose while he was returning from a transatlantic cruise to Germany. With the sinking of the *Titanic* and the *Lusitania* still in his memory, Giesel feared that he and his wife would not survive the storm. To alleviate his fears, he scribbled some words on a piece of stationery, imagining himself contributing to the ship's ability to withstand the storm by writing verses with anapestic rhythm duplicating the engine's chugging sound. Thus out of a storm was born the familiar and beloved writing style of Dr. Seuss.

Theodor Giesel went on to create a legacy that has touched millions of children and adults worldwide, selling more than two hundred million copies of his books in fifteen languages. When Giesel learned the Nazis were rolling into Paris in 1940, he took a hiatus from children's books and dedicated his talents to overcoming American isolationism by illustrating political cartoons. Through these political cartoons, Giesel reproved those who sat on the fence doing nothing about the spread of evil around the world. In 1999, historian Richard H. Minear compiled around two hundred of Seuss' political cartoons in a book entitled *Dr. Seuss Goes to War*.

Like those who preferred isolationism during World War II, many Christians are content to "sit on the fence," halting between two opinions. A carnal Christian is content with his salvation but refuses to commit to the spiritual war effort against Satan. Parliamentarian Edmund Burke (1729–1797) once said, "The only thing necessary for the triumph of evil is for good men to do nothing." Don't sit on the fence of indecision; join the fight.

A Vital Conduit

3 March 1965

Abide in me, and I in you. As the branch cannot bear fruit of itself, except it abide in the vine; no more can ye, except ye abide in me.—**John 15:4**

During the Vietnam War, North Vietnamese military forces regularly supplied communist sympathizers in South Vietnam via a supply route called the Ho Chi Minh Trail. The trail was used daily to send weapons, manpower, ammunition, and other supplies to insurgent forces operating in the south. Although it was initially just a crude series of jungle tracks, the Ho Chi Minh Trail became a sophisticated conduit of truck and foot routes stretching from mountain passes to communist sanctuaries and providing life-sustaining war materials to communist forces. At any one time, as many as 100,000 people were employed along the trail with the sole purpose of keeping the trail open. Had it not been for the Ho Chi Minh Trail, the North Vietnamese Army could not have successfully carried on the war.

On 3 March 1965, more than thirty US Air Force fighter bombers struck multiple targets along the trail in an attempt to sever this crucial supply network, but their efforts proved futile as North Vietnamese and Vietcong troops immediately repaired the damage.

In the Christian life, we have a life-sustaining conduit of spiritual nourishment as well, and that is our connection to Jesus Christ. The Lord used the word picture of a vine to help His disciples understand the necessity of this relationship. Without the nourishment that comes from abiding in the Vine, our branches will wither and die.

Sin can block this conduit if we allow it to grow in our lives. Satan will attack the conduit by throwing temptations in to block the flow. The only way to keep receiving the nourishment from the Vine is to keep the conduit clear. Is there anything in your life that has blocked your supply of spiritual nourishment? Get in the Word of God today and ask God to help you clear the conduit that is vital to your spiritual fruit.

No Return

4 March 1519

And Jesus said unto him, No man, having put his hand to the plough, and looking back, is fit for the kingdom of God.—**Luke 9:62**

Following Christopher Columbus' famous voyage in 1492, the Spanish financed multiple expeditions to explore the Americas. Hernán Cortés sailed to the Caribbean with hundreds of men and eleven ships. He landed in Veracruz on 4 March 1519. The Aztec king Montezuma sent an emissary to meet with Cortés. Upon seeing the gold jewelry worn by their Aztec host, Cortés reportedly said to the emissary, "We have a disease of the heart, that can only be cured by gold. Do you have more?" The emissary nonchalantly declared that he had lots of it.

Motivated by greed, Cortés decided to make the arduous trek inland, which included crossing mountain peaks of up to fifteen-thousand feet to reach the Aztec capital. Because he knew his men would not be persuaded to go with him, Cortés destroyed all his ships, which had carried him and his men to the New World. With no means of retreat, the men had no other option but to join him on his excursion to the city of Tenochtitlán and his ultimate capture and annihilation of the Aztec peoples.

A familiar hymn contains a stanza that reads, "I have decided to follow Jesus—no turning back, no turning back." As followers of the Lord Jesus Christ, Christians should resolve to have a "no return policy," refusing to go back to the worldly flesh and lusts.

Turning back to the world, however, is easier than we may think. For example, consider the first-century helper of Paul named Demas, who is mentioned three times in the New Testament. In Colossians and Philemon, Paul mentions Demas as a fellow laborer, but in 2 Timothy 4:10 Paul writes, "For Demas hath forsaken me, having loved this present world, and is departed unto Thessalonica." Instead of being faithful, Demas chose to return to the world. May it never be said of us that we have returned to the former lusts of this world instead of growing and moving forward to a victorious Christian life.

A Second Return

5 March 2018

Much more then, being now justified by his blood, we shall be saved from wrath through him.—**Romans 5:9**

On 5 March 2018, the USS *Carl Vinson* aircraft carrier made a port call in Vietnam. The supercarrier anchored in Da Nang Port, which had served as America's major staging post for the American war effort in the 1960s. To develop better relations between the once warring countries, the US and Vietnamese navies trained and participated in cultural activities together. In the 1960s, the Carl Vinson was a symbol of war and destruction. But its presence in 2018 symbolized peace and stability between former enemies.

More than two thousand years ago, the Prince of Peace entered this world in a manger. His mission was "to seek and to save that which was lost" (Luke 19:10). When Jesus came the first time, He brought peace to mankind through salvation. But there is coming a day when Jesus will come for a second time. And at this Second Coming, He will bring judgment for the sin and unbelief of this world. The book of Revelation describes His return as a time of wrath as He smites the nations. "And out of his mouth goeth a sharp sword, that with it he should smite the nations: and he shall rule them with a rod of iron: and he treadeth the winepress of the fierceness and wrath of Almighty God" (Revelation 19:15).

Christians have no need to fear Jesus' Second Coming, for we will be fighting alongside Him. We have been saved from His wrath by believing and trusting only in Him for eternal life. Rest in His promise today that we can know His peace, and in knowing that peace, we can share it with others so they too can be saved from the wrath to come. "For God hath not appointed us to wrath, but to obtain salvation by our Lord Jesus Christ, Who died for us, that, whether we wake or sleep, we should live together with him" (1 Thessalonians 5:9–10).

Re-Fortification

6 March 1916

For which cause we faint not; but though our outward man perish, yet the inward man is renewed day by day.—**2 Corinthians 4:16**

During World War I, the Battle of Verdun became synonymous with meaningless slaughter. Ranked the longest-running battle of the war, Verdun resulted in more than a million casualties with almost a year of fighting. The battle began in February 1916 with the Germans attacking the fortress city of Verdun, and the goal was to "bleed the French white" and destroy their morale.

Knowing the Allies planned to start a major offensive along the Somme River in July, the German high command decided to shift the focus from the inner ring of defenses that protected Verdun to the outer flanks surrounding the city. On 6 March 1916, the Germans attacked along the West bank of the Meuse River, but were unable to prevail over Verdun. The Germans had underestimated the strength of the French fortifications as well as their ability to repair the damaged fortifications during battle lulls. The French soldiers, undoubtedly tired in the midst of repairing and re-fortifying their defenses, persisted. And, their efforts were crucial to the French defense of the city, as well as their ultimate victory in the Battle of Verdun in December 1916.

As Christians, we often will tire of the constant attacks by the world, the flesh, and the devil. In many cases, our defenses may be torn down or weakened. It is at these times that we must rally and renew our inner man so that we may live to fight another day. Even when our physical bodies are weak, we can receive spiritual strength to continue in the spiritual battle.

Second Corinthians 4:18 gives us the key: "While we look not at the things which are seen, but at the things which are not seen: for the things which are seen are temporal; but the things which are not seen are eternal." As Corrie ten Boom said, "If you look at the world, you'll be distressed. If you look within, you'll be depressed. If you look at God, you'll be at rest." So, look to Him today.

Filling the Power Vacuum

7 March 1936

That ye put off concerning the former conversation the old man, which is corrupt according to the deceitful lusts.—**Ephesians 4:22**

The Rhineland is a strategic border region between France and Germany. Germany gained control of the region after the Franco-Prussian War of 1870–71, but lost it to France in the Versailles Treaty of World War I.

From 1919–1930, unrest and conflict continued between the French and the Germans concerning the Rhineland. Tired of the constant conflict, in 1930 France withdrew her troops from the region entirely, leaving a power vacuum.

On 7 March 1936, Adolf Hitler filled that vacuum as he marched three battalions of German troops into the Rhineland. The French and British did nothing to prevent this, nor did they attempt to oust the Germans from the Rhineland. Undoubtedly, Hitler saw their reaction as a sign of appeasement and weakness, which emboldened him to begin his drive toward world dominance, ultimately leading to World War II.

In most cases throughout history, a power vacuum does not take long to fill. Because selfish leaders thrive on power, a territory that has no political powers controlling it does not stay in a vacuum for long; someone always takes control.

As Christians, we are called to replace our former sinful behaviors with righteous ones. Scripture doesn't merely command us to stop what is wrong; it tells us to begin what is right. Throughout the New Testament we see the terminology "put off . . . put on." You see, when a Christian puts off the old, he leaves a vacuum. If we don't fill that vacuum with righteous behaviors, it leaves that territory open for the reentry of wicked habits. "That ye put off concerning the former conversation the old man, which is corrupt according to the deceitful lusts; And be renewed in the spirit of your mind; And that ye put on the new man, which after God is created in righteousness and true holiness" (Ephesians 4:22–24).

Not Your Typical Weapons

8 March 1966

Some trust in chariots, and some in horses: but we will remember the name of the L*ORD our God.*—**Psalm 20:7**

In modern wars, guns are the obvious choice of the foot soldier. In World War II, one soldier preferred to fight with bow and arrow and a sword rather than to use modern weapons. John Malcolm Thorpe Fleming Churchill, better known as "Mad" or "Fighting Jack," was renowned for his adventurous and anachronistic approach to modern combat.

Trained as a British commando, "Mad" Jack Churchill was so skilled with the bow that he competed in the world archery championship in 1939. During the war, he led his two commando groups into battle while waving his sword and uttering battle cries, reminiscent of medieval times. In one particular battle, he played his bagpipes in the landing craft while going to shore. "Fighting Jack" Churchill's colorful life came to an end on 8 March 1996 at the age of ninety.

John Churchill's unusual trust of ancient and medieval weaponry in modern combat reminds us of the Christian's weapons of choice. Second Corinthians 10:4 specifically tells us that our weapons are not "carnal," meaning "of the flesh": "For the weapons of our warfare are not carnal, but mighty through God to the pulling down of strong holds." According to Ephesians 6, our two offensive weapons in spiritual combat are the Word of God and prayer: "And take the helmet of salvation, and the sword of the Spirit, which is the word of God: Praying always with all prayer and supplication in the Spirit, and watching thereunto with all perseverance and supplication for all saints" (Ephesians 6:17–18).

Our world often claims that the Bible and prayer are out of date, but that is not the case. Both still have the power to give victory because God is the source of both. Hebrews 4:12 says, "For the word of God is quick, and powerful, and sharper than any twoedged sword, piercing even to the dividing asunder of soul and spirit, and of the joints and marrow, and is a discerner of the thoughts and intents of the heart."

A Clean Slate

9 March 1831

And their sins and iniquities will I remember no more.—**Hebrews 10:17**

King Louis-Philippe I (1773–1850) created the French Foreign Legion by royal ordinance on 9 March 1831. The Legion has always been known for its toughness and has been involved in nearly every French battle campaign since the nineteenth century.

The Foreign Legion was led by French officers and consisted of a single regiment of seven battalions, with each battalion containing eight companies. The training regimen was notoriously brutal because of the areas they would be assigned to fight. Between the brutal treatment and the instilled discipline, the Legion's unofficial motto became "march or die."

During the Legion's inception, it attracted malcontents, criminals, and assorted outcasts from other countries in Europe. These men saw joining the Legion as a way to start fresh. Many signed up with assumed names, as well as gave up their national allegiance in order to join this special task force.

When we trust Christ as our Saviour, He does something better than ignore our past. We get a far better gift. God wipes our sin debt clean and justifies us through the blood of Christ. Justification means "to declare righteous." Once God has declared us righteous, He also assures us that He does not remember—or call to mind—our past sins and iniquities. He gives us a truly clean slate. Second Corinthians 5:17 assures us, "Therefore if any man be in Christ, he is a new creature: old things are passed away; behold, all things are become new."

The forgiveness we have in Christ gives us the freedom to press forward into the future. We, too, can choose to trust our past to the blood of Christ and move forward for Him. As Paul stated in Philippians 3:13–14, we have not yet attained victory: "Brethren, I count not myself to have apprehended: but this one thing I do, forgetting those things which are behind, and reaching forth unto those things which are before, I press toward the mark for the prize of the high calling of God in Christ Jesus."

Rewards for Service

10 March 1813

And if a man also strive for masteries, yet is he not crowned, except he strive lawfully.—**2 Timothy 2:5**

The Iron Cross was instituted on 10 March 1813 by the king of Prussia, Friedrich Wilhelm III. As the most famous and striking of Prussian military decorations, this award is given for bravery in the field of battle. First given during the Napoleonic Wars, it became the first European military decoration issued for gallantry regardless of the military rank or social status of the recipient.

As originally designed, the Iron Cross had three degrees, Second Class, First Class, and Grand Cross. The construction of the medal was a blackened iron center, with silver trim around the edge. Ribbon widths varied in length. In World War II, Adolf Hitler added five additional degrees as a morale booster. As the war progressed, silver and iron became scarce and were replaced with alloy and brass.

After the awards ceremony, the medal was usually sent to the recipient's home while the ribbon was worn on their uniform. Later, a bar was made from the ribbon and worn on the left chest along with various other wartime ribbon bars.

The Iron Cross has not been awarded since the end of World War II. During the Cold War, however, Germans living in West Germany exchanged their swastika-bedecked, Nazi-era awards for the more traditional ones. An authentic Iron Cross today is a five-figure investment and their value continues to rise among collectors.

Soldiers don't receive their awards in the middle of the battle; they receive them after the battle has ended. Even so, you and I will receive the rewards Christ has promised to us after this life. These eternal rewards will not be cheaply-comprised substitutes, and we will never need to exchange them. So stay faithful, Christian soldier. Jesus promised, "And, behold, I come quickly; and my reward is with me, to give every man according as his work shall be" (Revelation 22:12).

A Fulfilled Promise

11 March 1942

And if I go and prepare a place for you, I will come again, and receive you unto myself; that where I am, there ye may be also.—**John 14:3**

The attack on Pearl Harbor in December of 1941 caught America by surprise. A day after the attack, Japan also invaded the Philippines, an American territory at the time. After losing much of his air support and with no promise from Washington, DC regarding reinforcements, General Douglas MacArthur was forced to leave Corregidor with his family and a few staff officers, leaving behind thousands of Allied troops on the islands.

Before leaving his troops, MacArthur falsely assured them that thousands of fresh troops with strong air support were on their way to relieve the beleaguered American and Philippine forces on Bataan. He ordered them to fight on until these reinforcements arrived, but MacArthur's unrealistic order to his troops to fight on for a hopeless cause condemned them to even greater suffering in the Bataan Death March.

On 11 March 1942, MacArthur departed in a patrol torpedo boat for Australia where, upon arrival in Melbourne, MacArthur delivered a memorable speech to reporters. Concerning the loss of the Philippine Islands to the Japanese, he promised, "I shall return." He fulfilled this promise in 1944 after a victory over the Japanese at Leyte Gulf.

While MacArthur's promise to return may have been an attempt at self-promotion and was not something MacArthur could ultimately ensure, the Lord Jesus Christ's promise to return is different. It is absolutely certain because God cannot lie (Titus 1:2).

God has given thousands of promises in the Bible just for us. Some have been fulfilled as in the case of Jesus' first coming, death, and resurrection for the sins of men. Some promises, such as His promises to return, are yet to be fulfilled. But whatever the promise, we can trust that His Word is true, and that He is indeed coming again. This assurance fills us with hope. "Looking for that blessed hope, and the glorious appearing of the great God and our Saviour Jesus Christ" (Titus 2:13).

Friendly Fire

12 March 1918

The beginning of strife is as when one letteth out water: therefore leave off contention, before it be meddled with.—**Proverbs 17:14**

On 12 March 1918, the HMS *D3* British submarine was days from completing her patrol when lookouts spotted an object over the horizon. The British sailors identified it as a French airship on patrol and signaled recognition rockets to ensure that the French airship knew they were friendly. The French, however, mistook the identification rockets as an act of aggression and began strafing the hull of the submarine.

Realizing the airship had bombs aboard, the British commander gave the order to dive as the crew frantically scrambled back inside the submarine before the airship could unload her payload. As the *D3* disappeared beneath the waves, the airship dropped bombs, which exploded about sixty-five feet from the submarine. Heavily damaged from the attack, all but four crew members sank to the bottom of the English channel with the destroyed submarine.

As the French airship descended to take prisoners, they heard the survivors speaking English and realized their mistake. Now attempting to rescue them, the airship couldn't reach them, and since they were unable to radio for help, they had to head to shore to relay the location. By the time a vessel did reach the area, the four survivors had joined their crew mates in the watery grave of the HMS *D3*.

Too often, Christians strive with one another which causes division within churches and families and ultimately hurts the cause of Christ. Friendly fire is never truly friendly, and it leaves many casualties. Rather than firing back a quick retort or returning evil with evil, reach out with an effort to restore peace. The next time contention rises with family, a friend, a co-worker, or another Christian remember these words: "Let nothing be done through strife or vainglory; but in lowliness of mind let each esteem other better than themselves" (Philippians 2:3).

Man's Best Friend

13 March 1942

A man that hath friends must shew himself friendly: and there is a friend that sticketh closer than a brother.—**Proverbs 18:24**

The US military began using dogs during World War I to carry messages, to alert soldiers to the presence of chemical gas, and even to attack enemy soldiers. Following the "war to end all wars," the practice was largely abandoned. During World War II, however, the American Kennel Association and an organization called "Dogs for Defense" asked dog owners to consider donating healthy canines to the US Army's Quartermaster Corps (QMC).

On 13 March 1942, the QMC began training dogs for its newly established K-9 Corps. Training lasted around twelve weeks, after which the canine "soldiers" were then sent through one of four specialized schools to prepare them for duty as sentries, scouts, messengers, or mine-detectors. The most decorated canine hero of World War II was Chips, a German Shepherd mix who served with the 3rd Infantry Division during the Allied invasion of Sicily. Trained as a sentry, Chips broke away from his handler and ran toward machine gun fire that was pinning down Allied troops during an amphibious landing. He attacked a gun nest, biting German soldiers and pulling the smoking machine-gun from its base. When Chips dragged a German soldier from the pill box, the rest of the stunned Germans followed with their hands up. Later that day, Chips helped capture ten other enemy soldiers, suffering minor wounds in the process. He was awarded the Distinguished Service Cross, Silver Star, and the Purple Heart for his heroic and selfless efforts.

In our Western world, dogs have been described as a "man's best friend" because of their loyalty to their owners. But in reality, we have one Friend that "sticketh closer than a brother" (Proverbs 18:24), and His name is Jesus. He took on the enemy of sin and death; He protects us from harm; and He speaks to us through His Word. We have no Friend who is more faithful and loyal to us than He.

Falsely Accused

14 March 1991

Blessed are ye, when men shall revile you, and persecute you, and shall say all manner of evil against you falsely, for my sake.—**Matthew 5:11**

The Irish Republican Army (IRA) is a paramilitary terrorist force dedicated to an independent Ireland, free from British rule. Since 1919, the IRA has waged war against the British military and police, primarily relying on bombing as its main method of attack.

In 1974, members of the IRA bombed two pubs in Birmingham, England, killing 21 people and injuring 182 others. A year later, six men (called the Birmingham Six) were found guilty of the bombings and sentenced to life in prison. Hugh Callaghan, Paddy Hill, Gerry Hunter, Richard McIlkenny, Billy Power, and Johnny Walker spent sixteen years in prison before their convictions were overturned on the basis of evidence fabrication, unreliable scientific evidence, and evidence suppression. On 14 March 1991, the Birmingham Six were exonerated and collectively received millions of pounds in compensation for their wrongful conviction.

When the Pharisees and the Sadducees accused Jesus before Pontius Pilate, the ruler said he found "no fault in this man" (Luke 23:14), but then Pilate sentenced Christ to be crucified.

As followers of Christ, Christians are also falsely accused. Since we are children of the King of Heaven, Satan and the unbelieving may try to find ways to "revile you, and persecute you, and shall say all manner of evil against you falsely" because of your relationship with Christ. When this happens, Matthew 5:12 says we are to "rejoice, and be exceeding glad: for great is your reward in heaven: for so persecuted they the prophets which were before you." Don't worry about the false accusations from the world, and don't retaliate in anger. Instead, take comfort in knowing that Christ understands, and respond as He responded: "Who, when he was reviled, reviled not again; when he suffered, he threatened not; but committed himself to him that judgeth righteously" (1 Peter 2:23).

Overconfidence Yields Failure

15 March 44 BC

Wherefore let him that thinketh he standeth take heed lest he fall.
—1 Corinthians 10:12

"Beware the Ides of March" has become synonymous with the assassination of Julius Caesar on 15 March 44 BC. Beginning with his rise to consul in 59 BC, Caesar continued to rise to power through his victories in the Gallic Wars and Rome's civil war.

Following the civil war, the Roman Senate gave him temporary dictatorial control, which Caesar used to carry out reform and revisions that would aid the growing Roman Empire. Becoming overconfident in his popularity and power, Caesar did not concern himself with the growing animosity from the Senate. When Caesar declared his intentions to make his dictatorship permanent, the Senate made plans to assassinate him and to restore the Roman Republic. Although suspicious of some of the senators, Caesar was still confident that his power would triumph over any plot devised. This overconfidence ultimately led to his death at the hands of those he had trusted most.

Overconfidence in our strength or talents will leave us open for failure. In Joshua 7, the Israelites became overconfident with the victory at Jericho and turned to attack the smaller city of Ai without asking for the Lord's guidance first. They failed in what had seemed to be an easy victory because God was not in the battle with them. Had they simply sought God's guidance, He would have revealed Achan's hidden sin which kept them from victory. While God will often have us make plans, He still wants to be a part of those plans. First Corinthians 1:25 says, "The foolishness of God is wiser than men; and the weakness of God is stronger than men."

While the world often portrays people with power as successful, God points out that He has "chosen the weak things of the world to confound the things which are mighty" (1 Corinthians 1:27). It is not weakness to rely on God instead of ourselves. We will be stronger with His strength than any we can formulate on our own.

Rescue the Perishing

16 March 1968

And others save with fear, pulling them out of the fire; hating even the garment spotted by the flesh.—**Jude 23**

War atrocities are nothing new. Since the time of armed conflict, combatants have often chosen to abrogate the laws of war to engage in outright murder. In the twentieth century, places like Babi Yar and Malmedy come to mind when pondering man's inhumane actions toward other men. During the Vietnam War, one of the most heinous acts ever to be perpetrated on innocent civilians was committed by young American males.

On the morning of 16 March 1968, three companies of soldiers from the 11th Infantry Brigade entered the village of My Lai near the Quang Ngai province on the south central coast of Vietnam. For reasons that remain unclear to this day, a heavily armed combat unit brutally murdered over five hundred unarmed Vietnamese civilians: women, children, and old men. Despite the horror that unfolded, a glimmer of mercy was found in helicopter pilot Hugh Thompson, Jr.

Flying over the village, he observed US troops from the air and thought they were firing on enemy forces. Once he realized what was happening, he landed his helicopter and persuaded the hiding Vietnamese to come out. He ordered his gunner to shoot any American soldier who opened fire on the civilians. None did. Thompson then radioed for another helicopter to evacuate the group. His actions undoubtedly spared many from death.

We live in a world filled with death and decay. The Bible tells us that "the wages of sin is death" (Romans 6:23), and the only remedy is in the Person of the Lord Jesus Christ. When we share the message of salvation with others, we, as the hymn by Fanny Crosby states, rescue the perishing:

> Rescue the perishing, care for the dying,
> Snatch them in pity from sin and the grave;
> Weep o'er the erring one, lift up the fallen,
> Tell them of Jesus the mighty to save.

Priceless

17 March 2016

Which is the earnest of our inheritance until the redemption of the purchased possession, unto the praise of his glory.—**Ephesians 1:14**

You've heard the phrase, "one man's trash is another man's treasure." This was certainly the case for the Whiteman family on 17 March 2016.

At a thrift store in Mesa, Arizona, Laura Hardy stumbled upon a Purple Heart medal, priced at $4.99. Laura purchased it in order to find the rightful owner and to return it to the family of the veteran. Fortunately, the recipient of a Purple Heart always has his or her name inscribed on the back of the medal. This medal's inscription read *Private First Class Eual H. Whiteman.*

Through the help of Tina Cook of Veteran Buddy Finder, Laura was able to find a living relative in Missouri—Whiteman's sister-in-law Phyllis Lawson. Tina and Laura contacted Mrs. Lawson and returned Eual's Purple Heart to the family. For Laura, this mission had been personal because her grandfather was also a Purple Heart recipient. Whiteman's Purple Heart held little monetary value, but the sacrifice it symbolizes is priceless.

Do you ever feel worthless? Does your life seem as if it has no purpose? Feelings of worthlessness may come from the reminder of past failures or from the lack of acceptance by others. Satan, called "the accuser of our brethren" in Revelation 12:10, looks for ways to put us in the "junk pile." But God has already purchased us at a great price, the precious blood of Jesus Christ. The price He paid for us shows the depth of His love for us.

Ephesians 2 shows us just how much God values us: "But God, who is rich in mercy, for his great love wherewith he loved us, Even when we were dead in sins, hath quickened us together with Christ, (by grace ye are saved;) And hath raised us up together, and made us sit together in heavenly places in Christ Jesus: That in the ages to come he might shew the exceeding riches of his grace in his kindness toward us through Christ Jesus" (Ephesians 2:4–7).

Holding On

18 March 1965

Set your affection on things above, not on things on the earth.—**Colossians 3:2**

During the Space Race, the United States and Soviet Union competed to see which nation would be the first to land a man on the moon. The United States won that race when Neil Armstrong walked on the moon in July 1969, but the Soviet Union garnered the accomplishment of having the first man to walk in space four years earlier. On 18 March 1965, Soviet Cosmonaut Alexei Leonov became the first human to venture outside a spacecraft and enter the void of space. After opening the air-lock of his space capsule, the Soviet cosmonaut floated above Earth for twelve minutes, tethered to his ship by a sixteen-foot cable. That cable was the only thing connecting Leonov to his transport.

He came close to never making it back inside the capsule when his suit began to balloon out of shape and the fabric stiffened. His hands slipped from his gloves, his feet came out of his boots and he could no longer fit through the air-lock. Thinking fast, Leonov bled some air from the suit to deflate it just enough to slip back inside the air lock.

Any of us in Leonov's situation would want desperately to get back into the space capsule and back to our loved ones. As Christians, our home is now above, and our affections should be there too. God calls us to set our affection, and by implication our attention as well, on things above.

What has your attention today? Who or what was first on your mind this morning? Are your affections more on Christ or more on this world?

Sometimes our lives, like Leonov's space suit, are so inflated with ourselves and things of this world that we can't seem to focus on Christ. When we instead purposefully turn our focus to the eternal, we let out some of that empty focus and can once again see clearly. "While we look not at the things which are seen, but at the things which are not seen: for the things which are seen are temporal; but the things which are not seen are eternal" (2 Corinthians 4:18).

Air Support

19 March 1916

Now we exhort you, brethren, warn them that are unruly, comfort the feebleminded, support the weak, be patient toward all men.—**1 Thessalonians 5:14**

Air support has been used in war since the Chinese used kites for gathering military intelligence; however, airplanes became the main type of military air support in World War I. Although America did not participate in the early years of World War I, an eleven-month mission into Mexico prepared our military to fight in more ways than one.

After receiving permission from Mexico's government, President Wilson sent Brigadier General John J. Pershing with seven thousand US troops into Mexico to pursue and capture the bandit revolutionary Pancho Villa. After leading his guerillas in a brutal raid against the town of Columbus, New Mexico, Pancho Villa fled back into Mexico to escape American justice. On 19 March 1916, America used planes in combat for the first time. During the eleven months that the First Aero Squadron helped US troops in Mexico, they flew hundreds of missions and gained the valuable experience needed for when America entered World War I.

It is interesting to note that on this same month and day in 1928, another "first" was accomplished by combat air support: Marine Aviation conducted the first US dive bombing mission to ward off Nicaraguan guerrillas during their civil war.

Just as our military depends on air support, so we as Christians must learn to support those who need help in their spiritual warfare. Many times, Christian brothers and sisters need support from their church families in order to endure their spiritual battle. It might be a sick loved one or a job lost, but whatever the trial, we should be there to support them in their weakness.

"I have shewed you all things, how that so labouring ye ought to support the weak, and to remember the words of the Lord Jesus, how he said, It is more blessed to give than to receive" (Acts 20:35). Who do you know today that is going through a trial to whom you can give your support?

A Prayer for Peace

20 March 1797

For they have healed the hurt of the daughter of my people slightly, saying, Peace, peace; when there is no peace.—**Jeremiah 8:11**

As Governor of Massachusetts, Samuel Adams proclaimed a "Day of Fasting" on 20 March 1797. In his address, Adams stated:

> And as it is our duty to extend our wishes to the happiness of the great family of man, I conceive that we cannot better express ourselves than by humbly supplicating the Supreme Ruler of the world that the rod of tyrants may be broken to pieces, and the oppressed made free again; that wars may cease in all the earth, and that the confusions that are and have been among nations may be overruled by promoting and speedily bringing on that holy and happy period when the kingdom of our Lord and Saviour Jesus Christ may be everywhere established, and all people everywhere willingly bow to the scepter of Him who is Prince of Peace.

Someone once said, "Warfare is the engine that turns the wheel of history." Since man has been on the Earth, wars and rumors of wars have continued to frustrate the hope for peace. "And ye shall hear of wars and rumours of wars: see that ye be not troubled: for all these things must come to pass, but the end is not yet" (Matthew 24:6).

Samuel Adams understood that peace will only come when the Prince of Peace is ruling this Earth. Until true world peace does exist during the Millennial Reign of Jesus Christ, it would be expedient for state and federal representatives to lay aside political rhetoric and beseech the only One who can truly bring peace to our world.

Because Satan is still "the prince of the power of the air, the spirit that now worketh in the children of disobedience" (Ephesians 2:2), world peace is not possible; however, peace for the individual or within a nation is possible if that nation will humbly acknowledge and pray for the peace of God as Samuel Adams did in 1797.

Symbol Versus Idol

21 March 630

He removed the high places, and brake the images, and cut down the groves, and brake in pieces the brasen serpent that Moses had made: for unto those days the children of Israel did burn incense to it: and he called it Nehushtan. **—2 Kings 18:4**

The hope of obtaining religious relics was among the various motivations for the Knights Templar to battle the Muslims in the Crusades. The prospect of garnering the crown of thorns worn by Christ, the bones of an Apostle, or perhaps even the cross of Golgotha itself caused a great deal of fervor among this group of religious crusaders. But none caused more controversy than the quest to return the "true cross" to Jerusalem.

The legend of the "true cross" began in AD 326 when Empress Helena, mother of Constantine I, allegedly discovered a remnant of Jesus' cross in a cavern outside Jerusalem. Helena encased the cross in gold and precious stones and placed it in the Church of the Holy Sepulcher. In 614, Persian King Khosrow II moved it to his own land after capturing Jerusalem.

On 21 March 630, Roman Emperor Heraclius defeated Khosrow II and retook the cross, which he moved to Constantinople and later returned to Jerusalem. Legend claimed that the cross remained hidden there until the Battle of Hattin in 1187 when Saladin captured it. Although the "true cross" was an inspiration and death sentence to many brave knights, it has disappeared from historical records. Even if it does exist somewhere, God would not condone enshrining it as an object of worship.

The cross is a symbol of the sacrifice for a sinful people that was paid by Jesus Christ. Over the centuries, however, many have made the cross into an idol, worshipping it instead of Christ Himself. A symbol is a reminder, but an idol is worshiped. The Bible instructs us to keep ourselves from anything that replaces the worship of the Lord. "And we know that the Son of God is come, and hath given us an understanding, that we may know him that is true. . . . This is the true God, and eternal life. Little children, keep yourselves from idols. Amen" (1 John 5:20–21).

Co-Equal with the Father

22 March 238

I and my Father are one.—**John 10:30**

As was so often the case in the ancient Roman Empire, the Senate did not always like their emperors. When Maximinus Thrax became emperor after his predecessor was assassinated in AD 235, the Senate quickly disagreed with his unfair tax policy and ill treatment of the poor and sought for ways to rid themselves of him. Things came to a head when one of Maximinus' tax collectors was murdered by a disgruntled nobleman in the province of Carthage, North Africa.

Deciding they wanted a new emperor, the provincial nobles burst into the home of Africa's governor Gordianius, threw a purple cloak around him, and demanded at sword point he become the new Roman emperor. He reluctantly accepted, but because of his advanced age, he insisted that his son Marcus Antonius Gordianus become co-emperor with him. On 22 March 238, the aged Gordianius arrived in Carthage as Gordian I with his son as Gordian II. The Roman Senate approved this and accepted the Gordians as Rome's co-emperors. Neither Gordian held power over the other; they were co-equal in every respect.

Despite what some religions teach, Jesus is not a created god, or in any respect inferior to God the Father. The Bible teaches, and Christ Himself declared, that Jesus Christ is equal with the Father. "Therefore the Jews sought the more to kill him, because he not only had broken the sabbath, but said also that God was his Father, making himself equal with God" (John 5:18).

Philippians 2:5–7 is clear that when Jesus became flesh, He did not give up His position in Heaven as the equal of God. "Let this mind be in you, which was also in Christ Jesus: Who, being in the form of God, thought it not robbery to be equal with God: But made himself of no reputation, and took upon him the form of a servant, and was made in the likeness of men." This fact is one of the most important details of our salvation, because only as God could Jesus have the power to save us from sin and death.

Just One More

23 March 2006

For the Son of man is come to seek and to save that which was lost.—**Luke 19:10**

On 23 March 2006, one of America's most courageous Army corporals passed away at the age of eighty-seven—Desmond Thomas Doss, a veteran of "Operation Iceberg."

"Operation Iceberg" was a joint US Army, Navy, and Marine Corps effort to displace the Japanese military from the island of Okinawa in order to use it as a staging point for the planned invasion of mainland Japan during World War II. Among the various battles within the two-month struggle, the Battle for Hacksaw Ridge was particularly fierce as dug-in Japanese soldiers waited until US infantry ascended the steep Maeda Escarpment before attacking them.

Hacksaw Ridge is noteworthy for the heroism and life-saving efforts of Desmond Thomas Doss. Joining the Army in 1942, Doss assumed that his conscientious objector status would guarantee him a slot as a medic. Instead, Doss was sent to the infantry and ordered to fight on Okinawa, even though he refused to hold a weapon. His fellow soldiers saw him as a liability but Doss held to his convictions. Eventually, Doss got his wish and climbed Hacksaw Ridge as a combat medic. His steely determination and dauntless courage resulted in his saving seventy-five men that day, despite never using a weapon and being wounded four times. In Doss' reflection on the battle, he said, "I was praying the whole time. I just kept praying, Lord, please help me get one more."

During the course of that battle, Doss embodied the mission of Christ who came to Earth to "seek and to save that which was lost." In the parable of the lost sheep, Jesus said, "What man of you, having an hundred sheep, if he lose one of them, doth not leave the ninety and nine in the wilderness, and go after that which is lost, until he find it? And when he hath found it, he layeth it on his shoulders, rejoicing . . . I say unto you, that likewise joy shall be in heaven over one sinner that repenteth, more than over ninety and nine just persons, which need no repentance" (Luke 15:4–5, 7).

Klansman Turned Christian

24 March 1863

Therefore if any man be in Christ, he is a new creature: old things are passed away; behold, all things are become new.—**2 Corinthians 5:17**

On 24 March 1863, Confederate General Nathan Bedford Forrest captured Brentwood, Tennessee, taking 759 prisoners and destroying a railroad bridge and blockhouse a short distance from Nashville. General Forrest became known as the "Wizard of the Saddle" for his revolutionary use of cavalry. Despite having no previous military training, Forrest rose from the rank of private to lieutenant general. General J. R. Chalmers, a man who served under Forrest, remarked that Forrest "was certainly the greatest revolutionary leader on our side. He was restrained by no knowledge of law or constitution. He was embarrassed by no preconceived ideas of military science. His favorite maxim was, 'War means fighting, and fighting means killing.'" After the war, he served as the Ku Klux Klan's first Grand Wizard.

But in 1869, Forrest withdrew from the Klan and ordered it to be disbanded. Not only did he cease to have dealings with the Klan, but Forrest appeared at an early civil rights convention during which he advocated equality for all Americans. A few years later, in 1874, he volunteered to bring to justice those responsible for continued violence against African Americans. Why the turnaround? It's simple. Forrest became a Christian, and that changed him from the inside out. In *Nathan Bedford Forrest's Redemption*, author Shane E. Kastler likens Forrest's conversion to Christianity with that of the murderous Saul of Tarsus who became Paul. Years after his salvation, Paul wrote to Timothy, "This is a faithful saying, and worthy of all acceptation, that Christ Jesus came into the world to save sinners; of whom I am chief" (1 Timothy 1:15).

Forrest's life is a reminder that no matter how sinful we have been, God's grace is always available. It is also a reminder to never give up on praying for and witnessing to someone who needs the Lord.

Mire of Despair

25 March 1420

Deliver me out of the mire, and let me not sink: let me be delivered from them that hate me, and out of the deep waters.—**Psalm 69:14**

For centuries, mounted knights ruled the battlefield, but in the fourteenth century, the balance of power shifted from heavily armored knights on horseback to skilled infantrymen on the field. In the early fifteenth century an important battle marked the zenith of infantry's rise during warfare.

A Hussite revolt broke out against the Roman Catholic authority in Bohemia. A one-eyed man named Jan Žižka (John Zizka) led the Hussites in one of the most lopsided battles in medieval history. On the morning of 25 March 1420, a force of four hundred Hussites—mostly comprised of women and children—retreated from the city of Pilsen and mounted a defense in the nearby village of Sudom. Two thousand Catholic knights pursued the Hussite army thinking them to be an easy victory. The terrain, however, was wet and marshy, quickly capturing the Catholic knights in its mire. The smaller and lightly armored Hussite infantry quickly dispatched the hapless knights.

In Psalm 69, David pleaded with God to deliver him from the mire of despair. King Saul and his men were seeking to find and kill David, which drove David into a deep sense of abandonment and depression. God not only delivered David from Saul, but He also delivered David from despair.

The trials of life sometimes make us feel trapped like those knights at Sudom. But unlike the knights who were defeated because of the mire, God delights in coming to our rescue and giving us victory from the mire. As David wrote in Psalm 40:2, "He brought me up also out of an horrible pit, out of the miry clay, and set my feet upon a rock, and established my goings."

If you are discouraged or depressed today, find comfort in the knowledge that God knows, and He is ready and able to help you. Cry out to Him in prayer, and turn to His Word for comfort and assurance in His promises.

Slanderer

26 March 1950

He that hideth hatred with lying lips, and he that uttereth a slander, is a fool. **—Proverbs 10:18**

The Red Scare of the 1950s was a time of hysteria and finger pointing primarily caused by one man, Senator Joseph McCarthy. In early February 1950, McCarthy announced that he possessed the names of 205 card-carrying Communists employed in the US Department of State. This declaration ignited a fire-storm of paranoia and the Senate demanded that he produce evidence to support his claim. McCarthy insisted that he had definitive evidence on at least one Communist who had worked for the State Department. On 26 March 1950, McCarthy named Owen Lattimore as a Soviet spy.

American-born Lattimore, who had lived in China with his English-teaching parents, taught at Johns Hopkins University. Because of his in-depth knowledge of Chinese history and culture, President Roosevelt appointed him as a special representative to the Nationalist Chinese government of Chiang Kai-Shek during World War II. When accused of being a Soviet spy, Lattimore denied it several times before charges were eventually dropped for lack of evidence. However, by this time, Lattimore's reputation and career had taken an unredeemable plunge.

Senator McCarthy used hearsay and intimidation to establish himself as a powerful and feared figure in American politics. He leveled charges at many who disagreed with his political views, costing the reputations and jobs of his victims, such as Lattimore.

Over the centuries, many have been destroyed by a slanderous tongue, including Jesus Christ. The Bible says in Psalm 101:5, "Whoso privily slandereth his neighbour, him will I cut off: him that hath an high look and a proud heart will not I suffer." When we gossip or lie about someone in order to lift up ourselves, God is not pleased. Don't fuel the fire of slander and strife. "Where no wood is, there the fire goeth out: so where there is no talebearer, the strife ceaseth" (Proverbs 26:20).

Muster Roll

27 March 1942

And Enoch walked with God: and he was not; for God took him.—**Genesis 5:24**

One of the most chilling announcements aboard a ship is "man overboard!" On the morning of 27 March 1942 at 1031, this announcement shook the crew of the USS *Washington* to its core.

The *Washington* had been assigned to a thirteen-vessel task force on its way to rendezvous with British navy ships near Scotland. The freezing rain and snow on this particular morning was so abysmal that visibility was significantly impaired. Despite two other ships in the taskforce coming alongside to assist, the man was lost at sea.

Naturally, a complete roll-call became an immediate priority to identify the missing crewman. Mysteriously, however, every officer and enlisted sailor was called and accounted for. The executive officer then ordered a recount, mandating that his officers make eye contact with each man under his charge as his name was called. The recount yielded the same results as the first: all officers and men were accounted for.

An officer was sent to submit the report to Rear Admiral John W. Wilcox, but he discovered the admiral's cabin was empty. Where was the admiral? Although the entire ship was searched, the crew soon realized that the mysterious man in the water had been the only man not listed on the ship's muster roll—Admiral Wilcox. A board of inquiry revealed several inconclusive reasons for Wilcox's fall, but it found no one aboard the *Washington* to be negligent in Wilcox's death including Wilcox himself.

One day, there will be a final muster roll when God will call His children to join Him in Heaven. The Bible tells us that we will vanish from this Earth "in a moment, in the twinkling of an eye, at the last trump: for the trumpet shall sound, and the dead shall be raised incorruptible, and we shall be changed" (1 Corinthians 15:52). Will you be included in this final muster roll, or will your life be lost at sea?

If you have not yet trusted Christ as Saviour, today is the day! If you have questions or doubts, reach out to a Bible-believing pastor or friend.

Internal Controls

28 March 1979

Unto the pure all things are pure: but unto them that are defiled and unbelieving is nothing pure; but even their mind and conscience is defiled.—**Titus 1:15**

Nuclear reactors have been used for a variety of reasons. Whether supplying power to a nuclear submarine or to a city, superheating water into steam makes for a more efficient means of generating power. On 28 March 1979, the pressure valve on the number two nuclear reactor at Three-Mile Island failed to close. As a result, contaminated coolant drained from the valve into neighboring facilities and the core began to overheat.

The designers of the nuclear reactor built in an internal control in the form of emergency cooling pumps, which automatically went into effect once an overheated alarm was triggered. Left alone, these safety controls would have prevented what has become known as the worst nuclear disaster in US history. Human operators in the control room misconstrued contradictory readings and decided to shut off the emergency cooling pumps. By early the next morning, the core of reactor two had heated to over four thousand degrees—only one thousand degrees shy of a complete meltdown.

God has built into man certain "internal controls." For an unsaved person, it is the conscience allowing him to understand and perceive the difference between good and evil. "For when the Gentiles, which have not the law, do by nature the things contained in the law, these, having not the law, are a law unto themselves: Which shew the work of the law written in their hearts, their conscience also bearing witness, and their thoughts the mean while accusing or else excusing one another" (Romans 2:14–15).

In addition to the conscience, a Christian also has the Holy Spirit to direct him. "I say the truth in Christ, I lie not, my conscience also bearing me witness in the Holy Ghost" (Romans 9:1). When we attempt to circumvent our own conscience or the Holy Spirit, we are in effect shutting down the emergency controls God gave us to prevent us from falling into sin and temptation.

Deserved Thanks

29 March 2017

His lord said unto him, Well done, good and faithful servant; thou hast been faithful over a few things, I will make thee ruler over many things: enter thou into the joy of thy lord.—**Matthew 25:23**

Historically, America has been a country that has honored and thanked her military personnel for serving overseas and for fighting for freedom here at home and around the world. Photos and videos often show the celebrations for these soldiers, sailors, airmen, and marines who return home after a long struggle against the enemy.

Sadly, America had one war during which political viewpoints looked past the sacrifice of our military and went directly to the feelings the media and protest frenzy had created. Upon returning home, the Vietnam War veterans saw a sad display of violent crowds of protesters shouting obscenities, pounding on vehicles, throwing items, and spitting at them. Many of the American military who served in Vietnam were labeled "baby killers" and were ostracized by society.

On 29 March 2017, Congress signed into law the Vietnam War Veterans Recognition Act. Pennsylvania's Veterans of Foreign Wars State Commander Thomas A. Brown stated, "All Vietnam War veterans deserve high honor and respect that many of them did not get when they returned home from war. Designating March 29 of each year to say 'welcome home' and 'thank you' to our Vietnam War veterans is a strong signal that America appreciates the service of these special patriots of freedom."

As believers, we may not always receive a "thank you" for our labor for Christ. Often, we will be misunderstood or even mistreated like the Vietnam veterans. Nevertheless, God says to stay as His good and faithful servant. When He calls us home to Heaven one day, there will be rejoicing and celebration for the work done for Him. "And whatsoever ye do, do it heartily, as to the Lord, and not unto men; Knowing that of the Lord ye shall receive the reward of the inheritance: for ye serve the Lord Christ" (Colossians 3:23–24).

No Favoritism

30 March 1870

Then Peter opened his mouth, and said, Of a truth I perceive that God is no respecter of persons:—**Acts 10:34**

The Declaration of Independence declared "that all men are created equal, that they are endowed by their Creator with certain unalienable Rights, that among these are Life, Liberty and the pursuit of Happiness." But up until 1865, those born into slavery did not experience the freedom that the Declaration describes. When the Civil War ended, slavery was abolished by Amendment 13 of the Constitution, and former slaves were proclaimed US citizens by Amendment 14. However, some Americans continued to keep the freedmen from voting and enjoying the benefits of American citizenship.

Finally, on 30 March 1870, Congress passed Amendment 15, which stated that the right to vote would not be denied an American citizen on account of race, color, or previous conditions of servitude. Although these amendments did not rid our country of prejudice and segregation, they were an important step toward equality and the fulfillment of our American ideals expressed in the Declaration of Independence.

Thankfully, we have a God in Heaven who is no respecter of persons. The ground is level at the cross. Christ died for the sins of the entire world—not just for the sins of a few. Furthermore, we all come to Christ the same way—through the blood of Jesus. "For there is no difference between the Jew and the Greek: for the same Lord over all is rich unto all that call upon him. For whosoever shall call upon the name of the Lord shall be saved" (Romans 10:12–13).

Because we serve a God who does not show favoritism and because every person is created in the image of God, we should treat others with respect, dignity, kindness, and love. Seeing and loving others as God does will help us share the gospel with everyone around us. No one is beyond the reach of God's saving grace, and no one should be beyond the reach of our love and compassion.

A Meddlesome Pilot

31 March 1943

He that passeth by, and meddleth with strife belonging not to him, is like one that taketh a dog by the ears.—**Proverbs 26:17**

During World War II, the China-Burma-Indian (CBI) Theatre was the site of a great deal of action. Most World War II history books give scant coverage to the CBI, which is unfortunate, since the fighting here was as decisive as the D-Day landings of the Atlantic.

On 31 March 1943, a squadron of US B-24 bombers was attacked by Japanese Zeros. The co-pilot of one of the bombers, Lieutenant Owen J. Baggett, bailed out with four other crew members when his plane was hit and caught fire. Not satisfied with the exploding B-24, the Japanese pilot went after the crew who were mid-air and parachuting to land. He circled around the floating targets, shooting two of the crew dead. On seeing this happen, Baggett did the only thing he could think to do: he played dead.

When the Japanese pilot pulled his Zero up to Baggett at near stall speed and opened his canopy to check on his horrendous work, Baggett drew his .45 automatic pistol from his side and fired four shots into the cockpit, one of which struck the pilot in the head. The Zero spun out of sight and crashed. Baggett landed safely and was captured by the Japanese. He survived two years in a Japanese prison camp in Singapore and eventually retired from the US Air Force as a colonel. Baggett became the only person in World War II to shoot down a plane with a pistol.

Had the Japanese pilot left Baggett alone, the pilot may have survived the war. His meddlesome investigation cost him his life. God's Word cautions us against involving ourselves in matters that are really none of our business. Proverbs 20:3 tells us, "It is an honour for a man to cease from strife: but every fool will be meddling." Only fools meddle in what does not concern them. Too often we make matters worse by becoming involved with something that is not in our realm of concern.

APRIL

The Greatest Love

1 April 1970

Greater love hath no man than this, that a man lay down his life for his friends.
—John 15:13

Sergeant Gary Beikirch received the medal of honor for actions displayed on 1 April 1970 in Camp Dak Seang, Vietnam. The US special forces and civilian combatants were stationed here to monitor and disrupt the flow of supplies on the Ho Chi Minh Trail. At twenty-three, Beikirch was one of two medics responsible for the health of those in the camp.

During the early hours of 1 April, the North Vietnamese Army started an assault on this camp. Beikirch was hit three times, with one shot partially paralyzing him. Despite his wounds and paralysis, Beikirch continued to treat the wounded and to fight the enemy. Deo, a friend and Vietnamese boy who helped carry Beikirch to the wounded, threw himself over the sergeant when he heard a rocket coming toward them. Deo's action cost him his life, and saved Sergeant Beikirch. Beikirch, now a Christian, once explained the profound sacrifice Deo made for him with these words:

> I've taught my students that there's a big difference between success and significance. Significance is when you are part of somebody's life and they are part of yours and you both walk away changed. Deo never reached his 16th birthday, never graduated from high school, never went to college—but he had the most significant impact on my life. He was able to love, to care, to sacrifice.

For a contrast between success and significance, consider the life of Christ. By some earthly measurements, Jesus' life could have appeared unsuccessful. But it certainly was not insignificant. His sacrifice for us is everything.

How about your life? Are you focusing all your goals on earthly definitions of success? Or are you sacrificially investing your life in others? In the end, eternal significance matters far more than earthly success.

An Incriminating Letter

2 April 1840

Christ hath redeemed us from the curse of the law, being made a curse for us: for it is written, Cursed is every one that hangeth on a tree:—**Galatians 3:13**

On 2 April 1840, French author and journalist Emile Zola was born in Paris. Zola is best known for writing the "J'Accuse" ("I accuse!") letter during the Dreyfus Affair.

Alfred Dreyfus, a French-Jewish artillery captain, was convicted of spying for the Germans in 1894. The physical evidence used to convict him was a slip of paper found in a German military trash can with a promise to deliver a French artillery manual. Although handwriting experts could not conclusively link the note to Dreyfus, the captain was sentenced to life imprisonment.

In the same German office two years later, French intelligence discovered another piece of paper promising new deliveries of French military secrets. The handwriting proved identical to the piece of paper used to incriminate Dreyfus, but since Dreyfus was serving time, he could not be the guilty party for either crime. Upon learning of these new developments, French military intelligence initiated a cover-up to save the military's reputation. Emile Zola discovered the cover-up and published an open letter to the president of France entitled "J'Accuse." Zola's letter accused French army officials of antisemitism and obstruction of justice in the Dreyfus case. Although Zola was found guilty of libel, Dreyfus's account was reopened and he was pardoned. In 1906, Zola was found innocent and exonerated.

Zola's willingness to act cost him public scorn and punishment, however, he was not willing to stand idle while a gross miscarriage of justice unfolded. He chose to act, despite the outcome.

Could the same be said of you? Are you willing to stand for Christ no matter the outcome? Jesus bore shame and reproach for us. Let's be bold to stand for Him even when others misunderstand us. Standing for Christ is not often the most popular of decisions, but it is the right one.

Help Refused

3 April 1948

Let us therefore come boldly unto the throne of grace, that we may obtain mercy, and find grace to help in time of need.—**Hebrews 4:16**

Following the unexpected death of President Franklin D. Roosevelt in 1945, Harry S. Truman became the thirty-third President of the United States, inheriting the daunting task of leading our nation through the end of World War II and post-war recovery. The war had left a great deal of Europe in ruins. Bombs, artillery shells, and rockets had ruined crop fields and destroyed vital infrastructure. In 1947, Secretary of State George C. Marshall proposed the European Recovery Program, a thirteen billion dollar economic aid package designed to bail Europe out of its post-war devastation.

On 3 April 1948, President Truman signed the proposed Marshall Plan into effect. The plan played a key role in ushering in an era of prosperity and political stability throughout Western Europe. While Truman also offered the plan to the Soviet Union, they rejected it outright. As a result, the Soviet Union and its satellite countries of Eastern Europe remained impoverished for decades while Western Europe rebuilt and flourished.

Today, many people try to recover from financial troubles, health problems, or sin problems. Organizations have been established for those needing to recover from alcohol or drug addictions. Companies have been established for the sole purpose of helping people manage financial debt. Therapy centers help those with physical ailments, and there are even places that help with anger management and emotional therapy.

Unfortunately, many of these secular programs do not include the One who has graciously offered His help in time of need. God Himself is the source for lasting help, recovery, or healing that we may need. "Bless the LORD, O my soul, and forget not all his benefits: Who forgiveth all thine iniquities; who healeth all thy diseases"(Psalm 103:2–3) Don't mirror the Soviet response to the Marshall Plan and reject God's spiritual recovery program. Take your needs to the throne of grace, and receive God's help.

Misguided Men

4 April 1968

Wisdom is the principal thing; therefore get wisdom: and with all thy getting get understanding.—**Proverbs 4:7**

Guided missiles have been around since World War II. The German V-2 rocket would ultimately become the modern-day cruise missile. In the late 1950s, America used German technology to establish her first successful cruise missile. Since World War II, our country has grown in our weaponry and strategic guidance systems.

While our guidance systems expanded during the 1950s, Dr. Martin Luther King, Jr. observed that something far more important had diminished: "Our scientific power has outrun our spiritual power. We have guided missiles and misguided men." Unfortunately, Dr. King, one of the most important leaders in the Civil Rights Movement, was assassinated on 4 April 1968.

King's statement about misguided men epitomizes the day in which we live. The technological breakthroughs in micro computing, weapons development, and communication since the 1960s, while amazing, have not paralleled an advance in human character. Over the decades, America has increased her knowledge on so many levels, but, over the same time period, has refused the wisdom of God. In this age of pluralism, Americans are acting as the Israelites during the time of the Judges when "every man did that which was right in his own eyes" (Judges 21:25) rather than following the Word of God. The guidance map of Scriptures has been denied in public education, in government, in homes, and sometimes even in churches. Yet people wonder why America seems to have lost her way.

Christian, my challenge to you today is to follow the map. Allow the Holy Spirit to guide you through His Word and give you direction for the choices and actions of today. "Howbeit when he, the Spirit of truth, is come, he will guide you into all truth: for he shall not speak of himself; but whatsoever he shall hear, that shall he speak: and he will shew you things to come" (John 16:13).

A Promise Kept

5 April 1856

If a man vow a vow unto the LORD, or swear an oath to bind his soul with a bond; he shall not break his word, he shall do according to all that proceedeth out of his mouth.—**Numbers 30:2**

On 5 April 1856, Booker Taliaferro Washington was born to slave parents in Hale's Ford, Virginia. When the Civil War ended in 1865, Booker T. Washington was only nine years old. Washington went on to become the founder of Tuskegee Institute, an orator, and an author. In 1901, he published his autobiography entitled *Up From Slavery*. In his book, Washington relays the account of meeting an ex-slave from Virginia:

> I found that this man had made a contract with his master, two or three years previous to the Emancipation Proclamation, to the effect that the slave was to be permitted to buy himself, by paying so much per year for his body; and while he was paying for himself, he was to be permitted to labor where and for whom he pleased. Finding that he could secure better wages in Ohio, he went there. When freedom came, he was still in debt to his master some three hundred dollars. Notwithstanding that the Emancipation Proclamation freed him from any obligation to his master, this black man walked the greater portion of the distance back to where his old master lived in Virginia, and placed the last dollar, with interest, into his hands. In talking to me about this, the man told me that he knew that he did not have to pay his debt, but that he had given his word to his master, and his word he had never broken. He felt that he could not enjoy his freedom till he had fulfilled his promise.

The worldly maxim "promises are made to be broken" is not only false; it's destructive. When we make promises and then renege, we hurt the ones we promised and destroy our credibility. The same is true when we make a vow to God and break it. Not only should we keep our promises to God, but we should do so remembering that He has *never* failed on a promise He has made to us. "God is not a man, that he should lie; neither the son of man, that he should repent: hath he said, and shall he not do it? or hath he spoken, and shall he not make it good?" (Numbers 23:19).

The General's Folly

6 April 1862

It is the spirit that quickeneth; the flesh profiteth nothing: the words that I speak unto you, they are spirit, and they are life.—**John 6:63**

During the Civil War's Western Theater, General Ulysses S. Grant was a force to be reckoned with. Following his success in capturing Confederate Forts Henry and Donelson in February 1862, Grant chose to rest and refit his bedraggled army at Pittsburg Landing along the Tennessee River. Seeing a chance to catch Grant's army unawares, Confederate General Albert Sidney Johnston attacked the unfortified Union position on 6 April 1862 near Shiloh Church.

As the battle progressed, Major General Stephen A. Hurlbut's men moved into a peach orchard and halted the Confederate advance. Frustrated at the inability of his men to oust Hurlbut's men from the peach orchard, Johnston personally led a charge of troops to encourage his men to swarm the orchard. As he watched his men advance, he jokingly commented about a bullet that had grazed the bottom of his foot, ripping open his boot sole during the charge: "They almost tripped me up that time."

Unbeknownst to the joking general, another bullet had sliced through the back of his calf, hitting a major blood vessel causing his boot to fill with blood. Johnston had a tourniquet in his pocket, but because he was unaware of the secondary wound, he bled to death on the battlefield.

How tragic that Johnston had a life-saving device on his person that could have spared him had he chosen to apply it. Mankind has the life-saving source of the Word of God as well as the truth of God "written in their hearts, their conscience also bearing witness" (Romans 2:15). Jesus Himself mentioned that the Word of God was more needful than food when He was tempted by Satan in the wilderness. "But he answered and said, It is written, Man shall not live by bread alone, but by every word that proceedeth out of the mouth of God" (Matthew 4:4).

Are you being sustained by the life-source of God's Word today? You have it available, but are you using it?

A Preserving Force

7 April 1975

(For he saith, I have heard thee in a time accepted, and in the day of salvation have I succoured thee: behold, now is the accepted time; behold, now is the day of salvation.)—**2 Corinthians 6:2**

When the United States military pulled out of Vietnam in 1973, a vacuum was left which North Vietnamese forces were quick to exploit. At this time, more than two-thirds of South Vietnam had fallen under Communist control.

On 7 April 1975, the North Vietnamese Army (NVA) launched the "Ho Chi Minh Campaign," the final phase of the North Vietnamese plan to conquer South Vietnam and make it Communist. Following the evacuation of US forces, the NVA attacked the lightly defended province of Phuoc Long north of Saigon and overran the provincial capital of Phuoc Binh. By 27 April, they had pushed the South Vietnamese Army as far south as possible and completely encircled Saigon. Three days later, the South Vietnamese surrendered, ending the ten-year civil war and resulting in a Communist-controlled Vietnam.

Although controversy surrounds America's involvement in the Vietnam Civil War, the presence of US forces did considerably hinder the Communist take-over of South Vietnam. Despite the lack of public support for America's involvement in the war, no one can deny that if not for the US military's presence, Vietnam would have succumbed to Communism far earlier than 1975.

Similarly, the Holy Spirit's presence on Earth is a restraining force over Satan. The Bible tells us that when the Holy Spirit lifts his restraint, Satan's forces will wreak unprecedented havoc upon the Earth: "For the mystery of iniquity doth already work: only he who now letteth will let, until he be taken out of the way" (2 Thessalonians 2:7). Thank God that the Scriptures promise that the devil's "day in the sun" will be cut short by the Second Coming of Jesus Christ, but it also warns that men and women should not put off accepting Christ as Saviour. Today is the day of salvation.

A Word of Encouragement

8 April 1981

A word fitly spoken is like apples of gold in pictures of silver.—**Proverbs 25:11**

On 8 April 1981, America lost the last of her five-star Army generals, Omar Nelson Bradley. Bradley commanded the largest American force ever united under one man's leadership during World War II. General Eisenhower was so impressed with Bradley's ability that he assigned him the task of figuring out why the US II Corps suffered such defeat against the Germans at the Battle of the Kasserine Pass in February 1943.

An astute tactician, General Bradley suggested some vital changes to his superior General Patton, which led to a sound victory when the II Corps encountered the Germans again. Bradley next commanded the II Corps during Operation Husky, the Allied invasion of Sicily. After the war, he became the first Chairman of the Joint Chiefs of Staff. Given his distinguished military career, it would seem as if Bradley was always meant to be a soldier. However, that was not the case.

When Bradley was just fourteen years of age, he lost his father. Bradley's mother then moved the family to Moberly, Missouri, where Omar worked odd jobs to help pay the bills. Graduating high school in 1910, Bradley planned to attend the University of Missouri until his Sunday school superintendent suggested that he apply to West Point instead. Bradley agreed and ended up graduating 44 out of 164 cadets, one of whom was Dwight D. Eisenhower.

Everyone has influence, and as Christians our influence should include encouragement. Never underestimate the power of encouragement. World history could have told a different story if not for the encouraging influence of Bradley's Sunday school teacher. Look for someone today whom you can encourage along a wholesome path with your words. "Wherefore comfort yourselves together, and edify one another, even as also ye do" (1 Thessalonians 5:11).

Access Granted

9 April 1942

And the blood shall be to you for a token upon the houses where ye are: and when I see the blood, I will pass over you, and the plague shall not be upon you to destroy you, when I smite the land of Egypt.—**Exodus 12:13**

The notorious Bataan Death March began on 9 April 1942 after Allied forces surrendered the Battle of Bataan to the Japanese. The march became infamous for the cruel brutality meted out upon defenseless captives.

One of the few Americans who survived managed to escape from a porthole of a Japanese boat. Swimming to a nearby island, he hid in the jungle and lived off coconuts and raw fish. After five weeks, he ventured to the other side of the island where he heard the unmistakable voice of Americans. Cautiously, he poked his head from the underbrush and gazed upon a detachment of US Marines! His joy quickly turned to dismay when a Marine guard halted him with his M-1 rifle. After so many weeks on the island, the American soldier looked nothing like an ally anymore.

Despite the prisoner's pleas and explanations, the Marine barked, "I got orders to shoot anybody who doesn't know the password . . . so give me the password and I'll let you in." Noticing the Marine's finger begin to take the slack from the trigger, the soldier screamed, "Let me at least pray!" "Okay, you have ten seconds," said the Marine. "Father, I'm going to meet you now. I have lived like the devil and disappointed you over and over. Lord, please don't remember my sins, only remember the blood your Son shed for me on Calvary." As the man finished his prayer, he looked up to a lowered rifle and an open gate. The Marine said, "The password is 'blood' . . . come on in."

When the children of Israel were preparing to escape Egypt, God commanded that they place the blood of a lamb on their doorposts so that the death angel would pass over them. This first Passover was a symbol of Jesus Christ's blood that would be shed on the cross to pay for the sins of the whole world. Access to Heaven requires His blood.

The Father's Presence

10 April 1979

What time I am afraid, I will trust in thee.—**Psalm 56:3**

No matter where one gets stationed in the military, the weather is often an adjustment for newly-installed families. Whether dealing with snow at Minot Air Force Base or humidity at Barksdale Air Force Base, families have to learn to handle the weather. "Terrible Tuesday" is an ominous phrase that those stationed at Sheppard Air Force Base use for the mile-wide F4 tornado that annihilated Wichita Falls, Texas, on 10 April 1979.

When my family was stationed at Sheppard, we learned to deal with the tornado season during the spring months. Seemingly every time I was at my off-duty job in Fort Worth, a tornado warning would sound for base housing. Because we had no basement, my wife would gather our two boys in a closet in the center of the house. To get their minds off of the danger, she would read Bible stories or sing Sunday school songs to them. As soon as I heard of the tornado warnings, I would call my family to reassure them, and they would take great comfort in just hearing my voice. Although I was not physically next to them, they knew I was aware of their trouble and praying for them.

God is our loving Father, and unlike an earthly father, He is always with us. In Psalm 139:8–12 the psalmist emphasizes the omnipresence of God:

> If I ascend up into heaven, thou art there: if I make my bed in hell, behold, thou art there. If I take the wings of the morning, and dwell in the uttermost parts of the sea; Even there shall thy hand lead me, and thy right hand shall hold me. If I say, Surely the darkness shall cover me; even the night shall be light about me. Yea, the darkness hideth not from thee; but the night shineth as the day: the darkness and the light are both alike to thee.

Due to God's eternal presence, we should not fear the storms of life. "The LORD is my light and my salvation; whom shall I fear? the LORD is the strength of my life; of whom shall I be afraid?" (Psalm 27:1). Whatever fears you may have today, God knows about them and He is there for you.

Stolen Tags

11 April 2018

Notwithstanding in this rejoice not, that the spirits are subject unto you; but rather rejoice, because your names are written in heaven.—**Luke 10:20**

On 11 April 2018, Fox News ran a story about the arrest and sentencing of a historian who had been stealing dog tags and other memorabilia from the National Archives in College Park, Maryland. The Justice Department reported that the man had taken the identification tags over a period of six years before being caught. Most of the dog tags belonged to American airmen who had been shot down over Europe. The thief sold off the majority of the stolen dog tags at online auction sites. He mostly sold them for money, but he sometimes traded them for experiences such as sitting in a Spitfire airplane at an aviation museum.

A federal judge ordered the convicted man to pay back over $40,000 in restitution to those who had purchased the stolen items, as well as sentencing him to a year in prison. US archivist David Ferriero remarked, "The theft of records from the National Archives amounts to stealing from the American people."

While the stolen dog tags or the names engraved on them may never find their way back to the National Archives, the Word of God assures us that for those who have placed their faith in the finished work of Christ, our names are written in the Lamb's Book of Life. Praise the Lord that once your name is written there, it cannot be removed, stolen, or erased.

We have a tendency to rejoice in the immediate circumstances of our lives, including the things God allows us to do for Him here on Earth. But these opportunities come and go, whereas the surety of our names in Heaven remains forever. This is why Jesus told His disciples that the greatest thing they could rejoice in was that their names were written in Heaven.

Is your name in the Lamb's Book of Life? If you have trusted Christ as your Saviour, it is, and you can rejoice in this fact. If not, it can be written there today, and you will have new reason to rejoice!

Life is Like a Swift Sparrow

12 April 627

How then shall they call on him in whom they have not believed? and how shall they believe in him of whom they have not heard? and how shall they hear without a preacher?—**Romans 10:14**

The seventh-century kingdom of Northumbria, located in present-day northern England and south-eastern Scotland, was ruled by the pagan Anglo-Saxons, descendents of the Germanic tribes that drove out the Romans nearly two hundred years prior. On 12 April 627, Paulinus, the first Bishop of York, presented the gospel to the Anglo-Saxon King Edwin at one of the king's advisory meetings. After hearing Paulinus, one of Edwin's chief advisors responded to his king with this observation:

> Your Majesty, when we compare the present life of man on earth with that time of which we have no knowledge, it seems to me like the swift flight of a single sparrow through the banqueting-hall where you are sitting at dinner on a winter's day with your counsellors. In the midst there is a comforting fire to warm the hall; outside the storms of winter rage. This sparrow flies swiftly in through one door of the hall, and out through another. While he is inside, he is safe from the winter storms; but after a moment of comfort, he vanishes from sight into the wintry world from which he came. Even so, man appears on earth for a little while; but of what went before this life or of what follows, we know not. Therefore, if this new teaching has brought any more certain knowledge, it seems only right that we should follow it.

After considering the words of Paulinus and his own advisor, Edwin promptly converted to Christianity, thus becoming the first Christian Anglo-Saxon king in England.

I admire the courage of Paulinus who was bold enough to tell his king the truth of the gospel. May we have the same boldness to witness for our King and declare the truth of the death, burial, and resurrection of Jesus Christ for our sins to those who are lost.

Stones from the Sky

13 April 1360

And it came to pass, as they fled from before Israel, and were in the going down to Beth-horon, that the Lord cast down great stones from heaven upon them unto Azekah, and they died: they were more which died with hailstones than they whom the children of Israel slew with the sword.—**Joshua 10:11**

Throughout history, the term "Black Monday" has referred to a turbulent event that happens on a Monday—like the stock market crash on 19 October 1987. The National Football League (NFL) uses the term to refer to the Monday after the regular season ends, in which coaches and general managers around the league receive a "pink slip" notifying them that they no longer have a job.

One of the first instances that "Black Monday" was used was on 13 April 1360 to describe a freak hail storm that killed an estimated one thousand English soldiers in Chartres, France. The storm and the devastation it caused was seen as divine intervention by English King Edward III and he immediately began negotiating the Peace Treaty of Bretigny with the French.

Like the Black Monday of 1360, God used a hailstorm to assist Joshua in his fight against the Amorites. Joshua 10:14 says, "And there was no day like that before it or after it, that the Lord hearkened unto the voice of a man: for the Lord fought for Israel." Joshua and the Israelites had victory against the Amorites because God fought the battle for them.

The Book of Joshua is often called the "warfare manual" for the Christian, as it is a type of the spiritual warfare believers face today. Too often we fight our Black Mondays in our own strength when God's command to us is, "Put on the whole armour of God, that ye may be able to stand against the wiles of the devil" (Ephesians 6:11). Notice this verse does not say to fight or attack the temptation or trial, but to stand with God's armor on. In a battle, this would not be a natural reaction to an attack, but as David said to Goliath, "the battle is the Lord's, and he will give you into our hands" (1 Samuel 17:47).

Salvation Just out of Reach

14 April 1912

But what saith it? The word is nigh thee, even in thy mouth, and in thy heart: that is, the word of faith, which we preach;—**Romans 10:8**

On the night of 14 April 1912, the *RMS Titanic* struck an iceberg and sank about two hours later. The tragedy of the sinking *Titanic* is that these people could have been saved.

Most people familiar with the *Titanic* sinking know that loss of life was caused by insufficient lifeboats aboard. What is less known is that another ship less than seven miles away could have rescued those who died.

Steamship *SS Californian* was the nearest ship to the *Titanic* and had radioed the *Titanic* at approximately 1900 hours to beware of ice which the *Californian* had nearly collided with herself. Captain Stanley Lord of the *Californian* ordered his ship to stop for the night, as it was too dangerous to proceed. The *Californian* radioed another warning to the *Titanic*, but received the reply: "Shut Up. Shut Up. I am Busy." Ten minutes later, the *Titanic* struck ice.

After striking the iceberg, the crew of the *Titanic* fired white flares instead of red flares. Red flares signal an emergency; white signals a "stay away" order. The *Californian* did not consider the white flares to be distress signals and therefore took no action. Salvation lay just a few miles and minutes away, yet the *Titanic*'s failure to properly call for help cost the lives of over 1,500 souls.

Sadly, not everyone who dies has eternal life in Heaven. Like those on the *Titanic*, there are people who will not be saved from eternal death because they don't simply put their faith in Christ and His sacrifice on the cross to save them from their sins. They may be refusing the warnings of those who have the truth, or they may be trusting in the wrong signals as their way to escape death. Only one way exists to be saved from eternity in Hell, and that is God's simple plan of salvation. "Jesus saith unto him, I am the way, the truth, and the life: no man cometh unto the Father, but by me" (John 14:6).

When the War Is Over

15 April 1450

Ye are of God, little children, and have overcome them: because greater is he that is in you, than he that is in the world.—**1 John 4:4**

The signature war of the Middle Ages was the conflict between France and England known as the Hundred Years' War. The war began in 1337 with King Edward III of England laying claim to the French throne. Throughout the long war, Europe saw military technology transform from mounted French knights to the English longbow to canons. On 15 April 1450, the Battle of Formigny essentially ended the Hundred Years' War. The French commander used cannons to mow down the dense pack of English longbow-men. Because the cannons' ranges far outweighed longbows, the English archers were unable to return fire. Seizing the moment, a second French company attacked from the other direction and collapsed the English line, killing or capturing most of the English army.

In the wake of the Hundred Years' War, France emerged as the master of its own territory with the creation of a modern army under Charles VII. England, on the other hand, emerged physically and financially exhausted and less than two years later, found herself embroiled in a series of civil wars known as the Wars of the Roses.

Our enemy Satan has weapons that can overwhelm us Christians, and the world has more ways to beat us down. When we try to fight Satan and the world in our own strength, the battle seems endless and we often fall into temptations of the flesh. There are two things, however, that we should remember about this battle: first, God is greater than all of our enemies combined. Only He has the power to weaken and conquer them. He lives within us and has the given us His armor and His power to defend ourselves against these enemies, but we must use what He gives to win our battles. Second, the war is already won. Sure, we might lose a battle or two when we try to fight in our own strength, but ultimately, the Lord wins the war. When eternity begins, Satan, the flesh, and the world will be destroyed, and we will live in eternal victory.

A Christian's USO

16 April 1981

As we have therefore opportunity, let us do good unto all men, especially unto them who are of the household of faith.—**Galatians 6:10**

The founder of the United Services Organization (USO), Mary Shotwell Ingraham, died on 16 April 1981. Mrs. Ingraham was a social reformer and the first woman to receive the United States Medal for Merit award. During World War II, she saw the need to create an organization that would help our soldiers have a "home away from home." Since 1941, the USO has been the nation's leading organization to serve both active duty and retired US military and their families. Aside from entertaining the troops stationed overseas, USO airport centers offer around-the-clock hospitality for traveling service members and their families.

On a recent vacation, our family was able to make use of the USO at the Tampa Airport during a five-hour layover. Tampa's USO had recliners, video games, televisions, computers, blankets, food, soft drinks, and toys for children. It was like visiting a close friend's home. When it was time to head to the gate for our flight, we didn't want to leave the hominess and service of the USO.

Just as the USO serves those in our military, church members are called upon to serve one another with a spirit of humility and love. The body of Christ is designed to serve as the "USO" of the local church. Whether it's singing in the choir, working in the nursery, teaching a Sunday school class, ministering to a child, or serving as a deacon, the need for every member to serve in their local church is essential. Galatians 5:13–14 exhorts, "For, brethren, ye have been called unto liberty; only use not liberty for an occasion to the flesh, but by love serve one another. For all the law is fulfilled in one word, even in this; Thou shalt love thy neighbour as thyself."

Do you serve in your local church? If not, find a place to serve today—you're needed!

A Successful Failure

17 April 1970

Make you perfect in every good work to do his will, working in you that which is wellpleasing in his sight, through Jesus Christ; to whom be glory for ever and ever. Amen.—**Hebrews 13:21**

Following on the heels of the Mercury space program missions, which succeeded in placing a man into space, the Apollo program was destined to put a man on the moon. After a series of successful and unsuccessful missions, the Apollo 13 mission was slotted to be the third moon landing. Given the term "successful failure," the mission of Apollo 13 would change to one of survival.

A little over fifty-five hours into the mission, an electrical failure caused an explosion which led to the failure of both oxygen tanks and loss of power on the command module. Being about 250,000 miles from Earth, Commander Lovell made his now famous distress call to mission control, "Houston, we've had a problem." Quick thinking led the three-man crew to use the lunar module as a "life raft" since the command module was unsuitable for life support.

The world held its breath as the survival of the crew hung in the balance. NASA engineers on Earth corresponded with the Apollo crew to overcome multiple situations in order to successfully get the crew back to Earth safely. After five harrowing days in space, Apollo 13 reentered Earth's atmosphere and touched down safely in the Pacific Ocean on 17 April 1970. They were finally home.

Often the best way to succeed is to fail. The Bible says, "For a just man falleth seven times, and riseth up again" (Proverbs 24:16). Thankfully, God does not expect perfection from us, but He does desire for us to have a growing Christian walk. Our relationship with Christ gives us the ability to work through our failures, learn from them, and press forward in spiritual growth. "But the God of all grace, who hath called us unto his eternal glory by Christ Jesus, after that ye have suffered a while, make you perfect, stablish, strengthen, settle you" (1 Peter 5:10).

The Eternal Cornerstone

18 April 1506

Therefore thus saith the Lord God, Behold, I lay in Zion for a foundation a stone, a tried stone, a precious corner stone, a sure foundation: he that believeth shall not make haste.—**Isaiah 28:16**

During the fourth century, Roman Emperor Constantine erected a basilica in what is now known as Vatican City. Through erosion and the passing of time, the basilica fell into disrepair. On 18 April 1506, Pope Julius II laid a new cornerstone for the basilica. The renovation project took 109 years to complete and with artwork from well-known Renaissance figures, such as Michelangelo and Raphael, the basilica is now one of the most visited attractions in Vatican City.

Of the many names of the Lord Jesus Christ given in Scriptures, one that is mentioned in both the Old and New Testaments is "Chief Cornerstone." A cornerstone is the first stone set in the construction of a building foundation. All the other stones are then placed in reference to the cornerstone. If the cornerstone is not right, the building will suffer from a faulty foundation, as was the case with the basilica started by Emperor Constantine.

As Christians, we can rest assured that our Cornerstone is perfect. He will never require renovation or repair, and therefore, the foundation on which we stand is solid. Ephesians 2:19–21 speaks of our relationship with Jesus as the Chief Cornerstone. "Now therefore ye are no more strangers and foreigners, but fellowcitizens with the saints, and of the household of God; And are built upon the foundation of the apostles and prophets, Jesus Christ himself being the chief corner stone; In whom all the building fitly framed together groweth unto an holy temple in the Lord."

Jesus was "the stone which the builders refused" as stated in Psalm 118:22. This refers to the rejection Jesus suffered on the cross. While Jesus is still rejected by our world, a Christian can trust that by making Him the Cornerstone of our lives we will have lives that are stable and secure on its foundation.

Operation Mincemeat

19 April 1943

For many shall come in my name, saying, I am Christ; and shall deceive many. **—Mark 13:6**

On 19 April 1943, the British submarine, HMS *Seraph* set sail for the Spanish coast. The *Seraph* contained a most unusual cargo—the body of dead Welshman Glyndwr Michael. To the Germans, the dead Welshman would be known as Major William Martin—the man who never was.

A necessary part of wartime strategy is deceiving the enemy. In January 1943, the Allied forces selected Sicily for a crucial amphibious landing. Wanting the Germans to think the landing would occur in Greece and Sardinia rather than Sicily, Allied intelligence devised an elaborate ruse and code-named it Operation Mincemeat.

Using the dead body of Glyndwr Michael, the Allies dressed him in a Royal Marine uniform, placed fictitious papers on his person, and jettisoned the body from the Seraph on 30 April. The body also had a briefcase attached that contained false information about an Allied landing in Greece and Crete. When the body washed ashore in Spain as planned, German military investigated and developed a plan to stop the supposed invasion. Some of Germany's best divisions and companies were moved to Greece over the next two months allowing the Allies to make their invasion of Sicily with far less opposition than they would have had if Operation Mincemeat had failed.

Satan's *modus operandi* is deception. "For such are false apostles, deceitful workers, transforming themselves into the apostles of Christ. And no marvel; for Satan himself is transformed into an angel of light" (2 Corinthians 11:13–14). The Bible cautions us that Satan's deceptions will often look good. Sometimes, he uses "good people" to teach unholy doctrine. Often, he makes sin look pleasurable and deceives Christians into thinking there will be no consequences for their sin. As you make choices today, make sure to be discerning and aware—"lest Satan should get an advantage of us: for we are not ignorant of his devices" (2 Corinthians 2:11).

Setting the Example

20 April 1789

Not because we have not power, but to make ourselves an ensample unto you to follow us.—**2 Thessalonians 3:9**

On 20 April 1789, George Washington was sworn in as America's first president. He set many precedents which presidents have followed for over two hundred years. Some precedents became tradition like adding the phrase "so help me God" to the end of the inaugural oath. Others have made their way into official policy such as a two-term limit on presidential service.

One precedent that Washington established first took place while he served as Commander of the Continental Army during the Revolution. Washington issued a General Order from Valley Forge that directed "Divine services be performed every Sunday at 1100 in those Brigades to which there are Chaplains . . . those which have none [chaplains] attend the places of worship nearest them . . . it is expected that officers of all ranks will by their attendance set an example to their men."

General Washington not only recognized the importance of providing religious services to his troops, but he also understood the need to be the example in attending the services. People do what people see, thus Christians who lead should make church attendance a priority. "Not forsaking the assembling of ourselves together, as the manner of some is; but exhorting one another: and so much the more, as ye see the day approaching" (Hebrews 10:25).

Being present when your church family gathers is a way for a Christian to serve and to fellowship with other believers. For military personnel and first responders, church attendance may not always be possible because of the duties they have to protect and serve; however, each Christian should strive for a time to worship and be a part of a church family. Your faithful example in the church goes a long way to encouraging those who are coming behind you to be faithful as well.

Freedom from Bondage

21 April 1861

There hath no temptation taken you but such as is common to man: but God is faithful, who will not suffer you to be tempted above that ye are able; but will with the temptation also make a way to escape, that ye may be able to bear it. **—1 Corinthians 10:13**

Around midnight on 21 April 1861, two boats from the sloop-of-war USS *Saratoga* moved silently toward an unknown ship anchored near the mouth of the Congo River. Climbing aboard the unmarked ship, US sailors and marines discovered over nine hundred slaves chained below deck. The unknown ship turned out to be the USS *Nightingale*, a slave ship that was preparing to load more slaves before sailing to America.

Ironically, the American Civil War, of which slavery played a leading factor, had begun only nine days earlier and, upon further investigation, the hundreds of men, women, and children found on board the *Nightingale* had been illegally taken from the country of Liberia, a nation founded in 1822 as a refuge for freed slaves. The commander of the *Saratoga* placed a select crew aboard the captured slave ship and sent the passengers back to Liberia and freedom.

The tragedy of this story is that the enslaved people aboard the *Nightingale* had already been freed, only to be captured back into slavery. Had the *Saratoga* not come along, these people may have never known freedom again.

When Paul wrote to the church at Galatia, he pointed out that they, who had been freed from sin and from the judgment of the Law, were returning to a place of spiritual bondage. After laying out the doctrinal and theological reasons they could live in freedom, he admonished them, "Stand fast therefore in the liberty wherewith Christ hath made us free, and be not entangled again with the yoke of bondage . . . For, brethren, ye have been called unto liberty; only use not liberty for an occasion to the flesh, but by love serve one another" (Galatians 5:1, 13). Christ has set you free; don't let Satan bring you back into bondage.

A Refusal to Fight

22 April 1363

But if ye bite and devour one another, take heed that ye be not consumed one of another.—**Galatians 5:15**

The Battle of Canturino was fought on 22 April 1363 between two mercenary groups—one German-dominated and one English-dominated. German mercenary Konrad von Landau led the Great Company while English mercenary Sir John Hawkwood led the White Company.

The details of this battle that broke out at a bridge near Canturino are obscure, but we do know two facts about it: First, we know that when the two companies met for battle, they both dismounted their horses to fight. We also know that both companies hired Hungarians because what happened next turned the tide of the conflict. Landau's Hungarian horsemen refused to fight their countrymen in the opposing army and promptly deserted the field. As Landau shouted at his fleeing Hungarians, he was struck in the face by a rock, breaking his helmet's nose piece. He was subsequently captured and died shortly thereafter.

The decisive factor in Landau's defeat that day came when the Hungarian troops refused to fight their kinsmen. Like Landau, Satan is also deprived the victory when Christians refuse to fight other Christians. According to the Bible, the church at Corinth was a carnally minded church. The book of 1 Corinthians mentions the problems that they dealt with, including carnal divisions. "For ye are yet carnal: for whereas there is among you envying, and strife, and divisions, are ye not carnal, and walk as men? For while one saith, I am of Paul; and another, I am of Apollos; are ye not carnal? Who then is Paul, and who is Apollos, but ministers by whom ye believed, even as the Lord gave to every man?" (1 Corinthians 3:3–5).

God wants us to live peaceably with others, and especially with our own brothers and sisters in Christ.

Spare Not the Enemy

23 April 1014

For if ye live after the flesh, ye shall die: but if ye through the Spirit do mortify the deeds of the body, ye shall live.—**Romans 8:13**

During the late ninth century, Viking raiders established settlements along the eastern coast of Ireland, which challenged the indigenous Gaelic tribes. Over the next two hundred years, the tribes struggled to rid the land of the Viking invaders and to raise up a high king of Ireland.

In AD 1002, Brian Boru rose to power, becoming the uncontested high king of Ireland. As King Brian's power expanded, Irish-Viking relations eroded. On 23 April 1014, Sitric, king of the Dublin Vikings, rebelled against King Brian. Brian's son Murchad defeated the Vikings at the Battle of Clontarf near Dublin, but he failed to kill them all. Following the battle, the small Viking contingent who had escaped Murchad's sword, happened upon King Brian's tent and murdered the elderly king. While the victory at Clontarf may have broken Norse influence in Ireland, the country largely fell into anarchy after Brian's death.

Like the Viking invaders, if sin is permitted to reside and reign in our hearts, even if we think we have it mostly under control, it will eventually cause spiritual death. We must not tolerate little bits of sin assuming that it will stay small. Rather, we must recognize that sin will destroy us. Galatians 5:17 warns, "For the flesh lusteth against the Spirit, and the Spirit against the flesh: and these are contrary the one to the other: so that ye cannot do the things that ye would." Furthermore, 1 John 2:16 tells us, "For all that is in the world, the lust of the flesh, and the lust of the eyes, and the pride of life, is not of the Father, but is of the world."

Instead of dabbling with sin, God tells us, "Flee also youthful lusts" (2 Timothy 2:22). And God promises to always give us a way of escape when temptation comes knocking. "There hath no temptation taken you but such as is common to man: but God is faithful, who will not suffer you to be tempted above that ye are able; but will with the temptation also make a way to escape, that ye may be able to bear it" (1 Corinthians 10:13).

Code of Conduct

24 April 1863

Rejoice not when thine enemy falleth, and let not thine heart be glad when he stumbleth: lest the LORD see it, and it displease him, and he turn away his wrath from him.—**Proverbs 24:17–18**

During the American Civil War, a Prussian immigrant named Francis Lieber introduced the first code of conduct for war, which became a forerunner to the Geneva Convention. Lieber was an international law scholar who became deeply interested in the treatment of combatants and civilians during war. Some of this interest stemmed from having three sons fighting in the war, two for the Union and one for the Confederacy. After authoring several essays and newspaper articles on the subject, he advised Union General Henry Halleck on the method with which to treat Confederate guerilla fighters captured by Union troops.

On 24 April 1863, the Union Army adopted Lieber's suggestions into what became known as the Lieber Code. The code stipulated that enemy combatants were to be treated with civility and respect. Although not every soldier adhered to the code, it did make a difference. And it influenced other countries to adopt a similar code.

As Christians, we also have a "code of conduct" in the Bible that tells us how to treat others, including our enemies. While it is tempting to delight when someone we dislike falls upon hard times or is stricken, God's Word tells us not to rejoice in such things, as this displeases the Lord and could delay His dealing with the person.

The Bible goes on to tell us in Romans 12:20, "Therefore if thine enemy hunger, feed him; if he thirst, give him drink: for in so doing thou shalt heap coals of fire on his head." The natural man and the carnal man both would see this verse as showing weakness, but we must remember that the spiritual man should follow the Spirit's direction and not his fleshly desires. When we want to rejoice at an enemy's loss or misfortune, we should instead pray for them and do good. Who knows what the Lord will do in that situation.

Boldness

25 April 1983

Having therefore, brethren, boldness to enter into the holiest by the blood of Jesus.—**Hebrews 10:19**

In December 1982 after hearing President Reagan refer to the Soviet Union as the "evil empire," Samantha Smith, a fifth grade girl from Maine, took it upon herself to write Soviet Premier Yuri Andropov a letter:

> Dear Mr. Andropov,
>
> My name is Samantha Smith. I am ten years old. Congratulations on your new job. I have been worrying about Russia and the United States getting into a nuclear war. Are you going to vote to have a war or not? If you aren't, please tell me how you are going to help to not have a war. This question you do not have to answer, but I would like to know why you want to conquer the world or at least our country. God made the world for us to live together in peace and not to fight.
>
> Sincerely,
> Samantha Smith

On 25 April 1983, Samantha received a response. Premier Andropov's letter to Samantha said the Russian people wanted to "live in peace, to trade and cooperate with all our neighbors on this Earth—with those far away and those nearby. And, certainly, with such a great country as the United States of America." He ended the letter by inviting Samantha to visit Russia, of which she accepted. In the midst of this war of words and threats, a ten-year-old girl from Maine boldly asked a powerful leader some hard questions.

Christ is far greater than even the most powerful earthly ruler. But He invites us to come to His very throne room with great confidence. "Let us therefore come boldly unto the throne of grace, that we may obtain mercy, and find grace to help in time of need" (Hebrews 4:16). Take time to enter His presence today.

No Difference

26 April 1945

For there is no difference between the Jew and the Greek: for the same Lord over all is rich unto all that call upon him. For whosoever shall call upon the name of the Lord shall be saved.—**Romans 10:12–13**

During World War II, daring pilots battled it out in the skies over Europe, the Pacific, North Africa, and the Atlantic. At this time in our nation's history, racial segregation was still an unfortunate part of the US Armed Forces. Qualifications for a fighter pilot involved three main things: had to be male between the ages of 18 to 22, had to have a high school diploma, and had to be of the "Caucasian persuasion." However, various civil rights groups lobbied for the inclusion of black men into the Army Air Corps pilot program. In response, President Franklin D. Roosevelt announced that the Army Air Corps would train black pilots. In the summer of 1941, the first all-black fighter squadron, named the 99th Pursuit Squadron, was activated at Tuskegee Army Air Field in Alabama.

Nicknamed the "Red Tails," the 99th distinguished themselves time and again throughout the war. During one mission, the Red Tails shot down twelve German fighters within two days. In 1944, the 99th combined with three other fighter squadrons to become the 332nd Fighter Group. By the time the 332nd had flown its final combat mission on 26 April 1945, these "Tuskegee Airmen" had participated in more than fifteen thousand combat sorties in the war's final two years.

When the Lord Jesus Christ died for our sins, He broke down the "middle wall of partition" (Ephesians 2:14) that separated Jews and Gentiles. In Christ, there is neither Jew nor Greek, but all are accepted based on Jesus' blood alone. Christ's salvation is not for a select few, but rather, for all who will receive Him. At the cross, all are accepted by Christ; and in Christ, we are all family, regardless of the color of our skin.

Because of this truth, we should treat one another as "fellowcitizens with the saints" (Ephesians 2:19), and we should share the gospel with *anyone* who does not yet know Christ.

An Empty Tomb

27 April 1897

And he saith unto them, Be not affrighted: Ye seek Jesus of Nazareth, which was crucified: he is risen; he is not here: behold the place where they laid him.
—Mark 16:6

When I was a boy, a repeated riddle, made famous by Groucho Marx, was, "Who is buried in Grant's tomb?" Technically, the proper response to the riddle is "no one," since both Grant and his wife are entombed in stone caskets in an atrium above the ground rather than buried in the earth.

President Ulysses S. Grant died of throat cancer in 1885. One of his dying requests was to be buried next to his wife, which eliminated national and military cemeteries at the time because they disallowed the internment of women. Within hours of his death, the Mayor of New York City sent a telegram to Grant's widow offering New York for a final resting place for both Grant and his wife Julia. Grant's tomb (General Grant National Memorial) was officially dedicated on 27 April 1897.

Here's another question:"Who is buried in Joseph's tomb?" While less well-known than the popular Groucho Marx riddle, the answer is the same: "No one!"

Joseph of Arimathea was a friend of Jesus and allowed his tomb to be used to bury the body of Christ following His death on the cross. When the body of the Lord Jesus was laid in Joseph of Arimathea's tomb, it was temporary. Three days later, Jesus rose from the grave, leaving an empty tomb.

Grant's tomb does have the remains of him and his wife, but the garden tomb where Jesus was buried is empty because Jesus conquered death that we may one day live eternally. We have no need to fear death or the grave because we know we have victory over both through Christ. "O death, where is thy sting? O grave, where is thy victory? The sting of death is sin; and the strength of sin is the law. But thanks be to God, which giveth us the victory through our Lord Jesus Christ" (1 Corinthians 15:55–57).

1 Kings 1–2 // Luke 19:28–48

Transforming Behavior

28 April 1789

Being confident of this very thing, that he which hath begun a good work in you will perform it until the day of Jesus Christ.—**Philippians 1:6**

On 28 April 1789, near the island of Tofua, Fletcher Christian and twenty-five seamen seized the merchant ship HMS *Bounty* in one of the most infamous maritime mutinies in history. Ultimately, the reason for the mutiny centered around the harsh treatment of the sailors by its captain, William Bligh. However, we can learn some important leadership lessons from this story.

Prior to mutiny, the ship had been moored in Tahiti for five months. Without the daily struggles of sailing a ship, Bligh's crew became lax and undisciplined. When leaving for England, Bligh overstepped and became a tyrant aboard ship in order to gain back control of his men. Fletcher became rebellious to Bligh's extreme discipline and led the mutiny against him. When Bligh and eighteen others were set adrift in an overcrowded long boat in the middle of the Pacific, Captain Bligh had to quickly change his leadership tactics. By remarkable seamanship and a more unified approach, Bligh and his men reached Timor, East Indies, in June, after a voyage of about 3,600 miles.

Bligh's willingness to change his leadership style was the main reason he and his crew made it back to England. How about you? When confronted with a criticism, do you push against it or look to change it? In order to make a positive change, the first step is humbling yourself enough to admit fault. "For whosoever exalteth himself shall be abased; and he that humbleth himself shall be exalted" (Luke 14:11). The second step is to identify actions or habits that must change. With this step, comes a close third step of allowing the Lord to instigate the change in your heart and mind: "Be ye transformed by the renewing of your mind, that ye may prove what is that good, and acceptable, and perfect, will of God" (Romans 12:2). This transformation does not happen overnight, but rather with a daily decision to allow God to continue the work in you.

Faithful Service

29 April 1990

Let no man despise thy youth; but be thou an example of the believers, in word, in conversation, in charity, in spirit, in faith, in purity.—**1 Timothy 4:12**

On 29 April 1990, the Discovery space shuttle touched down at Edwards Air Force Base after completing a mission to place the Hubble telescope into orbit. This space shuttle served as America's longest-serving orbiter, flying more missions than any of its sister ships and spending 365 days in space. Additionally, the Discovery flew every type of mission known to the era of space shuttles, several of which were firsts: she carried the first non-astronaut into space, was flown by the first African American commander, and was piloted by the first female spacecraft pilot. In March 2011, the Discovery was retired and placed on display at the Smithsonian's National Air and Space Museum in Virginia. Throughout all of its missions, the Discovery faithfully served the 251 crew members who flew on her into space.

When we think of the qualities that provide great usefulness, sometimes we forget the importance of faithfulness. Yet, without faithfulness, every other quality becomes useless.

In Luke 16, Jesus spoke of a steward who had not been faithful in his master's employ. The master gives the steward another chance to make it right, and he does by serving his master as he originally should have. In Luke 16:10, Jesus concludes the parable with this challenge: "He that is faithful in that which is least is faithful also in much: and he that is unjust in the least is unjust also in much." Missionary Hudson Taylor is quoted as saying, "A little thing is a little thing, but faithfulness in a little thing is a great thing." No matter what service Jesus has called us to, our mission is to be faithful.

Are you faithfully carrying out your mission here on Earth? A day is coming when we will retire to our home in Heaven. Will God be able to commend us for faithful service to Him?

1 Kings 6–7 // Luke 20:27–47

The Idol Self

30 April 1030

I protest by your rejoicing which I have in Christ Jesus our Lord, I die daily.
—1 Corinthians 15:31

On 30 April 1030, Mahmud of Ghazni died at the age of fifty-nine. Mahmud is famous as the first ruler to use the title *sultan*. An able military commander, he conquered the region that is present-day Iran, Uzbekistan, Afghanistan, and India.

While conquering, his practice was to destroy all the idols in every city he encountered. When he attacked the city of Gujarat, he encountered a fifteen-foot idol built by the Brahmins. As he ordered it destroyed, the Brahmins of the temple immediately fell at his feet, proclaiming, "Great Mahmud, spare our god, for the fortunes of this city depend upon him."

After a moment's pause, Mahmud said that he would rather be known as the breaker of idols rather than the seller of idols. He and his soldiers struck the idol with battle-axes, and the idol soon lay in pieces. Unbeknownst to Mahmud, the idol was hollow, used as a receptacle for thousands of the city's precious gems. The city's fortunes actually depended on the jewels within the idol, not on the statue itself. Only when Mahmud destroyed the idol was the wealth of any value.

Many times, we are like the Brahmins in this incident, unwilling to break the idol of self in order to use the jewels beneath. We declare that if we allow self to stand, it gives us pleasures and treasures. Scripture, however, tells us that true pleasure and lasting joy is found in the presence of God: "Thou wilt shew me the path of life: in thy presence is fulness of joy; at thy right hand there are pleasures for evermore" (Psalm 16:11). When we die to self, the Holy Spirit's presence becomes more evident in our lives.

"I beseech you therefore, brethren, by the mercies of God, that ye present your bodies a living sacrifice, holy, acceptable unto God, which is your reasonable service" (Romans 12:1). The challenge with sacrificing self is that, as a living sacrifice, it tends to get up off the altar. This is why Paul suggested that Christians have to die daily to self (1 Corinthians 15:31).

MAY

Best Laid Plans

1 May 1915

For that ye ought to say, If the Lord will, we shall live, and do this, or that. **—James 4:15**

On 1 May 1915, the RMS *Lusitania* set sail on a journey from New York to Liverpool, England. Despite warnings of U-boats sinking British ships in the newspapers, the ship's captain nevertheless pressed ahead, confident the *Lusitania's* speed was no match for slow-moving German submarines. Six days later, the *U-20*, commanded by Kapitänleutnant Walther Schwieger, launched a single torpedo into the hull of the *Lusitania*, sinking her in eighteen minutes. Among the 1,195 lost were 123 Americans.

While the sinking of the *Lusitania* was the not the sole reason America would enter the fight of World War I, the sinking was the catalyst that escalated tensions between America and Germany. Almost a year after the *Lusitania*'s sinking, President Woodrow Wilson declared war on Germany.

So often in life, we manipulate circumstances to achieve our own outcome. Even when we recognize the potential folly of a decision, we are quick to refuse godly counsel and press ahead with our own plans. Like the commander of the *Lusitania* discovered, sometimes it's better to listen to counsel.

But even beyond listening to human counsel, we are wise to remember that God's sovereign will overrides the best laid plans of man. Consider Moses. Acts 7:25 tells us that well before his burning bush experience, Moses already knew that "by his hand would deliver [the Israelites]." Unfortunately, rather than trusting God and waiting on *His* timing, Moses took matters into his own hands and killed an Egyptian man, thinking he was helping to free his people. It was forty years and a burning-bush surrender later before God could use Moses to free the children of Israel.

When you believe you know exactly God's plan for your life, follow Him by faith. But don't take matters into your own hands and presumptuously go against what He has already directed in His Word or through wise and godly sources of human counsel.

Be Not Forgetful

2 May 334

And you, that were sometime alienated and enemies in your mind by wicked works, yet now hath he reconciled.—**Colossians 1:21**

Alexander the Great is considered one of the greatest military commanders of all time. During the battle of the Granicus River in May 334 BC, Alexander the Great and his Macedonian army squared off against the Persians in what is modern-day Turkey.

During the heat of the battle, Alexander was struck by an axe on his helmet from a Persian nobleman named Spithridates. Before Spithridates could deal a death-blow, Cleitus the Black, one of Alexander's trusted generals and personal friends, killed Spithridates and saved Alexander's life. Alexander went on to conquer all of Persia. How did Alexander repay Cleitus for his act of heroism? During a drunken party six years later, Alexander got angry with Cleitus' disapproval of a decision and threw a javelin through his heart, killing him instantly. He mourned the loss of his friend for the remainder of his life.

It seems that sometimes Christians forget how good God has been to them and, in the heat of the moment, complain against Him or doubt His goodness to them. David said, "Bless the LORD, O my soul, and forget not all his benefits" (Psalm 103:2). When we really grasp the incredible mercy God has shown us, we feel compelled to offer our lives to Him because it is the only reasonable response. That was the conclusion of the psalmist: "What shall I render unto the LORD for all his benefits toward me? . . . O LORD, truly I am thy servant; I am thy servant, and the son of thine handmaid: thou hast loosed my bonds" (Psalm 116:12, 16).

Unlike Alexander the Great, we should remember the great salvation we have been given, and we should continue to love and serve the Lord with our whole hearts. Don't forget who you were and what Christ's work on the cross saved you from! Let the memory of God's great mercy compel you to continue to love and serve Him for the remainder of your life.

1 Kings 12–13 // Luke 22:1–30

A Call for Prayer

3 May 1990

And he spake a parable unto them to this end, that men ought always to pray, and not to faint;—**Luke 18:1**

During the early days of the Constitutional Convention in America, meetings were rampant with arguments and debates. No real work had been done in writing a Constitution that all thirteen colonies would sign because the delegates could not agree. Eighty-year-old Benjamin Franklin then suggested that every meeting be started with prayer.

> We shall be divided by our little partial local interests; our projects will be confounded; and we ourselves shall become a reproach and by-word down to future ages. . . . I therefore beg leave to move—that henceforth prayers imploring the assistance of Heaven, and its blessings on our deliberations, be held in this Assembly every morning before we proceed to business, and that one or more of the clergy of this city be requested to officiate in that service.

This was not the only time that leaders have called for prayer in the midst of a crisis. Many of our Presidents, including President Lincoln during the Civil War, have called for a national day of prayer. In 1988, President Ronald Reagan made the first Thursday in May the official National Day of Prayer. Just a few years later, on 3 May 1990, President Bush stated, "The great faith that led our Nation's Founding Fathers to pursue this bold experience in self-government has sustained us in uncertain and perilous times; it has given us strength and inspiration to this very day. Like them, we do well to recall our firm reliance on the protection of Divine Providence."

Missionary Hudson Taylor once said, "When we work, we work; but when we pray, God works." It is the height of pride to attempt a good and godly work without depending on the power of God through prayer. Never begin a day or a project without prayer for God's protection, power, and divine enabling.

1 Kings 14–15 // Luke 22:31–46

Warning System

4 May 1982

Nevertheless, if thou warn the wicked of his way to turn from it; if he do not turn from his way, he shall die in his iniquity; but thou hast delivered thy soul.
—Ezekiel 33:9

In the spring of 1982, Argentina decided to invade the British-occupied Falkland Islands, located about four hundred miles off the South American coast. Argentina had long laid claim to these islands, and military dictator General Leopoldo Galteri decided the invasion was the best chance to retake the islands before the 150th anniversary of British rule.

Because of British superior military strength, the invasion was somewhat one-sided; however, the Argentinians did score a significant propaganda victory on 4 May 1982. An Argentinian fighter sent a French-made Exocet anti-ship missile into the British destroyer HMS *Sheffield*, sinking her beneath the South Atlantic waters. Exocet anti-ship missiles, known as "flying fish," are unique because they are designed to skim the ocean's surface, rendering them tough to spot on radar. This, however, was not the reason the *Sheffield* sank. The HMS *Sheffield's* missile tracking system was programmed to ignore Exocets as "friendly" because France was an ally. When the Argentinian fighter fired the Exocet at the *Sheffield*, the ship's internal warning system recognized the inbound bogie as French-made and ignored it. Sadly, the *Sheffield* sunk because the tracking system ignored a missile it "knew" was coming.

As important as warning systems are for the military, God's method of warning people is even more important. Not only do we have His Word as a warning system, but we also have other Christians to help us against Satan's attacks. Even when his attacks appear as "friendly" temptations, the Bible and godly counselors can keep us from our ignorance. God's desire is for those who have experienced His grace in their lives to warn others, and for those who are growing in grace, to listen to wise counsel. "For by wise counsel thou shalt make thy war: and in multitude of counsellors there is safety" (Proverbs 24:6). God's warning systems will keep you afloat.

Refuge

5 May 1877

The LORD also will be a refuge for the oppressed, a refuge in times of trouble. **—Psalm 9:9**

Chief Sitting Bull has become an iconic figure of the American frontier. Sitting Bull became the war chief for the Lakota Sioux tribe who inhabited northern Wyoming and southern Montana in 1857. In June 1876, General George Armstrong Custer of the Seventh US Cavalry led an attack on the Sioux and other American Indian allies near the Little Bighorn River in southeastern Montana. The Battle of the Little Big Horn is famous because Custer and 260 other US Army soldiers were massacred.

Concerned that their great victory would invite massive retribution from the US Army, the Indians scattered into smaller groups. The Army tracked down the majority of these groups and forced them onto reservations. Sitting Bull and his followers, however, managed to elude confrontation with the Army until Colonel Nelson Miles met with Sitting Bull and tried to persuade him to surrender. The old war chief refused Miles, who in turn, stepped up the Army's harassment of the Lakota Sioux. Tired of the harassment and dwindling numbers of buffalo, Sitting Bull and his followers crossed the border into Canada on 5 May 1877. This region of Canada offered them refuge and relative peace.

The Old Testament book of Numbers speaks about the "cities of refuge," which were cities that God appointed for those who were fleeing the "avenger of blood." The spiritual application of the Old Testament cities of refuge foreshadows the Great City of Refuge, the Lord Jesus Christ. Even as Sitting Bull sought refuge in Canada, so much more it is when a person flees to Jesus—He becomes our Refuge. When Satan hounds us with our past sins and failures, we have the refuge of Christ on which to depend. "Be merciful unto me, O God, be merciful unto me: for my soul trusteth in thee: yea, in the shadow of thy wings will I make my refuge, until these calamities be overpast" (Psalm 57:1).

A Witness of Surrender

6 May 1942

That at the name of Jesus every knee should bow, of things in heaven, and things in earth, and things under the earth;—**Philippians 2:10**

The island of Corregidor became the last Allied holdout during the Japanese attack against the Philippines. For months, American and Filipino troops held off the Japanese through savage fighting. Following the surrender at Bataan, thousands of Allied men in the Philippines were subjected to a brutal forced march known today as the "Bataan Death March."

General Douglas MacArthur's escape from the Philippines in March 1942 left General Jonathan Wainwright in command. After constant shelling and aerial bombardment, Wainwright was finally forced to surrender the Allied troops still in the Philippines to the Japanese on 6 May 1942. Along with some eleven thousand surviving Allied troops, General Wainwright remained a POW until 1945. Wainwright endured years of imprisonment, abuse, and starvation while also suffering remorse for having surrendered the Allied troops.

After his liberation in 1945, an emaciated Wainwright watched the official Japanese surrender ceremony on the deck of the USS *Missouri*. After years of trial and tribulation, General Wainwright was able to witness the surrender of an enemy who had subjected him to abuse for three years.

In like fashion, a day is coming when those of us who have been born again will get to witness our enemy surrender and bow the knee to the King of kings and Lord of lords. "And I heard a loud voice saying in heaven, Now is come salvation, and strength, and the kingdom of our God, and the power of his Christ: for the accuser of our brethren is cast down, which accused them before our God day and night. And they overcame him by the blood of the Lamb, and by the word of their testimony; and they loved not their lives unto the death" (Revelation 12:10–11). What a wonderful day that will be when we witness the final surrender of the enemy of God!

Not an Enigma

7 May 1941

For the king knoweth of these things, before whom also I speak freely: for I am persuaded that none of these things are hidden from him; for this thing was not done in a corner.—**Acts 26:26**

The sending, receiving, and interpreting of signal intelligence or secret codes has been around since the days of the Egyptian pharaohs. The role that code breaking played during the Battle of the Atlantic in World War II was paramount in the Allies being able to pinpoint where and when German U-boats would strike. The German Enigma machine, devised by Berlin engineer Arthur Scherbius, was complex and had millions of possible combinations, making it almost impossible to crack.

The early days of the Battle of the Atlantic proved highly successful for Admiral Dönitz and his "wolf packs." Not knowing when and where these "gray wolves" would strike was costly to the Allied war effort. Prior to the war, a Polish mathematician made an observation which was passed on to British intelligence. A group of Allied chess players, mathematicians, and other experts (code-named Ultra) began meeting at Bletchley Park in England to crack the Enigma code. Their first real break came on 7 May 1941 when a British destroyer obtained an intact Enigma machine and code book. With previous knowledge and new information, the Allies cracked the code, which turned the tide of the Battle of the Atlantic.

While the German Enigma was meant to be kept secret, the gospel of the Lord Jesus Christ is not. In attempting to witness to King Agrippa, Paul reminded him that the events of the gospel were "not done in a corner," or in secret. God placed the gospel on "the bottom shelf" so everyone could have access. It's not some secret code that must be figured out. God made salvation so simple that even a child can understand it. The world has created complex avenues to eternity, but Jesus plainly said, "I am the way, the truth, and the life: no man cometh unto the Father, but by me" (John 14:6). Proclaim the truth by giving out the gospel code!

Military Spouse Appreciation

8 May 1984

We give thanks to God always for you all, making mention of you in our prayers.
—1 Thessalonians 1:2

The Friday prior to Mother's Day is designated on our calendar as "Military Spouse Appreciation Day." While those who serve or have served in the military certainly do not need a specific day set aside to express appreciation to their spouses, President Ronald Reagan established one in 1984. For hundreds, even thousands of years, military spouses have been the ones who have kept the home fires burning, cared for the children, and endured a myriad of trials and tribulations as their loved ones were off serving their country.

Elizabeth Bacon "Libby" Custer often followed her flamboyant husband, George Armstrong Custer, into the field to see to his needs while on campaign. When not with Custer, Libby traveled to Washington, D.C. where she met and socialized with military and political figures in the hopes of advancing her husband's career. After Custer was killed fighting at the Battle of the Little Big Horn in 1876, Libby dressed in black for the remainder of her long life. In 1885, she authored the first of several books that countered the criticism that had been levied against her late husband.

My own wife, Denise, supported my twenty-five years of active duty Air Force career in ways I can never adequately repay. She traveled with me to places that were rarely her choosing and she took care of our family when I was assigned TDY (temporary duty) or otherwise engaged in some military capacity.

When reading Luke's account of the Lord Jesus healing the ten lepers (Luke 17:12–19), I am always amazed that only one returned to thank Him. What about the other nine? Why was it not important to thank the One who had instantly cleansed them from such a horrible condition? Sadly, their actions are typical of our society today. A simple "thank you" carries more weight than we may imagine. Let us practice the gratitude attitude today by thanking someone who has influenced our lives.

New Lease on Life

9 May 1671

For we are his workmanship, created in Christ Jesus unto good works, which God hath before ordained that we should walk in them.—**Ephesians 2:10**

England's Crown Jewels have stimulated both awe and temptation for over six hundred years. Known as the coronation regalia, they are arguably the most visited objects in Great Britain. The 140-piece collection of Crown Jewels are displayed at the Jewel House in the Tower of London. Having seen these myself, the Crown Jewels are truly a sight to behold.

On 9 May 1671, an Irish adventurer named Thomas Blood, commonly known as "Captain Blood" for his service in the English Civil War, became one of the world's most infamous thieves as he and his accomplices tried to steal the Crown Jewels. Captain Blood and his team of three knocked out the jewel keepers and stole the jewels. However, one keeper awoke and sounded the alarm before the thieves could escape the tower with the jewels. After being imprisoned for the crime, Blood refused to speak with anyone about it except King Charles II. The king was so impressed with Blood's audacity in the meeting that he pardoned Blood, restored his estates in Ireland, and made him a member of his court with an annual salary! Evidently, the king saw something in Thomas that he thought he could use in the royal courts.

Like Blood, we are all "thieves" in one way or another. We steal time, we steal objects of value, and we steal blessings from others. None of us is righteous on our own, and yet God in His rich mercy not only pardons us when we receive Christ, but He allows us to serve Him just as Charles did for Thomas Blood. "And I will cleanse them from all their iniquity, whereby they have sinned against me; and I will pardon all their iniquities, whereby they have sinned, and whereby they have transgressed against me" (Jeremiah 33:8).

It would have been foolish for Blood to refuse the pardon and position that the king offered him. Likewise, it would be foolish for us Christians to refuse to serve our King who pardoned us from all of our sin.

Prepare to Meet God

10 May 1863

. . . prepare to meet thy God.—**Amos 4:12**

Thomas "Stonewall" Jackson became a lieutenant general in October 1862, and was arguably General Lee's most capable battle commander. During the Battle of Chancellorsville in the spring of 1863, Jackson marched 28,000 troops approximately fifteen miles to Union General Joseph Hooker's exposed flank while General Lee engaged in diversionary attacks at the front. Jackson's surprise attack on the Union rear inflicted massive casualties on the superior force, forcing Hooker to withdraw only days later. However, the Confederate victory was not without cost.

At sunset, Jackson took some men to scout ahead. Mistaken for enemy cavalry, a North Carolina regiment opened fire, severely wounding Jackson. The bullet shattered the bone just below his left shoulder, causing the doctor to have to amputate his left arm. Infection and pneumonia set into his body. His wife, who had been called to his side, comforted him saying, "Do you not feel willing to acquiesce in God's allotment, if He will you to go today . . . Well, before this day closes, you will be with the blessed Saviour in His glory." Jackson died on 10 May 1863, at the age of thirty-nine.

Thomas "Stonewall" Jackson certainly did not expect or plan to enter eternity. However, his wife bears testimony to the fact that Jackson was prepared to meet the Lord. In fact, Jackson's example contributed to a great revival that broke out among Southern troops during the summer of 1863.

The Apostle Paul said in 2 Timothy 4:6, "For I am now ready to be offered, and the time of my departure is at hand." Like Paul, Stonewall Jackson was ready to leave this Earth. Are you? In 2 Peter 1:10, the Apostle Peter instructs, "Give diligence to make your calling and election sure." Being ready for eternity requires that we place our complete faith and trust in the finished work of the Lord Jesus Christ. And being eager to meet the Lord requires that we walk in obedience to Him until He calls us Home. Does your life reflect Jesus to those who are around you? Would another person know that something is different because of the way you live?

2 Kings 10–12 // John 1:29–51

The Faithfulness of God

11 May 1775

Thy faithfulness is unto all generations: thou hast established the earth, and it abideth.—**Psalm 119:90**

On 11 May 1775, the Second Continental Congress officially convened. Among the outcomes of that historic gathering was the appointment of Benjamin Franklin as the first postmaster general. A few years later, the US Post Office was created. The United States Postal Service took as its unofficial motto the familiar phrase, "Neither snow nor rain nor heat nor gloom of night stays these couriers from the swift completion of their appointed rounds." These words are chiseled in gray granite over the entrance to the New York City Post Office on 8th Avenue.

What many people do not realize is that the US Postal Service actually borrowed these words from the ancient Persians. During their war with the Greeks in the fifth century BC, King Xerxes used a system of horsemen—similar to the United States' Pony Express—to relay messages to his troops. The ancient historian Herodotus described the mounted courier system in Book 8 of his Histories: "These are stopped neither by snow nor rain nor heat nor darkness from accomplishing their appointed course with all speed."

When one thinks of faithfulness, the US Postal Service motto could come to mind. But even more faithful than mail delivery is the faithfulness of our God. His watchful care over us is as sure as the sun coming up in the morning. The psalmist said, "It is a good thing to give thanks unto the LORD, and to sing praises unto thy name, O most High: To shew forth thy lovingkindness in the morning, and thy faithfulness every night" (Psalm 92:1–2).

Despite the changing climate of our culture, God is faithful. Despite the trials and darkness that may come our way, God is faithful. No matter the day or time, God is faithful to answer us and meet with us. When you're in the midst of a trial and it seems as if no one is there for you, God is! Be encouraged today to depend and rest on His faithfulness.

A Significant Part

12 May 1607

In whom all the building fitly framed together groweth unto an holy temple in the Lord: In whom ye also are builded together for an habitation of God through the Spirit.—**Ephesians 2:21–22**

On 12 May 1607, the colony of Jamestown, Virginia, was founded. The following is a narrative from one of the earliest recorded histories of that settlement:

> Having pitched upon a place to settle, they called it James-Town, in honor of His Majesty then reigning, and every man fell to work. The Council contrived the Fort and of the rest, some cut down and cleared away trees to make a place to pitch their tents; some got clapboards to remake the ships, whilst others were employed in making gardens and nets, and providing other necessities and conveniences.

One cannot read the history of the Jamestown settlement and not be struck by the fact that people worked together toward a harmonious existence. Certainly, Jamestown was by no means a utopia, but the colonists learned that everyone's contribution, no matter how seemingly insignificant, was vital to the settlement's survival.

No one in the body of Christ is insignificant. We all have a specific gift or talent that Christ wants to use to further His kingdom here on this Earth. In fact, when a person is saved, God gives him or her spiritual gifts that are to complement other people's spiritual gifts so the entire church can labor together and accomplish a wonderful work of God.

In 1 Corinthians 12:12, Paul compares the body of Christ to our physical bodies. "For as the body is one, and hath many members, and all the members of that one body, being many, are one body: so also is Christ." Just as every member of our physical body is needed, so every member of the body of Christ—the local church—is needed. Don't ever feel as if you and your talents are not significant in the work of God. As part of the church body, God can and will use you if you stay yielded to Him.

2 Kings 15–16 // John 3:1–18

Little Drummer Boy

13 May 1937

Let no man despise thy youth; but be thou an example of the believers, in word, in conversation, in charity, in spirit, in faith, in purity.—**1 Timothy 4:12**

A few weeks into the Civil War, President Lincoln issued a call for volunteers to serve in the Union Army. John Lincoln Clem, resident of Newark, Ohio, was one of those who answered that call. Being that he was only nine years old at the time, however, the newly formed Third Ohio Regiment refused him. Not to be dissuaded, Clem joined the Twenty-Second Michigan and was assigned as a drummer boy.

Clem sawed down his musket to make it more his size and participated in the Battle of Chickamauga, where he shot a Confederate colonel who chided him for being just a boy. For his actions at Chickamauga, Clem was promoted to sergeant, the youngest soldier ever to become a noncommissioned officer in the US Army. He was also given the nickname "Drummer Boy of Chickamauga." After fighting and surviving the rest of the war, he was discharged at the age of thirteen. Five years later, he was nominated to West Point by President Grant and rose to the rank of Major General before retiring from service on the eve of America's entry into the Great War. Clem was the last Civil War veteran to actively serve in the US Army. The "Drummer Boy of Chickamauga" died at the age of eighty-six on 13 May 1937.

In a day when youth is often derided for a lack of character or maturity, we should remember that God can and does work through the younger generation to provide an example worth emulating. If you are a younger person reading this, be encouraged that God can use you. If you know a younger person, encourage them in the Lord and challenge them to fully engage in spiritual battle for Christ. "For ye see your calling, brethren, how that not many wise men after the flesh, not many mighty, not many noble, are called: But God hath chosen the foolish things of the world to confound the wise; and God hath chosen the weak things of the world to confound the things which are mighty" (1 Corinthians 1:26–27).

Affliction Brings Salvation

14 May 1948

I know that the Lord *will maintain the cause of the afflicted, and the right of the poor.*—**Psalm 140:12**

God often works and moves in ways we would never consider. When God created man, He gave us a free will. Sometimes men make evil choices and decisions that go against what God condones. God will, however, use the choices of these evil men to allow His plan to unfold.

For example, as horrific as the Holocaust was, the establishment of the State of Israel on 14 May 1948 may never have taken place without it. Because of the Holocaust, West Germany's reparations gave Israel the resources necessary to survive. The Holocaust also motivated large numbers of Jews to immigrate to Israel providing the necessary population. The Holocaust enabled Israel to pressure Germany into supplying an economic base necessary to build infrastructure and support within the new state. The Holocaust swayed world opinion so that the United Nations approved and accepted the State of Israel in 1948. The culmination of all of this was that Israel becoming a sovereign nation fulfilled no less than ten Bible prophecies concerning the Jewish people.

As Bible believers, we might wonder or be asked, "Why does God allow bad things to happen?" We will never know the full answer to the question this side of Heaven. But the simple answer is that God works through hard times to bring people to Him and to fulfill His larger plan. The harder part of this answer is accepting by faith that "all things work together for good to them that love God" (Romans 8:28). In the book of Acts and throughout the pages of history, Christians have been tortured and killed for the faith. But in so many of those cases, God used the testimony of the martyred to bring people to Him. We cannot know or understand the mind of God, but we can rest assured that He knows the end result of the hardship and He will align it to His perfect will. The evil that happens in our world will not last forever, and in the meantime, we can share with others the hope that we have in a powerful, all-knowing God.

Needed Changes

15 May 1969

Confess your faults one to another, and pray one for another, that ye may be healed. The effectual fervent prayer of a righteous man availeth much. **—James 5:16**

On 15 May 1969 at the Mare Island site of the San Francisco Bay Naval Shipyard, the nuclear powered attack submarine *Guitarro* (SSN-665) sank while tied up to the dock. After three years of construction, the ship was close to being completed and commissioned. However, the damages to the submarine cost the Navy over fifteen million dollars and a two-year delay for the commissioning.

The investigation revealed that "although the sinking of the USS *Guitarro* was accidental, the immediate cause of the sinking was the culpable negligence of certain shipyard employees . . . [and] inadequate coordination of both the ship construction activities and the assignment of specific responsibilities." In other words, better communication and attention to details would have saved a lot of money and time. Following this costly accident, the investigative committee identified several changes that had to be made in regard to future ship building all of which had to do with better communication and supervising procedures.

In our Christian lives, costly mistakes are often created by our failure to communicate on a regular basis with the Lord and by a lack of accountability to a godly Christian. Although our past mistakes cannot be erased, future mistakes can be avoided by making a few changes.

First, be sure you have a daily time when you meet with the Lord, glean from His Word, and spend time with Him in prayer. "My voice shalt thou hear in the morning, O LORD; in the morning will I direct my prayer unto thee, and will look up" (Psalm 5:3). Second, find a godly person whom you trust to keep you accountable in your Christian walk. "The way of a fool is right in his own eyes: but he that hearkeneth unto counsel is wise" (Proverbs 12:15). Clear communication with the Lord and godly accountability will go a long way toward keeping your ship afloat.

Inflammatory Words

16 May 2007

Even so the tongue is a little member, and boasteth great things. Behold, how great a matter a little fire kindleth!—**James 3:5**

On 16 May 2007, a National Guard F-16 Fighting Falcon flew a routine training sortie over New Jersey air space. While practicing the use of a self-defense system to mislead heat-seeking missiles, the Falcon dropped a flare from too low an altitude to be safe. The flare, still burning on impact with the ground, ignited to become the largest fire the state of New Jersey has ever experienced. The fire destroyed about twenty square miles at the edge of the Pinelands National Reserve, burned three homes, and caused the evacuation of over two thousand homes. More than one thousand federal, state, and local firefighters were tasked to battle the inferno.

This incident illustrates James 3:5, which compares the human tongue to fire kindling. Many times, we do not realize how inflammatory our speech can be to others. An unkind word, foul language, or gossip can do much to cause harm to those who hear us or to damage another's reputation. Sometimes, we may say something in jest, not realizing the hurt it is causing the person at the brunt of the joke. The unfortunate thing about our words is that they can never be taken back.

The Bible instructs, "Let your speech be alway with grace, seasoned with salt, that ye may know how ye ought to answer every man" (Colossians 4:6). Salt is a great seasoning when it's used correctly. For instance, a little salt will bring out great flavors within a dish, but too much salt will ruin a dish. So it is with our words: they can be used to edify those around you or to destroy another's spirit.

How are you doing with your speech? Are you starting fires or putting them out? Do you encourage others or embarrass them? Are you complimenting or criticizing your family? Are you the instigator of false tales or of faithful truth? We must all work on speaking good and not evil. "Hear; for I will speak of excellent things; and the opening of my lips shall be right things" (Proverbs 8:6).

The Book

17 May 1829

The cloke that I left at Troas with Carpus, when thou comest, bring with thee, and the books, but especially the parchments.—**2 Timothy 4:13**

During his lifetime, John Jay (1745–1829) was a Founding Father, a signer of the Treaty of Paris, the second governor of New York, and the first Chief Justice of the United States. He was unanimously confirmed in 1789 and remained on the bench until 1795. As this was an introductory position, most of Jay's duties involved establishing rules, precedents, and procedures.

In addition to his legal duties, Jay was also elected president of the Westchester Bible Society in 1818 and president of the American Bible Society in 1821. In 1824, Jay addressed the American Bible Society:"In forming and settling my belief relative to the doctrines of Christianity, I adopted no articles from creeds but such only as, on careful examination, I found to be confirmed by the Bible."

On 17 May 1829, as he lay dying, John Jay was asked if he had any last words for his children, to which he responded: "They have the Book."

As the Apostle Paul's execution at the hands of Nero drew near, he asked young Timothy to bring him some items. Paul was in prison and could have asked Timothy to bring him anything. The last four words of 2 Timothy 4:13, however, reveal what was most important to Paul: "but especially the parchments." This request is a reference to the Scriptures. Like John Jay on his deathbed, Paul regarded the Bible as most important.

We should ascribe the same value on the Book as Justice Jay and the Apostle Paul. Jesus said, "Search the scriptures; for in them ye think ye have eternal life: and they are they which testify of me" (John 5:39). The value of the Bible is far above anything the world has to offer in wealth or riches. It is worthy of our diligent study, careful obedience, and bold proclamations. Read it, study it, memorize it, share it, and live it. You will never regret time invested in God's Word.

Destruction of Greed

18 May 1701

But they that will be rich fall into temptation and a snare, and into many foolish and hurtful lusts, which drown men in destruction and perdition. **—1 Timothy 6:9**

The Atlantic slave trade represents one of the most horrific periods in world history. Across four hundred years, European and American slave traders purchased Africans from African rulers, merchants, and middlemen to sell in Europe, Brazil, and the Americas. These unfortunate souls were packed tight into the holds of slave ships for a grueling journey across the Atlantic called the "middle passage." One slave ship in particular stands out as an example of man's insatiable lust for greed.

The *Henrietta Marie* sailed for Barbados in 1699 with over 250 slaves on board. Upon reaching his destination, Captain Deacon sold his human cargo for commodities he planned to take back to London. Sugar, ginger, and a hundred elephant tusks earned Deacon a small fortune. He retired and new captain John Taylor sought to replicate the "success" of Deacon. In the spring of 1700, the *Henrietta Marie* embarked upon its second voyage to Jamaica. Prior to reaching Jamaica, Captain Taylor died on board along with half his crew and sixteen slaves. No one has been able to determine the cause of these deaths since the surviving crew disappeared when the ship sunk during a hurricane on 18 May 1701, just days after leaving Jamaica. There were no survivors.

The lust for money, even to the detriment of human lives, prematurely ended the career of the *Henrietta Marie*, a ship never intended for the slave trade. Had the crew of the ship never engaged in human trafficking, perhaps they would not have "drowned in destruction and perdition."

The Bible teaches that "the love of money is the root of all evil: which while some coveted after, they have erred from the faith, and pierced themselves through with many sorrows" (1 Timothy 6:10). Be careful not to get caught up in the hurricane of greed, for this world's riches will soon pass away.

God Preserves His Plan

19 May 1588

For, lo, he that formeth the mountains, and createth the wind, and declareth unto man what is his thought, that maketh the morning darkness, and treadeth upon the high places of the earth, The LORD, The God of hosts, is his name. —**Amos 4:13**

Up until the late sixteenth century, most of the countries of Europe were Roman Catholic. When Henry VIII decided to divorce his first wife Catherine of Aragon, he separated from papal authority and dissolved relations between England and Spain. When Henry's son Edward VI ascended the throne, he officially established Protestantism for the first time in England's history. Despite the attempts of "Bloody Mary" to reinstate Catholicism after Edward's untimely death, Queen Elizabeth I re-established Protestantism and steered England further from the Church of Rome.

King Philip II of Spain ordered the Spanish Armada to crush England and return her to the Catholic fold. On 19 May 1588, 130 vessels with more than 27,000 Spanish soldiers set sail from Lisbon. Poor weather delayed the Spanish arrival to England's southern coast until July, and by then the Royal Navy, led by Sir Francis Drake, was ready for them. The longer range guns of the British frigates thinned the ranks of the armada, forcing the Spanish ships to flee toward the North Sea where an intense storm battered the weakened armada. As they rounded Ireland, more ships were wrecked off the rocky coast. Of the original 130, only 51 ships bearing 10,000 survivors were able to limp back to Spain. When King Philip heard of the defeat, he said, "I sent the Armada against men, not God's winds and waves."

Undoubtedly, God's sovereign hand was at work in the defeat of the Spanish Armada, changing the course of history and more specifically the settlement of North America. The Bible speaks of many instances when God allows both victory or defeat in order to carry out His plan. "The king's heart is in the hand of the LORD, as the rivers of water: he turneth it whithersoever he will" (Proverbs 21:1).

A Useless Victory

20 May 1969

Neither give place to the devil.—**Ephesians 4:27**

The Battle of Ap Bia Mountain, better known as "Hamburger Hill," was arguably the one battle that epitomized the overall futility of America's involvement in the Vietnam War. The purpose of this battle was to rid the entire A Shau Valley of North Vietnamese Army (NVA) forces. The plan was code named "Operation Apache Snow" and involved landing lead elements of the 101st Airborne on Hill 937.

From the first day, the NVA put up stiff resistance and by the end of the second day, the Americans realized they had grossly underestimated NVA strength. Intense enemy resistance coupled with five friendly fire incidents demoralized and took its toll on American infantry. About halfway through the battle, *Associated Press* reporter Jay Sharbutt arrived to investigate the battle. After interviewing a number of US soldiers, Sharbutt's article home described the battle as a "meat grinder," horrifying readers back home.

At a time when support for the war was at a low 39 percent, the press coverage of the battle on Hill 937 set off a fire-storm of protest that spread all the way to Congress. On 20 May 1969 at 1000 hours, ten artillery batteries fired more than twenty thousand rounds on the mountain, while over two hundred tactical air strikes dumped ordnance and napalm over the summit. Most of the enemy was killed or fled the mountain following this attack. On 5 June, American troops received orders to abandon Ap Bia, after which the NVA troops re-occupied Hill 937.

"Hamburger Hill" signifies the frustration of Vietnam—the failed strategy of winning a costly battle only to allow the enemy to recapture the won territory. When a Christian gives Satan a foothold in his or her life, a similar frustration occurs. It is detrimental to the cause of Christ and a believer's personal testimony when he allows one foolish decision to undo years of what God has wrought in his life. When God gives you a victory, don't foolishly throw it away by giving the devil ground that has already been won.

God Cares

21 May 1881

Casting all your care upon him; for he careth for you.—**1 Peter 5:7**

On 21 May 1881, the American Red Cross was established. The person most responsible for founding this organization was a nurse named Clara Barton. When the Civil War broke out, Barton was one of the first volunteers at the Washington Infirmary to care for wounded soldiers. Eventually, Barton left the city hospitals to go among the soldiers in the field.

Clara's presence on the battlefield was inspiring. She loaded army wagons with medical supplies, trained able-bodied men to perform first aid, and treated both Union and Confederate soldiers alike. Her care and courage in the midst of battles earned her the name "Angel of the Battlefield." Barton once said, "I may be compelled to face danger, but never fear it; and while our soldiers can stand and fight, I can stand and feed and nurse them."

After the war, Barton worked long hours to find missing soldiers for families and helped prepare former slaves for their new lives in freedom. Depleted, Clara traveled to Europe to regain her health. While in Switzerland, she learned about the International Red Cross. Going home refreshed and renewed, she began to lobby for an American Red Cross. At first the government was not convinced that we would need one since we did not plan to fight any more civil wars. Promoting the Red Cross use for natural disasters and aiding the homeless, Clara finally convinced Congress and served as the organization's first president.

More than the care that the American Red Cross can offer, God cares for us. Like a nurse, He will comfort us in the battles we encounter. "Are not five sparrows sold for two farthings, and not one of them is forgotten before God? But even the very hairs of your head are all numbered. Fear not therefore: ye are of more value than many sparrows" (Luke 12:6–7). When you are hurting or depleted, know that our Father in Heaven is with you to give the comfort and rest you need. You can rest in His care.

The Great Pretender

22 May 1455

For there shall arise false Christs, and false prophets, and shall shew great signs and wonders; insomuch that, if it were possible, they shall deceive the very elect.
—Matthew 24:24

In the fifteenth century, the English throne was disputed by two families: the House of York and the House of Lancaster. This medieval conflict became known as the Wars of the Roses, because of the white rose of York and red rose of Lancaster displayed on each family's coat of arms. The war began on 22 May 1455 with periodic battles fought until 1475. The Battle of Bosworth Field ended Yorkist King Richard III's rule and ushered in the Tudor line with King Henry VII.

Two years after King Henry's coronation, the house of York tried to unseat Henry and install ten-year-old Lambert Simnel, the supposed rightful heir to the throne. The only problem with this plan was that Simnel was an imposter. King Henry VII vanquished the Yorkists at the Battle of Stoke Field and captured the young Simnel. Instead of prison, Henry banished him to serve in the palace kitchens. King Henry VII became the last English king to win his throne on the field of battle, and he ruled in peace following his marriage to Elizabeth of York, thus merging the warring houses.

Like Simnel, Satan has many pretenders and false teachers out there ready to deceive and destroy the reign of Christ in our hearts. During His earthly ministry, the Lord Jesus warned His followers on more than one occasion to beware of pretenders. "Beware of false prophets, which come to you in sheep's clothing, but inwardly they are ravening wolves" (Matthew 7:15). False christs and false prophets will arise in these last days to seduce people away from the truth. Thankfully, Scripture provides the litmus test to detect pretenders. This is one reason we must be diligent to study God's Word. "But continue thou in the things which thou hast learned and hast been assured of, knowing of whom thou hast learned them" (2 Timothy 3:14).

No Evacuations

23 May 2018

In my Father's house are many mansions: if it were not so, I would have told you. I go to prepare a place for you.—**John 14:2**

On 23 May 2018, German authorities evacuated a downtown area of the city of Dresden after discovering an unexploded bomb from World War II while doing some construction work.

During World War II, British and American forces carpet-bombed Dresden for two straight days in February 1945. What was unique about this particular attack was the use of high explosive incendiary bombs, which essentially set the entire city on fire. US Army Air Force General Curtis Lemay was a strong proponent of strategic bombing and believed firebombing major enemy cities would erode the enemy morale. While the bombing of Dresden killed an estimated 25,000 civilians and destroyed 75,000 buildings, Germany remained obstinate toward surrender until the fall of Berlin in May 1945.

Imagine the frustration of the Dresden residents, having to evacuate because of an unexploded bomb left over from a war that happened over seventy years ago. Thankfully, the Christian does not have to worry about evacuating Heaven because of repercussions from the war that Christ fought and won over two thousand years ago. When Jesus conquered death and the grave, He conquered it not with the power of man but rather the power of His own deity.

Jesus told us, "Let not your heart be troubled: ye believe in God, believe also in me. In my Father's house are many mansions: if it were not so, I would have told you. I go to prepare a place for you. And if I go and prepare a place for you, I will come again, and receive you unto myself; that where I am, there ye may be also" (John 14:1–3). Our mansions will be ready and waiting for us when we go home to Heaven. Once we're settled, we will have no cause to evacuate because they will be eternal homes, created by God Himself. No bombs or enemy will be left over for us to fear. Praise the Lord for His enduring promises.

An Unrepentant Princess

24 May 2018

The Lord is not slack concerning his promise, as some men count slackness; but is longsuffering to us-ward, not willing that any should perish, but that all should come to repentance.—**2 Peter 3:9**

The Holocaust was one of the darkest times in world history. The Nazi regime, motivated by a perverse ideology, sought to annihilate an entire group of people. Throughout the pages of Adolf Hitler's autobiography *Mein Kampf*, he developed the ideas that would characterize his Third Reich. Within Hitler's social order, he taught that Jews and Marxists were to blame for all of Germany's misfortunes: these two groups stood in the way of Germany's economic, political, and geographic expansion.

As Hitler took power in the 1930s, he surrounded himself with a hierarchy who were loyal to this belief system. One such man was Heinrich Himmler, head of the Nazi Schutzstaffel (SS). Under the guise of nationalism, Himmler supervised and planned the murder of over six million Jews during the war.

Himmler's only child, Gudrun Burwitz, not only survived the war, but also continued in the Nazi ideology. Known as a "Nazi princess," Burwitz joined a group who helped Nazi fugitives flee to South America. She also zealously denied the Holocaust and attended underground reunions of Nazi SS officers as recently as 2014. Burwitz died on 24 May 2018 at the age of eighty-eight and remained an unrepentant Nazi to the end.

Repentance means "to change one's mind." Salvation through Christ requires repentance. "From that time Jesus began to preach, and to say, Repent: for the kingdom of heaven is at hand" (Matthew 4:17). God calls us to change our minds about believing that we can reach Heaven on our own and forgives anyone who acknowledges their sin and calls out to Him for salvation. As Christians, God wants us to repent of sin as soon as He reveals it to us—not to be saved, but to have a clear and strong relationship with Him. He promises that "if we confess our sins, he is faithful and just to forgive us our sins, and to cleanse us from all unrighteousness" (1 John 1:9).

A Coming Change in Government

25 May 1660

And the seventh angel sounded; and there were great voices in heaven, saying, The kingdoms of this world are become the kingdoms of our Lord, and of his Christ; and he shall reign for ever and ever.—**Revelation 11:15**

During England's Second Civil War, Oliver Cromwell and his New Model Army defeated King Charles I at the Battle of Preston in 1648. A year later, King Charles I was tried, convicted of high treason, and executed at the Palace of Whitehall. His son and heir Charles II went into exile to escape the same fate.

Oliver Cromwell assumed rule as Lord Protectorate of the Commonwealth of England. Under his leadership, several changes occurred in England, mainly involving England's form of government. After Cromwell's death in 1658, his son Richard took over, but the Model Army removed him, fragmenting the government into military factions.

On 25 May 1660, exiled King Charles II landed at Dover and took the throne as rightful king of England, Scotland, and Ireland. His reclaiming of the throne began the Restoration Era in English government. Although the monarchy was restored, the king required the consent of Parliament in governmental decisions, effectively creating a parliamentary monarchy. The Glorious Revolution of 1688 would formally instill parliamentary democracy as England's long-term form of government.

When sin entered the world, God allowed Satan to have some earthly dominion, even referring to Satan as "the god of this world" (2 Corinthians 4:4). However, God will take back the dominion of Earth, and He will have us rule and reign with Him. Revelation 1:6 tells of this coming day: "And hath made us kings and priests unto God and his Father; to him be glory and dominion for ever and ever. Amen."

No, the world isn't now as it should be. But as Christians, we can rest in the fact that the rightful Ruler will once again sit on the throne, having defeated the usurper.

Sow a Thought, Reap a Destiny

26 May 1914

For as he thinketh in his heart, so is he: Eat and drink, saith he to thee; but his heart is not with thee.—**Proverbs 23:7**

The assassination of Austro-Hungarian Archduke Franz Ferdinand in June 1914 was the catalyst that launched the world into World War I. The assassin, a nineteen-year-old Serbian terrorist, left Belgrade on 26 May 1914 for the purpose of wreaking havoc on the leadership of the oppressive Austro Hungarian empire. Gavrilo Princip traveled with a small group of Black Hand members, a fanatical Serbian terrorist organization who feared further aggression from the mighty Austro-Hungarian Empire.

The conspirators lined the streets of Sarajevo on 28 June 1914, awaiting the opportunity to attack the car carrying the Archduke and his wife. The first man missed his chance, leaving the second man to throw a grenade at the car. The grenade's delay caused damage and injury to the car behind the archduke's car, and the conspirators thought their chance gone. However, after the Archduke made his speech he traveled back the same route, but his driver took a wrong turn. Gavrilo Princip happened to be standing on a street corner when the royal couple's car stalled. Taking the opportunity, he fired his pistol point-blank at the royal couple; both died within minutes.

Princip plunged the world into an unprecedented era of death and destruction by his one action. Some historians argue that if not for this one assassination the world may have escaped not only World War I but also World War II, the Cold War, Korean War, and Vietnam War. When one considers the millions of people who died during the aforementioned conflicts, the actions of one person had staggering results.

While my sons were growing up, my wife would often admonish them as they left the house, "Make good choices." It has been said, "Sow a thought, reap an action; sow an action, reap a habit; sow a habit, reap a character; sow a character, reap a destiny." What you sow today, whether it is a thought or action, will eventually have a harvest. All it takes is one bad decision to destroy your testimony and derail God's best for you.

Involved in a Great Work

27 May 1942

And I sent messengers unto them, saying, I am doing a great work, so that I cannot come down: why should the work cease, whilst I leave it, and come down to you? **—Nehemiah 6:3**

In early May 1942, the Battle of the Coral Sea took place between the US and Japanese navies. This battle was the first carrier battle in history, as well as the first naval battle in which opposing forces never saw one another. During the battle, the carrier USS *Yorktown* sustained a bomb hit that penetrated her flight deck, exploded, and killed sixty-six sailors. Although heavily damaged, *Yorktown* managed to 'limp' to Pearl Harbor for repair. When the *Yorktown* arrived on 27 May 1942, ship engineers estimated that her damage would take three months to repair.

However, US code-breakers had discovered the Japanese plan to attack Midway Island. Hoping to cripple the powerful Japanese Navy, Admiral Chester Nimitz planned an ambush for the beginning of June. He was counting on three aircraft carriers: the USS *Hornet*, the USS *Enterprise*, and the USS *Yorktown*.

Rather than three months, engineers and shipbuilders worked around the clock to repair the *Yorktown*. In three days, she was ready for duty and headed to Midway. In what became the turning point battle in the Pacific Theatre of World War II, the US Navy decisively defeated Japan's carrier fleet and put Japan on the defensive. The sole reason for US victory was the success of its carrier fleet.

Arguably, the laborers who toiled to get the *Yorktown* back in the fight were tempted to give up when faced with a seemingly impossible task. Nevertheless, those stalwart ship workers refused to stop the work and were rewarded with a victory. Like Nehemiah, they were involved in a "great work." The Christian life is work, seeming impossible at times, but when we put our minds to the work, God gives us the victory. "So built we the wall; and all the wall was joined together unto the half thereof: for the people had a mind to work" (Nehemiah 4:6).

Borrowed Shoes

28 May 1887

And base things of the world, and things which are despised, hath God chosen, yea, and things which are not, to bring to nought things that are: **—1 Corinthians 1:28**

Jim Thorpe has been called the twentieth century's "greatest athlete," playing both professional baseball and football. As a Native American from the Sauk nation, Jim was born with the name Bright Path on 28 May 1887.

Thorpe received his start at the Carlisle Indian School in Carlisle, Pennsylvania, which would become the US Army War College. He shocked coaches with his natural athletic prowess, and was chosen to compete in the Olympics in 1912. The final events of the 1912 Olympic Games were the long jump and the high jump. While prepping for these two events, he discovered his athletic shoes had been stolen, most likely by those who resented his Native American status and did not want him to compete.

Rather than quit, Thorpe rummaged through a garbage can and found a shoe that was too large, which he accommodated with an extra sock. He borrowed a second shoe from a teammate, which proved too small. Even while wearing shoes that did not fit properly, Thorpe managed to win two gold medals that day for the pentathlon and decathlon.

Countless Christians have quit on God because they did not think He could use them due to their checkered past or their current challenges. This world is attracted to riches, luster, fame, and fortune but God is attracted to our weaknesses. Paul told the Corinthians that God often chooses the weak things of this world to confound the mighty. In a world that has become more hostile toward God, He just wants Christians who stay in the race, regardless of our weaknesses or lack of privilege. God does not require us to have a great background, a lot of talent, or a stellar career. All He requires is that we are faithful and strive for the finish line. "And every man that striveth for the mastery is temperate in all things. Now they do it to obtain a corruptible crown; but we an incorruptible" (1 Corinthians 9:25).

Beware of the Dragon's Deception

29 May 1592

Lest Satan should get an advantage of us: for we are not ignorant of his devices.
—2 Corinthians 2:11

Imagine being a sixteenth century sailor about to engage in battle with an enemy fleet when the sudden appearance of a "sea monster" destroys your chance of victory. Something like this actually occurred on 29 May 1592 during the Battle of Sacheon.

The Battle of Sacheon was part of the Imjim War between Korea and Japan. Prior to the battle, Korea's foremost naval admiral Yi Sun-sin received a report that Japanese warships were harbored near the Japanese port city of Sacheon. Knowing a frontal assault would be pointless because Sacheon's cliffs surrounding the harbor would direct cannon fire down on his ships, Admiral Yi planned to lure the Japanese into open water, away from the security of their port.

Admiral Yi ordered his fleet to approach the Japanese harbor, and as predicted, the Japanese commander ordered all twelve of his warships to meet the attack. In a bold move, Yi's ships turned to feign retreat with the Japanese pursuing as planned. When the Japanese fleet entered open water, Yi ordered his famed turtle ship into the fray. The turtle ship's deck was dome-shaped with spikes protruding everywhere to discourage boarders. Made from inter-locking plates of metal, this ship was impervious to Japanese arrows and cannon-fire. Most terrifying was a dragon's head protruding from the bow of the craft, which belched smoke, flame, and cannonballs. Virtually unstoppable, Yi's turtle ship made short work of the Japanese fleet, sinking all twelve ships and winning the victory.

Revelation 12:9 refers to Satan as the great dragon. Like Admiral Yi, Satan attempts to lure us away from the "safe harbor" of morality and righteousness and into the "open waters" of temptation. Once there, we find that what looked promising turns out to be a raging dragon. The next time Satan tries to lure you out of the harbor, stay anchored to the Lord and rest in the knowledge that He will win the battle for you.

Now We See Through a Glass Darkly

30 May 1971

For now we see through a glass, darkly; but then face to face: now I know in part; but then shall I know even as also I am known.—**I Corinthians 13:12**

On 30 May 1971, the National Aeronautics and Space Administration (NASA) launched the *Mariner* 9 space probe, headed for the planet Mars to discover what the surface of the planet looked like. Sophisticated global mapping equipment, television cameras, infrared spectrometers and other scientific instrumentation comprised the spacecraft.

The journey to the "red planet" took 167 days, but by the time *Mariner* 9 arrived to Mars' orbit, the surface was obscured by dust storms. While the storm lasted, the only geographical features that could be photographed were the summits of what appeared to be mountains. Surface details were delayed significantly.

Once the storm cleared, *Mariner* 9 revealed a planet with enormous volcanoes and a canyon that lay across the planet's surface for three thousand miles. In all, more than 54 billion bits of scientific data was gathered, to include 7,329 photographs of the entire planet. In October 1972, the probe was deactivated but remains in orbit around Mars.

The Christian life is such that we often cannot see what is on the other side of the "door of faith" that God asks us to walk through. Most of us would admit that we desire to know the outcome before we are willing to simply trust God. However, that is not how faith works. The Bible instructs: "Commit thy works unto the LORD, and thy thoughts shall be established" (Proverbs 16:3). Living by faith is contradictory to human independence, but God promises us that one day the "dust will clear," and we will see as He sees.

When the world seems upended and evil seems to be winning, I have to remind myself that God is still in control. Someone once said, "I know not what the future holds, but I know the God Who holds the future." When the future seems bleak or obscured, faith is simply staying in communication with God and trusting Him for the outcome.

Demoralized by Satan

31 May 1915

And deliver them who through fear of death were all their lifetime subject to bondage.—**Hebrews 2:15**

In 1909, Count Ferdinand von Zeppelin invented the world's first dirigible (airship). At that time in history, zeppelins, as they were called, carried wealthy travelers on a serene and slow journey high above the surface of the water much the way airliners do today. Eventually, the German military saw utility in zeppelins and purchased some for use in World War I.

On 31 May 1915, an early example of strategic bombing occurred: a tactic used during both world wars to demoralize the enemy by slaughtering innocent civilians in order to bring about surrender. The German *LZ38* zeppelin glided silently over London and dropped several bombs on the unsuspecting civilians below. Because the first person killed in this raid was a three-year-old girl, the British dubbed the new weapon "baby-killer."

To counteract the zeppelin threat, the British began using incendiary bullets in their fighter planes which proved much more maneuverable than the slow-moving behemoths of the night. Nevertheless, the thought of a zeppelin attack struck terror into the hearts of many a Londoner.

Satan uses a similar tactic of intimidation to paralyze Christians with fear. If he can demoralize and discourage us, he can win a strategic victory. He knows he cannot take the Christian's salvation, but he can render us ineffective for the cause of Christ. We must always remember that "greater is he that is in you, than he that is in the world" (1 John 4:4).

Even though the British quickly found a way to overcome the zeppelins, the British public had a hard time overcoming their fear of attack. Fear does nothing but paralyze us to the fight, but regrettably fear is part of human frailty. When fears do arise, what we need is the courage of the Lord. Courage is not the immediate dissipation of fear, but rather the decision to press onward in spite of the fear. Remember, "God hath not given us the spirit of fear; but of power, and of love, and of a sound mind" (2 Timothy 1:7). Rely on this promise to stand in the courage of the Lord.

JUNE

The Right Fight

1 June 1941

No man that warreth entangleth himself with the affairs of this life; that he may please him who hath chosen him to be a soldier.—**2 Timothy 2:4**

In late May 1941, the German Wehrmacht invaded the island of Crete. With an invasion force comprised almost entirely of paratroopers, the Nazis overran the island in just over two weeks. On 1 June 1941, Crete officially fell to the Nazis. This type of airborne invasion was the first of its kind in military history, and while it yielded the Germans a victory, it was a pyrrhic one at best.

The term *pyrrhic victory* refers to a victory gained at too great of a cost. In 279 BC, a brilliant Greek general, King Pyrrhus (319–272 BC), was victorious over the Romans at the Battle of Asculum at a great cost, giving rise to the term *pyrrhic victory* to symbolize a costly victory. At Asculum, the Romans lost around 6,000 warriors while Pyrrhus lost over 3,500. When someone congratulated Pyrrhus, Plutarch records that he said, "If we are victorious in one more battle with the Romans, we shall be utterly ruined." Similarly, because of the heavy casualties suffered by Hitler's paratroopers during Operation Mercury, Hitler forbade any further large-scale airborne operations and there was never another German airborne operation during the rest of the war.

The invasion of Crete was a costly one for the German army and ultimately was not worth the cost. In the same way, for a spiritual Christian to put a priority on seeking after earthly things is a waste of time. We are chosen as soldiers of God. Soldiers do not entangle themselves with things that do not please their Commanding Officer.

What unhealthy pursuit draws your attention? Sometimes we wander and are tempted by the lures of this world. When we seek after what the world has to offer, we may be "victorious" in the short range. But in the end, we will lose out on the victories that really matter. We are chosen to wage a greater war—we are chosen to engage in spiritual battle every day. That is the right fight.

A New Citizenship

2 June 1924

Now therefore ye are no more strangers and foreigners, but fellowcitizens with the saints, and of the household of God;—**Ephesians 2:19**

On 2 June 1924, President Calvin Coolidge signed a bill granting full American citizenship to all Native Americans born within the territorial confines of the United States. Known as the Indian Citizenship Act, the bill stated:

> Be it enacted by the Senate and House of Representatives of the United States of America in Congress assembled, That all non-citizen Indians born within the territorial limits of the United States be, and they are hereby, declared to be citizens of the United States: Provided That the granting of such citizenship shall not in any manner impair or otherwise affect the right of any Indian to tribal or other property.

Prior to this act, Native Americans occupied an unusual status under federal law. Effectively, the only way for a Native American female to acquire citizenship was to marry a white man. Others received citizenship through military service or another special dispensation. The vast majority, however, were prevented from naturalization until the Indian Citizenship Act of 1924.

We do not have to ask Congress for our heavenly citizenship. It has already been granted to all believers. Meditate on the incredible blessing of being a citizen of the world to come. Simple faith is enough to join the saints in the skies.

God has no unreasonable demands to obtain our heavenly citizenship. You do not have to marry someone specific or do some praiseworthy deed. Christ Himself has already paid our way; thanks to Him, we are no longer foreigners to God's home for us. And, the best part is: anyone can be a citizen of Heaven! If you have not yet received Christ, now is your chance. "But as many as received him, to them gave he power to become the sons of God" (John 1:12). Trust Him—and Him alone—for your eternal citizenship.

A Better House

3 June 1800

Even unto this present hour we both hunger, and thirst, and are naked, and are buffeted, and have no certain dwellingplace;—**1 Corinthians 4:11**

On 3 June 1800, President John Adams became the first US president to officially reside in Washington, DC. Although he would not be able to move into the White House until later that year, he stayed at Union Tavern in nearby Georgetown while construction on the White House was finalized.

Influenced by Leinster House in Dublin, Ireland, architect James Hoban designed the neoclassical White House, which would house the next forty-five US Presidents. The day after President Adams moved in, he wrote to his wife about their new residence: "I pray heaven to bestow the best blessings on this house and all that shall hereafter inhabit it. May none but honest and wise men ever rule under this roof." After some weeks, Mrs. Adams joined her husband in their new dwelling, tagging it an empty "castle" because of its enormous living space. Soon after, a US Treasury appropriation in the amount of $15,000 was made to provide furnishings.

Not everyone can live in a white mansion. Jesus Himself said He had "not where to lay his head" (Matthew 8:20). In the verse above, Paul pointed out that he had "no certain dwellingplace." But there is coming a day when we all will have a better house. Even our physical bodies, housing our souls, will give way to glorified bodies. "For we know that if our earthly house of this tabernacle were dissolved, we have a building of God, an house not made with hands, eternal in the heavens" (2 Corinthians 5:1). Paul was not speaking about an earthly house but a heavenly tabernacle. While the White House is certainly spectacular, it pales in comparison to what our Lord has been preparing us since He ascended to Heaven.

The US Treasury will not furnish the average American's home, but as believers, we can rest in the fact that God will take care of us in this life (Matthew 6:28–33), and that even now, He is preparing a heavenly place for us (John 14:2).

The Grand Review

4 June 1927

For we must all appear before the judgment seat of Christ; that every one may receive the things done in his body, according to that he hath done, whether it be good or bad.—**2 Corinthians 5:10**

A Naval Review occurs when either the President of the United States or Secretary of the US Navy views the pride of the Nation's fleet. Similar to a pass and review of ground troops, the Navy Review provides leadership an opportunity to see how the Navy has used the opportunities and resources afforded it. On 4 June 1927 at Hampton Roads, Virginia, President Calvin Coolidge reviewed one armored cruiser, one light cruiser, one cargo ship, and three destroyers. A variety of naval vessels passed before Coolidge, each with its own unique purpose, yet all part of one navy.

One day, God will give each of us a thorough review. The Judgment Seat of Christ awaits every believer (1 Corinthians 3:11–15; 2 Corinthians 5:9–10). The Christian will not be judged on his eternal destiny, but rather to determine whether he deserves eternal rewards. All of our decisions, holy and unholy, will come to light before Christ Himself.

Each believer begins his spiritual life on the foundation of Christ, but he is responsible for how he builds on this foundation. The Lord will separate our good works from our bad works, just as the President would recognize the difference between well-made ships and poorly-made ones. Each of us are members of the body of Christ, yet each has a different function in the body (1 Corinthians 12:13–20). And all members are held to the same high moral standard—living in a Christ-like way.

God will see how you have used the resources He has granted to you individually. Have your skills and gifts made a difference in others' lives? How often has sin derailed you from godliness? In the end, it does not matter where you stand in relation to others, but in relation to your own God-given capacity. We need to live our lives ready for this "Grand Review" by God. After all, His opinion is so much more important than any president's or navy secretary's.

The God of Miracles

5 June 1967

I will send my fear before thee, and will destroy all the people to whom thou shalt come, and I will make all thine enemies turn their backs unto thee. **—Exodus 23:27**

The Six Day War of 1967 was largely a result of animosity over the 1948 declaration of Israel's Statehood. Surrounded by three major enemies—Jordan, Syria, and Egypt—Israel demanded that the Straits of Tiran be opened to Israeli shipping in accord with the 1956 promise from Egypt that the straits would remain open. When Egyptian President Gamal Nasser closed them in May 1967, Israel took this as an act of war. It launched a series of preemptive airstrikes against Egyptian airfields. Thus began the Six Day War, during which God miraculously intervened countless times on the behalf of His chosen people. Early on the morning of 5 June 1967, around 200 Israeli fighter jets sortied for Egypt. Jordanian air traffic controllers picked up the Israeli air force movements by radar and subsequently forwarded a coded warning to Egypt. Miraculously, the Egyptians had changed their message-coding equipment without notifying the Jordanians. The message never made it, giving Israel the element of surprise. Without time to react, the Egyptians suffered the loss of six airfields and over three hundred planes. In a single day, Israel had destroyed the Egyptian and Syrian Air Forces. Divine intervention occurred again on the second day of the war when an Arab tank commander surrendered his obviously superior army to an Israeli force of twelve tanks. He later stated that while only a few enemy tanks were present, a "desert mirage" must have made him see hundreds surrounding his position. What else could he do but surrender?

Even today, God is watching over His people. He has kept Israel as the apple of His eye (Deuteronomy 32:9–10). And His children, bought by the blood of His Son, are no less special to Him. Rest assured today that God is able to take care of you. He is just as capable of performing miracles today as He was in Bible times.

The Devil's Distraction

6 June 1944

Ponder the path of thy feet, and let all thy ways be established. Turn not to the right hand nor to the left: remove thy foot from evil.—**Proverbs 4:26–27**

For historians, the date of 6 June 1944 immediately evokes thoughts of Operation Overlord—the Allied landing on the Normandy coastline. The same day, however, another operation ensued which was just as important, yet often forgotten. In the early morning hours of D-Day, the British launched Operation Titanic. This clandestine operation involved a massive parachute drop of burlap dummies all over Normandy Beach. A force of forty British aircraft dropped 500 three-foot tall dummies in four separate locations along the coastal interior of France. Fire-crackers, rifle fire simulators, and two teams of Special Air Service soldiers (carrying recordings of loud battle noise) were also dropped to reinforce the deception. Operation Titanic moved in the hopes of diverting German troops away from the Allies' actual drop zones. The dummies were nicknamed "Rupert." Fabricated from burlap, they were fashioned into human form and stuffed with straw or sand. The British operation was so successful, it prevented an entire German reserve regiment from reaching Omaha and Gold Beach as they searched the forest for miniature paratroopers.

Deception thrives on distraction. The British operation turned the eyes and ears of the German forces away from the true battlefield and onto a fruitless search. How might the devil be deceiving and distracting you in your Christian walk? Remember, the devil never rests. He walks about like a lion, seeking his next victim (1 Peter 5:8).

Strengthen your commitment to God's task for you. Your ministry at your local church may feel insignificant, or you may believe that your service doesn't make a difference. But Operation Titanic was critical to the success of the famous D-Day. Though people may forget to express their appreciation and may not remember your efforts, remember that God sees all. And He will reward you (Hebrews 6:10).

Reputation rather than Riches

7 June 1837

A good name is rather to be chosen than great riches, and loving favour rather than silver and gold.—**Proverbs 22:1**

On 7 June 1837, Alois Johann Schicklgruber was born in Austria. As a young man, he first made a living as a shoemaker. At age eighteen, he joined the border police in Austrian customs service near Salzburg. Nine years into his employment with the customs service, Alois married a woman fourteen years his senior who died without giving him children. He married again in 1883, this time to a hotel cook named Franziska Matzelsberger. She bore Alois a son and daughter before passing away from tuberculosis less than two years into the marriage. In 1885, Alois married a third and final time to Klara Poelzl, his second cousin. Klara and Alois had a son named Gustav and a daughter named Ida. Both died in infancy.

In 1876, Alois' father, Johann, resurfaced after being away for several years and testified before a notary that he was the legal father of Alois Schicklgruber and wanted his son's name changed to match the family surname, which he recently had changed to Hitler. The local parish priest scratched out the name Schicklgruber and wrote in its place Hitler. Thirteen years later, Alois and Klara had a son they named Adolf.

As a Christian, it is better to be respected than to be rich. The name Hitler is avoided; it is improbable to find anyone with this name. The name's nefarious connotation remains because of one person who carried it. The Bible is clear: if one were to make a choice between wealth and reputation, the right choice is always reputation—"a good name."

Hitler would be remembered differently had he changed his behaviors. God gives us the ability to leave a legacy for His glory. Regardless of previous choices, we each have the option to begin a new way of living now. As someone aptly said, "Today is the first day of the rest of your Christian life." Are there areas in your life where character has been sacrificed for achievement? Act today so others who hear your name will smile tomorrow.

Bones of Contention

8 June 1809

He is not here: for he is risen, as he said. Come, see the place where the Lord lay. **—Matthew 28:6**

Prior to the Revolutionary War, radical author Thomas Paine wrote the pamphlet *Common Sense,* which caused many Americans to join the Patriot cause. After the war, Paine became something of a social outcast and lost favor with the common people. On 8 June 1809, Paine died penniless and largely forgotten. An English admirer named William Cobbett decided to give Paine the recognition he felt he deserved. Cobbett dug up Paine's remains. If America had forgotten Paine, Cobbett reasoned, he would rebury his bones in England. Cobbett packed Paine's bones in a standard merchandise crate with the intention of placing them in a mausoleum at Cobbett's expense. Unfortunately, Cobbett was never able to raise the funds to properly bury Paine's bones and upon his death in 1835, his oldest son tried to sell them off as part of the estate but failed. The bones ended up being individually sold as macabre souvenirs.

There are hundreds of thousands, perhaps even millions of people, who would like nothing better than that the bones of the Lord Jesus Christ would suddenly be unearthed from the borrowed tomb. The entire foundation of Christianity would collapse. As the Apostle Paul said, "And if Christ be not raised, your faith is vain; ye are yet in your sins" (1 Corinthians 15:17).

Thankfully, however, not a bone of the Lord's has ever been nor ever will be discovered because He arose literally and physically from the grave never to die again. The angel's proclamation of His empty tomb is just as true today, more than two thousand years later. In fact, there is coming a day when all mankind will see the risen Christ and give Him the honor due His name. "That at the name of Jesus every knee should bow, of things in heaven, and things in earth, and things under the earth; And that every tongue should confess that Jesus Christ is Lord, to the glory of God the Father." (Philippians 2:10–11).

Making a Difference

9 June 1672

That they do good, that they be rich in good works, ready to distribute, willing to communicate;—**1 Timothy 6:18**

Peter the Great was one of the most famous Russian Czars in history. Born 9 June 1672, Peter Alekseyevich became Czar upon the death of his half-brother Feodor in 1682. His war against the Ottoman Empire in 1685 convinced Peter that Russia was militarily deficient compared to other nations. He therefore made it his life's goal to remedy the issue and to modernize both the army and the Russian nation. Known as the "Czar Transformer," he brought in experts from the West. He encouraged advancements in metallurgy and textile manufacturing, and he implemented more than two hundred new factories. Russia may still have become a great power without Peter the Great, but there is no doubt that he hastened the process.

God expects us to habitually do good to those around us. Peter the Great is remembered for advancing the Russian nation and army. Instead of keeping money and resources for himself, he invested them into the progress of his own country.

God has given you resources. You may not be wealthy, but He has granted you some sort of job or income. What are you doing with what God has given you? When you see a Christian brother or sister in need, how do you respond? We have an amazing opportunity to give to others around us while we can. In fact, the Apostle John questioned how we could love God, yet turn a blind eye to another Christian in need (1 John 3:17). Look for those around you whom you can help.

The Bible teaches us that God created us unto good works and gives us opportunities to make a difference in the lives of those around us. Ephesians 2:10 tells us, "For we are his workmanship, created in Christ Jesus unto good works, which God hath before ordained that we should walk in them." How are you making a difference in the lives of others today?

Modest Majesty

10 June 1881

But made himself of no reputation, and took upon him the form of a servant, and was made in the likeness of men:—**Philippians 2:7**

Count Leo Tolstoy is best known for authoring two nineteenth century literary masterpieces, *War and Peace* and *Anna Karenina.* Tolstoy was from Russia and hailed from nobility. He fought in the Crimean War as an artillery officer. On 10 June 1881, Tolstoy shed his royal garments and disguised himself as a peasant. Shunning recognition, he then embarked upon a sixty-mile trek on foot to the Optina Monastery. When he arrived, the Monk in charge assumed Tolstoy to be a beggar and denied him a proper room. When he wandered into the monastery's bookstore, he encountered a woman asking for a copy of the gospels. Tolstoy reached into his pocket and pulled out the money to buy her one. The Monk then realized who Tolstoy was. Suddenly, he was given new clothes and offered a first-class room upholstered in velvet. Tolstoy declined.

Nobility is revered and respected, but does not come close to the majesty of the divine. Count Tolstoy went undercover to mask his noble status. But Jesus Christ, in taking human form, veiled *deity* in humanity. Rather than exploiting His divinity, Christ chose a life of servanthood—living to please God the Father. What a great sacrifice He made for us!

While describing a challenge to someone else, you may have heard (or said): "You don't know what it's like! You've never lived through it!" In putting aside the prerogatives of His deity, Christ lived life exactly as you and I do. Though he was a general and worthy of honor, Tolstoy was mistaken for a peasant and denied a room. Jesus Christ Himself did not receive a warm welcome; even the local inn turned Him away as a baby (Luke 2:7).

When you face a battle or struggle, remember: you're not alone. Jesus, as God, knows all. He experienced all of the same temptations you and I experience (Hebrews 4:15). Run to Him in prayer. Confess all that is on your heart. And, remember, He wore the same flesh that you and I wear daily.

The Need to Purge

11 June 1937

Every branch in me that beareth not fruit he taketh away: and every branch that beareth fruit, he purgeth it, that it may bring forth more fruit.—**John 15:2**

In November 1939, the Soviet Union invaded tiny Finland in response to their refusal to give over a large portion of the Karelian Isthmus. Finland fought bravely in subzero temperatures for months. On 12 March 1940, in response to overwhelming Soviet reinforcements, the Finns signed a peace treaty with Russia and ended the "Winter War." The following June, having watched Soviet casualties mount, Adolf Hitler broke the non-aggression pact with the Russians and launched the largest land invasion in the history of warfare against his former ally. Within weeks of storming across the Russian border, the Nazis inflicted severe losses on the Red Army.

One of the main reasons for the abysmal Russian performance against Finland and Germany stemmed in a series of purges that Stalin instituted on 11 June 1937. In a paranoid reaction, Stalin had his Secret Police (NKVD) purge hundreds of his commanders, military officers, and political rivals. From June through December 1937, 2,238 officers were arrested and 15,426 were discharged. Some were murdered, some dismissed. But unexpectedly, the purge also allowed three great men to rise to power. Ivan Kovnev stopped the Germans at Kursk in 1943. Marshal Chuikov masterminded the annihilation of the German Sixth Army at Stalingrad in 1943, and General Zhukov led his Red Army into Berlin in 1945. Had there been no purge, these brilliant generals may never have been thrust into a position to lead the Soviet Union to victory over the Germans during World War II.

Paranoia led to this military purging and, overall, certainly had mixed results. But from a spiritual perspective, there are times each of us *need* purging in our lives. God allows these times to bring greater fruitfulness to us. When humbling circumstances enter your life—when positions change or when God leads you elsewhere—don't be discouraged. God is preparing you to bear more spiritual fruit. Submit and be humble, and He will exalt you in His time (1 Peter 5:6).

A Ruined Roadblock

12 June 1987

For he is our peace, who hath made both one, and hath broken down the middle wall of partition between us;—**Ephesians 2:14**

President Reagan was known for being a great communicator. His speeches evoked a sense of confidence that came at a time when our nation needed it most—a time known as the Cold War. Arguably, one of his greatest speeches was delivered on 12 June 1987 to a crowd of West Berliners, during which he implored Soviet Premier Mikhail Gorbachev to "tear down" the Berlin Wall. The Wall was an iconic symbol of the repressive Communist era in a divided Germany. Two years later, Reagan's plea was answered as joyful East and West Berliners began to demolish the wall.

A figurative wall has stood between God and man ever since the first sin was committed in the Garden of Eden. Parts of the Berlin Wall remain today as a testament to the divisive nature of the Communist era of Germany. Yet, for believers, no wall stands between them and God. Christ Himself has torn down the "wall of partition" between God and man. His sacrifice allows us to have fellowship and communication with God as He intended. As relations between Russia and the US have improved since the threatening period of the Cold War, so each of us can experience a full and rich relationship with God.

President Reagan's statement, "Mr. Gorbachev, tear down this wall!" was a bold and decisive move. Yet, Reagan's bravery and initiative do not compare to the greatest sacrifice ever made: Jesus Christ's sacrifice for mankind. He is the one who *is* our peace. He wrought the ultimate harmony between God and man through His own death on the cross and His resurrection.

Take advantage today of your freedom in Christ. If you have received Him as your Saviour, you have the ultimate privilege of fellowship with God through prayer and His Word. But, you must make the daily decision to commune with Him. We must not allow ourselves to live as if we have no access to God. The roadblock, because of Christ, is gone forever!

Ezra 3–5 // John 20

An Extraordinary Messenger

13 June 1919

But ask now the beasts, and they shall teach thee; and the fowls of the air, and they shall tell thee:—**Job 12:7**

On 13 June 1919, one of the greatest heroes of World War I died at Fort Monmouth, New Jersey, from battle wounds. Just eight months earlier, Major Charles Whittlesey's "Lost Battalion" came under heavy enemy fire during the Battle of the Argonne Forest. During the intense struggle, messengers were sent from Whittlesey's position with requests for support. The first two were shot by Germans, but the third managed to make it to division headquarters in just under twenty-five minutes. Despite having been shot through the chest, blinded in one eye, covered in blood and with a leg hanging only by a tendon, this courageous messenger relayed the coordinates of the Lost Battalion, which prompted a speedy rescue.

Unable to save the leg, Army surgeons gave the brave hero a wooden one. After being personally escorted back to the United States by General John J. Pershing, the hero messenger of the Argonne Forest was awarded the prestigious Croix de Guerre Medal with a palm Oak Leaf Cluster for extreme heroism in the face of combat. Today, this brave messenger's body is on display at the Smithsonian Institution. Such a public display, to some, would seem macabre. But once you realize this brave hero was a female carrier pigeon, named Cher Ami, the tribute seems fitting.

An animal is not often considered a hero, but Cher Ami's dutiful flight saved the lives of the Lost Battalion. If a trained carrier pigeon can carry a much-needed message, how much more should we carry the gospel to those around us? Every day, we walk by people who know nothing of the saving grace of Jesus Christ. They do not have a clue how to escape the sad destiny of Hell. God has given us the chance to influence as many as we can toward the truth of God's Word. Even if we suffer some "battle scars"—persecution, shaming, or ridicule—is it not worth it so that the lost of this world have a chance to be saved?

Pressing Forward

14 June 1777

I press toward the mark for the prize of the high calling of God in Christ Jesus.
—Philippians 3:14

I love our nation's flag. When I retired from the US Air Force, the American Flag was formally presented to me in a highly dignified and respectful manner.

On 14 June 1777, the Second Continental Congress officially requested that 14 June be designated as Flag Day. One hundred years later, the first national observance of Flag Day happened on 14 June. Since that time, Americans have held parades honoring "Old Glory," and have proudly displayed the flag from a variety of buildings and vehicles.

But have you ever wondered why the US flag faces "backward" on a US military member's uniform? The next time you encounter a man or woman in uniform, look at their flag patch and you will notice them wearing the flag on their right shoulder with the blue or subdued field facing forward. Basically, the idea behind the backward American flag on US military uniforms is to make it look as though the flag is flying in the breeze as the person wearing it moves forward. This concept originated during the American Civil War; both mounted cavalry and infantry units would designate a soldier to carry the flag into battle. As that man charged, his forward movement caused the flag to stream back. Therefore, the flag is worn on the right shoulder, and wearing it backward gives the effect of the flag flying in the breeze as the wearer moves forward.

Are your daily actions and decisions more influenced by your past or your potential future for Christ? On the Civil War battlefield, one soldier was picked to keep the flag—the symbol of the reason for their fight and sacrifice—in front of the soldiers. In the same way, let us keep Jesus Christ and His Word up front as we daily fight a spiritual battle. He is the reason that we are in God's army. He is the reason we fight. And His glory needs to be our motive and purpose. Press on.

Operation Little Vittles

15 June 1948

Hereby perceive we the love of God, because he laid down his life for us: and we ought to lay down our lives for the brethren.—**1 John 3:16**

On 15 June 1948, Soviet authorities closed the Autobahn, effectively cutting off western Germany from Berlin. Shortly thereafter, they cut off all barge and rail traffic from entering West Berlin. The Berlin Blockade had begun. Rather than withdraw, Western Allies looked for a way to protest without turning the Cold War into an armed conflict. With the threat of nuclear war looming, finding another way to resupply the city was the only viable option.

A plan was quickly hatched to airlift vital supplies to West Berliners. Commodities like flour, milk, meat, and even coal were dropped by parachute into the city every three minutes. For the people of West Berlin, the event was stressful; but for the children, it was particularly frightening.

One man took it upon himself to show the children that someone cared. Air Force Lieutenant Gail Halvorsen began dropping candy from the sky. Known as "Operation Little Vittles," Halvorsen dropped small handkerchief parachutes of candy from the flare chute in the bottom of his plane. Halvorsen stated, "There's something magic[al] about a chocolate bar come floatin' out of the sky." One of the children who received Halvorsen's candy was West Berliner Ruth Cheever, who said, "We were hungry and, you know, for someone to come in and drop us some candy, I can only say, thank you." Halvorsen showed the children of West Berlin and the world that someone did indeed care.

As a songwriter acknowledged: "No one ever cared for me like Jesus." Make today a day where you meditate on all that God provided for you. God has given believers not only physical needs, but the greatest spiritual provision: a home in Heaven. He truly does care (1 Peter 5:7). Thank Him today for His love, and let it move you toward a small deed—a little gesture—that shows someone else God's care as well. Sometimes the smallest acts of service make the greatest difference.

A Mighty Lion

16 June 1815

Therefore being justified by faith, we have peace with God through our Lord Jesus Christ:—**Romans 5:1**

Around our globe, monuments, statues, and various memorials commemorate famous battlefields. At Gettysburg, tourists can enjoy more than 1,300 monuments. In the country of Belarus, a massive concrete likeness of a Soviet soldier's head juts out from a mountain, commemorating the defense of Brest during Germany's invasion of Russia in 1941. In Belgium, a most unlikely monument commemorates the Battle of Quatre Bass, fought on 16 June 1815.

This monument sits over 130 feet high atop a conical mound on the plain of Waterloo in Belgium. It is not of a famous general or soldier; rather, this statue is a great bronze lion. The bronze beast weighs 31 tons and is 15 feet high by 15 feet long. Said to be forged from the captured guns of Britain's foes, the lion's right front paw rests upon a sphere, symbolizing global victory. William I, the Prince of Orange, had the monument constructed to commemorate his command of the troops before handing over the reins to Lord Wellington later that day.

To reach the lion monument, one must pay a fee and walk up 225 steps. The beast's mouth is open and snarls through his teeth over the battlefield. One man who took the time to observe this bronze visage remarked, "When I saw it last, one spring noonday, a bird had built its nest right in the lion's mouth, twining the twigs of the downy bed where the fledglings nestled around the very teeth of the metal monster, and from the very jaws of the bronze beast the chirp of the swallows seemed to twitter forth timidly the signal of peace."

Christ is the Lion of Judah (Revelation 5:5) who will one day bring justice as He reigns over all the Earth. But to us, He is not a threatening judge; He is our peace. We live in a cursed world but God is in control. We can trust the Lord. We can glorify His attributes and goodness. And we can rest in the peace He provides through His Son.

Nehemiah 4–6 // Acts 2:22–47

Prayer Takes Priority

17 June 1775

Pray without ceasing.—**1 Thessalonians 5:17**

The Battle of Bunker Hill was one of the early battles of the Revolutionary War. In an attempt to take control of Dorchester Heights in Boston, British troops began to amass forces just off the coast. A colonial militia, led by Colonel William Prescott, arrived to fortify the area around Bunker's Hill on the night of 16 June 1775. Prescott ordered his troops to take position by digging a formidable redoubt on nearby Breed's Hill. Upon hearing that the British troops had landed, Major General Joseph Warren rode over to Bunker Hill. It is said that Colonel Prescott signified his readiness to take orders from Warren due to his superior ranking, but Warren refused, stating he had come as a volunteer to take a lesson in warfare under such a well-tried officer. Warren then withdrew to spend two full hours in prayer. When he rose from his knees, there was no anxiety on his face; his countenance displayed peace and joyful trust in God. Warren gave a few simple directions, drank a cup of coffee, and left for the lines on Bunker Hill. Near Prescott's redoubt on 17 June, as he was endeavoring to rally the militia, General Warren was struck in the head by a musket-ball and instantly killed, becoming the first eminent sacrifice of the war.

The bravery of Christian soldiers in battle has been well attested. General Warren did not fear death because he knew his eternal destiny and he spent time doing the best thing he could do prior to entering the uncertainty of war . . . he prayed.

The general prayed for two hours straight. Unless dire circumstances call for it, many Christians do not pray for such long stretches. God does not place a specific time requirement or expectation for us as Christians. In fact, He tells us to "pray without ceasing"—to pray continually.

Is prayer a priority in your life? Do you set aside time to seek God's face and then continue in prayer throughout the day? We would do well to act on the biblical truth which the general displayed: prayer is not an option, but a necessity.

Waterloo

18 June 1815

For all seek their own, not the things which are Jesus Christ's. **—Philippians 2:21**

On Sunday, 18 June 1815, two countries joined forces. A coalition army led by Arthur Wellesley (Duke of Wellington) and a Prussian army led by Gebhard Leberecht von Blücher soundly defeated Napoleon Bonaparte's Grand Army at Waterloo. The severity of the battle's scope and drama has caused its name to become synonymous with an absolute, crushing defeat.

At Waterloo, the Duke of Wellington assumed overall command of five different armies from five different nations. Each spoke a different language. On paper, Waterloo was a recipe for disaster and confusion. Nevertheless, the Seventh Coalition soundly defeated Napoleon in what Wellington later described as a "near run thing." Had it not been for the Prussian arrival late into the battle, victory would have likely gone to Napoleon. Yet, Wellington was adamant that the Anglo-Austrians, rather than the Prussians, get the lion's share of the credit. After all, it was Wellington's coalition army that counter-attacked the French center once the Prussians entered from the east.

Credit for Waterloo's monumental victory cannot go merely to the Duke of Wellington. It was not a success due to a single strategy or person, and disaster may have resulted if any element failed. Yet, we need to ask ourselves: how often do we selfishly seek our own pursuits—our own glory? Paul knew well that it is a part of the human condition that "all seek their own." Though pride is a temptation for all of us, acting on it is never God's plan.

Instead of seeking all the credit for your life's achievements, remember how important the Prussian army was to the Anglo-Austrians. Whatever blessings you have, there is no doubt that someone helped you along the way. Write someone a quick note of thanks. Share the credit for your successes. Be grateful to others. And remember that God deserves the ultimate praise and glory for the great things He has done.

Secret Service

19 June 1942

But when thou doest alms, let not thy left hand know what thy right hand doeth: That thine alms may be in secret: and thy Father which seeth in secret himself shall reward thee openly.—**Matthew 6:3–4**

On 19 June 1942, the US Army activated the Military Intelligence Training Center at Fort Ritchie in Cascade, Maryland. Over 19,000 men were training at Fort Ritchie, among whom was a group of 9,000 Jewish soldiers who had fled Nazi Germany for America. The American military harnessed the enormous spirit of these young men who had escaped the Nazis and returned to their homelands with Americans to turn the tables. Known as the "Ritchie Boys," these men were able to speak fluent German and understood the land and culture. Their mission in Germany included interrogating prisoners of war, sabotage, and deception. Due to the nature of their operations, the Ritchie Boys were a highly secretive unit and are often credited with bringing an early ending to the war in Europe. Until a recent exhibit at the Holocaust Memorial Center revealed the existence of this unit, the exploits and heroism of the Ritchie Boys had been largely untold.

The Ritchie Boys were willing to risk their lives without accolades or recognition. Would be to God that Christians would have the same attitude when it comes to serving others and supplying needs. President Reagan is often quoted as stating, "There is no limit to the amount of good you can do if you don't care who gets the credit."

Serve, and let God do the rewarding. The Ritchie boys were willing to enter a continent torn by violence and hatred in order to accomplish their mission, even if their names would not be known until decades later. Humble servants are given a promise that they will one day get the rewards they deserve (Luke 14:11). Until the day of rewards, be content as a "secret servant." God will eventually reward you openly.

Unaware of War

20 June 1898

And Elisha prayed, and said, LORD, I pray thee, open his eyes, that he may see. And the LORD opened the eyes of the young man; and he saw: and, behold, the mountain was full of horses and chariots of fire round about Elisha. **—2 Kings 6:17**

The Spanish-American War erupted in 1898 over the explosion of the *Maine*—a US naval vessel in Havana, Cuba. The United States intervened, seizing several Spanish-held islands in the process. On 20 June 1898, the USS *Charleston* was ordered to land at Guam, seize the port, destroy all fortifications, and capture Spanish soldiers and government officials. When the *Charleston* entered the harbor at Guam, the ship's captain ordered that his guns fire thirteen shots to evoke a Spanish response. However, they were shocked to watch the handful of Spanish soldiers stationed there begin to board the *Charleston*. They apologized for not returning what they thought was a salute and then asked if they could borrow some gun powder to return the friendly gesture. Then, the Charleston's captain informed these men that they were prisoners of war and could not leave the ship. Chagrined, the men then realized their own government had never bothered to notify them that the United States and Spain were at war.

Like the Spanish soldiers, some Christians have forgotten a critical truth—the reality of spiritual warfare. The world, the flesh, and the devil oppose us. The souls of men and women are at stake. It is not a battle we can see physically, but it is real.

Because the soldiers knew nothing of the war, they were not prepared. And no Christian is prepared for spiritual battle when he is distracted by the world. Our spiritual armor is a support that we are able—and commanded—to put on (Ephesians 6:11–18). What has distracted you from the spiritual battle at hand? The only way to win a war is to be aware that it is happening. Ask God today to show you any temptation or time waster that may be keeping you from living a spiritually aware life.

Ambush Awareness

21 June 217 BC

For among my people are found wicked men: they lay wait, as he that setteth snares; they set a trap, they catch men.—**Jeremiah 5:26**

In the early Roman Republic, Carthaginian General Hannibal Barca crossed the Alps and invaded Italy during the Second Punic War. Hannibal's mixed army of Carthaginians, Numidians, Greek mercenaries, and Celts battled the Romans across the Western Mediterranean for a period of some seventeen years. Under the leadership of Gaius Flaminius, the Roman army decided to take up a position to defend Rome. On the morning of 21 June 217 BC, Roman troops marched eastward along a road running near the northern edge of Lake Trasimene.

Spoiling for a fight, Flaminius pushed his men hard and hastened the soldiers in the rear. Hannibal then sent a small force to draw the vanguard away from the front of the marching column to split the Roman forces. Once all the Romans had finally marched through the foggy, narrow path skirting the lake, they blew the trumpets, signaling a general attack. Hannibal's cavalry and infantry rushed down from the surrounding hills, blocked the road, and hit the unsuspecting Romans from three sides. Surprised and outmaneuvered, the Romans had no time to prepare and were forced to fight a desperate hand-to-hand battle without the benefit of forming into their famous maniples. The Romans were quickly split into three parts and annihilated. With another victory to his credit, Hannibal had successfully planned and executed the greatest ambush in history.

In his overconfidence, Flaminius let his guard down, making it easy for Hannibal to defeat him. The devil never stops his efforts to derail Christians (John 10:10). People are watching Christians' business dealings. They scope out any questionable activities we choose. While God does not expect paranoia from Christians, He does command caution. In fact, Paul commanded, "See then that ye walk circumspectly" (Ephesians 5:15). When you encounter a new opportunity, always proceed with prudence. Ask God for wisdom, and He will surely grant it to you (James 1:5).

Beautiful Feet

22 June 1000

. . . How beautiful are the feet of them that preach the gospel of peace, and bring glad tidings of good things!—**Romans 10:15**

In his *History of Normandy and England* (1851), Sir Francis Palgrave writes of Duke Robert of Normandy, "Arletta's pretty feet twinkling in the brook gained her a duke's love and gave us William the Conqueror." Palgrave was describing an incidental encounter in the life of Robert of Normandy, who was born on 22 June 1000.

As Robert was gazing one day from a castle tower, he spied a beautiful maiden rinsing her feet off in a stream. The young woman was Arletta of Falaise. She was tramping out dye used to tan leather. When she sat down to dip her feet into the brook to wash the dye from them, Robert was so taken with how beautiful her feet were that he immediately ordered her to be brought to the castle. She ended up becoming his mistress and gave birth to an illegitimate son named William I. Prior to his invasion of England in 1066, William was known as William the Bastard, due to his own illegitimate birth. But following the defeat of King Godwinson at the Battle of Hastings in 1066, he was forever known as William the Conqueror.

Had Arletta not attracted Duke Robert, King Godwinson would not have fallen at Hastings. There would have been no Anglo-Norman dynasty. No British Empire would have emerged. And our English language, as we know it, would never have been created. One can ponder at length the "what ifs" of this scenario; however, it is indeed compelling that, had Arletta's feet been unattractive or repulsive to Robert, men like William Tyndale, Charles Spurgeon, and other British heroes of the faith might never have influenced the world for Christ as they did.

We don't often consider whether or not one's physical feet are attractive, and certainly not the way Duke Robert did. But the Bible tells us that any feet that bring the gospel to others are beautiful indeed. Your feet are beautiful when they take you to places where you can proclaim the gospel.

A One-Man Army

23 June 1765

For who hath despised the day of small things?—**Zechariah 4:10**

On the morning of 23 June 1765, a ship dropped anchor at City Point, Virginia. Two men, rowing a longboat, quickly deposited a young five-year-old boy on the wharf and returned to their ship. The young boy was Pedro Francisco—and he would one day prove himself valiant and crucial to the American cause.

Pedro, called Peter by his new caregivers, was soon taken in by Judge Anthony Winston, an uncle of Patrick Henry. When the Revolutionary War began, fifteen-year-old Peter, influenced by Patrick Henry's famous line "Give me liberty, or give me death," begged Judge Winston to grant permission for him to enlist. The guardian agreed, on the condition that Peter wait one year.

Francisco saw much combat in his time as a soldier and endured a wound to his leg during the Battle of Brandywine in 1777. Having been involved in the Germantown and Valley Forge battles, he reenlisted as soon as his tour of duty expired. During the famed Battle of Camden in 1780, Francisco distinguished himself in combat against the British and saved the life of his commanding officer. Until the end of the Revolutionary War, Francisco would end up wounded six times, garnering the attention and admiration of General Washington. In fact, Washington is quoted as saying about Francisco, "Without him, we would have lost two crucial battles, perhaps the war; and with it, our freedom. He was truly a one-man army." A historical marker stands where Francisco was first found on the Virginia wharf.

Francisco's life stands as a testimony to the truth that even someone with an unknown name and background can change the course of history. Do you feel forgotten, or that your service for God is insignificant? Never "despise the day of small things." Never assume that a great God cannot use the dedicated service of unknown people. Small deeds prepare Christians for great spiritual accomplishments.

Stopping Short

24 June 1866

But ye, brethren, be not weary in well doing.—**2 Thessalonians 3:13**

In June 1866, the kingdom of Prussia declared war on the Austrian Empire. Known as the Austro-Prussian War, it began due to a dispute regarding the control of Danish territory. Commanding the Austrian South Army was Field Marshal Albrecht Friedrich Rudolf Dominik. The son of the only Austrian general to defeat Napoleon, Albrecht was commissioned as a colonel in the Austrian army at age thirteen and had proved himself in battle during the Battle of Novara in 1849. On 24 June 1866, Albrecht led 75,000 Austrian soldiers against 200,000 Italians at the Battle of Custoza in northern Italy. Incredibly outnumbered, Albrecht won a decisive victory over the Italians, but he neglected to pursue the Italians because he reasoned his men were too exhausted to press the fight. While the Austrians won the battle of Custoza, they lost the war the following month.

Had Albrecht continued the fight, he might have won the war. Will the Christian life sometimes be tiring? Yes. Will there be obstacles and unforeseen challenges? Absolutely. But God promises to bless our persistent efforts, so you do not have to stop short. "And let us not be weary in well doing: for in due season we shall reap, if we faint not" (Galatians 6:9).

Today, you can start fresh. If you've given up in some area of your walk with God or Christian service, today you can decide to get back on course and persist for the Lord Jesus Christ. If you have felt your work is futile, remember God's promise, and press forward.

The Christian life is not a walk in the park, nor does God ever suggest it is. Rather, He compares the Christian life to a battlefield and admonishes, "Thou therefore endure hardness, as a good soldier of Jesus Christ" (2 Timothy 2:3).

Victory in the past does not guarantee victory in the future. Albrecht rested on his laurels—and lost. Christian, until God calls you home, fulfill each next step of faith. God will restore your strength as you trust Him and continue doing the right thing: moving forward (Isaiah 40:28–31).

Custer's Crash

25 June 1876

Pride goeth before destruction, and a haughty spirit before a fall.
—Proverbs 16:18

On 25 June 1876, 268 soldiers of the US 7th Cavalry were annihilated by a combined force of Sioux, Cheyenne, and Arapahoe Indians near the Little Big Horn River in Montana. George Armstrong Custer was the man at fault for this tragedy. At the age of twenty-three, he had been promoted directly from captain to general, becoming one of the youngest generals ever in the history of the US Army. Yet, he had no command experience. Custer was always seeking glory and high positions; his arrogance displayed itself on numerous occasions. Just before Little Big Horn, Custer boasted to one of his Indian scouts about the rewards he would receive once he became President of the United States.

As General Terry led three columns into Sioux territory that summer of 1876, Custer broke from General Terry's group to pursue the Sioux on his own. When Terry offered Custer several Gatling guns to take along, Custer turned them down; he was anxious to attack the Sioux unencumbered so he could claim all the glory. Moments before clashing with the Indians, Custer still dismissed warnings from his scouts about the size of the Indian force. Disoriented, the US troops fumbled with their single-shot rifles, and the Indians picked them off with repeating rifles. Those unfortunate troops who managed to escape the murderous rifle fire were gruesomely dispatched with war clubs, knives, and tomahawks. Chief Rain-in-the-Face, a survivor of Little Big Horn, said in a 1903 interview for *Outdoor Life* magazine it "was just like killing sheep."

Custer brushed off warnings about the size of the Indian army. He declined help, and destruction ensued. God hates pride. In fact, in a list of sins God despises, He put pride first (Proverbs 6:16). God does not desire for us to live independently of Him, but rather to humbly rely on Him daily. If pride has filled your heart, today is a good day to confess it to Him, and He will gladly forgive you (1 John 1:9). Confess before you crash!

Job 3–4 // Acts 7:44–60

Rodney's Ride

26 June 1784

But as many as received him, to them gave he power to become the sons of God, even to them that believe on his name:—**John 1:12**

Most people are familiar with Paul Revere's midnight ride to warn patriots that the British had arrived. There was, however, another patriot who made a nighttime ride by horseback who is lesser known. On 26 June 1784, Caesar Rodney—one of Delaware's most famous patriots—died. Rodney is best remembered for his overnight ride from Dover, Delaware to Philadelphia. He rushed to cast the deciding vote for the Declaration of Independence in the Continental Congress on 2 July 1776. An image of Rodney on horseback appears on the Delaware 1999 quarter.

Rodney made haste to cast his vote at the Continental Congress. The freedom of the colonies, and the future United States of America, depended on it. While we can be grateful for Rodney's decisive eagerness in an earthly cause, many people today are far less eager to make the most important spiritual decision of their lives. Receiving Christ is perhaps the simplest choice on Earth—placing one's full faith and trust in the work of Jesus Christ alone in paying our sin-debt. No choice is more important or has greater eternal consequences. Yet, many postpone the decision, like some who responded to Paul's gospel presentation with the procrastinating phrase, "We will hear thee again of this matter" (Acts 17:32). Delaying a decision for Christ is itself a denial of Christ (Matthew 12:30).

Doubtless, it is an honor to be remembered on a monetary piece in Delaware. Many Presidents and public figures have been thus celebrated. But, as Christians, we are commanded not to lay up our treasures on Earth, but rather to seek heavenly things (Matthew 6:19–20; Colossians 3:1). When life is all over, and God takes Christians home, the main thing that will matter is others, not ourselves. How often did we sincerely share the gospel? Who will be in Heaven specifically thanks to you? Seek to help others know him and "believe on His name." That is a greater glory than earthly honor, for it pleases our heavenly Father—the one we will dwell with for eternity.

The Burden Bearer

27 June 2010

Cast thy burden upon the LORD, and he shall sustain thee: he shall never suffer the righteous to be moved.—**Psalm 55:22**

My grandfather served in the US Navy during World War II. He saw action in the Mediterranean while serving aboard a patrol craft (sub chaser), and served during all six years of the war. For most of my early childhood, I remember his trips in and out of mental hospitals after he returned from war. My mother even told me he was routinely subjected to electric shock treatments, a barbaric and horrible procedure supposedly designed to rid the patient of mental illness by changing their brain chemistry. His malady was Post Traumatic Stress Disorder (PTSD). Often relegated to prescription medication, PTSD is a serious affliction that affects hundreds of military personnel. The suicide rate among active-duty service members is at an all-time high—probably largely due to PTSD. People suffering from it often do not know how to deal with the emotional and mental anguish caused by their experiences serving our country. Thankfully, in 2010 the US Senate designated 27 June as National PTSD Awareness Day to raise consciousness of this crippling disorder.

God has not forgotten those who carry the burden of PTSD. If you are one who struggles with this, or any other emotional or mental burden, let God minister to you as you cast your burden upon the Lord. The Bible reminds us that, even when we have seen dangers beyond our power to process, God is near. As the second stanza of the old hymn "What a Friend We Have in Jesus" says,

> O what peace we often forfeit, O what needless pain we bear,
> All because we do not carry everything to God in prayer!

If you struggle with the burden of PTSD, never forget that, though others may not understand it, God does. And He cares for you (1 Peter 5:7). He promises to "sustain thee"—to keep and help you through it. So, seek His face and cast your burden on Him today.

See the Need, Take the Lead

28 June 1703

After these things Paul . . . came to Corinth; And found a certain Jew named Aquila . . . with his wife Priscilla . . . and came unto them. And because he was of the same craft, he abode with them, and wrought: for by their occupation they were tentmakers.—**Acts 18:1–3**

The Battle of Monmouth was fought on 28 June 1778 between Washington's Continental Army and the British. Like most battles waged during the Revolutionary War, the Battle of Monmouth involved musket-armed soldiers and cannons. Fought near modern-day Manalapan, New Jersey, this battle is noteworthy for two reasons. First, it was the war's longest one-day battle, featuring the largest artillery exchange during the entire war. Second, legend has it that a most uncharacteristic, unenlisted "soldier" manned a cannon during the heat of battle and helped repel the British attack. The surprise soldier was Mary Ludwig Hays—commonly known as Molly Pitcher—who allegedly took up a rammer and helped fire the field gun previously operated by her mortally-wounded husband.

After her husband's enlistment, Mary moved in with her parents so she could be closer to her husband's regiment. The primary job of her husband, William Hays, was firing cannons. Mary began to take care of support duties for the camp including laundry, cooking, sewing, and serving as a "water girl" to cool down the cannon barrels.

While bringing water, Mary saw her husband collapse from a bullet wound. Fearlessly, she immediately rushed to clean the ramrod and load the cannon herself and fought the rest of the day. Apparently, Mary was nearly hit by a cannon ball that passed between her legs, ripping her dress. She is said to have responded, "Well, that could have been worse."

Mary, like Priscilla the tent-maker, eagerly served others alongside her husband, even though it meant leaving her comfort zone. If we are to accomplish anything worthwhile as Christian soldiers, it will require leaving our comfort zones to minister to others. See a need, and take the lead. God will reward your service for Him.

Spared by Grace: The Personal Testimony of Denise Wells

29 June 1986

For by grace are ye saved through faith; and that not of yourselves: it is the gift of God: Not of works, lest any man should boast.—**Ephesians 2:8–9**

My journey to salvation began soon after I was married. Having grown up Catholic, I desired my children to follow Catholicism. However, I started to question my Catholic upbringing, especially due to our priests' strange admonition that we get our first son Joshua baptized as soon as possible. Baptizing someone so young just did not make sense to me. Around this same time, one of my husband's co-workers invited me to attend her Baptist church. As the Catholic church had advised me against attending other groups' church services, I reluctantly agreed to go. It was Sunday, 29 June 1986. Almost as soon as I entered church, a dear lady named Susan Hauenstein posed me a straightforward question.

"If you died today, would you know for sure you would enter Heaven?"

Uncertain, I replied, "No . . . how can anyone know that?"

She assured me that she could show me the answer from Scripture. Mrs. Hauenstein led me to a quiet area and showed me from the Bible how Christ died for my sins, was buried, and rose again three days later. She explained that doing good deeds or getting baptized does not save. Salvation comes by grace.

She asked, "Would you be willing to simply believe, and to trust only in the finished work of the Lord Jesus Christ?"

"Yes," I affirmed.

And right there, in the basement of Charity Baptist Church, I received Christ as my Saviour. My life, now and eternally, was wonderfully and miraculously changed.

Salvation is still by grace—God's undeserved kindness to us through Jesus Christ. Just as I put my faith in Jesus Christ alone, so can you. Your sins can be forgiven. But it's not of your own doing; it is thanks to Christ alone.

Salvation's Simplicity: The Personal Testimony of Randy Wells

30 June 1986

For whosoever shall call upon the name of the Lord shall be saved.
—Romans 10:13

The first time I ever attended a church in my life was when I got married at St. Thomas Catholic church in Zanesville, Ohio. My parents did not attend church, and religion was never truly addressed in our family. When I proposed to my Catholic soon-to-be fiancée, Denise, she expressed her desire for me to follow in her faith. I agreed. Shortly after our marriage, I began attending Continued Catholic Development classes. I did not benefit much from the sessions; my heart was really not inclined toward spirituality. I just wanted to be on the same page with my wife "religiously." On 29 June 1986, my wife attended a Baptist Sunday evening service. After the service, she informed me she had been saved.

"Saved? Saved from what?" I asked.

As a twenty-one-year-old newlywed, I remember becoming frustrated; I wondered if my wife would remain Catholic or join this new church. My wife reassured me that the next day some churchgoers would answer my questions. On Monday, 30 June 1986, our doorbell rang. I peered through the peephole and spotted a man in a wheelchair along with his wife. The couple were Mike and Susan Hauenstein. Sue had led my wife to Christ the previous evening at their church. Mike—a Vietnam veteran who had been rendered a paraplegic after being shot in battle—wheeled himself to our kitchen table. For over two hours, in response to every question I had about God or church or spiritual things, he was able to turn to an answer in his King James Bible. Finally, he asked me if I would be willing to receive Jesus Christ as my Saviour. "It can't be that easy," I responded. He assured me that salvation indeed was as simple as believing in Christ. At 78 Dickman Drive, Wright-Patterson Air Force Base, Ohio, I bowed my head at my kitchen table and trusted Christ as my Saviour.

JULY

An Unseen Shield

1 July 1097

For thou, Lord, wilt bless the righteous; with favour wilt thou compass him as with a shield.—**Psalm 5:12**

During the late eleventh century, Pope Urban II inaugurated the First Crusade. By 1097, the Crusaders were advancing across the arid territory of Anatolia. In order to feed the massive army, the Crusade's leaders divided their forces in half. The vanguard was led by Bohemond I of Taranto and the second contingent by Godfrey of Bouillon. On 1 July 1097, the Seljuk Turks, led by Sultan Kilij Arslan, attacked the Crusaders' camp near Dorylaeum. The Seljuks were renowned for their ability to fight from horseback and their signature tactic was to ride up to the enemy, unleash a hail of arrows and then feign retreat only to shoot down their pursuers. As the Seljuks advanced upon the Crusaders, Bohemond soon discovered his forces were surrounded. Rather than ordering his mounted knights to pursue the Seljuks' feigned retreat, he ordered his knights to dismount and form a protective shield wall around the horses, camp supplies, and unarmored noncombatants. To their surprise, the swift archery of the Seljuks proved futile against a solid wall of Crusader shields. Bohemond's men stayed the course until the arrival of the second contingent under Godfrey, who delivered a devastating charge into the harassing Seljuks. In a panic, the Seljuks fled the field, and the Battle of Dorylaeum was a Crusader victory.

The Bible speaks about the "fiery darts of the wicked" (Ephesians 6:16), which are the attacks we face from Satan. In 2 Kings 6:17, we read the account of Elisha's servant and his fear before the surrounding Syrian army. And yet, Elisha prayed and asked the Lord to open the spiritual eyes of the servant and he immediately saw that there were horses and chariots of fire that surrounded them. Similar to the Crusaders' shield wall, God promises that He will compass those who are His with a wall of protection. We need not fear the fiery darts of the wicked when our Saviour is our shield wall.

Bitterness

2 July 1881

Looking diligently lest any man fail of the grace of God; lest any root of bitterness springing up trouble you, and thereby many be defiled;—**Hebrews 12:15**

In 1880, James Garfield was elected president of the United States. After only a few months in office, a disgruntled constituent named Charles Guiteau shot him in the back with a .44 caliber revolver on 2 July 1881 at a train station. Ironically, Garfield fought in the Civil War for the 42nd Ohio Volunteer Infantry, yet never suffered so much as a scratch during the war.

After being shot, Garfield never lost consciousness. At the hospital, the doctor probed the wound with his little finger to seek the bullet. He could not locate it, so he tried a silver-tipped probe. Still, he could not locate the bullet, so Garfield was transferred back to Washington, D.C. Despite the summer heat, caretakers tried to keep him comfortable. As he grew weak, teams of doctors tried locating the bullet, probing the wound repeatedly. In desperation, they asked telephone inventor Alexander Graham Bell to see if he could locate the metal inside the President's body. He ultimately failed. The President survived through July and August, but on 19 September, he finally died. Surprisingly, he passed away from an infection, not from the gunshot wound. The repeated probing—which physicians had performed to help Garfield—actually resulted in his death.

A similar process happens in our lives when we become bitter. Whatever the original offense committed against us was does not have the power to destroy us. But if we allow bitterness in our hearts, it becomes an infection that spreads throughout our lives and, as the verse above mentions, spreads to hurt others as well. Many were hurt as a result of Garfield's death. Obviously, his family suffered, and Garfield's supporters had to endure the loss of their President-elect. Bitterness does not hurt only you. Left unchecked, it will surely affect many others. This is why we are to guard against bitterness. What thoughts might you be nursing that are giving a foothold to bitterness? What resentful thoughts do you mull over? Choose biblical thoughts as the replacement for bitter ones.

Prepare with a Prayer

3 July 1878

Yet have thou respect unto the prayer of thy servant, and to his supplication, O Lord my God, to hearken unto the cry and to the prayer, which thy servant prayeth before thee to day:—**1 Kings 8:28**

On 3 July 1878, George M. Cohan was born in Providence, Rhode Island. As a Broadway composer, Cohan is perhaps best known for writing the song lyrics to the World War I tune "Over There." First published in June 1917, the song rapidly became America's favorite anthem of World War I, and one of the country's great patriotic anthems. The famous lyrics read:

Over there, over there,
Send the word, send the word over there
That the Yanks are coming, the Yanks are coming
The drums rum-tumming everywhere.
So prepare, say a prayer,
Send the word, send the word to beware—
We'll be over, we're coming over,
And we won't come back till it's over, over there.

In recognition of Cohan's achievement, he became the first entertainer to receive a Congressional Gold Medal in 1936 from President Roosevelt.

Notice the line, "So prepare, say a prayer." Although a war-time anthem and recruiting song, these five words tucked in the lyrics are heavy with spiritual significance. Prayer may be a mere suggestion to some. But, for the child of God, prayer should not be viewed simply as an option or a line in a song. It should be our very lifeline and constant source of communion with God.

Jesus Christ Himself set aside time for prayer. Mark 1:35 tells us, "And in the morning, rising up a great while before day, he went out, and departed into a solitary place, and there prayed." And 1 Thessalonians 5:17 encourages us to continually seek God in prayer with the instruction, "Pray without ceasing." It is a good habit today—and every day—to prepare with prayer.

The Real Enemy

4 July 362 BC

But if ye bite and devour one another, take heed that ye be not consumed one of another.—**Galatians 5:15**

On 4 July 362 BC, Theban general Epaminondas led an army against the ancient Spartans at the Second Battle of Mantinea. For years, the Peloponnesian Peninsula had been wracked with war over which city-state would claim hegemony over ancient Greece.

Warfare during this time primarily included light and heavy infantry, chariots, war elephants, and cavalry. The two armies met near Mantinea, now called Arcadia. As was typical of classical Greek combat, both sides gave battle by charging one another with their heavy hoplite phalanxes. But on this occasion, Epaminondas elected to have his Theban hoplites march in column formation across the face of the enemy line, then had them execute a sharp right turn into the enemy right flank. Epaminondas personally led this column but was mortally wounded in the fight.

Despite having won the battle, and watching the flight of the Spartans, Epaminondas instructed his men to make peace. Lacking their leader and weakened by losses, both the Thebans and Spartans proved vulnerable to the rising power from the north—Macedonia. Less than a quarter century later, Phillip II of Macedon would conquer the entire portion of southern Greece, effectively ending the Theban and Athenian dominion.

Disagreements and disputes have led to real combat and bloodshed. Paul instructs Christians to be careful not to "bite and devour" one another. Christians must be on guard for division—for pointless argumentation or greediness that divides us and distracts us.

Christian, you may know the facts and be a better debater. But winning an argument with someone isn't truly a victory. Satan seeks to steal, kill, and destroy (John 10:10). Refuse to give him a foothold (Ephesians 4:27). Disagree gently and only when you need to, remembering who the real enemy is (1 Peter 5:8).

Carry On

5 July 1983

Therefore I take pleasure in infirmities, in reproaches, in necessities, in persecutions, in distresses for Christ's sake: for when I am weak, then am I strong.—**2 Corinthians 12:10**

On the afternoon of 5 July 1983, I boarded an airplane bound for San Antonio, Texas. When the plane landed, I took a bus—along with several other young men—to Lackland Air Force Base. It was late into the evening by the time the bus arrived. Our group was told to stand quietly on pre-painted footprints on a concrete tarmac. After several minutes, the sound of metal taps could be heard as three training instructors approached. Orders began to be screamed out, and it was at that moment it finally sank in: I'm in boot camp. For the next few weeks, the Air Force conformed my civilian identity to their military mold. By the time I graduated boot camp, I "ate, slept, and thought" Air Force principles. During my training, every time I asserted my own way or tried doing things outside of prescribed instructions, I received a reprimand. But when I conformed, things progressed smoothly.

Boot camp is a harsh test of endurance, character, and physical strength. All Christians are in God's army and must endure a series of adverse circumstances and events. Tests are part of the Christian life. A good soldier, however, remembers why he serves—for his beloved country. Knowing that God is the one for whom we live our lives, we can embrace the challenges of the Christian life with grace.

Most people do not like feeling weak or powerless. Pride can keep us from seeking help. The military certainly expects strength of will and physical toughness from each individual. But, we do not have to go through the Christian life alone. There are going to be times we feel weak in the face of difficulty. But Paul said that in his weakness, he realized true strength—strength through Christ. Paul could carry on in his weakness and disappointment. With God by your side, you can carry on, too.

Comfort the Feebleminded

6 July 2009

Now we exhort you, brethren, warn them that are unruly, comfort the feebleminded, support the weak, be patient toward all men.—**1 Thessalonians 5:14**

Robert S. McNamara served his country during the Kennedy and Johnson administrations. During his tenure as Secretary of Defense, he lobbied for an increase in America's role in the Vietnam War—a decision that made him quite unpopular. By 1966, the war in Vietnam had escalated. The majority of draft-eligible men were unavailable; many had avoided service by attending college or serving in the National Guard of Reserves. So McNamara devised a plan known as "Project 100,000." The plan entailed drafting men who had scored too low on the mental aptitude test required for enlistment. McNamara lowered the standard to the point that, by the war's end, 354,000 men unprepared for combat were sent to Vietnam. Tens of thousands of them were wounded, and a total of 5,478 low-IQ men died during the war. McNamara became one of the most hated men in America by Vietnam veterans. He died on 6 July 2009, having refused to apologize or admit his error in sending countless young men to a premature death.

Not everyone who was sent to Vietnam had the mental capacity to obey orders on a hectic battlefield. Paul gives Christians a direct command to "comfort the feebleminded." This may refer to Christians who easily become discouraged in the face of difficulty, or it may refer to those with mental disabilities. In either case, we should reach out to strengthen those who struggle. When you encounter someone with a mental disability, do you show kindness to them? Someone once said, "The test of a man's character is how he treats people less fortunate than him."

Consider how Jesus treated the maniac of Gadara (Mark 5:1–15). Jesus treated this demon-possessed man who experienced great mental anguish with compassion, not contempt. Others, no doubt, feared and ridiculed the maniac. But, Christ saw him as a man in need. Find someone today who is less fortunate than you, and comfort them. A smile or kind word can go a long way. Compassion is simply a part of being Christ-like.

One of Our Own?

7 July 2018

For I know this, that after my departing shall grievous wolves enter in among you, not sparing the flock.—**Acts 20:29**

On 7 July 2018, a US Army soldier was killed, and two others wounded, in an apparent "insider attack" in Afghanistan. At the Uruzgan airport, an Afghan soldier—recognized as "friendly" by US forces—turned his weapon and opened fire on American troops who were there in support of NATO's mission. This marked the first incident of this nature since August 2017, when a Romanian NATO soldier was killed.

The soldier who seemed like a friend turned out to be a foe. The Apostle Paul warned the church at Ephesus of "insider attack." He cautioned them about "grievous wolves" (deceivers and false prophets) who would enter local churches filled with "sheep" (believers). The term "wolf in sheep's clothing," of course, comes directly from this metaphor.

Have you noticed any influences in your life pulling you away from the truth of God's Word? Even a Bible teacher can be misled. When someone brings you an unfamiliar doctrine, make sure to "prove all things"—test it using the filter of the Word of God (1 Thessalonians 5:21). Be careful that you do not allow someone to undermine the basic truths of God's Word, such as the inspiration of Scripture, the divinity of Jesus Christ, the physical resurrection of Jesus, or salvation by grace alone.

Some people ask questions to sincerely seek truth; they are unintentionally ignorant or ill-advised. But, some people deliberately do not "spare the flock." In these cases, the deceiver knows full well he is in the wrong. The false teacher is "deceiving, and being deceived" (2 Timothy 3:13). He or she continually sows seeds of dispute and doubt about God's Word. This is why you must study God's Word to know what it says and what you believe (2 Timothy 2:15). Only as we prepare to defend our faith can we be secure that we won't fall prey to someone who pretended to be a sincere believer.

The Great Virtue

8 July 1986

A reproof entereth more into a wise man than an hundred stripes into a fool. **—Proverbs 17:10**

US Navy Admiral Hyman G. Rickover passed away on 8 July 1986. Known as the "Father of the Nuclear Navy," Rickover is best remembered for developing the atomic-powered submarine, the first of which—named the *Nautilus*—was launched in 1954. He had a well-deserved reputation for doing whatever it took to see a project through to completion. The admiral was famous for ignoring traditional naval customs and circumventing existing organizational red tape. He demanded the highest standards not only from himself, but also from his staff. Rickover followed a brutal interview process for young officers desiring to join the program. He was once quoted as saying, "It is necessary for us to learn from others' mistakes. You will not live long enough to make them all yourself."

As an old saying goes, "To err is human." Admiral Rickover made a wise observation about the need to learn from mistakes. How is your spirit toward counsel or advice? Do you listen when someone challenges you or points out a need to grow? Do you respond well when you are rebuked? We never arrive in our Christian lives—instead, we are "works in progress" as God continues to mold us into Christ's image.

A fool is convinced he is right—even a "hundred stripes [lashes]" couldn't convince him there is a better way. But a wise person humbly chooses to receive guidance.

Luke 14:11 says, "For whosoever exalteth himself shall be abased; and he that humbleth himself shall be exalted." The greatest people in history displayed humility in their daily affairs. Paul himself—considered by many to be the greatest Christian—wrote about the fact that he had not apprehended or reached perfection (Philippians 3:13–14). When you seek to remain teachable and embrace this great virtue in your daily life, you please God, and you put yourself in company with some of the world's most accomplished and respected people.

A Botched Battle

9 July 1755

The way of a fool is right in his own eyes: but he that hearkeneth unto counsel is wise.—**Proverbs 12:15**

The French and Indian War, also known as the Great War for Empire, started over control of the Ohio Valley. Following the Treaty of Aix-la-Chapelle in 1748, France established a series of forts along major waterways connecting the Great Lakes with New Orleans. Nestled between this line of French outposts and the edge of the Appalachians lay four hundred miles of expansive territory ripe for the picking.

France built a fort named Duquesne around the Ohio River's fork into the Allegheny and Monongahela Rivers. When word reached the English crown, British Major General Edward Braddock was dispatched to secure England's North American colonies. Braddock's official mission was to eliminate Fort Duquesne.

On 9 July 1755, Braddock led a force of around 2,200 British and American troops toward the fort, which housed around 600 Indians and 30 French troops. Within ten miles of reaching the fort, Braddock's forces were ambushed. The few natives accompanying Braddock tried to warn him, but he ignored their advice. The French and Indians, having hidden behind trees and boulders, massacred Braddock's forces. Braddock was left with a mortal wound. In the ensuing melee, French and Indian warriors subjected the British Redcoats to a humiliating defeat.

Braddock lost his life and suffered great casualties because he ignored advice from Native Americans who were well-qualified and experienced in the type of warfare Braddock was about to find himself. The general stubbornly followed his own goal instead.

In Proverbs 1:5 the Bible tells us, "A wise man will hear, and will increase learning." Wisdom and stubbornness do not mix. Instead, wisdom is found in a willingness to listen—even when it means admitting our wrong. Are you listening to those who have more experience or wisdom than you do? Lend an ear, and you will not have to regret a misinformed decision.

A Dispute Dissolved

10 July 1898

Blessed are the peacemakers: for they shall be called the children of God.
—Matthew 5:9

During the late nineteenth century, leaders representing several European powers attended the Berlin Conference with the intent of regulating European colonization and trade in Africa. The outcome of this historic meeting initiated what came to be called the "Scramble for Africa" as Germany, England, France, Spain, Belgium, Portugal, and Italy competed for a piece of the "continental pie." Among the major powers, France and England both desired the Upper Nile Valley in the Sudan. An expedition composed of Egyptian and British forces had reached the Upper Nile Valley in 1885 to rescue troops from Mahdi fanatics in Khartoum. Failing, the Anglo-Egyptian force departed the region, which left it open for control. The French then sent a force of 142 soldiers, led by Major Jean-Baptiste Marchand, to occupy an area called Fashoda. Marchand and his men arrived in Fashoda on 10 July 1898 after a fourteen-month trek. Upon hearing this, British forces under Lord Horatio Kitchener arrived two months later to contest the region. When the two leaders met, the imperial pride of both nations inflamed. In fact, the two nearly went to war over the issue. Both nations began to mobilize their fleets, but much can be said to the credit of Marchand who remained a cool head throughout the crisis. In the end, the French and British agreed that the Nile and Congo rivers would mark the frontier between their spheres of influence.

Though we do not involve ourselves in territorial disputes, we certainly encounter conflicts on a daily basis. Children play a game called "king of the hill"—they try to be the only one on top of a mound, pushing others aside if it is necessary to claim victory. Even Christians may argue about who will get the credit for someone coming to Christ. Sometimes believers want to be the best at any cost—even at the cost of a relationship with other Christians. Bring a gentle and peaceful demeanor toward others, and you will doubtless develop a reputation for being like your Saviour.

Sergeant's Beach Baptism

11 July 1988

When thou passest through the waters, I will be with thee; and through the rivers, they shall not overflow thee: when thou walkest through the fire, thou shalt not be burned; neither shall the flame kindle upon thee.—**Isaiah 43:2**

While stationed overseas in the Azores, my wife and I—as a saved couple—felt convicted to get baptized. We had been saved prior to transferring overseas, but we had not yet been baptized. We spoke with our pastor and let him know that we were ready to take the first step of obedience as Christians.

Since our tiny church on the island did not have a baptistery, it was agreed that we would be baptized in the Atlantic Ocean on 11 July 1988. An area known as Sergeant's Beach was chosen; it was close and could accommodate the church family that wanted to be there and take photos.

We walked out into the ocean wearing church clothes and holding hands. Our pastor then baptized both of us. The assembly rejoiced with us, and we headed home to change and dry off. Amazingly, the very next day Sergeant's Beach was designated off-limits to military personnel because it was discovered that the entire area was infested with Portuguese man o' war—a highly venomous jellyfish that can deliver a powerful sting to its victim. Thankfully, we were not stung.

A close encounter with a dangerous creature will hopefully never be in your future. But, whenever you face dangerous life circumstances, you can rely on God's promise to be with you. In Hebrews 13:5, He gives the assurance, "I will never leave thee, nor forsake thee." And in Isaiah 43:2 (above), He promises that whether you pass through water or fire—and by implication, any difficult situation in between—His presence will be with you.

As Christians, you and I never need to fear obeying what God has called us to do. Whatever the outcome of our obedience, we know that God will be with us. Jesus Himself promised that He will be with us until the end of the world (Matthew 28:20).

Where is Your Trust?

12 July 1944

The fear of man bringeth a snare: but whoso putteth his trust in the LORD shall be safe.—**Proverbs 29:25**

CBS News correspondent Edward R. Murrow once said, "We will not walk in fear, one of another. We will not be driven by fear into an age of unreason, if we dig deep in our history and our doctrine, and remember that we are not descended from fearful men."

On D-Day, Brigadier General Theodore Roosevelt, Jr. (son of President Teddy Roosevelt) was the only general officer to land with American troops. He was also the oldest man to storm the beach. At age fifty-six, his repeated requests to accompany his men was grudgingly granted by his commanding officer, General Barton. Roosevelt was in one of the lead landing craft and personally led his men across Utah Beach under heavy enemy fire. Pinned down, Roosevelt led his men over the sea wall. He then realized other troops were trapped back on the beach and cut off, so he turned around and led these men to join the attacking force. Amazingly, he repeated this action several times, continually under heavy fire.

For his gallantry, Roosevelt was awarded the Medal of Honor. Roosevelt was a Great War combat veteran, during which he had been permanently injured by a gunshot to the knee. Yet, the crippled general stormed Utah Beach with a cane in one hand and a .45 pistol in the other! Sadly, on 12 July 1944 (six days later), a heart attack took his life. He is buried in France. He has been called the "toughest man on the longest day."

Roosevelt, Jr.'s heart of service to others and his trust in the men he led proved a stronger influence than his fear of combat. What do you fear today? The fear of man will bring a snare—a trap. It will trick you into living for the praise of others. True safety lies in trusting the One who is always faithful and true—God Himself.

When fearful circumstances enter your life, rather than giving in to fear, pray with the psalmist, "What time I am afraid, I will trust in thee" (Psalm 56:3).

Bruised, but Not Bitter

13 July 1943

And forgive us our debts, as we forgive our debtors.—**Matthew 6:12**

The Olympic runner Louis Zamperini—whose story was publicized in the 2010 bestseller *Unbroken*—enlisted in the US Army Air Corps in 1941. He was assigned as a bombardier aboard a B-24 Liberator. As a result of combat damage, Zamperini's aircraft crashed in the Pacific Ocean. When the Japanese Navy spotted them near the Marshall Islands on 13 July 1943, he and two surviving crew members had been drifting at sea for forty-seven days. The men were held captive and beaten severely throughout the remainder of the war. Zamperini was most often tormented by one specific guard—a Japanese corporal nicknamed "the Bird" by the POWs.

Following the war, filled with hatred toward the Japanese, Zamperini began abusing alcohol. But Louis' wife persuaded him to attend a gospel crusade in 1949. During the second night of the crusade, Zamperini was born again. Forgiveness and the love of Christ filled his heart, and the hatred and nightmares ended.

Returning to Japan, he visited many of the guards from his POW days and let them know he had forgiven them. His trip included a visit to Sugamo Prison in Tokyo, where many war criminals were imprisoned. Zamperini was even able to lead some of the men to Christ. Four days before his eighty-first birthday, Zamperini ran a leg in the Olympic Torch relay for the 1988 Winter Olympics in Nagano, Japan—a location not far from one of the camps where he had been held. While there, he tried to meet with "the Bird"—the man who had inflicted so much torment and suffering. The man refused to see Zamperini. But Louis sent him a letter expressing his forgiveness and inviting him to trust Christ. It is unknown if "the Bird" even read the letter; Zamperini received no response.

Because Christ has forgiven Christians their sin debt, they should also forgive their "debtors"—those who have wronged them. Some, like "the Bird," may spurn our efforts to forgive. But we are never more like Christ than we when we, freely and sincerely, offer forgiveness anyway.

Battle at the Bastille

14 July 1789

Wherefore take unto you the whole armor of God, that ye may be able to withstand in the evil day, and having done all, to stand.—**Ephesians 6:13**

The Bastille, originally built in 1370, was first used as a state prison during the seventeenth century, and its cells were reserved for upper-class felons, political malcontents, and spies. Often, they were imprisoned without a trial. Standing 100 feet tall and surrounded by a moat more than 80 feet wide, the Bastille was an imposing fortress in the Parisian landscape.

In 1789, France was quickly moving toward revolution as severe food shortages were coupled with resentment over the rule of King Louis XVI. Mobs began rioting that June as King Louis tried to quell an uprising by the Third Estate, represented mainly by commoners. At dawn on 14 July, a huge crowd of revolutionaries—armed with muskets, swords, and various homemade weapons—began to gather around the Bastille. As the number of Parisians around the Bastille grew, a company of French Army deserters dragged cannons into the courtyard and turned them on the Bastille. The military governor of the Bastille raised a white flag of surrender over the fortress. The rioters took him into custody, seized the weaponry inside, and freed seven prisoners.

The capture of the Bastille symbolized the end of the *ancien* [former] regime and ignited the French Revolution. Joined by a majority of the French Army, revolutionaries took control of Paris and the entire French countryside. They forced King Louis to accept a constitutional government. In 1792, the monarchy was abolished; a year later, Louis and his wife Marie-Antoinette were beheaded for treason.

The Bible tells us that the spiritual battle we are in is "not against flesh and blood, but against principalities, against powers, against the rulers of the darkness of this world, against spiritual wickedness in high places" (Ephesians 6:12). For this reason, we need to wear the armor God has provided and stand strong for Him.

This Wasn't the Plan

15 July 1918

But Naaman was wroth, and went away, and said, Behold, I thought, He will surely come out to me, and stand, and call on the name of the Lord his God, and strike his hand over the place, and recover the leper.—**2 Kings 5:11**

Approximately four months before the Great War ended, the Germans initiated what they believed would be their *coup de grâce* for winning the war. General Erich Ludendorff, head of the German general staff prepared to attack Flanders—an area stretching from northern France to Belgium. In his view, it posed the best route to German victory. On 15 July 1918, four entire German armies advanced, finding that the French had set up a line of fake trenches, manned by just a few defenders. The real front line of trenches was further in; it had barely been touched by the German's pre-attack bombardment. As the Germans approached the real Allied front, they were hit with a ferocious barrage of French and American fire. Trapped and surrounded, the Germans suffered heavy casualties—and their hope of winning the war was lost.

Naaman, like the German army, jumped to conclusions. They both assumed things would proceed "according to plan," whether it meant a dramatic display of God's miraculous power in healing a leper or a military victory. How about you? Do you approach life leaning strictly on your own thoughts and intellect? Or does the Word of God fill your mind and influence your decisions? Proverbs 21:30 assures us, "There is no wisdom nor understanding nor counsel against the Lord." Embrace the opportunity to serve God with a mind saturated with the Word of God. Joshua told the children of Israel to meditate in the Scriptures, for "then thou shalt make thy way prosperous, and then thou shalt have good success" (Joshua 1:8). Do you desire God's help in your life? Let the Word of God fill your mind and heart daily. And when God redirects your plan, you'll be satisfied, knowing He knows best. "Trust in the Lord with all thine heart; and lean not unto thine own understanding. In all thy ways acknowledge him, and he shall direct thy paths" (Proverbs 3:5–6).

The Destroyer of Worlds

16 July 1945

And fear not them which kill the body, but are not able to kill the soul: but rather fear him which is able to destroy both soul and body in hell.—**Matthew 10:28**

The secret operation to develop and test the world's first atomic bomb was code-named the Manhattan Project. Contrary to what many believe, the United States was not the only nation during World War II that worked to develop the bomb. Nazi Germany and Japan also attempted to develop and test nuclear weapons but were not successful. On 16 July 1945, the US development team tested the atomic bomb at the Trinity test site of New Mexico. When he saw the fireball, the head of the Project—Robert Oppenheimer—invoked a famous quote from a Hindu scripture. "Now I am become Death," he mused, "the destroyer of worlds." The most destructive weapon ever built by humankind was ready for war. Doubtless, Oppenheimer felt the great gravity of the weapon's destructive power, and understood his own responsibility for the destruction that would soon occur in Japan's Hiroshima and Nagasaki.

Rumors about and use of nuclear weapons have led to great global fear. Yet, the Lord Jesus reminds us not to fear man, but rather to fear the One who has ultimate power over eternal life and death—God Himself. Human beings in warfare have inflicted pain. They have taken the lives of others. But their power ends when their lives end. God's power, on the other hand, is eternal. He has established the two places of Heaven and Hell—eternal places of bliss on one hand or torment on the other.

Knowing that those who reject God will enter Hell for all eternity, how should Christians respond? Shouldn't they strive to bring others to the saving knowledge of Jesus Christ? As terrifying and destructive as a nuclear bomb is, its destruction pales in comparison to the Lake of Fire's eternal and final destruction (Revelation 20:11–15). Let the words of Jesus serve as a reminder. Far more important than the fears of the here and now is what awaits everyone around us in the hereafter.

Fake News

17 July 1870

Every word of God is pure: he is a shield unto them that put their trust in him. **—Proverbs 30:5**

In the years leading up to German unification, Prussia's Prime Minister, Count Otto von Bismarck, sought for a means to draw the pro-Catholic Southern German states into what was then termed the North German Confederation. Religious differences separated pro-Lutheran Northern Germany from Catholic Southern Germany. Bismarck reasoned that something significant would need to occur to bring all the German states together in unity.

In early July 1870, France's ambassador to Prussia, Count Vincente Benedetti, met with Prussia's king, Wilhelm I, who was enjoying the healing waters at a spa near Koblenz. Benedetti asked Wilhelm to guarantee that he would not encourage a Prussian (Hohenzollern) to assume the recently-vacated Spanish throne. Wilhelm graciously refused. And a member of Wilhelm's cabinet then sent a telegram to Bismarck with the meeting details. When Bismarck received the telegram, however, he selectively deleted certain words from the original telegram to give the provocative impression that each side had insulted the other. Bismarck then ensured that the amended version was released to the newspapers on 14 July (France's Bastille Day) and telegraphed to all of Prussia's foreign embassies. On 17 July 1870, the Kingdom of Württemberg, a Southern German state, mobilized and pledged their allegiance with the Northern German Confederation. France was so incensed, they declared war on Prussia, which is what Bismarck wanted all along.

Words are of monumental importance, and this is especially true when it pertains to the inerrant Word of God. There is no such thing as an insignificant word within the pages of Scripture. Although there are some who might desire certain words to be stricken from God's message to us, we can rest assured that every "jot and tittle" (Matthew 5:18) is there for a reason, and God desires we read and meditate on His every word.

Tares and Wheat

18 July 1861

But when the blade was sprung up, and brought forth fruit, then appeared the tares also.—**Matthew 13:26**

Widely considered the first major battle of the American Civil War, the First Battle of Manassas or First Battle of Bull Run, was fought near a railroad junction in Manassas, Virginia, on 21 July 1861. Three days before the battle actually started, however, there was fighting, known as the Skirmish of Blackburn's Ford, between Union and Confederate forces.

On the morning of 18 July 1861, the First Division, led by Union General Daniel Tyler, marched to Centreville, Virginia, near a crossing point over Bull Run Creek called Blackburn's Ford. Tyler's intent was to probe Confederate defenses in an attempt to determine enemy strength. Unbeknownst to Tyler, Confederate General James Longstreet had concealed a brigade of Virginia and North Carolina infantry in the woods at Blackburn's Ford. By late morning, Tyler spotted a Confederate battery across Bull Run but was unable to determine rebel strength. He ordered four Union regiments to investigate. Due to a lack of standardization in Union uniforms, the First Massachusetts charged forward dressed in gray, which confused soldiers on both sides since Confederate troops also wore gray. The ensuing skirmish convinced Tyler's boss, General Irvin McDowell, to attempt a crossing of Bull Run around the Confederate left flank three days later, which resulted in a decisive Union defeat.

Among the many parables of Jesus, one concerns the tares and the wheat (Matthew 13:24–30, 36–43). Tares, or weeds as we might call them, resemble wheat stalks, but are a different plant entirely. When the lifestyle of a Christian looks no different than the unsaved world, it sends a mixed message like those Union troops dressed in Confederate gray and makes it difficult to witness to those who need Christ. The Apostle Paul admonished Timothy, "Let every one that nameth the name of Christ depart from iniquity" (2 Timothy 2:19). As believers, we must strive to let our lifestyle "be as it becometh the gospel of Christ" (Philippians 1:27).

A Nurse with a Big Heart

19 July 1817

But we were gentle among you, even as a nurse cherisheth her children: **—1 Thessalonians 2:7**

On 19 July 1817, Mary Ann Ball was born near Mount Vernon, Ohio. In 1847, she married Robert Bickerdyke, and together they had two sons. Tragically, Robert died just twelve years after they were married. Mary Ann then supported their family by serving as a nurse in Galesburg, Illinois.

Two years after Robert's death, the Civil War broke out. Upon hearing of the filthy conditions of the military hospital at Cairo, Illinois, the citizens of Galesburg collected $500 worth of hospital medical supplies, and they selected Nurse Bickerdyke to deliver them. Once Mary arrived, she took it upon herself to organize the Cairo hospital. General Ulysses S. Grant noticed her efforts. He was so impressed, he appointed Bickerdyke as Chief of Nursing. She traveled with various Union armies throughout the war, setting up hospitals where needed. Even after dark during battle, Mary would routinely risk her own life to retrieve the wounded, carrying a lantern into the crossfire. Whether Confederate or Union, Mary only wished to ease their suffering. She was known affectionately to her "boys," the grateful solders, as "Mother Bickerdyke."

By the war's conclusion, Mary had established three hundred hospitals and helped Union veterans obtain their pensions. In 1886, Congress awarded her a pension for her work in the Union Army. A life-sized bronze statue of Mary administering care to a wounded soldier stands in front of the Knox County Courthouse. A hospital ship, the SS *Mary Bickerdyke*, is named in memory of her outstanding contribution to the field of nursing.

The Apostle Paul compared the manner in which he, Silvanus, and Timothy cared for the church at Thessalonica to a nurse who cherishes her children (1 Thessalonians 2:7). Those in church leadership have a biblical mandate to care for the spiritually wounded and downtrodden like a nurse. Mother Bickerdyke is an excellent example, not only for pastors, but for every Christian who has an opportunity to care for someone in need.

When Will Evil End?

20 July 1944

The L*ORD* *hath made all things for himself: yea, even the wicked for the day of evil.*—**Proverbs 16:4**

As German fuhrer, Adolf Hitler's schedule for 20 July 1944 included a meeting with his top military leaders at his "Wolf's Lair" in Eastern Prussia. As the men assembled and began taking their seats, an explosion rocked the conference room. Hitler was thrown across the room; many others were severely injured. For a brief time, it appeared that the plot to kill Hitler—code named Operation Valkyrie—had succeeded. German Colonel Claus von Stauffenberg was the man primarily responsible for carrying out the attack. Before the other men arrived, he had placed an explosive-laden briefcase behind one of the conference room's table legs. Shortly after the meeting began, he excused himself to take a phony phone call. Stauffenberg made a hasty escape before the timer set off the explosion. Plans immediately went into effect to replace the Nazi regime and end the nightmare that had characterized Hitler's reign. But it was not to be. Somehow, Hitler managed to survive the blast with only minor injuries. Colonel Stauffenberg and his accomplices were quickly rounded up and executed. It would be another nine months before Hitler's fall.

It is sometimes hard to understand why God allows evil people to continue their nefarious deeds. But God will not allow anyone, including Hitler, to walk away from their evil unpunished. God has a record of all our deeds—good or bad (Ecclesiastes 12:14)—and will judge righteously. The wicked, God says, are made for the "day of evil"—Judgment Day.

Meanwhile, we wonder why evil people seem to prevail. Why doesn't God smite the evil around us? We may never fully understand the answer to these questions, but we can rest assured there is coming a day when God will banish all evil from His sight. But, until then, we can choose to trust God and believe His promise to His own in Romans 8:28: "And we know that all things work together for good to them that love God, to them who are the called according to his purpose."

Stonewall Jackson

21 July 1861

But sanctify the Lord God in your hearts: and be ready always to give an answer to every man that asketh you a reason of the hope that is in you with meekness and fear:—**1 Peter 3:15**

At the age of eighteen, Thomas Jonathan Jackson entered West Point and began training for service in the US Army. A West Point cadet witnessed to Jackson, who then received Christ as his Saviour. Jackson graduated West Point in 1846, served in the Mexican War, and taught at the Virginia Military Institute for ten years. With the outbreak of the Civil War, Jackson and his cadets received orders to report to the newly formed Confederate Army. Prior to leaving, Jackson knelt with his wife at their bedside and read from 2 Corinthians 5:1, "For we know that if our earthly house of this tabernacle were dissolved, we have a building of God, an house not made with hands, eternal in the heavens." He then got up and marched out of the house, never to return.

On 21 July 1861, "Stonewall" Jackson earned his now-famous nickname during the Battle of Bull Run. While serving as a general officer, Jackson took it upon himself to witness to his fellow soldiers and led many to Christ. To set an example of faithfulness, Jackson never took a leave since beginning his army service. Jackson was accidently shot by his own men during the Battle of Chancellorsville; General Lee said that losing Jackson was like losing his own right arm. Jackson's death eight days after being wounded was keenly felt across the Confederacy. He had been a great man of prayer, and he prayed fervently that he would honor God.

Think back to that unknown West Point cadet who witnessed to his fellow student. The cadet had no way to know that Jackson would later become a prominent general, nor that he, in turn, would share the gospel with many soldiers under his command. When we share the gospel, we do not know whom we have influenced. Perhaps the next person you witness to will end up as a great preacher or leader or educator. Let us keep sharing the gospel, leaving the results to God.

Disastrous Denial

22 July 1942

But though he had done so many miracles before them, yet they believed not on him:—**John 12:37**

On 22 July 1942, Nazis began deporting Jews living in the Polish Warsaw ghetto to the Treblinka concentration camp, located about fifty miles northeast of Warsaw. Of all the grim and horrific events of the Second World War, none is so unfathomable as the systematic murder of more than six million Jews. Yet, shockingly, millions today deny the Holocaust even happened. Despite eyewitness testimony from those who survived it and those who perpetrated it, and despite written documentation and photographic and physical evidence, two-thirds of the world's population do not know the Holocaust happened—or they blatantly deny its truth.

The human heart can be obstinate. Jesus Christ's actions and words have eyewitness testimony, written documentation, and physical evidence backing them. Yet, just like Holocaust deniers, some simply choose not to believe in Him. The Gospel of John tells us that even the people who had personally watched as Christ performed miracles did not believe on Him. Jesus even confronted two of His disciples who, after His resurrection, still didn't understand why He had come and that He was indeed the Christ. Luke 24:25–27 records, "Then he said unto them, O fools, and slow of heart to believe all that the prophets have spoken: Ought not Christ to have suffered these things, and to enter into his glory? And beginning at Moses and all the prophets, he expounded unto them in all the scriptures the things concerning himself."

Whether it is a lost person denying Christ's deity or a saved person denying His power, the results are tragic. Don't be in denial of the most important event of all of human history: Christ's death on the cross, His burial, and His resurrection for your sins. And don't be "slow of heart to believe" what Scripture tells us about the power of Christ. Trust Him today. And if you have friends or family who have not yet trusted Christ, remind them again why denying His offer of salvation is a tragic mistake.

Tested and Proven

23 July 1759

But strong meat belongeth to them that are of full age, even those who by reason of use have their senses exercised to discern both good and evil.—**Hebrews 5:14**

The HMS *Victory*—widely considered to be the world's most famous warship—owes her fame to Admiral Horatio Nelson's victory over the French at Trafalgar in 1805. This first-rate ship of the line was the brainchild of Sir Thomas Slade and carried an accompaniment of 104 guns, making *Victory* the largest warship of the British fleet. *Victory*'s keel was laid down on 23 July 1759. Her name was given due to Britain's many victories during her involvement in the Seven Year's War.

Around 150 men were tasked with building the *Victory*'s frame. The task required six thousand mature oak trees that had been seasoning in storage for fourteen years. This process ensured the incredible longevity of the *Victory* as she saw use during the Revolutionary War, Anglo-Spanish War, and the Napoleonic Wars. Today, the *Victory* is still a popular tourist attraction in Portsmouth, England.

Undoubtedly, the longevity and usefulness of the HMS *Victory* was, in part, due to the six thousand mature and seasoned oak trees from which she was built. There are two lessons for us regarding spiritual maturity that we can learn from the *Victory*.

First, when it comes to seeking counsel, look for people who are seasoned and mature Christians. Learn from those who have a solid foundation on the Word of God, those who "by reason of use have their senses exercised to discern both good and evil." The foolish man in the Bible built his house on the sand, so when the storms came, the house fell. But the wise man built on a rock (Matthew 7:24–27). Learn from those who have built their lives on the Christ the Rock.

Second, determine to grow into a seasoned mature Christian yourself. Hebrews 5:14 tells us that the way we do that is by "reason of use." It is by learning God's Word and applying it to the daily situations of life that, over time, gives spiritual maturity and stability.

A Foreign Destination

24 July 1969

Giving thanks unto the Father, which hath made us meet to be partakers of the inheritance of the saints in light:—**Colossians 1:12**

The Apollo 11 mission is noteworthy for a number of reasons, especially Neil Armstrong's walk on the moon. However, returning safely to Earth was just as important to those three astronauts as getting to the moon. On 24 July 1969, the crew of Apollo 11 splashed down in the Pacific Ocean, some eight hundred nautical miles from Hawaii. The USS *Hornet* dispatched helicopters to retrieve the heroes. Before they could walk among the crew of the *Hornet* or come into contact with other humans, the crew had to don protective biological isolation garments so they would not infect others with an unknown pathogen from outer space. The three were then scrubbed with a solution of sodium hypochlorite and were quarantined for three weeks inside a thirty-foot-long quarantine facility known as the Lunar Receiving Laboratory (LRL).

As the astronauts arrived from the foreign abode of space, so we will one day arrive in Heaven from foreign Planet Earth. Paul, under the Holy Spirit's inspiration, expects Christians to be "giving thanks unto the Father." Think of it! One day, we will enter the very area where God makes His abode—that which we refer to as the "third heaven," above outer space (the second heaven) and Earth's atmosphere (the first heaven). Paul recognized the gratitude that should fill us when we understand the privilege of joining the saints in this celestial paradise.

Thanks to God, we are made "meet to be partakers" of the saints' inheritance. "Flesh and blood cannot inherit the kingdom of God," Paul said, "neither doth corruption inherit incorruption" (1 Corinthians 15:50). God will give us new bodies one day, but permanent and eternal ones (unlike the astronaut's protective garments). In these new bodies, we will be able to dwell with God for all of eternity. What a glorious opportunity it is that God has prepared us for living eternally with Him!

Breakthrough

25 July 1944

And he spake a parable unto them to this end, that men ought always to pray, and not to faint . . . And shall not God avenge his own elect, which cry day and night unto him, though he bear long with them?—**Luke 18:1, 7**

The invasion of Normandy, code-named Operation Overlord, allowed the Allies to breach Hitler's "Fortress Europe." However, simply landing on the five beaches was not enough. A breakthrough into the French interior would be required to establish a firm Allied presence in Nazi occupied France. On 25 July 1944, a massive Allied bombardment kicked off Operation Cobra. The aerial assault constituted the largest carpet-bombing of the entire war, resulting in nearly 3,300 tons of bombs dropped northwest of Saint-Lô. This breakthrough was no easy task, as the dense hedgerow of the agrarian French countryside proved a formidable obstacle to Allied armor and infantry alike. By the end of July, through much effort and trepidation, the Allies successfully isolated the Cotentin Peninsula and captured Saint-Lô. Ultimately this offensive would open the road to invade Germany.

Mark 9:29 records Jesus telling His disciples, "This kind can come forth by nothing, but by prayer and fasting." How many times have we given up in prayer and fasting when the "breakthrough" was perhaps one more prayer away? Like those Allied soldiers in July 1944, we must strive for the breakthrough by continually bombarding God's throne with our prayers and supplications. Only then may we be confident of victory.

God invites us to come directly to His throne with our petitions: "Let us therefore come boldly unto the throne of grace, that we may obtain mercy, and find grace to help in time of need" (Hebrews 4:16). And He even helps us in prayer: "Likewise the Spirit also helpeth our infirmities: for we know not what we should pray for as we ought: but the Spirit itself maketh intercession for us with groanings which cannot be uttered" (Romans 8:26). So, don't give up praying!

The Danger of Pride

26 July 1941

Likewise, ye younger, submit yourselves unto the elder. Yea, all of you be subject one to another, and be clothed with humility: for God resisteth the proud, and giveth grace to the humble.—**1 Peter 5:5**

On 26 July 1941, General Douglas MacArthur was recalled to active duty as commanding general over all military forces in the Philippines. At that time, the military planners in Washington had devised a plan called Rainbow Five, which essentially made defeating Hitler in Europe the priority of the war. This meant that the Philippine Islands were expendable. MacArthur was furious at this and demanded an amendment to the plan. He claimed that if he were provided with long-range bombers, there would be no need to retreat to the Bataan Peninsula as outlined in Rainbow Five.

In reality, military planners recognized it was almost impossible to defend the Philippines with its eight thousand islands and combined length of shoreline exceeding the United States' shoreline. Nevertheless, MacArthur's reputation convinced the Army Chief of Staff to divert war supplies to the Philippines. Unfortunately, they did not arrive in time to make much of a difference. When the Japanese invaded the Philippines nine hours after attacking Pearl Harbor, the fallacy of MacArthur's boastings came to light. MacArthur's forces were rapidly overrun and his air force destroyed. He ordered a retreat to the Bataan Peninsula and then escaped to Australia. The men he left behind on Bataan nicknamed him "Dugout Doug" for his actions.

Pride is an insidious sin which all of us must fight. The Bible has much to say about the sin of pride. "These six things doth the Lord hate: yea, seven are an abomination unto him: A proud look . . ." (Proverbs 6:16–17). It's interesting how pride is the first thing that God lists in those things that He hates. Pride is almost always the root of our sin and often the cause for unrepentence. "When pride cometh, then cometh shame: but with the lowly is wisdom" (Proverbs 11:2). Pride must be constantly acknowledged and denied in our lives.

One Word Made the Difference

27 July 1945

But let your communication be, Yea, yea; Nay, nay: for whatsoever is more than these cometh of evil.—**Matthew 5:37**

During the waning days of World War II, President Truman and other Allied leaders delivered Japan an ultimatum known as the Potsdam Declaration. Essentially, the declaration called for Japan's unconditional surrender. As early as April 1945, factions within the Japanese government wanted peace on any terms, even unconditional surrender. On the other hand, Japanese War Minister General Korechika Anami argued that the terms of Potsdam were too rigid and urged his government to issue a rebuttal. While high-ranking Japanese military leaders discussed the declaration with their civilian war ministry, the United States awaited a response. On 27 July 1945, officials in Tokyo concluded that the only possible course for the moment was to remain silent. As a result, they issued a one-word statement: *mokusatsu*, which could be translated "to withhold comment" or "to ignore." Once the Japanese government made the terms and response public, Japanese newspapers interpreted *mokusatsu* as "rejection by ignoring." The Japanese War Ministry realized that their response had been misinterpreted, but Truman assumed the Japanese had spurned the Potsdam Declaration and went ahead with the decision to drop the atomic bomb. Who can tell to what extent the misunderstanding of this one-word response may have influenced the horrible, final days of the war?

When the Lord Jesus Christ uttered that one final word *tetelestai* on the cross, He left no chance for misinterpretation. "When Jesus therefore had received the vinegar, he said, It is finished [*tetelestai*]: and he bowed his head, and gave up the ghost" (John 19:30). When Jesus died on the cross for the sins of mankind, there was no question that He completed the payment required for our sin. He did all that was required for our salvation. One word made the difference. "So Christ was once offered to bear the sins of many; and unto them that look for him shall he appear the second time without sin unto salvation" (Hebrews 9:28).

A Declaration of War

28 July 1914

And I will put enmity between thee and the woman, and between thy seed and her seed; it shall bruise thy head, and thou shalt bruise his heel.—**Genesis 3:15**

Exactly thirty days following the shocking assassination of Archduke Franz Ferdinand of the Austro-Hungarian Empire, Austria-Hungary declared war on Serbia on 28 July 1914. Culminating what was called the "July Crisis," Austria-Hungary set in motion a series of events that transformed the European continent into a battlefield of yet to be seen carnage when Germany, France, Russia, and Great Britain joined the conflict. Dozens of additional nations mobilized troops, and in four years, some 9.5 million soldiers would die in the "war to end all wars," and yet, the armistice did not end the killing. Life in Europe had become too unhinged. Relations among nations remained unsettled, and many young men, who knew nothing but war, found that there was nothing for them at home.

Man likes to think that the present conflict will be the last one and that world peace is possible. But the Bible teaches that world peace will not be possible on Earth until the conflict between Satan and God is over. When God issued the first Messianic promise in Scripture in Genesis 3:15, He instantly identified the two sides of the cosmic conflict. The words "her seed" refers to the Messiah, the Lord Jesus Christ, while the words "thy seed" refers to Satan's offspring. Jesus told the unsaved Jews in John 8:44, "Ye are of your father the devil, and the lusts of your father ye will do. He was a murderer from the beginning, and abode not in the truth, because there is no truth in him. When he speaketh a lie, he speaketh of his own: for he is a liar, and the father of it." Since that day in the garden, a war has waged between those two seeds and will continue until Satan is cast into the Lake of Fire.

Thankfully, God does give personal peace to Christians who have put their trust in Him and who are growing in His grace. "Peace I leave with you, my peace I give unto you: not as the world giveth, give I unto you. Let not your heart be troubled, neither let it be afraid" (John 14:27).

Blinded

29 July 1014

In whom the god of this world hath blinded the minds of them which believe not, lest the light of the glorious gospel of Christ, who is the image of God, should shine unto them.—**2 Corinthians 4:4**

The Byzantine-Bulgarian wars began when the Bulgars settled in the Balkan Peninsula early in the fifth century. As their empire expanded south, they frequently clashed with the Byzantine Empire, which was formed from the fragmented Western Roman Empire upon its demise in AD 476.

On 29 July 1014, Byzantine Emperor Basil II marched his forces from Constantinople to the Rupel Pass in central Macedonia with the goal of wiping out his rival Bulgarians. Upon reaching the Rupel Pass, he found it heavily defended and was unable to pass through. Basil II sent one of his generals to lead his forces around a mountain and attack the Bulgarians from the rear, while he continued the frontal assault on the pass. When it was over, the Byzantines had routed the Bulgarians and captured eight thousand prisoners. A thirteenth century Byzantine chronicler reported that Basil II blinded all but eighty of the eight thousand prisoners. The eighty who had not been blinded would lead the others home.

Those without Christ have been spiritually blinded by Satan, meaning they are incapable of discerning spiritual truth. Similarly, a Christian, through continued sin, can sear his conscience whereby the Holy Spirit's conviction no longer makes an impact. "Speaking lies in hypocrisy; having their conscience seared with a hot iron" (1 Timothy 4:2).

Jesus encouraged His disciples to have spiritual perception when He said, "But blessed are your eyes, for they see: and your ears, for they hear" (Matthew 13:16). And Paul prayed for the Ephesian believers something we should each pray for ourselves as well: "The eyes of your understanding being enlightened; that ye may know what is the hope of his calling, and what the riches of the glory of his inheritance in the saints" (Ephesians 1:18).

Battle of the Crater

30 July 1864

Whoso diggeth a pit shall fall therein: and he that rolleth a stone, it will return upon him.—**Proverbs 26:27**

On 30 July 1864, Union General Ambrose Burnside committed one of the greatest blunders in military history in what became known as the Battle of the Crater. The retreating Confederate army was entrenched at Elliot's Salient near Petersburg, Virginia. One of General Burnside's men convinced him to tunnel beneath the Confederate position, plant four tons of explosives in a mineshaft, and blow the Rebels sky high. Impressed, Burnside agreed and the engineer burrowed a tunnel some five hundred feet into the area beneath Elliot's Salient. While the mineshaft was packed with the explosives, General Burnside planned the infantry attack, which would immediately follow the explosion of the mine.

During the early morning hours of 30 July 1864, the fuse was lit and a tremendous explosion shattered the earth. Although 278 Confederate troops were vaporized in the blast, the Union infantry discovered a horrifying reality: the blast had created a crater approximately 170 feet long, 120 feet wide, and 30 feet deep. As Union troops poured into the crater, they became disorganized and trapped. Surviving Confederate soldiers quickly amassed along the rim of the crater and fired into the mass of Union troops. One Rebel soldier described it as a "turkey shoot" as more than five hundred Union soldiers were gunned down while trying to find a way out of the crater.

Many times in life, the problems we face are of our own creation. Blaming others for hardships may give a temporary reprieve to feelings of guilt, but when we confess our sins to God, He will always give forgiveness and cleansing. "If we confess our sins, he is faithful and just to forgive us our sins, and to cleanse us from all unrighteousness" (1 John 1:9). The psalmist wisely prayed, "Search me, O God, and know my heart: try me, and know my thoughts: And see if there be any wicked way in me, and lead me in the way everlasting" (Psalm 139: 23–24).

Chameleon Christians

31 July 1938

And now thou sayest, Go, tell thy lord, Behold, Elijah is here: and he shall slay me.—**1 Kings 18:14**

When one mentions the name Henry Ford, the thought of assembly line mass production comes to mind. Ford was responsible for the Ford Motor Company as well as giving the average American an opportunity to own one of his Model T motorcars. What many may not know about Ford was his allegiance to Nazism and Adolf Hitler. On 31 July 1938, Ford was presented the Grand Cross of the Supreme Order of the German Eagle for his persuasive voice towards the Nazi cause. In the 1920s, Henry Ford, an avowed anti-Semite, published and distributed a series of four pamphlets entitled "The International Jew: The World's Problem." A letter written by Reichsführer Heinrich Himmler in 1924 described Ford as a valuable and important Nazi. Interestingly, Ford is the only American given favorable mention in Hitler's *Mein Kampf.*

In 1 Kings 18, Obadiah is confronted by the prophet Elijah. Their conversation reveals a shifting allegiance in Obadiah's heart between wicked King Ahab and God. Obadiah can be likened to a carnal Christian who makes alliances with people who have no use for God or the Bible. "Because the carnal mind is enmity against God: for it is not subject to the law of God, neither indeed can be" (Romans 8:7).

Like Henry Ford, a carnal Christian is a chameleon, conforming and aligning himself to who he is around. Ford was happy to enjoy the fame of being called a "great American" for his economic contributions, and yet he openly admired and supported one of history's most horrific despots. "For to be carnally minded is death; but to be spiritually minded is life and peace" (Romans 8:6). The ever-changing ideals of a carnal Christian lead one away from God even as they lead to continuing conformity to the world's idealogies. A carnal Christian can renew his mind by surrender to God and transformation through God's Word (Romans 12:1–2).

AUGUST

Weariness

1 August 1942

But ye, brethren, be not weary in well doing.—**2 Thessalonians 3:13**

In late June 1942, a sealed dispatch stated that the First Marine Division would attack the Japanese in the Tulagi-Guadalcanal region on 1 August 1942. Because the division did not land on Fiji until 28 July, the attack was pushed back to give them time to rehearse the landings.

On the morning of 7 August, US Marines clambered down the transport's cargo nets to embark into landing craft heading for the beach. When they hit the beach between Koli Point and Lunga Point, they were shocked to discover the absence of Japanese soldiers. By nightfall, eleven thousand marines were ashore setting up bivouac areas. Over the next few weeks, the Marines did encounter sporadic resistance, but other than that, all seemed well. In September, this all changed.

By 12 September, the Japanese sent six thousand infantry to Guadalcanal which attacked the US troops in an attempt to clear the high ground south of Henderson Field. The battle became known as "Bloody Ridge," because of the casualty ratio of ten Japanese for every one American. By December, the exhausted men of the First Marine Division were finally relieved and the campaign ground to a halt. By 9 February 1943, all remaining Japanese troops had evacuated the area. For the remainder of the war, Guadalcanal mostly fell under American control. This first major land offensive by Allied forces against Japan was successful in launching the Allied strategy of "island hopping" toward Japanese shores.

No doubt, the US Marines felt like giving up many times during the protracted fighting for Guadalcanal; nevertheless, they stayed faithful to the cause. Often, Scripture compares the Christian life to a battle. Paul told Timothy to "endure hardness, as a good soldier of Jesus Christ" (2 Timothy 2:3). In life as in battle, weariness sets in, and we are tempted to give in to the enemy. When this happens, remember the consequences of giving in: losing a battle means becoming a prisoner of the enemy. Endure the weariness and know that relief is coming your way soon!

A Word Fitly Spoken

2 August 216 BC

A word fitly spoken is like apples of gold in pictures of silver.—**Proverbs 25:11**

On 2 August 216 BC, the mighty Roman army suffered the worst defeat in the history of warfare. A Carthaginian general named Hannibal Barca lured a superior-numbered Roman force into a pitched battle near the village of Cannae. Hannibal's brilliance led to the total encirclement of his enemy, and some seventy thousand Romans perished over a period of about six hours. (To place this statistic in perspective, over nineteen thousand British soldiers died on the opening day of the Battle of the Somme [1916]. Most of those were killed either by artillery or machine-gun fire, neither of which existed in 216 BC when all of the combat at the Battle of Cannae was up close and personal.)

Prior to the battle, Gisco, one of Hannibal's trusted commanders, expressed fear concerning the astonishing odds against them. Hannibal replied, with a serious countenance, "There is one thing, Gisco, yet more astonishing, which you take no notice of. In all those great numbers before us, there is not one man called Gisco!" That word of encouragement spread throughout the Carthaginian ranks, and undoubtedly, contributed to a great victory for Hannibal.

When a good word is said in the proper setting, much can be accomplished. Proverbs 25:11 tells us that the words we say are like apples of gold—they are of great value. However, if words are not said in the proper setting, they may go unnoticed or unheeded. If Hannibal would have complimented Gisco while celebrating a great victory rather than right before a strategic battle, the value of the words may have been missed or forgotten.

Praise and encouragement offered to the right person at the right time will be valuable. Be sensitive to who the Holy Spirit puts on your heart to encourage. Today, the Lord may want to use your good word to lift someone's spirits.

Leadership Is Influence

3 August 1108

Look not every man on his own things, but every man also on the things of others.
—Philippians 2:4

On 3 August 1108, Louis VI was crowned king of France. Although he was known later in life as "Louis the Fat" due to his obesity, in his younger days he was quite athletic. He fought numerous wars and always preferred to lead from the front.

During one battle, an enemy soldier grabbed the reins of Louis' horse and exclaimed, "The king is taken! The king is taken!"

Crying out "No sir!" Louis swung his battle axe down and killed the soldier. Afterward, he cried, "A king is never taken, not even in chess!"

By the end of his reign, which lasted twenty-nine years, Louis VI had established an impressive reputation as the most powerful French king since Charlemagne. As he lay dying, Louis told his son and heir to the throne, "Always bear in mind that the royal authority is a charge imposed upon you, of which, after your death, you must render an exact accounting."

Leadership is influence. Many of us are privileged to lead others, whether it be in the military, at a secular job, in a church ministry, or as a parent. God has given us a responsibility to wield our influence wisely and we should be mindful that one day, we will "render an exact accounting."

Perhaps one of the most influential leaders in the Bible was Moses. How would you like the responsibility to lead millions of people across a wilderness over a forty-year period? This was the leadership position to which God called Moses. With enemies constantly on the attack and with numerous other challenges, Moses had to lead a complaining and often rebellious group of people. Yet, through Moses' leadership, the children of Israel defeated enemies, received the law of God, and experienced many miracles. Moses also influenced Joshua, who became the next leader of Israel and the one who would bring them into the Promised Land. Today, remember that God has given you leadership and influence. Use them wisely!

Our Protection

4 August 1912

Much more then, being now justified by his blood, we shall be saved from wrath through him.—**Romans 5:9**

During the opening years of World War II, Hungary was an ally of Nazi Germany. When mounting defeats caused the Hungarian regime to seek an armistice with the western Allies, German troops occupied Hungary in March 1944. Shortly thereafter, the pro-German government installed in Hungary began deporting Hungarian Jews to Auschwitz-Birkenau concentration camp in Poland. By July 1944, nearly 440,000 Hungarian Jews had been sent to concentration camps, and Hungarian authorities intended to deport the remaining 200,000 Jews in compliance with Nazi requests. Thankfully, a savior was on his way to help.

Born 4 August 1912, Raoul Wallenberg was recruited by the US War Refugee Board (WRB) in June 1944 to travel to Hungary in the hopes of saving Hungarian Jews. Assigned to the Swedish legation in Hungary, Wallenberg arrived in July 1944. Despite a total lack of experience in diplomacy and secret operations, he led one of the most extensive and successful rescue efforts during the entire Holocaust. Shortly after his arrival, Wallenberg used his neutral Swedish government's authorization to begin distributing certificates of protection to Jews in Hungary. Any Jew who had possession of one of Sweden's certificates of protection was exempt from deportation, a fate that almost certainly meant death. His work with the WRB prevented the deportation of thousands of Hungarian Jews.

Thanks be to God that we have a Protector from a "far off country" who makes available to each man, woman, boy, and girl the means whereby we might escape eternal death. Our "certificate of protection" is found in receiving the Lord Jesus Christ as Saviour. In John 10:27–28, Jesus promises, "My sheep hear my voice, and I know them, and they follow me: And I give unto them eternal life; and they shall never perish, neither shall any man pluck them out of my hand."

A Line to God

5 August 1858

Likewise the Spirit also helpeth our infirmities: for we know not what we should pray for as we ought: but the Spirit itself maketh intercession for us with groanings which cannot be uttered.—**Romans 8:26**

Communicating with someone we love is a luxury many of us either take for granted or work to improve. In August 1857, the wealthy investor Cyrus West Field made the first attempt at laying a transatlantic telegraph cable from Europe to America with the help of British and American ships. This attempt proved unsuccessful when the cable snapped. Soon, other problems mounted as well. The next attempt began in America, but again, efforts were stopped when the cable broke.

The third attempt to lay the cable was deemed a success followed by failure. Reaching the shores of Newfoundland 5 August 1858, the cable stretched almost two thousand miles across the Atlantic at a depth of more than two miles. Three weeks later, President James Buchanan and Queen Victoria exchanged formal introductory and complimentary messages via Field's transatlantic telegraph. Although the cable failed again on 1 September, the company continued improvements and attempts until they were finally successful in 1866.

Prior to the fall, Adam and Eve enjoyed uninterrupted fellowship with God. One might say they had a successful "cable" directly to God. But Adam and Eve's fall into sin broke the cable line of fellowship. God established temporary lines of communication through the priests and the prophets, but nothing was direct until the coming of the Lord Jesus. When Jesus paid for our sin, He also reestablished the direct line of communication between us and God. "For there is one God, and one mediator between God and men, the man Christ Jesus" (1 Timothy 2:5). We do not have to go to a priest or wait for a prophet to take our messages to God, we have direct access through Christ. "According to the eternal purpose which he purposed in Christ Jesus our Lord: In whom we have boldness and access with confidence by the faith of him" (Ephesians 3:11–12).

Vanished Without a Trace

6 August 1930

Then we which are alive and remain shall be caught up together with them in the clouds, to meet the Lord in the air: and so shall we ever be with the Lord.
—1 Thessalonians 4:17

One of the strangest missing persons cases in American history involved New York Supreme Court Justice Joseph Force Crater. During his career as justice, Crater issued two published opinions, both dealing with fraudulent activities. In July 1930, Crater and his wife were vacationing in Maine when he received a mysterious telephone call, prompting him to return alone to New York. He told his wife he would return a few days later.

On 6 August 1930, Crater was seen getting into a taxi around 2130 hours and that was the last anyone ever saw of him. He disappeared without a trace, which caused a massive manhunt. The case has been referred to as "the missingest man in New York," and the phrase "pulling a Crater" entered public usage as a synonym for going AWOL. Nine years later, Crater's wife declared him legally deceased. To this day, no one knows what happened to Crater. It remains a mystery.

There is coming a day when all who have received Jesus Christ as their Saviour will "pull a Crater" as they will vanish from this Earth without a trace. However, unlike Crater, there will be an explanation.

As we see in 1 Thessalonians 4, the Bible is clear that when the trumpet sounds, the Lord will return in the air to catch His Bride away. Can you imagine the man-hunts that will take place when we are raptured to Heaven? People will panic and search, but they will be searching the wrong places. The Bible will be the only answer in the midst of this chaotic time.

Unfortunately, because our world has moved further away from the Bible, many people will deny the truth during this time. The Antichrist of the Tribulation will gain power, more than likely through the explanation and comfort he will give when millions of people disappear. As we prepare for the Rapture of the church, let us be bold witnesses to those around us so that they can be part of the vanished and not part of the deceived.

Misunderstood Symbol

7 August 1920

For the preaching of the cross is to them that perish foolishness; but unto us which are saved it is the power of God.—**1 Corinthians 1:18**

The date was 7 August 1920, and the place was the Salzburg Congress. Recognized as far back as three thousand years, a symbol that once meant life, power, strength, and good luck would now symbolize a movement, a national identity.

The ancient Indian language of Sanskrit was the first to use the symbol and attach the word *suastika* to it, which meant well-being. Ancient Greek pottery and coins show that this symbol was commonly used as far back as 1000 BC. This symbol even shows up in the artwork of multiple Native American tribes and has a variety of meanings between the tribes. In the early twentieth century, this symbol still held positive connotations when an American infantry division and the Finnish air force adopted it during World War I.

On that day in August of 1920, however, one man decided that his nation needed its own insignia and flag. For Adolf Hitler, the swastika became "a symbol of our own struggle," with *our* meaning the Aryan race. Not long after, the swastika became a symbol for hatred, antisemitism, violence, death, and murder. What once symbolized life, good fortune, and strength will forever symbolize a time of horror and holocaust.

In contrast, the symbol of the cross was once a symbol of shame at the hands of Roman public executioners, yet now, the cross evokes a more powerful reminder than even the swastika. The cross symbolizes the end of man's struggle against sin and the hope each of us finds in the eternal redemption by Jesus' blood shed on that cross. No longer do we go to God through a priest and the sacrifice of an animal, because Jesus died with our sins on the cross. "But God forbid that I should glory, save in the cross of our Lord Jesus Christ, by whom the world is crucified unto me, and I unto the world" (Galatians 6:14). Be encouraged by the cross today, and share the hope it can bring to lost and hurting hearts.

Psalms 72–73 // Romans 9:1–15

Attention to Detail

8 August 1942

Because thou hast made the Lord, *which is my refuge, even the most High, thy habitation; there shall no evil befall thee, neither shall any plague come nigh thy dwelling. For he shall give his angels charge over thee, to keep thee in all thy ways. They shall bear thee up in their hands, lest thou dash thy foot against a stone.* **—Psalm 91:9–12**

On 8 August 1942, the Japanese sank three American aircraft carriers during the Battle of Savo Island. On board the USS *Astoria*, Signalman Third Class Elgin Staples was thrown overboard when his ship was hit by enemy fire. Although dazed and wounded, Staples survived and attributed his survival to his US Navy M-1926 life belt that had been secured around his waist.

While traveling home, Staples examined the life belt that had saved his life and was surprised to discover that it had been made in his hometown of Akron, Ohio, at the Firestone Tire and Rubber Company. He also noticed a curious set of numbers stamped onto the belt, but thought nothing of it.

Upon arriving home, Staples relayed his harrowing account to his mother. His mother responded to the story by mentioning her work in the local Firestone plant. To contribute to the war effort, she checked for defects on the life belts and approved their readiness.

Stunned, Staples jumped from his seat and grabbed his life belt from his sea bag. "Look at that, Mom, this belt was made right here at your plant," Staples announced.

Taking the life belt in her hands, Mrs. Staples leaned closer and noticed the set of numbers. Her jaw dropped as she barely whispered, "Son, I am an inspector at Firestone. This is my inspector number!"

This mother's careful attention to details saved her son's life, over eight thousand miles away. What details have your focus today? The Bible says in Isaiah 26:3, "Thou wilt keep him in perfect peace, whose mind is stayed on thee: because he trusteth in thee." Keep your mind fixed on the Lord; He is the "life belt" that will give you peace in times of turbulence.

The Failing Arm of Flesh

9 August 378

(For the weapons of our warfare are not carnal, but mighty through God to the pulling down of strong holds;)—**2 Corinthians 10:4**

During the declining days of the Roman Empire, various barbarian tribes began encroaching upon Roman territory in a series of migrations. One such tribe the Visigoths sought permission from Emperor Flavius Julius Valens to cross the Danube River in AD 376 to escape pressure from the Huns. Shortly after settling in Thrace, Roman officials began exploiting the Visigoths, and by 378, starvation forced the Visigoths to lay siege to the city of Adrianople in order to find food.

On 9 August 378, Emperor Valens dispatched an army and marched to Adrianople to relieve the besieged city. When Valens approached the city, he estimated the barbarian force to be around ten thousand men. Unbeknownst to Valens, most of the Visigoth cavalry was off on a foraging mission. Seizing what he thought was the opportune moment, Valens ordered a full attack, initially driving the Visigoths away from Adrianople.

The returning Visigoth cavalry attacked the Roman right flank. Visigoth leader Fridigern then ordered his barbarians to attack the Roman center and left flank, encircling the Roman army. Thus positioned, they slaughtered Valens and two-thirds of his army. One contemporary historian relates that it was the worst Roman defeat since Hannibal's victory at Cannae.

Like Emperor Valens, Christians often think they can embark upon spiritual warfare in their own strength. Scripture tells us otherwise. In 2 Chronicles 32:7–8, King Hezekiah of Judah told his besieged and outnumbered army, "Be strong and courageous, be not afraid nor dismayed for the king of Assyria, nor for all the multitude that is with him: for there be more with us than with him: With him is an arm of flesh; but with us is the LORD our God to help us, and to fight our battles."

We can never hope to defeat the forces of Satan in the "arm of flesh," for they will outnumber us. With God fighting on our side though, we far outnumber the enemy.

Declaration of Independence

10 August 1776

If the Son therefore shall make you free, ye shall be free indeed.—**John 8:36**

The beginning of the Revolutionary War was many things to many people. For British soldiers serving in America, it was a local uprising of British citizens living in Massachusetts. For the colonists, it was a struggle against unfair taxation. For King George III, it was a full-fledged colonial rebellion against the English Crown. In 1776, political activist Thomas Paine clarified the exact nature of the Revolutionary War's meaning in his pamphlet entitled *Common Sense.*

Paine argued that as long as the colonies were tied to England, no colonist could ever truly feel safe. Paine's *Common Sense* quickly reached the masses as more than half a million copies sold in just a short time. By the spring of that same year, support for a declaration of independence had swept through the colonies. In June and early July, a document was drafted, ratified, and signed, declaring American independence from Great Britain.

While many of the Founding Fathers, as well as local militia, considered themselves emancipated from British rule upon signing the declaration, the document did not reach the king in London until 10 August 1776. For the next seven years, a war for independent sovereignty would rage along the Eastern Seaboard of the United States, culminating in American victory.

Hearing news that Americans considered themselves free from British tyranny no doubt stunned the English government. However, there was nothing they could do to undo the Declaration of Independence. Similarly, Christ's atoning work on Calvary is the child of God's "declaration of independence" from the world, the flesh, and the devil. Nothing can take away from that transaction.

Sadly, some Christians still live tied to their former masters when the war for our eternal independence has already been fought and won. My challenge to you today is do not live in the bondage from which you have been saved. Live in the freedom that Christ has given to us. "And ye shall know the truth, and the truth shall make you free" (John 8:32).

Work until Jesus Comes

11 August 1972

Therefore, my beloved brethren, be ye stedfast, unmoveable, always abounding in the work of the Lord, forasmuch as ye know that your labour is not in vain in the Lord.—**1 Corinthians 15:58**

The Vietnam War has gone down in history as an American political and military debacle. Aside from being an unpopular war, Vietnam was in many ways a seemingly fruitless effort, especially to the quintessential infantryman on the ground.

US combat units would engage in fierce fire fights against North Vietnamese or Vietcong insurgents either to achieve a "body count" or to gain ground. What proved immensely frustrating to these brave soldiers was their own government's insistence that the enemy be allowed to retake much of the ground for which US troops had fought.

On 11 August 1972, the last ground combat unit in South Vietnam departed for the United States. As part of President Nixon's plan to end the war, members of the US 21st Infantry Regiment boarded a "freedom bird" and headed back to the States. For the soldiers of the 21st Infantry Regiment, their tour of duty in a hostile land was over. They had been whisked away from the danger of enemy fire, hidden snares, and tropical disease. Once they landed in America, they never again had to set foot in Vietnam. The war officially ended for the United States a year later. In 1975, North Vietnamese communists took over the country.

Our world has become more and more hostile to Bible-believing Christians. One day soon, soldiers of Christ will escape the "fiery darts of the wicked," his "hidden snares," and leave this world behind. However, while we are still fighting against the evil in this world, let us remember to fight in the power of the Lord, to bring hope to the enslaved, and to fulfill the duty of a Christian soldier while we are still in battle. Like the soldiers of the 21st Infantry Regiment, may we do our duty until the Lord returns for us. "The night is far spent, the day is at hand: let us therefore cast off the works of darkness, and let us put on the armour of light" (Romans 13:12).

Help Refused

12 August 2000

Wherefore comfort yourselves together, and edify one another, even as also ye do.
—1 Thessalonians 5:11

On 12 August 2000, one of the greatest maritime disasters ever to splash across world headlines occurred in the Barents Sea. As part of a series of war games, the Russian military mobilized aircraft, ships, and submarines to the Arctic Circle. One of those submarines, the *Kursk*, was scheduled to fire a test torpedo resulting in a couple of explosions in the front portion of the *Kursk*. While it is still unclear how the explosion happened, it sent the vessel to the bottom of the ocean floor.

For several days, the 118-man crew of the Kursk stayed alive on portable oxygen canisters while composing letters to loved ones. Many nations immediately volunteered to help in the rescue effort; however, the Russian government refused any assistance.

After a week at the bottom of the sea, Russian divers reached the *Kursk* but found no signs of life: all 118 men aboard were dead. When the *Kursk* was finally raised the following September, most of the front portion of the submarine was left on the ocean floor, rendering it impossible to accurately assess what went wrong.

Just as pride kept the Russians from accepting help, a Christian's pride might often prevent him or her from receiving the help and encouragement God wants to send them. God created man for fellowship, primarily with Himself, but also with one another. The Word of God instructs us to "consider one another to provoke unto love and to good works" (Hebrews 10:24). When such overtures of help are refused, the one needing help will suffer in the long run. As Psalm 73:6 describes, "Pride compasseth them about as a chain." The *Kursk*'s crew could have survived this disaster at sea if the Russians had accepted help. Unfortunately, chains of pride kept them in the ocean depths far longer than the life-giving oxygen allowed. Don't let the chains of pride steal your joy as a Christian. Allow others to help and encourage you!

A Good Defensive

13 August 1864

Be sober, be vigilant; because your adversary the devil, as a roaring lion, walketh about, seeking whom he may devour:—**1 Peter 5:8**

During the waning days of the American Civil War, Confederate General Robert E. Lee withdrew his forces to the city of Petersburg, Virginia. Petersburg was essential to the supply of Lee's Confederate Army as well as the Confederate capitol of Richmond. In what stretched out to be nine months of trench warfare, Union General Ulysses S. Grant tried numerous times to break through Lee's position. These series of engagements became known as the Deep Bottom Run campaigns.

Sensing a weakness in the Confederate defenses, General Grant sent troops to cross Deep Bottom Run and attack an area of trenches Grant was certain would falter. Grant based his plan on a report that stated General Lee had shaved off a significant portion of his forces to support General Early in the Shenandoah Valley. Grant ordered General Hancock and his men across the James River on the evening of 13 August 1864.

The report Grant depended on was false, and Hancock's company was driven back by Confederate troops for which Grant had been unprepared. This battle in the Deep Bottom Run campaign ended with Grant ordering his men back across the James. Eventually, the Union Army was successful the following April, but Lee's stubborn defense during the Deep Bottom Run Campaign frustrated Grant's plans for victory in 1864.

Much like General Grant's Union troops at Deep Bottom Run, Satan relentlessly tries to breach through a Christian's defensive network in order to gain some measure of victory. General Lee believed his defensive lines were adequate; however, repeated Union attempts to breach his lines eventually paid off. Satan never takes a day off in his fight against the child of God. Therefore, we must always be vigilant and protected by the armor of God in order to thwart his attacks. The Lord has given us His Word, godly mentors, and strength for each day. Staying behind His defense line will not allow for a breach.

Boast Not of Tomorrow

14 August 1914

The lot is cast into the lap; but the whole disposing thereof is of the LORD. **—Proverbs 16:33**

Kaiser Wilhelm II was the Emperor of Imperial Germany during World War I. Shortly before sending his troops into France and Belgium, the Kaiser assured his army that they "would be home before the leaves fall from the trees."

On 14 August 1914, the Battle of Lorraine began. This battle was one of a series of major offensives which represented a collision between the military strategies of the French Plan XVII and the German Schlieffen Plan. The French fought hard to regain territory they had lost to the Germans during the Franco-Prussian War, and the Germans fought harder to keep them out. Rather than being home before the leaves fell, the German military would continue to fight throughout World War I, costing the German Empire some 1.7 million men.

Kaiser Wilhelm II was so confident in the power of his military that he boasted a quick victory. Little could he realize the titanic struggle and bloodshed that would ensue over the next four years. As humans, we tend to make plans without taking into consideration that God is sovereign and may choose to alter our plans. God cautions us, "Boast not thyself of to morrow; for thou knowest not what a day may bring forth" (Proverbs 27:1).

In 2020, no one could have anticipated the global pandemic that would stop the world. Graduates made plans, families planned vacations and trips, political parties anticipated election campaigns, and businesses planned for a great economic year. Nothing went as planned for anyone. Schools and work went virtual; campaigns and trips were postponed. The boasts of 2020 were disappointed.

Although God does not desire for us to just "wing it" each day, He does want us to be flexible and sensitive to His changing of our plans. If we stubbornly boast of our plans, we will surely find our plans thwarted and ourselves forced to remember just how dependent we are on Him.

A Praying Leader

15 August 1945

And Solomon stood before the altar of the LORD in the presence of all the congregation of Israel, and spread forth his hands toward heaven:—**1 Kings 8:22**

President Harry S. Truman became our thirty-third president under less than ideal circumstances. President Franklin D. Roosevelt suffered a brain hemorrhage and suddenly died in April 1945. As Vice President, Truman was suddenly thrown into making decisions regarding Japan and the end of World War II. One decision that he had to make was the orders to drop the atomic bombs on Japan, thus forcing their unconditional surrender on 15 August 1945.

Truman, a World War I veteran, was cognizant of his weaknesses and shortcomings as he entered the highest office in the land. He once stated this prayer:

> Oh! Almighty and Everlasting God, Creator of Heaven, Earth and the Universe: help me to be, to think, to act what is right, because it is right; make me truthful, honest and honorable in all things; make me intellectually honest for the sake of right and honor and without thought of reward to me. Give me the ability to be charitable, forgiving and patient with my fellowmen—help me to understand their motives and their shortcomings—even as Thou understandest mine! Amen, Amen, Amen!

President Truman was forced to make tough decisions, and he acknowledged the need for divine assistance. The Bible teaches us to pray for those in leadership, but it is equally important that any leader recognize the need to daily beseech the wisdom and guidance of Almighty God. Paul requested of the church of Rome, "Now I beseech you, brethren, for the Lord Jesus Christ's sake, and for the love of the Spirit, that ye strive together with me in your prayers to God for me" (Romans 15:30). Paul also told the Christians at Corinth, "Ye also helping together by prayer for us, that for the gift bestowed upon us by the means of many persons thanks may be given by many on our behalf" (2 Corinthians 1:11). Prayer is vital for a leader.

Distracted Duty

16 August 1812

But Jesus said unto him, Follow me; and let the dead bury their dead. **—Matthew 8:22**

The War of 1812 has often been referred to as America's Second War for Independence. Britain's lack of respect for American ships, citizens, and western lands led to the outbreak of war in June 1812. During the early days of the war, the British defeated American troops in their attempts to seize upper Canada.

One of these defeats was at the American-held Fort Detroit in the Michigan Territory on 16 August 1812. British and Native American forces surrounded the fort and demanded surrender. General William Hull, commander of the fort, was concerned by the presence of his grandchildren within the fort and decided to surrender without firing a shot.

As it turned out, enemy numbers were considerably less than Hull's strength, indicating that had he fought, he would likely not have had to surrender at all. Because of his decision, British morale was boosted and they gained an important post in the western theater of the war. Hull was tried by court martial and sentenced to death. President Madison commuted his sentence from death to dismissal from the Army, mostly in recognition for his honorable service in the Revolutionary War. The interesting thing is that Hull's predecessor was William Henry Harrison, who became a war hero and future president.

For General Hull, a distraction cost him defeat and an honorable finish to his career. When we allow other things to distract us from our duty as Christians, we hurt the cause of Christ. While those distractions may not be specifically sinful, anything can become sinful that distracts us from following the Lord. We need to always remember that the Christian life is a full-time calling. "Brethren, I count not myself to have apprehended: but this one thing I do, forgetting those things which are behind, and reaching forth unto those things which are before, I press toward the mark for the prize of the high calling of God in Christ Jesus" (Philippians 3:13–14).

He Knows Your Name

17 August 1943

Because he hath set his love upon me, therefore will I deliver him: I will set him on high, because he hath known my name.—**Psalm 91:14**

One of the more significant Allied operations during World War II was known as Operation Husky, which involved landing American, British, Canadian, French, and Australian troops in Sicily. US Army General Matthew B. Ridgway, a 1917 West Point graduate, was the chief planner for the American airborne portion of the invasion of Sicily. The operation ended on 17 August 1943 and was considered a success because it caused the collapse of Mussolini's regime.

General Ridgway was fiercely loyal to his troops and used a unique way of showing that loyalty. At West Point, he developed the ability to memorize and associate names of large groups of people. By the end of his first year, he knew all 750 cadets by name. Incredibly, Ridgway literally knew the names of thousands of soldiers under his command throughout World War II and the Korean War. Soldiers were in awe when their commander called them by name.

How much more should it awe us that the Supreme God of the universe knows our names! Scriptures speak of the fact that He knows us before conception and has a plan for us. "Before I formed thee in the belly I knew thee; and before thou camest forth out of the womb I sanctified thee, and I ordained thee a prophet unto the nations" (Jeremiah 1:5). In Psalm 139:15–16, the Bible tells us how God individually fashioned us for a purpose: "My substance was not hid from thee, when I was made in secret, and curiously wrought in the lowest parts of the earth. Thine eyes did see my substance, yet being unperfect; and in thy book all my members were written, which in continuance were fashioned, when as yet there was none of them." In a world where people are so busy that they often forget appointments or special days of family and friends, each of us should be comforted by the fact that God has not and will not forget about us.

Leaving a Legacy

18 August 1227

But as many as received him, to them gave he power to become the sons of God, even to them that believe on his name:—**John 1:12**

In the thirteenth century, perhaps no other name evoked more trepidation than that of Genghis Khan, the Mongol chieftain who forged an empire stretching across most of Asia. Khan earned the distinction of conquering more territory than any other person in history, and his Mongol warriors were some of the most fearsome horse soldiers in military history. While his exploits are legendary, his reputation for fathering many children became a topic of conversation after a genealogical study in 2003 discovered that over sixteen million men are genetic descendants of Genghis Khan. That number is 0.5 percent of the world's male population. Genghis Khan died on 18 August 1227, but his lineage continues to this very day.

When the Lord Jesus Christ confronted a group of Pharisees in John 8, they were quick to proclaim that they were children of Abraham, and therefore, children of God. Jesus quickly corrected them in John 8:44: "Ye are of your father the devil, and the lusts of your father ye will do. He was a murderer from the beginning, and abode not in the truth, because there is no truth in him. When he speaketh a lie, he speaketh of his own: for he is a liar, and the father of it." A person is not automatically a child of God simply because they attend church, have Christian relatives, or perform good deeds. The Bible is clear that being a child of God is only for those who have received Christ as Saviour. "But as many as received him, to them gave he power to become the sons of God, even to them that believe on his name: Which were born, not of blood, nor of the will of the flesh, nor of the will of man, but of God" (John 1:12–13).

While a legacy on Earth may be important, what type of eternal legacy are you leaving behind? Will your legacy be one of worldly treasure that will one day burn up, or will it be of eternal treasure that will last forever? "Lay up for yourselves treasures in heaven, where neither moth nor rust doth corrupt, and where thieves do not break through nor steal" (Matthew 6:20).

Mobility Ready

August 1990

Be ye therefore ready also: for the Son of man cometh at an hour when ye think not.—**Luke 12:40**

Operation Desert Shield commenced in August 1990. Initially, Desert Shield was America's response to Iraq's invasion of Kuwait, but it would prepare the US for Operation Desert Storm in January 1991. Desert Storm became the second largest coalition war in history. (World War II was the largest with forty-six nations allied against the Axis.) Approximately thirty-five nations stood with the United States to combat Iraqi aggression under the Saddam Hussein regime.

In 1990, my family and I were stationed at Sheppard Air Force Base in Wichita Falls, Texas, where I was assigned as an instructor at the USAF School of Health Care Sciences. In light of the massive buildup for Desert Shield, many active duty and reserve personnel received the order to be "mobility bag ready." My mobility bag was a large, olive bag designed to hold only the material needed to deploy at a moment's notice. I was required to maintain my bag so that upon notification of transport, I could grab it quickly. I recall that my wife hated that bag, which I kept in our home near the front door. She didn't mind its location, but she disliked the constant reminder that I could be gone at a moment's notice.

As Christians we should always be "mobility ready" to meet the Lord, whether that be via the Rapture of the saved or through death. The Apostle John, in 1 John 2:28, cautioned believers, "And now, little children, abide in him; that, when he shall appear, we may have confidence, and not be ashamed before him at his coming."

Every moment of our days should be spent anticipating and waiting to meet our God. While we don't have a bag to pack for our journey to Heaven, will we be bringing any souls into eternity—our own or those we lead to Jesus? For those who are living with Christ's return always in mind, seeing Him will be a joy. For those Christians living as if this life is all there is, seeing Christ will be a shock. Are you ready to see the Lord?

The Legion of the United States

20 August 1794

Brethren, be followers together of me, and mark them which walk so as ye have us for an ensample.—**Philippians 3:17**

Following the *Treaty of Paris*, which officially ended the Revolutionary War, Great Britain refused to evacuate the Northwest Territory. To harass American colonists, the British maintained forts throughout the Ohio country and supported Indian attacks against the settlers.

Washington's Continental Army had disbanded after the Revolution, leaving the newly liberated colonies woefully unprepared for conflict. The defeat of Major General Arthur St. Clair's rag-tag assembly of American soldiers in 1791 at the hands of fifteen hundred Indian warriors convinced President Washington to act.

Secretary of War Henry Knox had a clear vision for how the government should respond: copy the ancient Roman army. Knox had long been an admirer of the Roman legions, as was Washington's first Inspector General, Baron Friedrich Wilhelm von Steuben. Together, Knox and Steuben reorganized the US Army as the "Legion of the United States." From ancient Rome they took logical structure and the power of adaptable, standardized units to form an effective combined-arms army. Commanded by "Mad Anthony" Wayne, the newly formed US Legion finally ended Indian incursions into the Ohio country at the Battle of Fallen Timbers on 20 August 1794.

Following Wayne's death in 1796 and Washington's death in 1799, Congress dismantled the Legion and reorganized the troops into the 1st, 2nd, 3rd, and 4th Regiments of the US Army. Thus, just like the Roman Legion, the US Legion disappeared, never to be resurrected.

Many voices and personalities clamor for our emulation. Whether someone on social media, an athlete, a celebrity, or mentor, make sure the influences in your life sharpen you spiritually and are worthy of your emulation. Paul said, "Be ye followers of me, even as I also am of Christ" (1 Corinthians 11:1).

Unshackled

21 August 1831

Stand fast therefore in the liberty wherewith Christ hath made us free, and be not entangled again with the yoke of bondage.—**Galatians 5:1**

Slavery was one of the causes for America's bloodiest war—the Civil War. More than 650,000 men perished in that terrible conflict and the aftereffects reverberate to this very day. Some thirty years prior to the start of the war, a slave named Nat Turner instigated what became the bloodiest slave revolt in US history.

Turner often claimed he heard voices and signs telling him of a coming conflict between black and white spirits. In early 1831, he witnessed a solar eclipse that he took for a sign that the time was right to rise up. On 21 August 1831, Turner gathered fellow slaves and killed an estimated fifty-five white men, women, and children in Southampton County, Virginia, before finally being captured and executed weeks later.

While the means with which Turner went about to obtain freedom may not have been the best course of action, he nevertheless wanted to be free from the shackles of bondage. Whether people wish to admit it or not, sin is bondage. As the old saying rightly states, "Sin will take you further than you want to go, keep you longer than you want to stay, and cost you more than you want to pay." No amount of earthly resistance or revolting will free us from sin's shackles. Only the bondage breaker, the Lord Jesus Christ, can free a person from the bondage of sin. Galatians 5 begins with the challenge to not entangle ourselves again with the yoke of sin. Paul continues to tell the church of Galatia that no one is justified (made right before God) by following the law, because none of us can follow it perfectly. Only justification that comes from Christ's blood will free us from bondage.

Like Turner, we often fight against bondage with our own plans, walking according to our flesh. Paul continues to say in Galatians 5:16, "Walk in the Spirit, and ye shall not fulfil the lust of the flesh." By trusting in the powerful work of Christ, we can defeat the bondage of sin.

Hasty Orders

22 August 1638

The way of a fool is right in his own eyes: but he that hearkeneth unto counsel is wise.—**Proverbs 12:15**

In 1638, the French launched a major naval attack against Spain. The resulting attack left a shipyard destroyed along with sixteen Spanish galleons. Additionally, the French captured a key fortress at Fuenterrabia.

At that time, Spain's first minister was the nobleman Gaspar de Guzman, known as the Count-Duke of Olivares. Desperately wanting to take back the Spanish fortress, Olivares commanded his two naval fleets to meet and to sail together to relieve the fortress. His fleet in the Mediterranean was commanded by the flamboyant Antonio de Oquendo while a smaller fleet was stationed at La Coruna under the seasoned commander Lope de Hoces.

Because of the distance of Oquendo's fleet, his squadron would take longer to reach Hoces' fleet at La Coruna thus stalling the relief of the fort. In haste, Olivares ordered Hoces to sail at once, without waiting for Oquendo. Although Hoces attempted to point out that his twelve ships were no match for sixty-four French warships, Olivares refused to listen and overruled his admiral. On 22 August, thirty-three French warships trapped Hoces in the small port of Guetaria. The French admiral, Henri de Sourdis, decided to employ fire ships, setting fire to six of his own ships and sending them straight into the wavering Spanish line. Confusion broke out as flames spread throughout the fleet, and Hoces was forced to order his remaining ships burned to avoid capture. Before the battle was done, Hoces and a thousand of his men had to swim to shore. Three thousand Spanish perished while the French lost less than a hundred men.

Sometimes we think because we hold a position of high rank or importance, we are immune to the counsel of those under us. Had Olivares listened to the wise counsel of his subordinate, things may have turned out differently at the Battle of Guetaria. May we as leaders be willing to humble ourselves and ask for counsel instead of making hasty decisions that could ruin the lives of those we influence.

Copycat General

23 August 1941

But continue thou in the things which thou hast learned and hast been assured of, knowing of whom thou hast learned them;—**2 Timothy 3:14**

Shortly after the Germans invaded the Soviet Union in the summer of 1941, Hitler's tanks and infantry made stunning progress as Soviet defenses seemingly melted under the onslaught of the German *blitzkrieg*. On 23 August 1941, Hitler initiated the Battle of Kiev. Taking a page from the battle plan of an ancient general named Hannibal Barca, Hitler attempted one of the most difficult maneuvers in ground combat—a double envelopment of the enemy's forces.

By mid-September, German forces had completely encircled several Soviet armies in Kiev, resulting in the capture of over 600,000 Soviet troops: the largest encirclement in the history of warfare. As with Hitler, military leaders tend to imitate the plans of other leaders who have been successful in combat. They realize others have worked at certain areas and honed skills to elevate both themselves and their followers to a level of success. Although Hitler was not the best tactician, in this case he chose to emulate the tactics of one of history's greatest generals.

Just as a military tactician can learn from the skills of a seasoned general, we must learn from to the One who is the ultimate and perfect example: Jesus Christ.

Many Christians use the popular Christian catch phrase, "What would Jesus do?" We see people wear shirts or wrist bands with WWJD, but too often, it just remains a phrase without substance. If our goal is to be like Jesus and to do what He would do, we need to rely on something other than our own abilities and strength. The Bible says, "For even hereunto were ye called: because Christ also suffered for us, leaving us an example, that ye should follow his steps" (1 Peter 2:21). Jesus left us a wonderful example of how to live, but we must study and follow His life and ministry on Earth in order for our battles to be victorious. Copying Jesus will never steer us wrong.

Guarded Integrity

24 August 1936

Better is little with the fear of the LORD than great treasure and trouble therewith.
—Proverbs 15:16

On 24 August 1936, President Manuel Quezon of the Philippines conferred the title of field marshal on General Douglas MacArthur. As US Army Chief of Staff, MacArthur had served as head of all American and Filipino armed forces at the request of Quezon. When MacArthur learned of his new assignment, he sent a request to President Roosevelt asking that Dwight D. Eisenhower accompany him as one of his personal aides.

After the Japanese occupied the Philippines, Quezon was forced to live in exile in the United States. Quezon presented a check to Eisenhower for a substantial amount of money; some historians say it was over $100,000. When Eisenhower inquired the reason for such an exorbitant sum, Quezon replied that it was for the service he had rendered to the Philippine people as MacArthur's aide. When Eisenhower protested, Quezon informed him that General MacArthur had no qualms at all about accepting a similar gift of $500,000. Eisenhower promptly refused the money as it would have compromised his ethics. He stated, "I explained that while I understood this to be unquestionably legal, and that the President's motives were of the highest, the danger of misapprehension or misunderstanding on the part of some individual might operate to destroy whatever usefulness I might have to the allied cause in the present War."

While it would not have been illegal for Eisenhower to have accepted the check from Quezon, Eisenhower sensed it would have labeled him as a man who could be "bought," thus eliminating his usefulness as a military leader.

The Bible has much to say on financial matters. And a key verse to remember is 1 Timothy 6:10: "For the love of money is the root of all evil: which while some coveted after, they have erred from the faith, and pierced themselves through with many sorrows." Money itself isn't the root of evil, but the *love* of money has hurt many people. Don't allow the love of money to trip you up.

He Never Sleeps

25 August 1819

Neither is there any creature that is not manifest in his sight: but all things are naked and opened unto the eyes of him with whom we have to do. **—Hebrews 4:13**

On 25 August 1819, Allan Pinkerton was born in Glasgow, Scotland. While that name may be less familiar today, Mr. Pinkerton's name became synonymous with private eye and the slogan "We never sleep."

Pinkerton immigrated to Chicago, Illinois, in 1842 and began making barrels to support himself. While collecting wood for his barrels, Pinkerton stumbled onto a counterfeiting ring. After several days of observations and notes, he offered his innate sleuthing abilities to the local police department. Not long after this incident, Pinkerton formed his own detective agency known as Pinkerton's National Detective Agency with his signature logo featuring a wide open eye and the caption "We Never Sleep."

Specializing in embezzlement cases and railroad misconduct, Pinkerton caught the attention of President Lincoln when he foiled an assassination attempt on the newly-elected President. Lincoln was so impressed, he asked Pinkerton to form a secret service to root out spies in Washington, DC. To this day, the Pinkerton organization is still going strong and retains its iconic logo and slogan.

Although the Pinkertons can brag that they never sleep, we all know that that's only possible because there are many of them. How comforting to know that our God actually never does sleep but is always watching over us!

The fact that God never sleeps should also be challenging for us because He also sees all that we do, even when we think no one is watching. We think of Adam and Eve as foolish when they tried to hide from God in the Garden of Eden, but too often we act as they did, believing that God does not see us when we sin. Find comfort in knowing that God never slumbers, but also find the challenge that He sees you when you're alone. Live a life that is open and transparent before Him.

Mortifying the Old Man

26 August 1914

For if ye live after the flesh, ye shall die: but if ye through the Spirit do mortify the deeds of the body, ye shall live.—**Romans 8:13**

Most people associate the First World War with trenches along the Western Front, an area that stretched from the Swiss border to the English Channel. While there was much activity between the Allied and Central Powers on the Western Front, just as much fighting happened along the Eastern Front among German, Russian, Serbian, and Austrian troops. On 26 August 1914, Russian forces under the command of General Aleksandr Samsonov advanced into German-occupied East Prussia.

During the Russian occupation, one Prussian officer decided to direct artillery fire on his own house after the Russians took possession of it. What great courage was seen in the sacrifice of this Prussian soldier, willingly destroying his own home to destroy the enemy within.

After a person is saved, a battle rages between the flesh and the spirit, or between the "new man" and the "old man." The Apostle Paul taught that believers must be willing to mortify, or put to death, those deeds of our bodies that would lead us into sin. Romans 6:6 says, "Knowing this, that our old man is crucified with him, that the body of sin might be destroyed, that henceforth we should not serve sin."

Think of it like changing clothes. If I need to change out of my work clothes into freshly-laundered clothes, I first must remove the soiled clothes. A similar process must happen to put off the old man and put on the new. Paul explained it to the Ephesians this way: "That ye put off concerning the former conversation the old man, which is corrupt according to the deceitful lusts; And be renewed in the spirit of your mind; And that ye put on the new man, which after God is created in righteousness and true holiness" (Ephesians 4:22–24). As the Prussian soldier had to mortify the enemy within his house, so must we mortify the enemy within our hearts so we can live as dedicated Christians.

A Fence of Separation

27 August 1918

Know ye not that ye are the temple of God, and that the Spirit of God dwelleth in you?—**1 Corinthians 3:16**

Shortly before the end of World War I, United States troops found themselves engaged in a border skirmish with Mexico. On 27 August 1918, US troops based in Nogales, Arizona, clashed with Mexican military and civilian militias based in Nogales, Sonora-Mexico.

The trouble began when a civilian carpenter from Mexico crossed back into Mexico without having the bulky package he was carrying inspected by US customs officials. When officials shouted at him to comply by returning to US territory for inspection, the man became confused. A US Army private then fired a warning shot, which prompted Mexican officials across the border to fire in retaliation. Things quickly escalated as troops of the Mexican Federal Army amassed at the border and joined the fight.

US troops of the 35th Infantry Division along with Buffalo soldiers of the 10th Cavalry crossed into Nogales, Sonora, and began patrolling the streets. Late in the fighting, US troops placed a machine gun atop a stone building and fired into the Mexican positions, ending the skirmish. After the Battle of Ambos Nogales was over, a two-mile-long border fence was erected through the Ambos Nogales community, forming the first permanent border fence separating Mexico and the United States.

For Christians, God has placed an internal "fence of separation" within us in the Person of the Holy Spirit. A marked difference should exist between the life of a Christian compared to the life of an unsaved person. Sometimes we may want to jump the fence back into enemy territory, but remember, while the grass may look greener over there, Satan's grass is always artificial turf. Some Christians even like to straddle the fence, having one foot in the world and one foot in Christian living. However, as James 1:8 says, "A double minded man is unstable in all his ways." Eventually, one who straddles the fence will fall, and it's usually not on the right side of the fence.

Diligence Wins

28 August 1886

He becometh poor that dealeth with a slack hand: but the hand of the diligent maketh rich.—**Proverbs 10:4**

Andrew Higgins was born on 28 August 1886 in Columbus, Nebraska. In 1922, he started the Higgins Lumber and Export Company, importing various hardwoods from the Philippines, Central America, and Africa. In pursuing these ends, Higgins also took the initiative to acquire and redesign a fleet of sailing ships.

Higgins' small boat designs caught the attention of the US military. When tested in 1938 by the Navy and Marine Corps, Higgins' boats outpaced the performance of similarly designed Navy craft. Once the US Navy adopted his boat designs, the boats were re-dubbed "Landing Craft, Vehicle, and Personnel" (LCVP). To most of the world, they were simply called "Higgins boats." Higgins built about twenty thousand of his LCVPs for the Navy, which were then used during World War II.

On 6 June 1944, the Allied forces used more than one thousand Higgins boats when they landed on the five beaches of Normandy. General Dwight Eisenhower said, "Andrew Higgins is the man who won the war for us. If Higgins had not designed and built those LCVPs, we never could have landed over an open beach. The whole strategy of the war would have been different." Adolf Hitler also recognized Higgins' heroic war efforts in ship production, bitterly naming Higgins the "New Noah."

Andrew Higgins' diligence in the design and production of a small boat not only made him a wealthy man but also ensured safe passage for thousands of soldiers, sailors, and marines as they faced the enemy. In contrast, many people have lost money and even their reputations because of get-rich-quick schemes. The key to experiencing success is found in the laying of diligent plans and following through on those plans. Of course, wealth on this Earth should never be the primary goal for a child of God, and we certainly are not promised we will have it. But the principle holds in any endeavor: the key to success is diligence, not luck.

Allegiance: Not for Sale

29 August 1776

Watch ye, stand fast in the faith, quit you like men, be strong.
—1 Corinthians 16:13

On 29 August 1776, around thirty thousand British Redcoats attacked New York harbor, delivering a decisive setback to Washington's Continental Army. General Washington asked for a spy. Nathan Hale, a patriotic twenty-one-year-old teacher from Coventry, Connecticut, answered with a courageous: "I am willing to go. Send me."

Hale was raised in a godly Christian home, possessed a gentle spirit, and was always concerned for others. Doubtless, these admirable qualities endeared him to General Washington who commissioned him a captain upon his acceptance into the Continental Army.

Entering the enemy camps, Hale took notes, made sketches of fortifications, and hid the papers in the soles of his shoes. As he prepared to return to his own lines, the British captured him and discovered the papers in his shoes. He was condemned to be hanged as a spy before the following dawn. Prior to his hanging, a British officer tried to persuade Hale to switch sides by offering him a sum of money and a captaincy in the British Army. Hale refused to surrender his allegiance to his country for the money or the position. His dying words reveal even more his strength of character: "I only regret that I have but one life to lose for my country."

Nathan Hale could have accepted the British offer instead of submitting to an early death. Hale's allegiance, however, was not for sale, and he proved this with his death. In a day when Christians are flippant about where their allegiance should lie, may we emulate the values of Nathan Hale and refuse to compromise with the world. As the three Hebrew children said in the face of Nebuchadnezzar's threat of death: "If it be so, our God whom we serve is able to deliver us from the burning fiery furnace, and he will deliver us out of thine hand, O king. But if not, be it known unto thee, O king, that we will not serve thy gods, nor worship the golden image which thou hast set up" (Daniel 3:17–18).

Taking Advantage

30 August 1740

Lest Satan should get an advantage of us: for we are not ignorant of his devices.
—2 Corinthians 2:11

On 30 August 1740, David Bushnell was born in Connecticut. Most would be unfamiliar with Bushnell but for the fact that he is credited with inventing the first submarine used in battle.

Submarine warfare dates as far back as the American Revolution with Bushnell's "turtle." The vessel was designed to propel under water and used to attach explosives to British ships. Although mostly unsuccessful during the Revolution, Bushnell's craft proved to be the foundation of submarine development. By World War II, nearly all combatant nations used submarines, although the German U-boat gets most of the publicity due to movies, books, and media attention.

The USS *Trout* (*SS*-202) was a Tambor-class American submarine that began her service the day Japan attacked Pearl Harbor. The *Trout* completed a total of ten war patrols before being lost in the East China Sea. Aside from firing torpedoes at Japanese surface vessels, the *Trout* was directed to plant a series of naval mines during her eighth patrol off the coast of Borneo. Unlike a torpedo, which is propelled through the water to a target, a naval mine is a contact weapon that explodes whenever a vessel approaches or strikes it. Since they float in the water like a fishing bobber, they are not that difficult to spot. Provided a lookout does his job properly, naval mines are entirely avoidable.

Like a submarine, Satan's tactics are often below the surface. His attacks, like the submarine's torpedoes, can be sudden and quick. But they can also be like mines, planted along our path to destroy us when we come in contact. When we let down our guard, we become easy prey for his traps.

As you head into the sea of life today, be ready and prepared to do battle "against the wiles of the devil" (Ephesians 6:11). "Watch ye, stand fast in the faith, quit you like men, be strong" (1 Corinthians 16:13).

Born Abroad

31 August 1987

For our conversation is in heaven; from whence also we look for the Saviour, the Lord Jesus Christ:—**Philippians 3:20**

On 31 August 1987, our second and youngest son, JohnMichael, was born while we were stationed in the Azores, Portugal. Because of that, the events surrounding his birth were somewhat atypical.

First, he was delivered by Captain America. That's right, the first name of the Air Force obstetrician who delivered him was America, and she was a captain at the time. Perhaps that explains JohnMichael's love of Marvel comics to this day.

Second, his birth certificate was unique in that it read: "United States of America Citizen Born Abroad." Unlike federal installations in the States, the Air Base on the Azores Island was Portuguese territory. Although he was born outside the geographical United States, he was (and is) legally and positionally an American citizen.

God's Word tells us that as Christians, our citizenship is in Heaven. Like our son who experienced a physical birth in the Azores but is a US citizen, a Christian's spiritual citizenship is in Heaven even though he has experienced the spiritual rebirth on Earth.

For any of us who have been abroad for weeks and months, coming home to America is a singularly comforting emotion. Depending on where a soldier has been, he or she may even express the emotion by kissing the ground of American soil. Now, imagine stepping onto the streets of our heavenly home for the first time. It won't be asphalt or dirt but gold that greets the soles of our feet. Instead of cheering crowds, our ears will pick up the chorus of angels. And for the first time, our faith will be sight as we look upon the face of our Saviour Jesus. What a day that will be! Revelation 21:4–5 describes it: "And God shall wipe away all tears from their eyes; and there shall be no more death, neither sorrow, nor crying, neither shall there be any more pain: for the former things are passed away. And he that sat upon the throne said, Behold, I make all things new."

SEPTEMBER

Where a Little Drift Leads

1 September 1983

Thy word is a lamp unto my feet, and a light unto my path.—**Psalm 119:105**

On 1 September 1983, Korean Airlines Flight 007 departed from Anchorage, Alaska, on a direct flight to Seoul, Korea. Unknown at the time, one of the crew members accidentally set the computer engaging the flight navigation system off by one and a half degrees. The mistake was unnoticeable at the point of departure. Yet, as the giant 747 continued through the Aleutians and out over the Pacific, that seemingly-insignificant error caused the plane to increasingly stray from its proper course. Eventually, it found itself flying over Soviet air space. Soviet radar picked up the plane, and because a US Air Force RC-135 was flying a secret mission in the same area, MiG-23 fighter jets quickly scrambled into the air to intercept what they perceived was an intruder. Over mainland Russia, the jets shot Flight 007 out of the sky, and everyone on board perished. Over 269 people lost their lives over a one and a half degree drift in course.

Unfortunately, spiritual drift is the norm rather than the exception. A hymn writer attested, "Prone to wander, Lord, I feel it, Prone to leave the God I love." Christians daily face the distractions of this world. If we are to walk in righteousness and truth—and if we are to stay the course for an entire lifetime—we must come back over and over to the Word of God for guidance.

The passengers of Flight 007 did not even realize they were off course until it was too late. Choose your direction well, and allow the Word of God to be a "light unto your path." Poor choices may seem insignificant at first. Disaster does not usually strike immediately. But unwise or disobedient choices made repeatedly over time can result in spiritual shipwreck.

Christian, do you desire to live out God's will in your life? Each day, seek God in His Word. Sincerely go to God looking for leadership in your life and, like the psalmist, you will also be able to attest to His guidance in your life as well.

Deliverance

2 September 1945

Who hath delivered us from the power of darkness, and hath translated us into the kingdom of his dear Son:—**Colossians 1:13**

The Vietnam War stands out as one of the most maligned and misunderstood wars of the twentieth century. More than 56,000 Americans perished in the war and hundreds of thousands were wounded, both physically and psychologically. On 2 September 1945, Ho Chi Minh—a staunch Vietnamese nationalist and Communist—declared Vietnam independent from five years of Japanese occupation. Borrowing from Thomas Jefferson, Ho Chi Minh began his speech by quoting directly from America's own Declaration of Independence. During the speech, speaking of French colonial rule, Minh stated of the French that "they have fleeced us to the backbone, impoverished our people, and devastated our land."

Doubtless, some Vietnamese did not agree with Ho's assertion that the French were responsible for such dreadful conditions. After all, French architecture and cuisine had dominated Saigon for nearly six decades. When the French were finally ousted after the Battle of Dien Bien Phu in 1954, a power vacuum existed that was rapidly filled by United States involvement as advisors. The decade-long Vietnam War followed.

This world is influenced by Satan. The "power of darkness" is present all around us. We can find it in news headlines, in ungodly music, and even in the colonial mistreatment experienced in so many nations. An old song says: "This world is not my home; I'm just passing through. My treasures are laid up somewhere beyond the blue." We can rejoice that this planet is not our home; it is a temporary holding place for us as we witness and live for Christ.

While an earthly kingdom has a definite beginning and end, the kingdom to which we have been "translated"—the kingdom of "his dear Son"—has no end. If you're a believer, give thanks to God today that He has given you the opportunity to have faith. One day, Christians will receive the mansions that Christ has promised (John 14:2–3).

Never Be Ashamed of the Gospel

3 September 1777

Thou hast given a banner to them that fear thee, that it may be displayed because of the truth. Selah.—**Psalm 60:4**

Banners have been used since Bible days as a standard or ensign to declare an army's allegiance. As symbols of nationality, they have helped direct soldiers before, during, and after a battle. On 3 September 1777, Colonial troops were involved in a skirmish with British Red Coats at the Cooch's Bridge in Delaware. General William Maxwell, commander of the Patriots, directed the newly designed stars and stripes be raised as his men moved to meet the enemy. This marked the first time the American flag was carried into combat by American forces, and it certainly was not the last time.

The psalmist observed that a banner is displayed "because of the truth." A flag stands for the values and truths embraced by a nation. But, think of the many truths that the Bible teaches us as Christians. We know that God is the Creator, the Saviour, the Sustainer, and the Protector of His people. You may not have a flag that visibly displays the great qualities of God. But there are other ways you can proclaim these truths to the world.

Perhaps one of the greatest ways to publicize these truths about God is through your testimony. "Thou hast given a banner," the psalmist wrote, "to them that fear thee." To be an effective Christian witness, one must live a biblically sound life. Our lives will never be perfect, but they can be sincere. Display the truth of God's Word today—not through a flag, but through your life, your obedient choices to Scripture, and your love for others. Someone once said: "Your face is God's billboard." Others are not only watching your behavior, but your attitude as well. No one will have to wonder whom you represent.

Another way to spread the truth of God is through speaking up for Christ through witnessing. Tell those around you of Christ, of the gospel, and of the joy it is to be a child of God.

Geronimo!

4 September 1886

I beseech you therefore, brethren, by the mercies of God, that ye present your bodies a living sacrifice, holy, acceptable unto God, which is your reasonable service. And be not conformed to this world: but be ye transformed by the renewing of your mind, that ye may prove what is that good, and acceptable, and perfect, will of God.—**Romans 12:1–2**

When I was young, my friends and I would often jump from the back of the press box at a local junior high school into a pile of foam designed to cushion the fall of pole vaulters. Each of us would cry out "Geronimo!" as we leapt some fifty feet into the foamy sponges. Have you ever wondered why people yell "Geronimo!" when they jump? It is connected to the legend of the famed Apache warrior.

For decades, Geronimo led raids and incursions against white settlers and the US Army because they had encroached upon his native land. Eventually, Geronimo was tracked down by a US soldier whom he respected. Captain Henry Lawton spoke Apache and was able to convince Geronimo to surrender. On 4 September 1886, the great warrior and his band of followers surrendered to General Nelson Miles in Skeleton Canyon, Arizona. He lived out the remainder of his days as a captive to the US Government. Exclaiming "Geronimo!" originates with the US Army Airborne from World War II, when Private Aubrey Eberhardt shouted "Geronimo!" as he parachuted from his plane during his first training jump.

Surrendering to an opposing army is never easy, and Geronimo required some convincing arguments. But Christians are commanded to surrender ourselves to one higher than a general or king: God Himself. And we can know that when we do, God only has good plans for us. Geronimo would have had real reason to not surrender. But we can surrender to God without reservation or fear, because He is good and loves us. In fact, Romans 12 tells us that when we wholly surrender to God, we will "prove what is that good, and acceptable, and perfect, will of God." Indeed, God's will is best and always worthy of our full surrender.

I Pledge Allegiance

5 September 1836

And Ruth said, Intreat me not to leave thee, or to return from following after thee: for whither thou goest, I will go; and where thou lodgest, I will lodge: thy people shall be my people, and thy God my God:—**Ruth 1:16**

I remember being stationed overseas with my family in the mid-1980s and singer Lee Greenwood came to sing his famous song "I'm Proud to Be an American" as part of a USO show for the troops. The US military went wild when he sang, affirming their allegiance to the United States.

Allegiance is most seen when it is tested. This was the case for Sam Houston. On 5 September 1836, Houston was elected President of the Republic of Texas following the same year's defeat of General Santa Anna at the San Jacinto River. Houston went on to assist Texas in becoming a US state in 1845. In 1861, as the American Civil War loomed on the horizon, Houston was forced to step down after refusing to swear allegiance to the Confederacy. His loyalty to the Texas he had defended remained steadfast, but he could not give loyalty to a cause which he believed would hurt the state he loved.

As Christians, it is essential that we determine where our allegiance lies. Is it with this world or with Christ? Ruth's loyalty to Naomi is easily seen in her promise, "Whither thou goest, I will go." Our devotion to God ought to be even greater than a daughter-in-law's devotion to her mother-in-law.

Jesus taught that believers are to live what they believe in such a way that those around them can easily see. "Neither do men light a candle, and put it under a bushel, but on a candlestick; and it giveth light unto all that are in the house. Let your light so shine before men, that they may see your good works, and glorify your Father which is in heaven" (Matthew 5:15–16).

History records the dying words of many martyrs. Their stories leave no doubt as to their allegiance. Their families, friends, and even persecutors all knew the depth of their faith. Would those who know you best say that you are a committed Christian? Let it be known today that God is the one to whom you have given your allegiance.

Little is Much

6 September 1915

Ye have not chosen me, but I have chosen you, and ordained you, that ye should go and bring forth fruit, and that your fruit should remain:—**John 15:16**

The trench warfare of World War I birthed several technological innovations, not the least of which was the development of the first battle tank. On 6 September 1915, British manufacturers rolled from the assembly line a prototype tank named Little Willie. The tank weighed fourteen tons, lacked any sort of main gun associated with modern tanks and could only travel at about two miles per hour. Although "Little Willie" never saw combat, its creation spawned a generation of tank research and design, which forever changed the face of the battlefield.

I am confident the designers of Little Willie never envisioned the potential of such modern tanks as the M-1 Abrams. Yet, God sees the potential of every child of God no matter how insignificant each might see himself. We see this in Jesus' words to His disciples in John 15 as He envisions for them a future of bearing fruit—of their lives having potential beyond themselves.

This fruit of which Jesus spoke would certainly include leading others to Christ. Do you tend to feel insignificant in the work of your witness? Do you perceive others as better soulwinners or better Bible students than you? Remember, God knew all your strengths and weaknesses. Yet, He has commanded all believers to preach the gospel to every creature (Mark 16:15). In your own view, you may not have the talents or skills that others possess. But, you are still a chosen child of God to help "bring forth fruit"—disciples—into this world.

It's important for us to remember that *God* is the one who uses us, and He is unrestrained by our inadequacies. As the title to the familiar song says, "Little Is Much When God Is in It." Be encouraged in the fact that you have been chosen to bear fruit for Christ, and trust that He will do what you cannot do: bear spiritual fruit that remains.

Secure in His Son

7 September 1940

To the praise of the glory of his grace, wherein he hath made us accepted in the beloved.—**Ephesians 1:6**

Peter Foster was a Royal Air Force pilot during World War II. Toward the end of the Battle of Britain, on 7 September 1940, three hundred German bombers raided London. For fifty-seven consecutive nights, the Germans bombed London in an attempt to get them out of the war so Hitler could focus on the Eastern Front. The raid became known as the London Blitz.

Among the aircraft used to defend London was the Royal Air Force Hawker Hurricane. A single-seat fighter, the Hurricanes resembled mosquitoes pestering the big German bombers. The Hurricane was effective except for one design flaw. The fuel lines were mounted alongside the cockpit. In a direct projectile hit, the pilot would instantly be engulfed in flames before he could eject. The consequences were often tragic. Some Royal Air Force pilots caught in that inferno would undergo ten or twenty surgeries to reconstruct their faces. Peter Foster ended up one of the downed pilots whose face was burned beyond recognition.

As Foster's release from the hospital drew near, he wondered about his family's acceptance. Fortunately, Foster had the support of his family and the love of his fiancée. She assured him that nothing had changed except a few millimeters of skin. Two years later, they got married. Foster said of his wife, "She became my mirror. She gave me a new image of myself. When I look at her, she gives me a warm, loving smile that tells me I'm okay."

Those who have received Christ are fully accepted and never need to wonder about their acceptance. God has made us "accepted in the beloved." On the merits of Jesus Christ, we have been received unconditionally. This means that nothing we do or don't do can affect His love for us or His acceptance of us as His children. If you are saved, you are secure in His Son. And that is a reason to rejoice!

A Wayward Wreck

8 September 1923

There is a way which seemeth right unto a man, but the end thereof are the ways of death.—**Proverbs 14:12**

A multi-ship pileup at sea has happened only once in recorded history. Officially known as Point Pedernales or Honda Point, the Devil's Jaw is located a few miles from the northern entrance of the heavily-traveled Santa Barbara Channel. A squadron of fourteen US Navy destroyers was traveling at twenty knots from San Francisco Bay along a southern course into the Santa Barbara Channel. The flagship *Delphy's* crew decided to use the imprecise technique of dead reckoning to navigate her course. Depth soundings could not be taken, as the ships were sailing at full speed. Instead, sea charts were cross-checked against Radio Direction Finding (RDF) signals from Point Arguello, a few miles south of Honda Point. They expected to sail into the Channel, but Point Arguello reported their position still too far north. RDF technology, though, was still new and unproven; the USS *Delphy* led its fleet eastward, ignoring its location information.

As the ships entered a thick fog that evening, the ship captains did not realize their vessels were several miles farther northeast than it seemed. About five minutes after making her turn, the *Delphy* slammed into the Honda shore and stuck fast. A few hundred yards behind, the USS *S. P. Lee* turned hard to port, but also struck the hidden coast to the north of *Delphy*. The USS *Young* behind the *S. P. Lee* had no time to turn before ripping her hull open on submerged rocks. The *Young* quickly capsized. Before it was all over, on 8 September 1923, seven of the fourteen destroyers resembled a derailed locomotive in shallow water. The Devil's Jaw disaster was the greatest peacetime loss of US Navy ships. The navigator and captain had dismissed their indicated bearings as erroneous. Eleven officers were court-martialed, and twenty-three sailors died.

Do you follow God's Word, or do you find yourself making life choices based on what "seems right"? Making decisions that are not in alignment with God's will lead to spiritual shipwreck (1 Timothy 1:19).

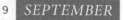

He Knows My Name

9 September 1987

But the very hairs of your head are all numbered.—**Matthew 10:30**

On 9 September 1987, I was sent on a TDY (temporary duty) to Andrews Air Force Base, Maryland, from Lajes Field, Azores, Portugal. My family and I had only been stationed on the island of Terceira in Portugal for about eleven months when I was directed to travel back to the States to learn how to perform medical ultrasound. My TDY was about six weeks, and while I was away we received permission to move from the local village where we resided, to on-base housing, which was on the other side of the island. With me being back in the States, it fell to my wife to move with our two sons, one of whom was newborn. Thankfully, my First Sergeant and some dear military friends helped her, but my wife handled the lion's share of the burden. After they moved into the new house, our twenty-three-month-old son, Joshua, began behaving strangely. He was terrified that, due to the move, I would not be able to find them when I returned from the States. In his mind, since the house was different and on a different part of the island, how would his daddy ever find him or be with him again? This caused such consternation in his heart that my wife would constantly reassure him that his daddy knew where to find us, what color his new room was, knew the street it was on, and even knew the house number. When I would call from the States, I would describe landmarks to him that he could relate to his new location. It worked, and he calmed down once he understood his father knew where he was.

There are times when we feel as if our heavenly Father does not know what we are going through. But if God has numbered "the very hairs of your head," He knows and sees each trial and temptation you may be facing today. Rest assured today that He knows all, sees all, and is always watching over us. Even a sparrow does not fall to the ground without the Father's knowledge (Matthew 10:29). Take comfort that God has not forgotten you, and give Him your burdens. He knows them, and He is willing to carry them for you.

Seasoned with Salt

10 September 1944

A soft answer turneth away wrath: but grievous words stir up anger.
—Proverbs 15:1

In the spring of 1944, Allied leaders began formulating a strategy for how best to pursue and defeat the German army following D-Day. General Dwight D. Eisenhower, Supreme Allied Expeditionary Force Commander, wanted to employ a broad-front strategy to keep the Germans from building up a firm defensive line. The alternative to the broad front strategy was a narrower, "pencil-like thrust" through Arnhem straight into Berlin.

The strategic debate between two high-ranking war officials escalated. Eisenhower and the ranking British officer of the war, Field Marshal Bernard (Monty) Montgomery, met together. This was in keeping with the custom that the senior officer should visit his subordinates. On Eisenhower, Montgomery once commented: "His ignorance as to how to run a war is absolute and complete." On 10 September 1944, aboard Eisenhower's aircraft parked on the tarmac at Brussels airport, the military meeting began innocently. But then Montgomery launched into an intemperate and foolish outburst. In language fit for a drill instructor addressing recruits, Montgomery berated Eisenhower's plan, insisting it would not work. Eisenhower patiently sat in stony silence. When Montgomery at last paused for breath, Eisenhower put his hand on Montgomery's knee and gently said, "Steady, Monty! You cannot speak to me like that. I'm your boss." Humbled, Montgomery muttered, "I'm sorry, Ike," and the meeting concluded.

How often, when you are angry, do you give a "soft answer"? Responding with fury to an injustice, even if the opposing party is in the wrong, is a sure way to erode a Christian's testimony. The Bible admonishes us that the best way to defuse an argument is by letting our speech be always with grace and "seasoned with salt" (Colossians 4:6). Salt, while used as a preservative for food, can also serve to preserve peace between Christian brothers and sisters. Be kind and, if you must disagree, do so with grace.

To Glory

11 September 1697

For the Lord God will help me; therefore shall I not be confounded: therefore have I set my face like a flint, and I know that I shall not be ashamed.—**Isaiah 50:7**

On the morning of 11 September 1697, Austrian commander Prince Eugene of Savoy could see an army of Turks crossing the Tisza River near the town of Zenta on their way to pillage Transylvania. The Turkish army, though twice the size of Eugene's imperialist force, foolishly divided itself on both sides of the river. A priceless opportunity presented itself for the young Austrian prince to prove his mettle against a feared and vaunted foe. A subordinate presented Prince Eugene with a letter from King Leopold, which he knew contained a petition for the Austrians to retreat. The letter stayed sealed. Eugene advanced.

The Turkish artillery ineffectively unleashed their volley against Eugene's army. The prince commanded his troops to flank the right side of those nearest to his side of the river. Forced into the river, thousands of Turks drowned under heavy loads of equipment. Eugene later said, "Men could stand on the dead Turkish bodies as if on an island." In the end, some twenty thousand dead Turks littered the field of battle, and ten thousand more drifted in the Tisza River. Eugene returned victorious to Vienna on 17 November to great fanfare. Two years later, the Ottoman Empire finally fell, and the Treaty of Karlowitz awarded the Habsburgs possession of both Hungary and Transylvania. Austria now ruled central Europe—and it all stemmed from the Battle of Zenta and an unopened letter requesting retreat.

Prince Eugene could have taken the easy way out and returned to Austria. After all, he had the king's permission to do it. Nevertheless, he chose to advance and won a great victory for king and country. Many times in life, Satan attempts to get our eyes off the "prize of the high calling of God in Christ Jesus" (Philippians 3:14) by offering an easier path. Like our Lord on His way to Calvary "set his face like a flint," determined to do the will of the Father, may we as Christian soldiers do the same for Christ.

A Legacy for the Lord

12 September 2012

Children's children are the crown of old men; and the glory of children are their fathers.—**Proverbs 17:6**

On 12 September 2012, Cooper Scott Wells was born. As our only grandson, he holds a special place in our hearts. When he was around two years old, I began teaching him about military history. I used a method I knew would resonate with him: plastic army men. But these were not your ordinary dime store bags of cheap plastic figures. I had begun collecting high-end 54mm plastic figures several years before he was born with the intent of teaching him about the world's various armies. By the time he was four, he could tell me the difference between a third century BC Carthaginian soldier and a medieval Norman man-at-arms from the 1400s just by glancing at the figurine. Cooper appreciates this activity not only because it gives him time with me, but also because he knows he descends from a long line of men on his father's side who have served in the military. I, his grandfather, served in the Air Force; his paternal great-grandfather served in the Marines during Vietnam. Both his paternal great-great grandfathers fought in World War II, and his paternal third great-grandfather was a combat engineer during World War I. His paternal fifth great-grandfather fought in the Civil War. To top it off, his paternal seventeenth great-grandfather fought with King Henry VI at the Battle of Towton in 1461!

Heritage is important—and, while a military heritage is commendable, a godly heritage is much more important. As parents and grandparents, we should always be mindful that someone is watching our lives. As parents, we will never be "the glory of children" by going AWOL from godliness and family devotion to God. Children are God's gifts to you. Let your godly life be your gift to them, and one day they can tell their own children how they grew up under the leadership of godly parents.

At a Moment's Notice

13 September 1759

But sanctify the Lord God in your hearts: and be ready always to give an answer to every man that asketh you a reason of the hope that is in you with meekness and fear:—**1 Peter 3:15**

Just past midnight on 13 September 1759, Major General James Wolfe and a force of more than four thousand British Redcoats rowed silently up the St. Lawrence River to launch an assault on the town of Quebec. French, Canadian, and Indian troops were stationed in the city and along miles of riverfront fortresses. Wolfe decided to send his army upriver to a sheltered cove called Anse de Foulon, where they could meet the French in open battle on the Plains of Abraham. The Major General gave strict orders for complete silence so as not to reveal their position. In the quiet September darkness, British forces embarked in rowboats. Their advance was spotted by a French sentry who assumed that the boats contained French supplies. He issued a call in French. The attack now hung in the balance. If the city defenders were alerted, the French could prevent the landing and realistically destroy Wolfe's men in their boats.

A quick-thinking Scottish Highlander immediately answered the challenge in perfect French. He convinced the sentry that the boats held cargo bound from settlements in the interior. The sentry was persuaded. Wolfe's men scaled the 175-foot bluffs and began a battle with the French that lasted only fifteen minutes at most. The British secured the city of Quebec for North America as the French retreated. Three years into the French and Indian War, the capture of Quebec had just decided the fate of North America, and General Wolfe was forever memorialized in the annals of British military history. It was all thanks to a Scotsman who was ready to answer a sentry's call.

As Bible believers, we must be ready at a moment's notice to give an answer to those who ask about our faith. Do you hesitate when given an opportunity to defend your beliefs? Or are you ready to share the gospel and tell others about Christ any time there is an opportunity or need?

Fit for the Occasion

14 September 1901

I will greatly rejoice in the LORD, my soul shall be joyful in my God; for he hath clothed me with the garments of salvation, he hath covered me with the robe of righteousness, as a bridegroom decketh himself with ornaments, and as a bride adorneth herself with her jewels.—**Isaiah 61:10**

The first time Theodore Roosevelt took the presidential oath of office on 14 September 1901, he was unprepared. His ascension to the presidency was so unexpected that he was forced to wear borrowed clothes to his own inauguration ceremony. Just hours before, he had been hiking high in the Adirondacks when he received word that President McKinley had died of a gunshot wound sustained in an assassination attempt. As vice president, Roosevelt urgently needed something fitting to wear. He scrambled to borrow a frock coat, a pair of striped trousers, a waistcoat, a neck tie and shiny leather shoes, in the hopes that he might be sworn in as president like a proper-looking gentleman.

When Judgment Day arrives, there is only one "suit" of clothes that will pass muster and it will not be the filthy rags of our own self-righteousness. Only those clothed in the perfect, spotless righteousness of the Lord Jesus Christ will enjoy eternity with the Lord. In Jesus' parable of the wedding feast, He told of many who were invited to a wedding for the king's son, but they refused to come. Then the king sent his servants out to invite not just the friends of the king, but *anyone*. Many came, but one man was not wearing a "wedding garment." (This garment would have been provided by the king. For the guest to refuse it was to spurn the king's provision.) The king asked him why he was not wearing the wedding garment. "And he was speechless. Then said the king to the servants, Bind him hand and foot, and take him away, and cast him into outer darkness; there shall be weeping and gnashing of teeth" (Matthew 22:12–13). And so it will be at the end of this world. Jesus has made every provision for us to wear the "garments of salvation" and a "robe of righteousness." If we do not trust Christ as our Saviour, we are spurning the provision He has made for us.

Sacrifice

15 September 1922

But God, who is rich in mercy, for his great love wherewith he loved us, Even when we were dead in sins, hath quickened us together with Christ, (by grace ye are saved;) And hath raised us up together, and made us sit together in heavenly places in Christ Jesus: That in the ages to come he might shew the exceeding riches of his grace in his kindness toward us through Christ Jesus.—**Ephesians 2:4–7**

Rin Tin Tin is a name associated with one of the most beloved animals in film history. The iconic German Shepherd, Rin Tin Tin, or Rinty as his owner called him, was rescued by an American World War I "Doughboy" during the Battle of Saint-Mihiel. Corporal Lee Duncan, a gunner for the 135th Aero Squadron, was on a scouting mission for a suitable airfield in the French village of Flirey when he happened upon a kennel containing a starving mother and five nursing Shepherd puppies. Heartbroken for the dogs, Duncan brought them back to his unit and cared for them until the pups were weaned. He kept a male and a female, whom he named Rin Tin Tin and Nanette. Later, Duncan parlayed the talented Rin Tin Tin into a silent film "star" in 1922. Some twenty-eight years after his death, Rin Tin Tin was honored with a star on Hollywood's Walk of Fame.

In many ways, we can all identify with that famous pup, starving and just waiting for someone to come along and rescue him. Like Corporal Duncan, the Lord Jesus Christ came to seek and to save the lost and He specializes in rescuing the perishing and giving purpose to those He has redeemed.

I love the phrases in the verses above that describe God as "rich in mercy" and as having a "great love wherewith he loved us." Christ did not die for us because of what He could get from us, any more than Corporal Duncan rescued Rin Tin Tin for what the corporal could gain. Duncan simply had compassion on a family of starving dogs.

Best of all for us, Christ not only rescued us from sin, but He gave us a new purpose: "to show the exceeding riches of his grace." Our very salvation showcases the grace of God.

Delays and Distractions

16 September 1620

Wherefore seeing we also are compassed about with so great a cloud of witnesses, let us lay aside every weight, and the sin which doth so easily beset us, and let us run with patience the race that is set before us, Looking unto Jesus the author and finisher of our faith; who for the joy that was set before him endured the cross, despising the shame, and is set down at the right hand of the throne of God.
—Hebrews 12:1–2

The story of the *Mayflower* is one of the most well-known and beloved historical facts in our nation's history. I recall learning about it as a grade-schooler and watching Thanksgiving cartoons about the Pilgrims and this famous vessel. While most know that the *Mayflower* landed in Massachusetts on 16 September 1620, what some don't know is that they could have arrived earlier had it not been for a sister ship called the *Speedwell*. The *Speedwell* sailed from the Netherlands to Southampton with the intent of sailing alongside the *Mayflower* to America. Three times, however, the *Speedwell* developed leaks and had to return to England, each time delaying the *Mayflower*. Frustrated with the enormous amount of time lost and their inability to maintain the *Speedwell*, those on board the *Mayflower* eventually made the decision to leave the *Speedwell* behind and sail on to America alone.

We can get sidelined and delayed in our goals in this life, and like the *Mayflower*, our timetable may not always be what we planned. Nevertheless, God encourages us to keep our focus on Jesus and to remember that His delays are always for our good.

Remember, God's delays are not necessarily God's denials. Perhaps there has been an unintentional problem or obstacle along the way and you feel beset by difficulty and unable to move forward. Trust God and His timing. Psalm 18:30 tells us, "As for God, his way is perfect." Above all, keep your eyes on Christ. He faithfully ran His race, and He will give you the grace and endurance to run yours.

Knowing Is Not Enough

17 September 1862

For the king knoweth of these things, before whom also I speak freely: for I am persuaded that none of these things are hidden from him; for this thing was not done in a corner.—**Acts 26:26**

As the summer of 1862 faded, Confederate General Robert E. Lee hoped that a decisive Confederate victory would persuade the British to recognize Southern independence and give their support. He determined to lead his Army of Northern Virginia into Maryland to divert Union pressure away from the Shenandoah Valley.

Assuming the Union army would require time to rebuild following their defeat at Second Manassas, Lee decided to divide his forces, sending General "Stonewall" Jackson's corps to take Harpers Ferry while General Longstreet proceeded towards Sharpsburg, Maryland. Lee informed his two generals of the strategy in a secretive plan known as Order Number 191. In a strange twist of fate, Lee's Order was found wrapped around three cigars in a field by a Union soldier and delivered to Union General George McClellan. With Lee's secret plan in Union hands, one would think McClellan would have capitalized on the new intelligence. Instead, he allowed seventeen hours to elapse before moving to face Lee's army on 17 September. The delay allowed the Confederates time to regroup, resulting in the Battle of Antietam that became the bloodiest single day in all of American history.

General McClellan failed to act quickly on a vital piece of military information, and it cost his troops dearly. But, King Agrippa made an even greater mistake. He heard the greatest news—the gospel—and yet he chose not to put his trust in Jesus Christ. Knowing is not enough. After all, King Agrippa is only one of the thousands of people throughout history who knew the gospel, yet failed to receive Christ. "Behold, now is the day of salvation," says 2 Corinthians 6:2. The consequences of neglecting enemy intelligence do not compare to the penalty of ignoring the gospel. Do not be guilty of simply *knowing*.

Exercise to Engage

18 September 1941

But refuse profane and old wives' fables, and exercise thyself rather unto godliness. For bodily exercise profiteth little: but godliness is profitable unto all things, having promise of the life that now is, and of that which is to come.—**1 Timothy 4:7–8**

In October 2017, I went to work for the Office of the Inspector General at Edwards Air Force Base, California. My job title is Senior Exercise Planner, which entails planning and executing various types of mission assurance and war readiness exercises. I help test the base's ability to respond to contingency situations. These activities are extremely rewarding, and they are part of a long tradition of military training.

Before the US entered World War II, there was a great need for logistical training of large-scale maneuvers in modern warfare. To this purpose, the US Army created the "Louisiana Maneuvers"—a massive exercise involving over 3,400 square miles of territory.

On 18 September 1941, some 400,000 troops assembled in northern and west-central Louisiana to evaluate their training, logistics, doctrine, and command. The soldiers were divided into two teams representing fictitious countries—Kotmk and Almat. (They were also called the Red Army and Blue Army respectively.) Through the training, our troops gained valuable practice experience, and many of the officers who would become leaders of World War II proved their leadership potential.

While physical exercise prepares a national soldier, spiritual exercise prepares a spiritual soldier. How are you doing with "exercising" yourself "unto godliness"? Are you regularly engaging in the spiritual disciplines that develop Christian growth? These include time in God's Word and prayer, regular church attendance, fellowship with God's people, and more. Hebrews 5:14 specifically tells us that there is some Christian maturity that comes only "by reason of use": "But strong meat belongeth to them that are of full age, even those who by reason of use have their senses exercised to discern both good and evil." Practice is the key to developing as a Christian soldier and being ready for the inevitable spiritual battles you will face.

Carrying the Hurt

19 September 1863

For I reckon that the sufferings of this present time are not worthy to be compared with the glory which shall be revealed in us.—**Romans 8:18**

Private Jacob C. Miller served in the 9th Indiana Volunteer Infantry during the American Civil War. On the morning of 19 September 1863, Private Miller was wounded at the Battle of Chickamauga, a battle considered the most significant Union defeat in the Western Theatre of the war. While hundreds of thousands of soldiers suffered wounds in the Civil War, Miller's wound was one of a kind. He was shot right between the eyes with a musket and left for dead. Shockingly, he survived. Miller regained consciousness and made his way back to his own lines with a hole in his head.

Seventeen years after Miller was shot at Chickamauga, the musket ball dropped out of his wound. And, thirty-one years after, another two pieces of lead came out. Imagine going about your daily life for decades—all with buckshot in your head!

While we do not all experience the type of physical pain Miller did, we all carry hurt. And sometimes we struggle to keep our hurts in perspective.

Romans 8:18 reminds us that the difficulties we face now are "the sufferings of this present time," and it tells us that, in light of the glory awaiting us in eternity, these present sufferings don't even deserve to be compared.

No matter how much you may endure in this life, don't lose sight of eternity. And when you do lose perspective, as all of us do at times, read Romans 8 to regain the larger, truer picture. Revelation 21:4 assures us, "God shall wipe away all tears from their eyes; and there shall be no more death, neither sorrow, nor crying, neither shall there be any more pain: for the former things are passed away." The old song says it this way: "There is coming a day when no heartaches shall come, no more clouds in the sky, no more tears to dim the eye." If you're carrying pain today, cast your burden on the Lord. He will sustain you (Psalm 55:22).

All In

20 September 1187

Again, the kingdom of heaven is like unto treasure hid in a field; the which when a man hath found, he hideth, and for joy thereof goeth and selleth all that he hath, and buyeth that field.—**Matthew 13:44**

The Crusades—a series of religious wars between Catholic and Islamic armies—took place in the eleventh and twelfth centuries. In 1185, King Guy of Lusignan was crowned King of Jerusalem upon the death of Baldwin V. On 20 September 1187, Muslim forces led by Egyptian Sultan Saladin began a siege of Jerusalem culminating in the Second Crusade.

During the Battle of Hattin in the summer of 1187, Guy's military forces were defeated by Saladin, who took him captive. Guy's wife, Queen Sybil, retreated to the city of Ascalon, along with her two daughters. For a year, she defended her city against Saladin's forces while pleading for her husband's release. Finally, in the fall of 1188, Sybil surrendered Ascalon to Saladin in exchange for the release of her beloved husband. Notably, during the twelfth century, women were not accepted as negotiators on behalf of a kingdom. Sybil proved a most unlikely mediator, motivated by her great love for Guy.

Queen Sybil prized her husband enough to fight for his release at great personal cost. In truth, love *always* costs something. Jesus loved us so much that He gave His life for us. Our love for Him, if it is genuine, will not be without sacrifice. Christ is so good and so worth our full loyalty that we should be like the man who found the treasure in the field and sold all he had so he could own it. What sacrifice for Christ is too great to make when we consider the great sacrifice He made for us on the cross?

Are you all in, or is living the Christian life a mere hobby? Let us follow the admonition of Romans 12:1, "I beseech you therefore, brethren, by the mercies of God, that ye present your bodies a living sacrifice, holy, acceptable unto God, which is your reasonable service." It is only reasonable that we would give 100 percent to Him who gave His all for us. It is our honor to be all in for Jesus Christ.

Salt of the Earth

21 September 454

Ye are the salt of the earth: but if the salt have lost his savour, wherewith shall it be salted? it is thenceforth good for nothing, but to be cast out, and to be trodden under foot of men.—**Matthew 5:13**

Often called the "last of the Romans," Flavius Aetius spent the majority of his military career in service of the Visigoths, who had taken him hostage upon his father's death.

Born at the turn of the fourth century, Aetius is perhaps best known for his temporarily delaying the disintegration of the Roman Empire. Aetius possessed a knack for playing one group of barbarians against the other, which led to his assembling a coalition of forces to battle the Huns. In 451, he amassed an army of Romans, Franks, and Visigoths to defeat an invasion of Gaul by Attila the Hun. His exploits likely saved Western civilization in the process, as Attila withdrew back across the Rhine. On 21 September 454, Aetius was assassinated by Emperor Valentinian III in Rome. It was later said that Valentinian had "cut off his left hand with his right." Twenty-two years later, the Western Roman Empire was divided, absorbed by barbarians, and ceased to exist.

Aetius did what he could to preserve the Roman Empire. Sadly, his efforts drew the ire of the very people he tried to help. The Lord Jesus exhorts us to be the "salt of the earth," as salt is a preservative. Like Aetius, our efforts are likely to be despised by the world, but that should never excuse us from being a preserving agent to stall the spiritual decline we see around us.

We should not be surprised when those who hate Christ also hate us. "Marvel not, my brethren, if the world hate you" (1 John 3:13). As long as we continue to live the Christian life as we should, unsaved people will present resistance to us and the godly principles for which we stand. Be the "salt" anyway—be a light shining in the darkness of this ungodly world. Some will notice and will desire your inner peace, joy, and wisdom. When they do, be sure to give God the glory. Stay distinct; point people to Christ.

An Unexpected Tactic

22 September 1914

For ye see your calling, brethren, how that not many wise men after the flesh, not many mighty, not many noble, are called: But God hath chosen the foolish things of the world to confound the wise; and God hath chosen the weak things of the world to confound the things which are mighty;—**1 Corinthians 1:26–27**

During World War I, U-boats proved a significant threat to Allied shipping. For instance, on 22 September 1914, the German U-boat SM *U-9* torpedoed and sank three British cruisers in less than an hour. Without the advent of sonar or radar, World War I U-boats were virtually undetectable unless they surfaced to launch an attack. Thanks to a device called a periscope, U-boat commanders could choose to attack completely submerged, essentially invisible to their prey. To accomplish this, they would raise the small periscope lens a few inches above the surface of the water to line up their quarry for a torpedo shot.

In response, the British sought for a way to take out these annoying submarines that were capable of disappearing at will. That's when the British noticed that the one weakness appeared to be the brief window of time when the periscope poked up through the water's surface. In an unorthodox approach, the British placed sailors on small boats and instructed them that, upon seeing a periscope, they were to sail close enough to have one man place a bag over it while another smacked it with a large hammer. It is amusingly reminiscent of the "Whack-A-Mole" game children enjoy today.

Sometimes, Christians incorrectly assume that God approaches problems as we would. In reality, God is not bound by man's methods or plans. In fact, God delights in using weak people and unlikely means to accomplish His will.

So, if you're facing a "periscope trouble" that leaves you at your wit's end for solutions, don't despair. And don't assume God can't use you as part of the solution. God doesn't look for the superb; He looks for the surrendered.

"I Have Not Yet Begun to Fight!"

23 September 1779

Now when he had left speaking, he said unto Simon, Launch out into the deep, and let down your nets for a draught. And Simon answering said unto him, Master, we have toiled all the night, and have taken nothing: nevertheless at thy word I will let down the net. And when they had this done, they inclosed a great multitude of fishes: and their net brake.—**Luke 5:4–6**

Long regarded as the "father of the modern Navy," John Paul Jones accepted a congressional appointment as a lieutenant in the nascent Continental Navy. Thanks to the efforts of Benjamin Franklin, he was granted a captaincy of the USS *Bonhomme Richard.* On 23 September 1779, he suddenly encountered two British vessels, the *Serapis* and the *Countess of Scarborough,* as they were escorting some merchant ships off the eastern coast of England. Impressively, Jones chose to engage the two warships in British waters.

In this skirmish known as the Battle of Flamborough Head, Jones succeeded in capturing the two British warships after a protracted and bitter duel. During the fight, Jones was famously reported to have shouted, "I have not yet begun to fight!" in response to his opponent's demand that he surrender the *Bonhomme Richard.* The battle proved a major embarrassment for the British Navy and forever cemented Jones' place in the annals of naval history.

Jones, with one ship, faced the enemy's force of two ships, yet succeeded. In contrast, Simon Peter felt discouraged in his one ship after a fruitless night of fishing. At Jesus' command, however, Peter let down the net, and drew a great multitude of fish.

When you do something courageous without God's leading, success isn't guaranteed. But when you, in obedience to Christ, "launch out" to do His will, you can count on God's presence to be with you all the way. God memorialized the names of those who stepped out in faith in Hebrews 11, including Abraham, Sarah, Isaac, Jacob, and Joseph. Acting in faith is better than self-reliant courage, for it pleases God (Hebrews 11:6).

Hero with a Horn

24 September 1942

But charge Joshua, and encourage him, and strengthen him: for he shall go over before this people, and he shall cause them to inherit the land which thou shalt see.—**Deuteronomy 3:28**

One of the most recognizable military officers of World War II never fired a shot in anger, never collected ribbons for gallantry, and never participated in a major battle. Glenn Miller, an accomplished trombone player, had formed a swing band in the 1930s that was earning a staggering $800,000 a year by 1940. Once the United States entered the war, Miller decided to leave his lucrative career as a bandleader so he could serve his country. On 24 September 1942, he officially broke up his band and was commissioned a captain in the US Army Air Corps. For the next two years, Miller served in the 418th Army Air Forces Band, encouraging the morale of countless soldiers, sailors, airmen, and marines. Sadly, the plane in which Miller was traveling mysteriously disappeared over the English Channel in late 1944, and he was never seen again.

Encouragement is a powerful force, and Glenn Miller knew how to use it. Sometimes we think of service for the Lord primarily in terms of the direct results of our labor—the people we personally are able to lead to Christ, teach, disciple, or minister to in some way. But we also serve the Lord as we encourage others in the fight. Think of Moses. Not only did he faithfully serve by leading the children of Israel out of Egypt and through the wilderness to the Promised Land, but he further served the Lord and Israel by encouraging Joshua to rise to *his* moment of leadership.

Do you know someone who is wavering about ministering for Christ? Remind them that He will be with them always, "even unto the end of the world" (Matthew 28:18–20). Do you know someone who struggles to overcome a fear of witnessing? Remind them that "the Lord will be [their] confidence" (Proverbs 3:26). Do you know someone grieving or hurting? Encourage them to cast their burden on the Lord (Psalm 55:22). In humility and in the right timing, seek to give others a Spirit-led word of support.

Black Hawk Down

25 September 1993

It seemed good unto us, being assembled with one accord, to send chosen men unto you with our beloved Barnabas and Paul, Men that have hazarded their lives for the name of our Lord Jesus Christ. We have sent therefore Judas and Silas, who shall also tell you the same things by mouth.—**Acts 15:25–27**

During the Clinton administration, the United States found herself embroiled in the factional fighting between rival warlords in the country of Somalia. As part of Operation Restore Hope, US Special Operations Forces deployed troops to Mogadishu, where the situation had worsened. On 25 September 1993, a US Blackhawk helicopter was shot down by Somali rebels. Almost immediately, US and Pakistani forces braved enemy fire, secured the downed aircraft, and evacuated the casualties. The incident was dramatized in the 2001 Hollywood film *Black Hawk Down*.

War is fraught with danger, and life for first-century Christians had its hazards as well. Acts 15 praises Paul and Barnabas for putting their own lives in danger for the sake of Christ. Preaching the gospel in first-century Rome could cost not only jail time, but also one's life. The Lord does not always ask us to put our lives in danger for others, but are we willing to share the gospel even when we face ridicule or mockery?

One of my favorite hymns is "Rescue the Perishing" by Fannie Crosby. The fourth stanza of that hymn begins with the words, "Rescue the perishing, duty demands it." Duty drove those brave US and Pakistani soldiers into dangerous territory to retrieve helicopter crewmen. And today, duty demands that we tell others that a "Saviour has died" for them.

The Lord Jesus Christ Himself has commissioned us. "And he said unto them, Go ye into all the world, and preach the gospel to every creature" (Mark 16:15). When was the last time you witnessed to someone? Does fear of ridicule or loss hold you back? If we believe that the gospel is the most important news anyone can receive, why would we keep it to ourselves? God has given us the "ministry of reconciliation" (2 Corinthians 5:18); let us never disregard our duty.

Soviet Missile

26 September 1983

Moreover by them is thy servant warned: and in keeping of them there is great reward.—**Psalm 19:11**

A chilling experience marked my first two months in the US Air Force. At the time referred to as the Cold War, there was a perpetual state of active tension between the United States and the Soviet Union. One wrong diplomatic, political, or military move could have disastrous results. A little after midnight on 26 September 1983, the Soviet Union's early warning missile detector system reported an incoming American intercontinental ballistic missile (ICBM). Thankfully, a Soviet officer realized that their warning system must have malfunctioned because an American-first strike would surely involve hundreds of missiles as opposed to just one. Had the officer acted in accordance with Soviet policy, he would have initiated an immediate and compulsory nuclear counterattack against the United States, which would surely have resulted in World War III. Today, we can all be thankful that someone recognized a glitch in the Soviet's early warning system.

God's Word is, in itself, a source of warning and admonition. It admonishes us of our need for a Saviour (John 3:36). Unlike the Soviet warning system, the Word of God is always correct. David testified that by God's judgements "is thy servant warned." He recognized the great guiding power of God's Word in helping him avoid sin.

Additionally, there is "great reward" in keeping the Word of God. When we follow the biblical admonition to pray, God grants us peace (Philippians 4:6–7). When we apply the command to wait on the Lord patiently, He renews our strength (Isaiah 40:29–31). And when we follow God's guidance to give to His work, He promises that we will reap as bountifully as we give (2 Corinthians 9:6).

Recognizing the reliability of God's warnings and the blessings of following His Word, we should be quick to respond to His warnings and careful to follow His commands.

Isaiah 1–2 // Galatians 5

Give Me Liberty

27 September 1941

Stand fast therefore in the liberty wherewith Christ hath made us free, and be not entangled again with the yoke of bondage.—**Galatians 5:1**

One of the most emblematic examples of America's mass production effort during World War II was in the manufacturing and launching of liberty ships. These ships were classified as cargo vessels, designed to carry both men and materials to the front lines. The United States was able to turn out approximately three liberty ships every two days for a total of 2,751 ships. In fact, the United States was able to make liberty ships faster than the enemy could sink them. The first liberty ship, the SS *Patrick Henry*, was launched on 27 September 1941, following a speech by President Roosevelt. The production program of these ships proved vital to the Allied war effort.

Patrick Henry, as the inspiration for the first liberty ship name, said the famous line, "Give me liberty, or give me death." But, beyond any liberties that people now enjoy in the US, Christ offers liberty from sin to all who will believe. Paul's admonition to us is that we "stand fast" in that liberty. The freedom Christ gives is not freedom *to* sin. Rather, the Lord gives us freedom to abstain *from* sin—to "be not entangled again with the yoke of bondage." Titus 2:11–12 tells us that God's grace gives us the power to deny sinful desires and live godly lives: "For the grace of God that bringeth salvation hath appeared to all men, Teaching us that, denying ungodliness and worldly lusts, we should live soberly, righteously, and godly, in this present world."

Do you experience the freedom Christ grants us from sin? Not all Christians do. That is why Paul, under the Holy Spirit's guidance, challenged us in Galatians to "stand fast" in that liberty. Whatever sin may have crept into your life, confess it. "If we confess our sins, he is faithful and just to forgive us our sins, and to cleanse us from all unrighteousness" (1 John 1:9). God stands ready to restore fellowship with you. Don't let anything rob you of the liberty Christ has purchased for you.

The Battle of Yorktown

28 September 1781

Thy testimonies also are my delight and my counsellors.—**Psalm 119:24**

On 28 September 1781, the Battle of Yorktown began. This historic battle would prove the defining moment for Washington's Continental Army and end further British land operations in North America. British Commander Lord Cornwallis retreated to the Yorktown peninsula in June 1781 to rest and refit his worn-out army. Meanwhile, General George Washington stationed his army outside New York in preparation of an assault. When news arrived that a thirty-four-ship armada of French ships, coming to aid the Continental Army, was heading for Virginia, Washington abandoned New York and ordered all available forces to relocate to Virginia in hopes of surrounding Cornwallis.

Knowing he was trapped, Cornwallis asked the British fleet and army in New York for help. The British fleet clashed with French ships off the Virginia Capes in one of the most important—yet least known—naval battles of history. The outnumbered British stuck to their rigidly conservative fighting instructions and sailed their ships in a tidy, straight line while French Admiral De Grasse battered the British ships in a two-and-a-half-hour struggle. The results destroyed any chance for Cornwallis to get reinforcements. On 19 October 1781, Cornwallis finally surrendered.

The British Navy's unrealistic and inept fighting instructions were greatly responsible for their ship losses. Christians, however, have an infallible set of life instructions that will never lead them astray. The psalmist described the words of God as his *delight* and his *counselors.* Do you rejoice in having access to the very Word of God? Do you turn to it for direction and counsel along life's path? When we do not follow God's Word and His prescription for life, we should not be surprised when we end up on the rocks and shipwreck. No matter how formidable a decision or situation you are facing today, the Bible can give you the counsel you need. "Thy word is a lamp unto my feet, and a light unto my path" (Psalm 119:105).

Accommodation Leads to Atrocity

29 September 1938

Neither give place to the devil.—**Ephesians 4:27**

One of the more demoralizing decisions British Prime Minister Neville Chamberlain made during his life was the signing of the Munich Pact on 29 September 1938. After becoming Chancellor of Germany in January 1933, Adolf Hitler set his sights on dominating Europe. In March 1938, Hitler annexed the nation of Austria as the western allies did nothing. The following month, he sought to grab the Sudetenland, an area in the northwestern part of the Czech Republic on the border with Germany that had been formally allocated to Czechoslovakia following Germany's defeat during World War I. Furious over the way Germany was treated at the Treaty of Versailles, Hitler wanted the Sudetenland back and planned to annex it like he had Austria.

A German politician in Czechoslovakia—Konrad Henlein—produced a series of demands known as the Carlsbad Program. The document detailed conditions for Sudetenland to be given to Germany. When the Czech government recognized Hitler's plans, they mobilized 400,000 troops. Riots followed. France and England expressed verbal support of Czechoslovakia but did little militarily. As Hitler's anger built, the neutral French government suggested the British Prime Minister should meet with Hitler. Chamberlain viewed this opportunity as a display of British strength; Hitler viewed it as a sign of weakness. Despite protests by British generals, Chamberlain caved to Hitler's demands and signed the Munich Pact, convinced he had won a great victory for democracy. Hitler strengthened his army and invaded Czechoslovakia in March 1939.

By giving place to Hitler, Chamberlain emboldened Hitler until he eventually ignited the bloodiest conflict in human history. As believers, we must always be wary of Satan's schemes. Like the pharaoh of the Exodus, he comes asking for a compromise, yet has a knife hidden behind his back. Do not "give place" to the devil. The more you accommodate his influence, the more he will hurt your fellowship with God.

Paid in Full

30 September 1961

Neither by the blood of goats and calves, but by his own blood he entered in once into the holy place, having obtained eternal redemption for us.—**Hebrews 9:12**

Most people are familiar with the famous Boston Tea Party in which American colonists dumped more than three hundred chests of tea from the British-owned East India Company into the water at Griffin's Wharf in Boston. The act was the first major demonstration of defiance against British tyranny and became a rallying cry for patriots to unite. What is less well known is that on 30 September 1961, the Mayor of Jackson County, Oregon paid $1.96 of the $4,966 total cost of the tea lost back in 1773. Mayor Snider figured that Oregon's share of the debt was $1.96, so he sent a check in that amount to the British government.

If the British government has ever expected full repayment from the US, Mayor Snider's check was not nearly enough to cover the debt owed by Americans due to the Boston Tea Party. But, if you are born again, God paid your sin debt in full. And it was all thanks to His Son's death, burial, and resurrection.

Historically, the "holy place" was the innermost part of the temple which contained the Ark of the Covenant with the "mercy seat" as its top. When the Lord Jesus Christ shed His blood on the cross and presented it on the mercy seat in Heaven, He was paying for a debt long owed by mankind. One Bible teacher noted that, during the Old Testament, God saved the saints "on credit" with the intent that He would "pay" for those sins later with the blood of His only begotten Son. This is why no one who died in grace during Old Testament times could enter Heaven. Rather, they went to a place called Abraham's Bosom (Luke 16:22) to await the day when the Son of God would pay for their sin, once and for all. When Jesus shed His blood and then cried out "It is finished" on the cross (John 19:30), He obtained "eternal redemption" for us. He did not make a partial payment for sin. Our sin is paid in full!

OCTOBER

On the Winning Side

1 October 331 BC

But thanks be to God, which giveth us the victory through our Lord Jesus Christ.
—1 Corinthians 15:57

The Battle of Gaugamela—sometimes called Arbela—was the third of four major battles fought by Alexander the Great during the fourth century BC. Alexander embarked upon an invasion of the Persian Empire having succeeded his father, Philip II. He defeated the Persians at the Battle of the Granicus River in 334 BC and emerged victorious again over Persian King Darius III at Issus in 333 BC. This battle, however, left Darius with an "axe to grind" with Alexander, particularly because Alexander had captured his wife and daughters. However, Darius was wise enough to realize that Alexander and his army posed a great threat to his reign. Therefore, he offered Alexander a deal. He would concede to him all the Persian territory west of the Euphrates River if Alexander would stop his eastward expansion. Alexander refused and instead marched into Mesopotamia in search of a final battle with Darius.

The two armies met on the plains of Gaugamela in modern-day Iraq. Plutarch, an ancient Greek historian, records that Darius kept his men up all night on the night before the battle so he could review them. Alexander, on the other hand, chose to spend the night sleeping. Parmenio, one of Alexander's trusted generals, had to call Alexander's name three times on the morning of 1 October 331 BC before he awoke from his slumber. Astonished, Parmenio asked Alexander how it was possible that, while anticipating the most important battle of his career, he could sleep as soundly as if he were already victorious. Alexander simply replied, "And are we not so?"

Alexander drew confidence from his military preparedness and strategy. But, we as Christians are never commanded to rely on our own strength. Our victory comes "through our Lord Jesus Christ." In the end—in the last chapter—we know that God wins. And if you're His child, you win, too! Rest in that knowledge.

Betrayal by Bagpipe

2 October 1746

Thou hast been in Eden the garden of God; every precious stone was thy covering, the sardius, topaz, and the diamond, the beryl, the onyx, and the jasper, the sapphire, the emerald, and the carbuncle, and gold: the workmanship of thy tabrets and of thy pipes was prepared in thee in the day that thou wast created. **—Ezekiel 28:13**

Most people would never consider the bagpipe to be a weapon. Nevertheless, the bagpipe was and still is the only musical instrument classified as a weapon of war. In 1745, Charles Edward Stuart, better known as "Bonnie Prince Charlie," led a series of revolts in an effort to reclaim the English throne for the House of Stuart. Initially, the young pretender was successful, capturing Edinburgh and invading England that December. Unfortunately, the Scottish highlanders, known as Jacobites, were finally defeated by the British at the Battle of Culloden in 1746.

Throughout the battle, a Jacobite piper named James Reid played his pipes. Unbeknownst to the British, Reid had embedded certain codes in his music, which facilitated a means of communication to the Scottish commander. Following the battle, Reid was tried in York and insisted he never took up arms against the British. He was merely a piper in support of Prince Charlie. The court refused this alibi and ruled that the bagpipes were indeed a weapon of war. They executed Reid on 2 October 1746.

Did you know that the greatest enemy the Christian has was initially created with an unprecedented talent for music? The book of Ezekiel describes Lucifer as a creature possessing both tabrets (tambourines) and pipes as a part of his physical makeup. In a sense, Satan was a living musical instrument designed by God to create heavenly music. Though God's purpose was for Satan to bring Him glory and honor through music, the devil today is certainly not bringing God praise.

Don't let the positive things God has granted turn to negative, selfish pursuits. Like James Reid who tried to appear neutral to the war effort, your actions will, sooner or later, betray your heart's desires.

No Wall of Division

3 October 1990

For he is our peace, who hath made both one, and hath broken down the middle wall of partition between us;—**Ephesians 2:14**

During the last part of World War II, Allied leaders met in the Crimean Peninsula at a resort town called Yalta. The aim of this meeting was to essentially parcel out portions of Germany to the nations that had contributed most to the Nazis' defeat: the United States, Britain, France, and the Soviet Union. With the advent of the Cold War, however, Germany ended up being divided into two blocs—East and West Germany—with the Berlin Wall becoming a tangible separation. For nearly thirty years, the two Germanys remained at odds.

Finally, in June 1990, the process of tearing down the wall began. And on 3 October 1990, East and West Germany officially reunited to become one Germany.

A physical separation caused great challenges for the people of Berlin. But, above the logistical and familial separation brought by the Berlin Wall, there stands a massive separation between God and mankind—"the middle wall of partition." Ephesians 2:1–18 details how because of our sin, we were separated from God and, as verses 11–18 describe, the Gentiles were even further alienated from God as they were "strangers from the covenants of promise, having no hope, and without God in the world" (verse 12).

However, when the Lord Jesus Christ died for the sins of man on Calvary, He made it possible for *all* men to have access to God. This truth has incredibly wonderful ramifications.

First and best, it means God has given us direct access to Himself through Christ.

Second, it means there should be no ethnic or racial divisions (as were common among the first-century Jews and Gentiles) among the people of God.

And finally, it means that we should do all we can to lead others to Christ that they, too, may know the joy of reunification with God.

Seeking Peace

4 October 1918

From whence come wars and fightings among you? come they not hence, even of your lusts that war in your members? Ye lust, and have not: ye kill, and desire to have, and cannot obtain: ye fight and war, yet ye have not, because ye ask not. Ye ask, and receive not, because ye ask amiss, that ye may consume it upon your lusts.—**James 4:1–3**

The First World War, or Great War, was a cataclysmic event that set the precedent for how wars in the twentieth century would be waged. While historians have debated a single cause for the Great War, the most plausible reason was that the nationalistic spirit of Austria-Hungary was threatened when Archduke Ferdinand was assassinated. The nations then tumbled into world war. After four years of bloody fighting, German Chancellor Max von Baden sent a telegram on 4 October 1918 to American President Woodrow Wilson asking for an armistice between Germany and the Allied powers. Five weeks later, the Great War ended.

All of us want peace with others, yet we do not always go about achieving it the right way. In fact, James 4 tells us that strife and division come about because we want something we cannot have and, rather than turning to God in prayer to give us what *He* would desire we have, we insist on manipulating to gain our way.

In the verses just prior to this passage, James contrasts a heart that is filled with conflict versus a heart that is wise to make peace: "But if ye have bitter envying and strife in your hearts, glory not, and lie not against the truth. For where envying and strife is, there is confusion and every evil work. But the wisdom that is from above is first pure, then peaceable, gentle, and easy to be intreated, full of mercy and good fruits, without partiality, and without hypocrisy. And the fruit of righteousness is sown in peace of them that make peace" (James 3:14, 16–18).

Would those who spend time with you consider you a strifebringer or a peacemaker? The world tells us that peacemakers are weak; God says they are wise.

Surprise Landing

5 October 1969

Lest Satan should get an advantage of us: for we are not ignorant of his devices.
—2 Corinthians 2:11

The fear of enemy air attack upon United States soil has been heightened since the attack on Pearl Harbor in 1941. Ever since World War II, the United States has maintained a highly technical air defense system, designed to identify and prevent enemy aircraft from harming US citizens or her assets. Yet on 5 October 1969, a Cuban Air Force pilot flew his Soviet-made MiG-17 (Fresco) fighter completely undetected through US air defense networks and successfully landed at Homestead Air Force Base in Florida. Alarmingly, the foreign pilot managed to land and taxi his jet right next to President Nixon's Air Force One! Thankfully, the pilot was a defector and meant the United States no harm.

While the consequences of the foreign pilot's undetected flight were mild, the effect of Satan's work in your life should not be underestimated. The devil has "devices"—tactics he uses to achieve his devious goals. He can sneak in undetected into our thoughts and hearts, getting an advantage over us. Spiritual attacks are often unexpected and come at times when we are unprepared to handle them.

God has given us a conscience to help discern between good and evil. We ought to be sensitive to its signals that we are doing something wrong. Further, the Holy Spirit is our God-given guide in this world. Jesus promised that the Spirit would guide us "into all truth" (John 16:13).

When you have a decision to make or are unsure of whether something is morally right, seek the Lord in His Word and let the Holy Spirit lead you. Satan can be tricky and deceiving—he can even appear as an "angel of light" (2 Corinthians 11:14). And he certainly intends to trick you with his "wiles" (Ephesians 6:11).

But God will never lead you astray. He *is* truth (John 14:6), and He never changes (Hebrews 13:8). You can safely follow Him.

The Safe Haven

6 October 1961

The Lord also will be a refuge for the oppressed, a refuge in times of trouble. And they that know thy name will put their trust in thee: for thou, Lord, hast not forsaken them that seek thee.—**Psalm 9:9–10**

The threat of global thermo-nuclear war loomed heavy on the hearts of most Americans during the tumultuous Cold War era. The prospect that the Soviet Union could launch a nuclear attack on American cities caused a deep disquiet that weighed heavily in the hearts of typical American families. On 6 October 1961, President Kennedy encouraged American families to build bomb shelters as protection against atomic fallout in the event that the US and Soviet Union had a nuclear exchange. The media capitalized on Kennedy's address and a *Life* magazine cover featured a story headlined "The Drive for Mass Shelters." The Office of Civil Defense even promoted how-to manuals for building shelters, and many Americans built them right in their own backyards.

Whether a homemade bomb shelter would protect you from a thirty-megaton nuclear blast is uncertain. But what *is* certain is the security we possess in a relationship with the Lord Jesus Christ. Unlike a bomb shelter, we never have to worry if Christ is good enough. He is.

No matter what threat or uncertainty you face today, the Lord can be your refuge. Sometimes, health crises come unexpectedly to a family or church. God cares. Relational burdens at times pain our hearts and make life dreary. The Lord listens. Nothing is too small to bring to the Lord. He can provide you with security and inner peace that you have never felt before.

Jesus lived as a man on this Earth; He understands your humanity and struggles and wishes to bear your burden: "For we have not an high priest which cannot be touched with the feeling of our infirmities . . . Let us therefore come boldly unto the throne of grace, that we may obtain mercy, and find grace to help in time of need" (Hebrews 4:15–16). Run to Him. True safety, security, and spiritual rest is found in God alone.

Rise Up

7 October 1944

Be sober, be vigilant; because your adversary the devil, as a roaring lion, walketh about, seeking whom he may devour: Whom resist stedfast in the faith, knowing that the same afflictions are accomplished in your brethren that are in the world.—**1 Peter 5:8–9**

The word *mutiny* refers to an uprising against authority, especially in a military sense. It typically evokes images of indolent seafarers refusing to serve the ship's captain. One famous example is the mutiny on the HMS *Bounty* in 1789. But, history records other kinds of uprisings as well.

On 7 October 1944, a mutiny took place that many would have deemed impossible. A group of Jews imprisoned by the Nazis at the Auschwitz-Birkenau death camp organized a mass resistance. They set fire to one of the crematoria, attacked Nazi guards known as the SS (*Schutzstaffel*), and cut through wire to escape. Sadly, the SS managed to track them all down. Three SS soldiers died and ten were wounded, while about 250 Jews died during the uprising.

There comes a time when evil must be resisted. If you are a believer, it is your duty to resist Satan's influence. Like those sadistic SS guards, Satan wants to eliminate us—or, as the Bible puts it, to *devour* us. In fact, the Greek word used for *devour* in 1 Peter 5:8 literally means to *swallow down*.

Let us be willing to rise up and resist the forces of evil in our world. If you find yourself in a situation under pressure from others to do something wrong, run! Proverbs 1:10 instructs, "My son, if sinners entice thee, consent thou not." When we give in to temptation, we risk tainting our testimonies and losing our God-given reward at the Judgment Seat of Christ. "Look to yourselves, that we lose not those things which we have wrought, but that we receive a full reward" (2 John 8).

Resistance to unrighteousness should be the norm for a Christian, rather than the exception. To be sure, it is always easier to give in than to resist. But one day when we all stand before God, we will be glad we chose the right way rather than the easy way.

Isaiah 28–29 // Philippians 3

Man Overboard

8 October 1988

Brethren, if a man be overtaken in a fault, ye which are spiritual, restore such an one in the spirit of meekness; considering thyself, lest thou also be tempted. Bear ye one another's burdens, and so fulfil the law of Christ. For if a man think himself to be something, when he is nothing, he deceiveth himself.—**Galatians 6:1–3**

The USS *Midway* was the oldest carrier of its time while in service. It launched on 20 March 1945. As one of the few non-nuclear-powered aircraft carriers still in active service, the *Midway* featured an unusual hull—not an aircraft carrier hull, but a battleship hull. The *Midway* was thus prone to extreme rolls at sea. Astoundingly, on 8 October 1988, the *Midway* withstood a record-breaking roll of twenty-six degrees to her starboard side during a typhoon near the Philippines. It was not supposed to survive a roll higher than twenty-four degrees.

The *Midway*'s crew practiced man overboard drills for emergencies and rolls like these. During the drills, the ship's klaxon would make a distinctive sound, tipping off the crew that a shipmate had fallen or been blown overboard. Immediately, the entire crew would assemble on deck and take accountability. If someone was absent, every man on board would begin intensely searching the ship for the missing sailor.

When someone we know goes "overboard" spiritually, we are to seek to restore them in the spirit of meekness. Too often, we tend to cast judgment when a former church attender cannot be found or makes a morally wrong decision. It is easier to judge them or to sign them off as "worldly," rather than working to restore them. If the US Navy would take such great measures to restore a sailor overboard, how much more should we, as spiritual people, seek to restore an erring brother or sister in Christ?

The Lord Jesus Christ told three parables about lost items in Luke 15, highlighting in each the joy of restoration. Christ was concerned for those who had gone astray. How is your attitude and response to those who have ended up "overboard"? Rather than standing in judgement over a repentant sinner, reach out to help the church restore.

Eye in the Sky

9 October 1999

The eyes of the Lord *are in every place, beholding the evil and the good.* —**Proverbs 15:3**

During the Cold War, the United States sought to develop and deploy reconnaissance aircraft (spy planes) that could not only photograph vital intelligence but also evade surface-to-air missiles and hostile aircraft. The U-2, while efficient, proved too easy to shoot down. This was evidenced by pilot Gary Powers' 1960 U-2 Incident, in which a Soviet missile shot down the U-2 while Powers was on an aerial reconnaissance mission to collect photographic intelligence. He ended up a prisoner of war for two years.

Four years later, Lockheed developed the SR-71 Blackbird. To date, no other plane can fly higher or faster than the Blackbird. Constructed from titanium and able to reach cruising altitudes of nearly 90,000 feet, the sleek spy plane could fly at speeds three times faster than the speed of sound (Mach 3). The Blackbird also sported high-resolution cameras that were able to look at 100,000 square miles of the Earth's surface every hour. When the Blackbird was on duty, everything was visible. On 9 October 1999, the Blackbird made its final flight. This plane model is now on display at various museums.

The Blackbird, as advanced as it was, had limits to its ability to inspect details on the Earth. Trees and other natural obstacles could block its view. But God has no limit to His knowledge, whether of good deeds or bad deeds. God sees everything. For mankind, this truth can be encouraging or convicting—depending on your perspective. The Bible says that God is the One "who both will bring to light the hidden things of darkness, and will make manifest the counsels of the hearts: and then shall every man have praise of God" (1 Corinthians 4:5). Do you welcome the gaze of God? Or do you seek to hide from it. First John 1:7 tells us, "but if we walk in the light, as he is in the light, we have fellowship one with another, and the blood of Jesus Christ his Son cleanseth us from all sin."

Wounded for Our Salvation

10 October 1927

But he was wounded for our transgressions, he was bruised for our iniquities: the chastisement of our peace was upon him; and with his stripes we are healed.
—Isaiah 53:5

On 10 October 1927, Army Chief of Staff General Charles Summerall directed that a draft bill be sent to Congress to "revive the Badge of Military Merit." Considered the oldest award still given to military personnel, the Purple Heart has its roots with George Washington who himself called it the "Badge of Military Merit." General Washington specifically qualified that the award was to be given to those who had shed their blood for America and that those who receive the award should be looked upon with reverence. Washington issued the award to just three soldiers during the Revolutionary War.

The Badge of Military Merit then ceased to be issued until after World War II, when interest in it resurfaced. During this time, considerable effort was placed into reintroducing the medal. In fact, the medal was redesigned completely, after which it became known as the Purple Heart. Today, the medal is heart shaped and includes a gold border that contains the bust of George Washington. The medal also includes Washington's coat of arms and, on the reverse side, reads, "For Military Merit."

The Lord Jesus Christ did not shed His sinless blood as a means to an honorary medal or award. He fulfilled the Father's plan of redemption by becoming "obedient unto death, even the death of the cross" (Philippians 2:8). Christ was "wounded" and "bruised" for our sin; He left Heaven's glory so we could have eternal life.

Whom have you told of His sacrifice lately? You may know the story well—you may have heard it for years. But there are countless people who do not understand salvation. Even if the next person you witness to does not trust the Lord that day, you know you will have pleased your Captain. And isn't that what matters most?

It's Not What You Get; It's What You Give

11 October 1899

For the love of money is the root of all evil: which while some coveted after, they have erred from the faith, and pierced themselves through with many sorrows. **—1 Timothy 6:10**

In the early nineteenth century, Britain colonized much of South Africa to include the Dutch Cape Colony. As a result of the encroachment upon the indigenous Dutch settlers (Boers), the Boers began an exodus into the tribal territory inhabited by the Zulus. In 1833, the Boers founded the Transvaal and Orange Free State, and for several decades, the Boers lived peaceably with their British neighbors until the British annexed the Boer diamond fields in 1872.

On 11 October 1899, the Anglo-Boer War officially began. The conflict pitted a small, agrarian culture against a highly industrialized nation. The smaller nation resorted to the strategy of guerilla warfare. After three years, Britain had won the great Anglo-Boer War—but at the cost of her reputation. Greed over diamonds discovered in South Africa propelled the British empire into a brutal war that resulted in thirty thousand deaths and the world's first use of concentration camps.

The lust for wealth has caused untold suffering in this world, and it continues to plague mankind. Money is not inherently wrong or bad—it is a necessary part of life. Money can be used to support missionaries or to care for your family. Yet, money can also cause sorrow and distress for those who come under its power, using it only for selfish gain. The key to honoring God with money is contentment. The Apostle Paul wrote, "Not that I speak in respect of want: for I have learned, in whatsoever state I am, therewith to be content" (Philippians 4:11).

Are you content? The riches of this world can never satisfy. If you do not have much down here, thank God for what you *do* have. And, focus on storing up treasures in Heaven by giving to the work of God on Earth (Matthew 6:19). Even the richest person must leave it all behind when they breathe their last, but you can store up treasure for eternity as you give.

Have they Forgotten?

12 October 1862

And even as they did not like to retain God in their knowledge, God gave them over to a reprobate mind, to do those things which are not convenient; —**Romans 1:28**

According to *The Library of Congress Civil War Desk Reference*, as of 2002, approximately 70,000 books had been published on the American Civil War. Since 2002, it is estimated that approximately 1,500 have been published each year on the topic, totaling about 95,550 books containing endless discussions of its riveting battle narratives, the heart-wrenching issue of slavery, and opinions regarding politics, tactics, and the war's effect on society. In the midst of this colossal military struggle, however, was a great outpouring of religious fervor that culminated in the Great Revival of 1863. It is estimated that as many as 300,000 men from both sides of the conflict came to Christ from October 1862 to May 1864. That number represents about ten percent of all Civil War soldiers who, in less than two years, had received Christ as Saviour.

The revival started on Sunday, 12 October 1862, as Reverend Scott preached to a group of Confederate soldiers near the Rappahannock River in eastern Virginia. While it was fairly commonplace for chaplains to conduct Sunday morning services for the men, Scott noticed a marked difference from the outset of that service. He stated, "From the beginning of these services it was evident that God's Spirit was working in many hearts. The men listened with the deepest attention, and seemed very reluctant to leave the ground when the benediction was pronounced." Other Army chaplains reported similar results. Revival had begun.

Amazingly, however, of about 100,000 books that have been written about the American Civil War, fewer than ten cover the Civil War revival. Many people simply do not value the things of God or "retain God in their knowledge." Of course, the Bible teaches that a man in his natural state "receiveth not the things of the Spirit of God: for they are foolishness unto him" (1 Corinthians 2:14). When God works, let's make it known.

A Change of Allegiance

13 October 1943

But above all things, my brethren, swear not, neither by heaven, neither by the earth, neither by any other oath: but let your yea be yea; and your nay, nay; lest ye fall into condemnation.—**James 5:12**

Shortly after Nazi Germany invaded France, fascist dictator Benito Mussolini declared Italy as one of Germany's Axis partners. For a period of three years, Italy tried in vain to impress Hitler by fighting in Africa, Greece, and Yugoslavia. It seemed, however, that no matter how hard Mussolini tried, his forces proved unable to effect any significant gains for the Axis cause. On 13 October 1943—after Mussolini's own people turned on him and he was deposed—the Italian government reversed course and declared war on its former Axis partner. Mussolini's former chief of staff had begun negotiations with General Eisenhower three months prior, which proved instrumental in the Allies landing in Salerno in September. Germany had *had* an ally, but now it had gained an enemy—and, thankfully, the Allied war effort was helped.

When it comes to where loyalties lie, vacillating seems to be a common human characteristic. Pontius Pilate epitomized this trait when he wavered back and forth on what to do with Christ (Matthew 27:24–26). The Bible admonishes us to be people of our word, firmly committed to what we say we are going to do and loyal to those to whom we have pledged allegiance.

Be a Christian who is steadily charging forward for the Lord, willing to adjust where necessary, but never vacillating in your loyalty to Christ. If you have chosen the wrong friends, the wrong influences, or made wrong decisions, it's not too late for a change of plans. But when it comes to your allegiance to Christ, remain firm.

The Bible says, "A double minded man is unstable in all his ways" (James 1:8). Choose not to be a double-minded Christian. Drop your loyalty to the world, but freely offer Christ your life. Ask God to examine your life today and see where your loyalties lie. Is it time for a change of allegiance?

Newfound Courage

14 October 1066

So then after the Lord had spoken unto them, he was received up into heaven, and sat on the right hand of God. And they went forth, and preached every where, the Lord working with them, and confirming the word with signs following. Amen. **—Mark 16:19–20**

On 14 October 1066, Duke William of Normandy crossed the English Channel with a combined force of ten thousand Norman soldiers in an attempt to claim England's throne. The resulting battle is known as the Battle of Hastings, and it ranks as one of the most decisive battles in world history. William's opponent, King Harold Godwinson (who would become the last Anglo-Saxon King of England), had an equal force.

The first half of the battle resulted in an English advantage, as Duke William's forces could not penetrate the shield wall the English had formed. But then, a rumor spread that Duke William had been killed, and William's men began retreating upon hearing this report. King Harold seized the opportunity and ordered his cavalry to break away from the shield wall to pursue the fleeing Normans.

William was actually alive, however, and he began riding through his ranks, reassuring his men with a loud voice. Like a football team after a pep rally, the Normans turned from retreating and stormed the English positions, now thinned from their pursuit of William's men. The English formation was disrupted when King Harold received a fatal shot to the eye. William and his men defeated the English. He was crowned King of England on 25 December 1066 in Westminster Abbey. History refers to Duke William as William the Conqueror.

Once William's men realized their king was alive, it changed everything. A much greater joy must have entered the disciples' hearts when they saw their risen Lord. Rather than cowering in fear, these men went forth boldly proclaiming the gospel to everyone they could. Take heart—no religion has what we have. Our risen Saviour gives us newfound courage, if we but remember that our King is alive.

Move On

15 October 1529

The discretion of a man deferreth his anger; and it is his glory to pass over a transgression.—**Proverbs 19:11**

Sultan Suleiman I, the Magnificent, was one of the most famous military leaders in world history. He enjoyed one of longest reigns of any sixteenth-century world monarch, which lasted forty-six years. During his reign, he expanded the Ottoman Empire farther than any Sultan had done.

In 1526, Suleiman defeated the king of Hungary at the Battle of the Mohacs. Flush with victory, he planned to move further west and attack Austria. In late September 1529, Suleiman led his Ottoman forces against the Austrian city of Vienna with the intent to lay siege. A string of bad weather prevented Suleiman from forcing Vienna's surrender. On 15 October 1529, the Ottomans withdrew back toward their homeland.

All of us experience times when we need to be "reeled in." We are quick to retaliate when threatened, quick to become angry when misunderstood. Discretion, however, teaches us to defer. James 1:19–20 instructs, "Wherefore, my beloved brethren, let every man be swift to hear, slow to speak, slow to wrath: For the wrath of man worketh not the righteousness of God."

One servant of the Lord who faced many difficult and demoralizing situations is the Apostle Paul. He gives us a sample of them in 2 Corinthians 11:24–26, writing, "Of the Jews five times received I forty stripes save one. Thrice was I beaten with rods, once was I stoned, thrice I suffered shipwreck, a night and a day I have been in the deep; In journeyings often, in perils of waters, in perils of robbers, in perils by mine own countrymen." Yet, Paul endured, "forgetting those things which are behind, and reaching forth unto those things which are before" (Philippians 3:13). When Paul was mistreated, rather than retaliating, he moved on. Paul's example reminds us of Jesus, "Who, when he was reviled, reviled not again; when he suffered, he threatened not; but committed himself to him that judgeth righteously" (1 Peter 2:23). You can trust God with your hurts. But don't let them hold you back. Reach forth for Christ.

This Means War

16 October 1859

And I will put enmity between thee and the woman, and between thy seed and her seed; it shall bruise thy head, and thou shalt bruise his heel.—**Genesis 3:15**

Pinpointing the final trigger that sparked the American Civil War is as debatable as it is difficult. Arguably, several different events provoked the war's hostilities. One seminal event, however, seems to eclipse all others in significance: John Brown's failed raid of the Harpers Ferry arsenal on 16 October 1859.

The US federal arsenal at Harpers Ferry, Virginia, held a cache of aged muskets, rifles, and ammunition. Brown intended to arm the thousands who would flock to his banner with this equipment. Once the raid was discovered, local militias set out to quell Brown's raiders. In a matter of hours, Brown and a dozen of his men were holed up in a brick fire engine house. A force of ninety US Marines led by Lt. Col. Robert E. Lee stormed the engine house, killing and wounding Brown's raiders. Brown was captured and later executed. His death stirred sentiments in the North and South for diametrically opposed reasons, and the raid on Harper's Ferry was the *casus belli* for what would become America's bloodiest conflict.

The Bible's first Messianic prophecy, found in Genesis 3:15, represents the *casus belli* for what Bible scholars call the "war of the seeds." The phrase speaks of the conflict between the seed of the woman (Christ) on one hand, and the seed of the serpent (Satan) on the other. Ever since the Garden of Eden until the death of Christ on Calvary, Satan has attempted to prevent the Promised Seed from fulfilling God's redemptive plan. But, Christ dealt a grand blow to Satan at the cross by providing a way of salvation, and will one day completely bruise Satan once and for all (Romans 16:20). The war will finally end when the devil is cast into the Lake of Fire for eternity (Revelation 20:10). What a grand day that will be for Christians once the "accuser of our brethren" (Revelation 12:10) meets his destined fate. He will forever cease to war with God's plan and His people.

A Recognized Citizenship

17 October 1978

Now therefore ye are no more strangers and foreigners, but fellowcitizens with the saints, and of the household of God;—**Ephesians 2:19**

Jefferson Davis was elected president of the Confederate States of America shortly after South Carolina seceded from the Union in December 1860. Davis would lead the Confederacy through four years of bloody civil war, costing the lives of nearly 700,000 Americans.

Following Lee's surrender at Appomattox Courthouse in April 1865, Davis fled for his safety. The following month he was apprehended by Union cavalry and imprisoned at Fort Monroe, Virginia, for two years. In 1868, President Johnson issued a presidential pardon and amnesty to "every person who directly or indirectly participated in the late insurrection or rebellion." But it wasn't until 17 October 1978 that President Jimmy Carter officially, albeit posthumously, restored full citizenship to Jefferson Davis.

A president can restore an earthly citizenship. But only Christ can allow you to become a "fellowcitizen with the saints." The Bible tells us that we enter this life already estranged from God—we are "foreigners" (Ephesians 2:19) and "without Christ" (Ephesians 2:12). Unsaved people live without any hope of an eternal home. Scripture says, "But as many as received him, to them gave he power to become the sons of God, even to them that believe on his name" (John 1:12). We are not citizens of Heaven until we receive God's pardon for sin. At that moment, we become members of "the household of faith" (Galatians 6:10).

Unlike Davis, no misdeed or missed deed can make one lose their citizenship with God in Heaven. Yes, as children of God, we will be chastised by the heavenly Father (Hebrews 12:6) when we stray. And yes, we should live in a way that brings honor to God (Titus 3:8). But we never need to fear that God will reject us or cast us out of His family. On the contrary, Jesus promised, "Him that cometh to me I will in no wise cast out" (John 6:37). If you're saved today, thank God for giving you such an incredible, permanent citizenship.

Earth's Evil Twin

18 October 1967

Who only hath immortality, dwelling in the light which no man can approach unto; whom no man hath seen, nor can see: to whom be honour and power everlasting. Amen.—**1 Timothy 6:16**

The planet Venus has been often referred to as Earth's twin due to its similarity in size to Earth. The orbit of Venus is also the closest to Earth's orbit of any planet in our solar system. Thanks to a series of probes that have landed on the planet, however, we now realize that Venus—on closer inspection—is a very different planet from our own.

On 18 October 1967, the Soviet Union's Venera 4 probe became the first probe to transmit information back to Earth regarding details of Venus. One surprising discovery was its atmosphere. It consists largely of carbon dioxide, causing surface temperatures that reach a blistering 870 degrees Fahrenheit. Moreover, the air pressure on Venus is about ninety times greater than Earth's. And, its clouds are made of sulfuric acid. Rather than being a planet that man could one day explore, the composition of Venus makes it entirely impossible for man to survive on the surface, let alone the atmosphere.

No one can visit Venus without special equipment, probes, and clothing. And if this is true of a planet in our own solar system, how much more true must it be of entrance into Heaven? It seems unclear to many people that there are preparatory steps to meet the God who created this universe. God dwells in light "no man can approach unto," and no one is ready to see God unless they have received His Son. Too many believe they are ready for Heaven simply because they go to church, have been baptized, or try to observe the golden rule.

Sin prevents man from being able to enter Heaven or abide there for eternity. The only way a man or woman is prepared to enter Heaven is by having their sin washed clean by the blood of the Lord Jesus Christ through receiving Him as Saviour. Only then are we prepared to exist in God's presence. Have you received Christ?

Reach Forth

19 October 1864

Brethren, I count not myself to have apprehended: but this one thing I do, forgetting those things which are behind, and reaching forth unto those things which are before, I press toward the mark for the prize of the high calling of God in Christ Jesus.—**Philippians 3:13–14**

On 19 October 1864, Confederate forces—under the command of Georgia-born Major General John B. Gordon—surprised the Union Army at Cedar Creek near Strasburg, Virginia. Gordon led his tired and hungry men across the icy, chest-deep Shenandoah River with the intention of wiping out General Philip Sheridan's Union Army. Gordon's men nearly did so, but Sheridan's troops quickly abandoned their camp and retreated to a new position eight miles north.

Gordon, an apt and experienced commander, wanted to press forward immediately and finish off the stunned Yankees. He asked his general, Jubal Early, for permission to continue the advance. Early shrugged off Gordon's suggestion and said, "This is glory enough for one day." While Early's men looted the abandoned enemy camp, General Sheridan made a ten-mile gallop back to the battlefield and completely reversed the Confederate gains by regrouping his own troops. The event—known as Sheridan's Ride—may never have been possible if General Gordon had been permitted to press his attack. Sheridan's unexpected victory was crucial to Lincoln's winning a second presidential term and continuation of the "hard war" against the South.

Unlike General Early, Christians cannot be content with half-measures. Too often, we rest on yesterday's victories or partial success rather than pressing forward into the future. When Paul wrote "forgetting those things which are behind," he was referring to the successes of yesterday as well as the failures. Paul wasn't content to reminisce on the past; he was determined to reach forth into the future. If you're surrounded by difficulty today, press on. If you're blessed with victory today, thank God and press on. The "prize of the high calling of God in Christ Jesus" lies ahead.

One of Us?

20 October 1947

They went out from us, but they were not of us; for if they had been of us, they would no doubt have continued with us: but they went out, that they might be made manifest that they were not all of us.—**1 John 2:19**

Following the end of World War II, the United States and Soviet Union entered a period of turmoil called the Cold War. President Harry Truman highlighted his foreign policy as one of containment, particularly of containing the spread of Communism. This policy instantly polarized the two superpowers of the US and the USSR, and each sought to stay a step ahead of the other. On 20 October 1947, the House Un-American Activities Committee began investigating communist influence within the confines of top American opinion makers, namely the Hollywood film industry. The committee also scrutinized numerous other American citizens to determine whether they were sufficiently loyal to the nation. As a result, a "blacklist" was compiled which banned over three hundred people from working in Hollywood. While some of the methods of this committee were questionable, there was a real problem that it was originally posed to address—specifically, subversive behavior by those who had access to national secrets. Some who posed as lovers of our country actually were undercover spies for the Communists.

By the same token, not everyone who claims to be a believer is truly a born-again Christian. John wrote of those who "went out from us, but . . . were not of us"—those who *seemed* to be believers, but never had been converted. It is fairly easy to pass oneself off as a true believer, but the Lord Jesus Christ told His disciples that there is coming a day when those who have truly received Him as Saviour will be separated from those who have rejected Him, like the wheat is separated from the tares (Matthew 13:24–30, 36–43). Heed Peter's admonition to "give diligence to make your calling and election sure" (2 Peter 1:10). Do not fret about who the unbelievers are; God knows. One day, they will be made manifest. But do make sure that you are a child of God, having placed your faith in Christ.

Faith to See It Through

21 October 1805

These all died in faith, not having received the promises, but having seen them afar off, and were persuaded of them, and embraced them, and confessed that they were strangers and pilgrims on the earth.—**Hebrews 11:13**

During the Napoleonic Wars, Britain and France vied for naval supremacy. In one of the most famous naval engagements in history, Britain destroyed the French fleet on 21 October 1805 during the Battle of Trafalgar without losing a single British ship. Britain's victory, however, was not without loss. British Admiral Lord Nelson, the architect of the victory, was shot by a sniper and died thirty minutes before the end of the battle.

Like Admiral Nelson never seeing the end of the battle, many Old Testament saints died before seeing the covenant promises of God fulfilled. Yet, they had the faith to believe the promises were real and to be faithful in the moment. Hebrews 11 tells us that they "died in faith, not having received the promises, but having seen them afar off." The chapter includes people like Abraham, who left for a land that God promised to show him and did not even know where he was going when he started out (Genesis 12:1, Hebrews 11:8). And there was Sarah who "judged him faithful who had promised." Though at first she laughed at God's promise, Sarah ultimately believed His word that she would conceive and bear a child past the age of childbearing (Genesis 18:14–15, Hebrews 11:11).

The Bible says, "Cast thy bread upon the waters: for thou shalt find it after many days" (Ecclesiastes 11:1). The things you do for God have a way of developing over time and developing into incredible results. Many people give up when they do not see immediate results. While we may not always see results from serving the Lord now, we know that He will reward us one day.

Embrace faith to see it through. Keep working in your area of ministry. Keep laboring to spread the gospel. Keep praying for that person who refuses to get saved. God will keep His promises to you. Keep looking to Him and have faith to see it through.

Preparing a Place

22 October 1986

In my Father's house are many mansions: if it were not so, I would have told you. I go to prepare a place for you.—**John 14:2**

In July of 1986, I received Permanent Change of Station (PCS) orders to report to Lajes Field, Azores, Portugal in October. I remember having to look at a globe to find out the location of this place. Once I broke the news to my wife Denise that we had PCS orders to the Azores, she began making preparations to move to this tiny island in the North Atlantic. One of the stipulations of the new assignment was I had to travel ahead of my wife and infant son Josh to secure housing before they could join me. With great trepidation, I said goodbye and boarded a C-130 that took me across the ocean.

I had to live in the barracks, but I spent my free time looking for a house. I finally found a two-bedroom house in a local village. Unlike the base housing we were used to, this house was made of cement, had no central air conditioning, and the shower only dripped water. We had one light in the living room which consisted of a solitary bulb hanging from the ceiling on a long cord. On windy days we had no electricity.

Elated to have anything at all, I shared the news, and my wife and son flew to meet me. When I picked them up from the airport, I reassured them the house was "not that bad" and that we only had to live there until we received on-base housing. Denise was underwhelmed when she walked through the front door. Chocolate brown walls and orange furniture from the 1960s met her gaze. A donkey braying near the window the first morning did not help the reception either! Yet, she began putting her touches on it to make this house a home.

I went ahead of my family and prepared a place for them. Jesus promised that He is preparing mansions for those who have received Him as Saviour. At some point, you may have needed to spend time in some lackluster hotels or a shoddy house. Yet, if Jesus is preparing a place for us, we can only imagine how magnificent it will be when we arrive in Heaven.

The Hungarian Hero

23 October 1980

Who, being in the form of God, thought it not robbery to be equal with God: But made himself of no reputation, and took upon him the form of a servant, and was made in the likeness of men: And being found in fashion as a man, he humbled himself, and became obedient unto death, even the death of the cross. **—Philippians 2:6–8**

On 23 October 1980, the world lost a true hero. Pinchas Tibor Rosenbaum, a Hungarian Jew, saved thousands of Jews during the Nazi occupation of Hungary during World War II. He dressed up as a Nazi *Schutzstaffel* (SS) officer, convincing the Germans, as well as a fascist group known as the Arrow Cross, that he was on their side. Only incredible courage and a love for his people could have compelled Rosenbaum to routinely risk his life.

By depending upon an underground intelligence network, Rosenbaum would learn in advance when the Arrow Cross planned to round up the Jews for extermination. Posing as a Lieutenant of the feared German SS, Rosenbaum would show up when the Arrow Cross was herding Jews into train cars and immediately countermand the orders of the Arrow Cross soldier in charge. Instead of leading the Jews to cattle cars, however, Rosenbaum guided them to the now famous "Glass House." There, he revealed his true identity, furnished them with a hiding place, and switched back into his false identity to save others. After the war, he settled in Switzerland, but continued working tirelessly for the State of Israel.

Long before Rosenbaum took on the identity of "the enemy," another Jew was born of a virgin, took on the likeness of those who were at enmity with God, and provided salvation through the blood of His cross. That Man, of course, is the God-Man, the Lord Jesus Christ, who completed the greatest "rescue mission" in history.

I can only imagine the gratitude the rescued Jews felt toward Rosenbaum. But do we not sometimes take the sacrifice of Christ for granted? Have you thanked Jesus today for His sacrifice for you?

Strings Attached

24 October 1954

Behold, as the eyes of servants look unto the hand of their masters, and as the eyes of a maiden unto the hand of her mistress; so our eyes wait upon the LORD our God, until that he have mercy upon us. Have mercy upon us, O LORD, have mercy upon us: for we are exceedingly filled with contempt.—**Psalm 123:2–3**

Prior to American involvement in the Vietnam War, US President Dwight D. Eisenhower wrote a letter to South Vietnamese President Ngo Dinh Diem on 24 October 1954. He promised financial support to South Vietnam; however, the assistance was conditioned on Diem's agreement to uphold certain standards of performance set by Eisenhower. These included both land reform and a decrease of Diem's corrupt government. Diem readily agreed, but he later reneged on Eisenhower's stipulations. As a result, the civil unrest in South Vietnam escalated, leading to the eventual downfall of the Diem regime.

Financial assistance often has strings attached; it is conditional, especially when political goals are in view. What is not conditional, however, is God's mercy, which the psalmist seeks in Psalm 123. Micah the prophet noted that "the LORD delighteth in mercy" (Micah 7:18). His mercy is not given to those who do right—after all, those who live righteously do not require mercy. God gives mercy to those who do wrong! It is unearned and undeserved. Do not try to earn what God did not ask you to work for. Salvation is a free gift of God (Ephesians 2:8–9).

God is not just loving and merciful to those who are believers but also to unbelievers. "He maketh his sun to rise on the evil and on the good" (Matthew 5:45). Furthermore, the Bible says, "Christ died for the ungodly" and that "while we were yet sinners, Christ died for us" (Romans 5:6, 8).

God's love has no strings attached. He knew all the sins you or I have committed or ever will commit, and He died for us anyway. He does not withdraw His mercy when we misbehave. "Where sin abounded, grace did much more abound," the Bible says (Romans 5:20). Meditate today on the blessing of His unconditional mercy and grace.

Redemption's Price

25 October 1945

What? know ye not that your body is the temple of the Holy Ghost which is in you, which ye have of God, and ye are not your own? For ye are bought with a price: therefore glorify God in your body, and in your spirit, which are God's.
—1 Corinthians 6:19–20

Japan was victorious over China in the First Sino-Japanese War of 1894–1895. The resulting agreement—the Treaty of Shimonoseki—ceded the island of Taiwan (previously known as Formosa) to the Japanese Empire. For the next fifty years, the Japanese would occupy the island and rule Chinese citizens in Taiwan. While the people of Taiwan probably thought that Japanese occupation would be perpetual, World War II changed this dynamic.

The surrender of the Japanese on the USS *Missouri* on 2 September 1945 ushered in the end of World War II. On 25 October 1945, the Japanese surrendered the island of Taiwan to Chinese nationalist leader Chiang Kai-shek. To the uninformed, it appeared Japan was giving up part of its own land under the formal surrender agreement. China, however, had previously owned Taiwan and thus was only receiving its rightful property back. China would no longer allow Japan to rule over its land.

The word *redemption* is a powerful word, and one that appears in the Bible fourteen times. It means "to regain a possession of something in exchange for a payment." It also refers to the "clearing of a debt." When the Lord Jesus Christ shed His blood on the cross of Calvary, He paid the debt of our sin.

The Bible tells us we are "bought with a price." As a result, we belong to the Lord. It is easy to fall into a habit of living life and making decisions based on what we want. But God has proved to us His love for us, He has purchased us with His blood, and He calls us to surrender our will to Him. Don't live to serve self. Live so that Christ will be glorified. After all, you belong to Him.

Honor to Whom It Is Due

26 October 2006

Render therefore to all their dues: tribute to whom tribute is due; custom to whom custom; fear to whom fear; honour to whom honour.—**Romans 13:7**

Military deployments are hard on families. Military members are often given very little notice of the need to pack up and fly to new overseas locations where they will serve for a period of six months to a year. During that time, they miss out on children's special days, miss holidays with loved ones, and must endure the loneliness and separation that comes with being deployed. Moreover, the spouse left at home has to shoulder the lion's share of parental responsibilities while maintaining the household.

Knowing first-hand the sacrifices my wife Denise has made to support my military career, including through deployment, makes me especially grateful for 26 October, which marks the official "National Day of the Deployed." The day was first observed in 2006, thanks to North Dakota resident Shelle Michaels Aberle. She petitioned her governor to proclaim a special day to honor those who have sacrificed by serving their country in foreign lands. By 2012, all fifty states were observing this day.

The Bible speaks of giving honor to whom it is due which, for American Christians, includes those who have served to protect our religious freedoms.

But the Bible also speaks of giving honor to our spiritual leaders. First Timothy 5:17 says, "Let the elders that rule well be counted worthy of double honour, especially they who labour in the word and doctrine." The word *honour* can mean financial remuneration, as in the sense of *honorarium*, but it can also apply to giving respect to spiritual laborers. Hebrews 13:17 shares the incredible responsibility they carry "as they that watch for your souls."

How long has it been since you thanked your pastor? Like spouses of deployed military, there are unseen burdens a pastor carries. Thank yours today for his faithful labor.

Faithfulness of a Father

27 October 1858

Come unto me, all ye that labour and are heavy laden, and I will give you rest.
—Matthew 11:28

On 27 October 1858, America's twenty-sixth president was born in New York City. Theodore "Teddy" Roosevelt gained notoriety for his imperialist foreign policy and brash leadership style. Roosevelt is perhaps best remembered for his involvement in the Spanish-American War in 1898, when he led the First US Volunteer Cavalry (Rough Riders) in the famous charge up San Juan Hill. He is one of the four US presidents to have their faces immortalized on Mount Rushmore.

But, strong as Roosevelt may have seemed, he was also a man of kindness. His father, Theodore Roosevelt, Sr., proved a great influence on his son, infusing into him such traits as gentleness, tenderness, and courage. Roosevelt once said of fatherhood, "It's a mighty bad thing for a boy when he becomes afraid to go to his father with his troubles, and it's mighty bad for a father when he becomes so busy with other affairs, that he has no time for the affairs of his children."

God has told us in His Word that we may come "boldly unto the throne of grace that we may obtain mercy, and find grace to help in time of need" (Hebrews 4:16). Unlike some earthly fathers, our heavenly Father is never too busy, cantankerous, or neglectful to welcome our approach at any time we need Him.

If you're a father, take it as a challenge today: have an inviting spirit with your children. Jesus told us, "Come unto me." As a dad, seek to adopt this attitude in your daily life at home, remaining approachable and sensitive to your children's needs. Your care and example could be what develops them into great citizens and, hopefully, better Christians as well.

If you're a child of God, take your heavenly Father up on His invitation to come boldly into His presence. He is available for you and able to help you beyond what any earthly father can provide.

Words that Help

28 October 1818

Let no corrupt communication proceed out of your mouth, but that which is good to the use of edifying, that it may minister grace unto the hearers. —**Ephesians 4:29**

Abigail Adams was the wife of John Adams, the second president of the United States. The two met in 1792 at a social gathering, where John was immediately smitten with the shy seventeen-year-old. The relationship between Abigail and John was unique; she was not just his wife, but also a loyal and trusted confidante. She is remembered for the copious letters she wrote to her husband while he stayed in Philadelphia during the Continental Congresses. John frequently sought the advice of Abigail, and their letters are filled with intellectual discussions on government and politics. Critics, in objection to Abigail's influence over her husband, began calling her "Mrs. President."

Historian Joseph Ellis discovered that the twelve hundred letters between the couple, "constituted a treasure trove of unexpected intimacy and candor, more revealing than any other correspondence between a prominent American husband and wife in American history." In Ellis' view, President Adams—considered one of the best letter writers of the age—falls short of self-educated Abigail's superb letter composition. Abigail, regarded as the more resilient and emotionally balanced spouse, is considered by Ellis to be one of the most extraordinary women in American history. On 28 October 1818, Abigail passed away at the age of seventy-three. Her husband died eight years later on 4 July.

The former President was blessed with a unique and helpful companion in Abigail Adams. As a nation, we owe a debt of gratitude for the character of this former First Lady. The Bible reminds us, "Let your speech be always with grace" (Colossians 4:6). It also says, "Wherefore, my beloved brethren, let every man be swift to hear, slow to speak, slow to wrath" (James 1:19). How gracious are your words to your spouse and to your friends? Help—don't hurt—with your speech.

Never Too Old

29 October 1998

As yet I am as strong this day as I was in the day that Moses sent me: as my strength was then, even so is my strength now, for war, both to go out, and to come in. **—Joshua 14:11**

John H. Glenn is famous for being the first American to orbit Earth. Prior to this accomplishment, he was a US Marine pilot who shot down three MiG fighters during the Korean War. Glenn was also one of the famed Mercury Seven astronauts. He experienced an exciting and fulfilling career as an aviator, astronaut, and politician. At the age of seventy-seven, Glenn chose to return to space on 29 October 1998, working as a payload specialist aboard the space shuttle Discovery. He became the oldest human to travel in space.

A common misconception among Christians is to believe that God cannot—or will not—use us in old age. That is not true! Caleb was forty years old when he spied out the land of Canaan, but Joshua 14 records his words as an eighty-five-year-old man. He confessed, "I am as strong this day as I was in the day that Moses sent me" and ambitiously stated, "Give me this mountain," referring to Hebron (Joshua 14:12). Caleb still pursued God, not just in his forties, but even in his eighties.

Abraham was seventy five years old when He departed from Haran to follow God's call (Genesis 12:4). Joshua died at 110 years old, having served God even in his old age (Joshua 24:29).

If John Glenn—past his youth—had enough passion to travel in space, can we not muster the passion to seek to serve God in the "golden" years? We may not be able to serve God in the same ways in old age as we did in our youth, especially as poor health begins to take its toll. But each of us can do *something* to serve Christ as the years progress. Seek to find a spot and serve, no matter your age. Your devotion and example will, no doubt, be a powerful influence on the next generation.

Real Danger or Radio Drama?

30 October 1938

And I saw the beast, and the kings of the earth, and their armies, gathered together to make war against him that sat on the horse, and against his army.
—Revelation 19:19

On the Sunday evening of 30 October 1938, nearly a million Americans—convinced our planet was at war with alien visitors—panicked. At 2000 hours, a CBS representative announced, "The Columbia Broadcasting System (CBS) and its affiliated stations present Orson Welles and the 'Mercury Theater on the Air' in *The War of the Worlds* by H. G. Wells." During the 1930s, Sunday evenings were considered prime-time as millions of Americans sat around their radios, in much the same way that Americans today sit in front of their televisions. At the beginning of this particular CBS program, however, most listeners were tuned in to Edgar Bergen's noted ventriloquist program, airing simultaneously on a rival radio station. Once Bergen's "Charlie McCarthy" ended at 2012 hours, people tuned to CBS. Listeners suddenly heard Welles' play unfold, having missed the introductory caveat explaining that it was only a dramatization.

Through clever sound effects and talented voice dramatization, possibly as many as a million listeners were convinced that a real martian invasion was afoot. Welles' story detailed that seven thousand National Guardsmen had been annihilated by poison gas. Immediately, terrified civilians clogged the highways. Electric companies were inundated with calls, asking to shut off residential lights so US homes would not be easily spotted by Martians. Some even asked the police for gas masks! Thankfully, the *War of the Worlds* was fake—it was merely an elaborate Halloween hoax. Welles' career as a filmmaker in Hollywood had now experienced its launch.

The coming Battle of Armageddon, however, will not be an elaborate ruse. For millions of people, it will be their final—and fatal—stand against God. Not only will the colossal conflict of Armageddon truly occur, but also eternity in the Lake of Fire will be the destination of many. Are you saved? It's the only way God will spare you from these perilous events.

The Sting of Death

31 October 1961

But if the Spirit of him that raised up Jesus from the dead dwell in you, he that raised up Christ from the dead shall also quicken your mortal bodies by his Spirit that dwelleth in you.—**Romans 8:11**

In the 1950s, the science-fiction genre dominated the silver screen. Concepts new to film were developed, including giant ants, radioactive dinosaurs, and a shrinking man. One unusual film in 1956, released by Allied Artists, was called *Invasion of the Body Snatchers.* It featured alien invaders duplicating human beings for the purpose of taking over the Earth.

On 31 October 1961, a real-life "body snatch" occurred when Soviet dictator Joseph Stalin's body was removed from Lenin's tomb in Moscow and re-interred in a nearby tomb. Vladimir Lenin was of course succeeded as Soviet leader by Joseph Stalin, who led his country to a hard-fought victory over Germany in World War II. Following the war, he ruled the USSR with an iron fist until his death in 1953, after which he joined Lenin in his tomb. Because of his brutality, Soviet authorities ordered his body removed from public display.

The sight of tombs and graves reminds us of our mortality. Our physical lives will one day be over. But Christians can take heart, as the same Spirit that raised up Christ from the dead also dwells in each of us! And God promises to "quicken"—raise up—our mortal bodies by His Spirit.

We even have hope as Christians that Christ could come back before we physically die. Paul spoke of those who "are alive and remain" during the time of the Rapture and how we will be "caught up together with them"—those who had died—"in the clouds" (1 Thessalonians 4:17). Christ could come any day, and if He comes very soon, you could find yourself never having to experience what 1 Corinthians 15:56 refers to as the "sting of death." Wouldn't that be an amazing way to begin eternity—to see your Saviour coming to receive you to Himself for all eternity? He could come—even today!

NOVEMBER

Strong Enough to Be Gentle

1 November 1861

And the servant of the Lord must not strive; but be gentle unto all men, apt to teach, patient,—**2 Timothy 2:24**

Following the Union defeat at the Battle of Bull Run, also called the First Battle of Manassas, General Winfield Scott resigned as President Lincoln's General-in-Chief. Lincoln felt he found a suitable replacement in General George B. McClellan. Like Scott, McClellan was a Mexican-American War veteran and a talented leader. His knack for military organization and drills likely impressed Lincoln, who wanted someone who could transform raw recruits into soldiers. From that perspective, McClellan was the man for the job. On 1 November 1861, Lincoln offered the position of General-in-Chief to McClellan.

From the start, however, McClellan's ideas about Union strategy collided with Lincoln's. McClellan repeatedly tried to convince the President he could not fight until he had more forces. From Lincoln's perspective, McClellan was too conservative—too unwilling to engage the enemy. A few weeks after his appointment, McClellan wrote his wife and disparaged Lincoln as "the original gorilla." In fact, until he was replaced by General Ulysses S. Grant in 1862, McClellan made no attempt to hide his disdain for President Lincoln. Nevertheless, Lincoln was willing to overlook McClellan's insubordinate conduct if he would only fight and win—something McClellan proved unwilling to do.

Amazingly, Lincoln, when mistreated, chose not to retaliate. Even when he replaced McClellan, it was not for personal reasons but because it was obviously necessary for the sake of the nation to win the war.

God does not ask us to deliberately place ourselves in situations of abuse and mistreatment. But, when rudeness or anger are aimed at us, we must be gentle. We are challenged by Christ's example, who never profaned nor mistreated His accusers (1 Peter 2:23). Don't be kind for the sake of merely your own reputation. Be gentle and patient for the sake of Christ and the gospel.

Distraction Leads to Disaster

2 November 1944

He that hath ears to hear, let him hear.—**Matthew 11:15**

Lieutenant Herb Dalliance was assigned to the First Platoon, Fox Company, 28th Infantry Division during World War II. Eager to prove himself in combat, Dalliance was always volunteering himself and his men for hazardous patrols. During the Battle for the Hürtgen Forest in November 1944, American troops were ordered to cross the Kall River to take the village of Schmidt. Dalliance assembled at the Battalion Command Post to hear the combat briefings and patrol orders for that morning. The company commander detailed the opposition that lay ahead in the village of Schmidt. He spoke of German troop strength, artillery pieces, and their tanks. During the speech, Dalliance erroneously chose to chitchat with another lieutenant with whom he had attended West Point. As the Colonel was ending the briefing, Dalliance *thought* he heard, "Men, this will be a picnic, as the Germans are vastly outnumbered." In reality, the Colonel said, "Men, this will be no picnic, as the Germans have us vastly outnumbered."

When they were all dismissed, Dalliance went back to his platoon and told the men that they didn't need to bring extra ammo or grenades. He explained that it was useless to arrange for another company to follow them in case they were cut off. The Colonel, after all, said it would be a picnic. On 2 November 1944, the 28th Infantry entered the Kall gorge and suffered one of the worst defeats in its history. The week-long battle was among the costliest division attacks of the war for the US Army, with casualties exceeding six thousand. Dalliance and all thirty-eight men of the First Platoon were slaughtered that day—all because he did not focus and listen.

Too often, husbands don't listen to wives and employees don't listen to employers. Most disastrous of all, sinners fail to listen to the Word of God, and Christians turn a deaf ear to the Holy Spirit. Eight times in the gospels, the Lord Jesus admonished His followers to listen carefully to what He had to say. Rather than being distracted by things of this world, we should listen to God's Word carefully and obey it diligently.

Humility in Leadership

3 November 1777

Who, when he was reviled, reviled not again; when he suffered, he threatened not; but committed himself to him that judgeth righteously:—**1 Peter 2:23**

During the American Revolution, General George Washington was apprised of a conspiracy intended to discredit his leadership of the Continental Army. On 3 November 1777, Washington discovered an unfavorable letter written by Inspector General Thomas Conway. Once Washington knew of Conway's letter, he wrote a letter of his own to Congressman Henry Laurens the following January. Rather than lambasting Conway in the letter, Washington chose measured language and even acknowledged humbly that he was not above scrutiny:

> But why should I expect to be exempt from censure—the unfailing lot of an elevated station? Merits and talents, with which I can have no pretensions of rivalship, have ever been subject to it. My heart tells me it has been my unremitted aim to do the best circumstances would permit; yet, I may have been very often mistaken in my judgment of the means, and may, in many instances deserve the imputation of error.

We easily jump to conclusions and lash out at those who we *think* may have wronged us. Washington's restraint reflects the teachings of Christ, who, "when He was reviled, reviled not again." The Bible further tells us that Christ "committed himself to him that judgeth righteously."

God knows the resistance you may be facing from those who wish you would not speak of the Lord or His Word. The Lord is watching; He has not forgotten you. Turn these times of chiding and resistance to prayer requests. Petition God to help you speak the truth in love (Ephesians 4:15). And, instead of seeking to "even the score," ask God to do so. Romans 12:19 admonishes us, "Dearly beloved, avenge not yourselves . . . for it is written, Vengeance is mine; I will repay, saith the Lord."

It is pride that tells us we deserve to lash out against those who criticize us. It is humility that acknowledges error when it is pointed out to us and, when we are innocent, trusts God to be the righteous judge.

A Simple Reminder

4 November 1979

But we preach Christ crucified, unto the Jews a stumblingblock, and unto the Greeks foolishness; But unto them which are called, both Jews and Greeks, Christ the power of God, and the wisdom of God.—**1 Corinthians 1:23–24**

A group of Iranian student protestors became aggravated after the deposed Shah of Iran received medical treatment in America. They stormed the US Embassy in Tehran on 4 November 1979 and captured fifty-two American diplomats and citizens. These Americans were held hostage for 444 days (4 November 1979 to 20 January 1981). They were finally released upon President Ronald Reagan's inauguration. During the captivity of these Americans, a "Yellow Ribbon" campaign began in the US. Thousands of yellow ribbons were tied around trees and hung on doors to remind Americans to pray for the hostages. The ribbon banded a nation together in intercession, and the symbol quickly unified the country's thoughts and prayers.

A cross has no meaning to the world, but it has deep meaning to Christians. "For the preaching of the cross is to them that perish foolishness; but unto us which are saved it is the power of God," declares 1 Corinthians 1:18. The cross is a powerful reminder of the suffering endured by Christ for us.

Have you ever felt that the Christian life should be easier? Christians are told by Christ to take up their "cross" (Luke 9:23)—a symbol of the surrender that God expects of him or her. The Holy Spirit guided Paul to write, "I am crucified with Christ: nevertheless I live; yet not I, but Christ liveth in me" (Galatians 2:20). To be crucified involves sacrifice and extreme difficulty.

God does not expect us to be grim people. But, these Scripture passages should remind us that the Christian life is a serious matter, and the cross is not a mere religious ornament. Let the cross remind you to endure when times get tough, "Looking unto Jesus the author and finisher of our faith; who for the joy that was set before him endured the cross" (Hebrews 12:2).

The Gunpowder Plot

5 November 1605

The grass withereth, the flower fadeth: but the word of our God shall stand for ever.—**Isaiah 40:8**

The Gunpowder Plot of 1605 was a failed assassination attempt against King James I of England by disgruntled Catholics. The Catholics in England had expected James to be more tolerant than his predecessor, Queen Elizabeth I, because he was the son of Mary Queen of Scots. However, James proved to be the opposite and ordered all Catholic priests to leave England. This so angered some Catholics that they decided to kill James and put his daughter Elizabeth Stuart on the throne, ensuring a Catholic would be the ruler. This led to a plot to kill not only King James I, but also everyone sitting in the Houses of Parliament when Parliament opened on 5 November 1605.

The plot was revealed to the authorities in an anonymous letter on 26 October. A search of the House of Parliament around midnight on 4 November revealed a man named Guy Fawkes guarding thirty-six barrels of gunpowder—enough to reduce the House of Parliament to rubble. Fawkes was arrested along with seven other conspirators. At their trial on 27 January 1606, they were convicted and sentenced to be hanged, drawn, and quartered.

Six years after this assassination plot, the fifty-four-member translation committee King James had appointed in 1604 finished their work on the King James Authorized Version of the Bible. Had Fawkes and his conspirators succeeded in the Gunpowder Plot, the King James Bible may never have come into being.

As far back as man's beginning in the Garden of Eden, Satan has attempted to question, corrupt, or destroy the Holy Bible. However, God in His providence has preserved His Word throughout the ages, just as He promised He would. Once again, God showed Himself faithful in 1605 by stopping this potentially devastating event. He has not stopped guarding His Word!

Provoked to Good Works

6 November 1528

And when they were come, and had gathered the church together, they rehearsed all that God had done with them, and how he had opened the door of faith unto the Gentiles.—**Acts 14:27**

On 6 November 1528, Spanish conquistador Álvar Núñez Cabeza de Vaca became the first European to set foot on what would become Texas soil. Núñez' unintentional landing, near what is now Galveston Island, was due to his flight from hostile Indians in Florida. With around ninety men, Núñez and his explorers scrambled aboard whatever boats they could find to avert certain disaster. Landing in Texas did not end their troubles, however, as Núñez and his men were taken captive by the Karankawa Indians. After two years in captivity, Núñez and his men were given freedom after he showed himself a skilled medicine man to the Karankawa. Over the next several years, they wandered through the tribes learning how the Indians lived and providing medical help. Finally, in 1536, his party encountered fellow Spaniards, who led them to Mexico City where they rehearsed their amazing odyssey to their fellow countrymen. Núñez' harrowing tale so inspired fellow explorers that they ramped up their exploration of the land that would one day become Texas.

Each year, our church hosts a missions conference. During this series of meetings, missionaries that our church supports rehearse what God has done in the respective countries where they are sharing the gospel. It is an exciting and inspiring time as hearing these accounts motivates God's people to pray and give so many others may also know the good news.

All of us can share with other Christians blessings of great things God has done in our lives. When you have a financial burden lifted, tell someone the story. When God gives you a unique opportunity to share the gospel, let another believer know. The Bible says, "Let us consider one another to provoke unto love and to good works" (Hebrews 10:24). When you let your blessings be known, others are encouraged to follow God that they may see His good hand in their lives as well.

Sheep among Wolves

7 November 1931

For I know this, that after my departing shall grievous wolves enter in among you, not sparing the flock.—**Acts 20:29**

On 7 November 1931, the Portland-class heavy cruiser USS *Indianapolis* was launched into service. One of the advantages of heavy cruisers is their great speed. This was due in that time to their steam turbine design that relied on oil, versus a reciprocating steam engine. This design came in handy when the *Indianapolis* was tasked with a top-secret mission to deliver atomic bomb components just hours after the bomb had been tested in New Mexico. The *Indianapolis* set a speed record, arriving at Tinian Island in the Western Pacific on 26 July 1945. After off-loading her top-secret cargo, the *Indianapolis* headed to Guam but was torpedoed and sunk by the Japanese submarine *I-58* en route. Hundreds of sailors abandoned the sinking vessel and were forced to endure three and a half days of incredible hardship before being spotted by naval rescue aircraft. Particularly horrifying was the fact that beneath the water's surface lurked an ominous threat. Hundreds of man-eating sharks terrified and attacked the weakened men. Of the 900 men who went into the water, only 316 survived. The rest succumbed to hyperthermia, dehydration, sharks, and suicide. Those who survived bore lasting scars from their ordeal.

Like sharks among the stranded sailors, so today there are wolves (false teachers) lurking among sheep (God's people). The Apostle Paul warned the church leaders at Ephesus about these wolves and referred to them as *grievous,* meaning "violent, cruel, and unsparing." Pray that God would grant your pastor clear vision to discern those who seek to sow discord and false doctrine in your church. And be on guard yourself. Jesus warned of "false prophets, which come to you in sheep's clothing, but inwardly they are ravening wolves" (Matthew 7:15). If you were in the ocean and knew there was a shark nearby, you would quickly move to safer waters. When you encounter someone who sows discord and false doctrine, no matter how benevolent their intentions appear, beware!

The X-Ray Discovery

8 November 1895

But whoso looketh into the perfect law of liberty, and continueth therein, he being not a forgetful hearer, but a doer of the work, this man shall be blessed in his deed.—**James 1:25**

On 8 November 1895, a German scientist named Wilhelm Conrad Roentgen conducted an experiment to test whether cathode rays could pass through glass. During the experiment, Roentgen noticed a strange glow coming from a nearby chemically-coated screen. He christened the rays that caused this glow "X-rays" because he was unable to explain their nature. For several weeks, Roentgen conducted more experiments with the mysterious X-rays until he learned they could penetrate human flesh, but they could not penetrate higher-density substances like bone. He also learned they could be photographed. Military physicians quickly recognized the usefulness of X-rays to see broken bones, bullets, and pieces of shrapnel in wounded soldiers. During the next few years, "Roentgen rays" helped diagnose injuries to troops in the Greco-Turkish War, the Russo-Japanese War, and the Balkan Wars. Mobile X-ray units accompanied field hospitals during World War I. Dr. Rontgen went on to garner numerous awards for his work, including the first Nobel Prize for physics in 1901, yet he remained humble and, from a desire to serve the widest number of people possible, never tried to patent his discovery.

As an X-ray technician, I can attest to a phrase that has become one of the maxims of radiology: "X-rays never lie." If there is a foreign object inside the human body, it *will* be revealed on an X-ray image. If someone has pneumonia, an X-ray *will* show it. God compares His Word to a mirror—which also never lies. When you look in a mirror, what you see is what is there. Unlike the mirrors in our homes, however, God uses His Word to reveal our *hearts*. The Bible is the "perfect law of liberty," and through it, the Holy Spirit reveals what is on the "inside" of our lives. If you want an accurate diagnosis of your spiritual life, spend time in God's Word through reading, study, and listening to it preached.

Time Is Short

9 November 1938

. . . Woe to the inhabiters of the earth and of the sea! for the devil is come down unto you, having great wrath, because he knoweth that he hath but a short time. —**Revelation 12:12**

On 9 November 1938, the Nazi Party launched a campaign of terror targeted against the Jews of Germany and Austria. Known as *Kristallnacht* or the "Night of Broken Glass," more than 7,000 Jewish businesses were destroyed, along with 117 private homes. An estimated 30,000 Jewish men were arrested, many of whom were sent to concentration camps. Kristallnacht represented a dramatic escalation of Nazi terror. The event would foreshadow Hitler's Final Solution, an effort to purge every Jew from Europe.

Satan knows he has only "a short time" on this planet. In these final days prior to Christ's return, our adversary has ramped up his attacks on God's people. Cultures worldwide are filled with profane language, indecent images, and a push toward living without God and the Bible. If he can dissuade you, Christian, from your calling to follow Christ, He will do it. Describing Satan, Jesus said, "The thief cometh not, but for to steal, and to kill, and to destroy" (John 10:10). Knowing these things provides all the more motivation for those who name the name of Christ to follow the instruction of 1 Peter 5:8, "Be sober, be vigilant; because your adversary the devil, as a roaring lion, walketh about, seeking whom he may devour."

How do we remain vigilant against the devil? The Bible gives us specific ways: Memorize God's Word. "Thy word have I hid in mine heart, that I might not sin against thee" (Psalm 119:11). Sing spiritual songs. "Speaking to yourselves in psalms and hymns and spiritual songs, singing and making melody in your heart to the Lord" (Ephesians 5:19). Guard your inner self—your heart—"for out of it are the issues of life" (Proverbs 4:23). Take the steps you can to steer clear of the devil's tricks. Though he will never stop tempting you, Christ will always be with you (Hebrews 13:5).

Help Wanted

10 November 2001

But when he saw the multitudes, he was moved with compassion on them, because they fainted, and were scattered abroad, as sheep having no shepherd. Then saith he unto his disciples, The harvest truly is plenteous, but the labourers are few; Pray ye therefore the Lord of the harvest, that he will send forth labourers into his harvest.—**Matthew 9:36–38**

When Islamic terrorists flew planes into the World Trade Center and Pentagon on 11 September 2001, life for Americans forever changed. Not since 7 December 1941 had enemies attacked American soil. Many were shaken to the core as a result of the dastardly and cowardly attack on our nation. On 10 November 2001, President George W. Bush addressed the United Nations to plead for support in combating international terrorism across the world. Unfortunately, the response was less than what he hoped.

If we were directly approached by the President of the United States with a request for assistance, we would be honored. If we were asked by the President for prayer, we would be faithful to pray for his request. How much more seriously should we take Jesus' prayer request? The Lord specifically asked us to pray for laborers who will take the gospel around the world.

The Bible tells us that as Jesus looked on the multitudes, He was "moved with compassion." Christians too often focus on what they cannot do in the harvest field. Perhaps a physical condition keeps them from traveling to be a missionary. For some, the obstacle is a deeply entrenched belief that God will not use them because of their lack of ability. But *all* of us can do *something*.

Definitely, each of us can pray for laborers, as Jesus asked us to. Each of us can also give to support the work of missions. And all of us can maintain a tender heart toward sharing the gospel everywhere we go. God does not ask all of us to serve in the same capacity, but He does ask us to be willing—to present ourselves "a living sacrifice" (Romans 12:1). If you are willing, God will make a way for you to be involved (2 Corinthians 8:12).

Patton's Pattern

11 November 1885

Lest Satan should get an advantage of us: for we are not ignorant of his devices.
—2 Corinthians 2:11

On 11 November 1885, one of the greatest military leaders in history was born. George Smith Patton, Jr., desired to be a war hero from an early age. He enrolled in the famed Virginia Military Academy in 1904 and graduated from West Point in 1909. Patton began his combat career chasing Mexican bandit Pancho Villa near the Texas-Mexico border. During World War I, Patton was a strong advocate of using armor and trained tank crews. In World War II, Patton was given command of the US Third Army, which swept across France, capturing town after town.

It is rumored that Patton was once asked the reason for his success. He supposedly replied that he kept two books on his night stand. One was the Holy Bible, which he read every day, and the other was a book by Erwin Rommel entitled *Infantry Attacks*. Rommel was one of the German Army's most respected and renowned generals. Patton studied Rommel, and thus was able to anticipate his adversary's moves.

One reason Satan enjoys victory over Christians is that they are ignorant of the way he works to undermine their witness for Christ. Satan has devices—regular schemes, plots, and tricks—he uses against us. Patton knew Rommel's tactics, but do you know Satan's strategies? Ancient Chinese theorist Sun Tzu said, "If you know the enemy and know yourself, you need not fear the result of a hundred battles."

We have a Book we can read every day to stay a step ahead of our adversary, the devil. Christians can never attain perfection—not even Paul did (Philippians 3:13). But, through His Word, God gives "doctrine . . . reproof . . . correction . . . instruction in righteousness" (2 Timothy 3:16). More than military victory, let us seek to have victory over spiritual wickedness and the devil (Ephesians 6:12). If you develop one habit in your life this year, let it be the habit of a daily walk with God. Seek to triumph in your spiritual battles with Him by your side.

Closed Door

12 November 1954

A window shalt thou make to the ark, and in a cubit shalt thou finish it above; and the door of the ark shalt thou set in the side thereof; with lower, second, and third stories shalt thou make it.—**Genesis 6:16**

Ellis Island is famous for many reasons, not the least of which is that during World War II it served as a hospital for wounded soldiers, a detention center, and a Coast Guard training facility. Better known as the "gateway to America," the once famous immigration center closed its doors on 12 November 1954 after having legally processed some twelve million immigrants since 1892. While other legal means now exist to enter America, Ellis Island has forever shut its doors to those seeking to immigrate to the US.

While a door and opportunity of salvation remains open in this age of grace, there is coming a day when it will be shut. There won't be another chance to be saved. When God instructed Noah to build the ark, He specified that there was to be only *one* door. And, once that door was shut, no one else was getting onto the ark. However, in His mercy, God delayed His judgment and commissioned Noah to preach a message of repentance for 120 years (Genesis 6:3). During this period of forbearance, all someone had to do was to enter the door, and they would be spared.

The Lord Jesus Christ said in John 10:9, "I am the door: by me if any man enter in, he shall be saved, and shall go in and out, and find pasture." We not only have the blessed opportunity of eternal life in Heaven, but also to show others the way. Perhaps you've never had the courage to give someone the gospel. Ask God for boldness. If you struggle with nervousness, you are in good company. Paul the Apostle asked the Ephesians to pray for him to be a bold soulwinner (Ephesians 6:19). Maybe no one has responded lately to your gospel witness. Even the most faithful soulwinners encounter those seasons. Continue telling others that Jesus is the way, the truth, and the life (John 14:6). Remember, God promises we will reap as we continue to sow (Galatians 6:9).

God Feeds the Forgotten

13 November 1942

I have been young, and now am old; yet have I not seen the righteous forsaken, nor his seed begging bread.—**Psalm 37:25**

The end of a harrowing experience in the life of Eddie Rickenbacker came on 13 November 1942. Rickenbacker and his crew of eight were flying a mission to deliver a top-secret message to General Douglas MacArthur. Rickenbacker's plane experienced navigational problems and malfunctioning equipment, and the crew frantically looked for their first stop on Canton Island. As their plane descended and sank into the sea, Eddie and the other seven men had scrambled into three life rafts. Rickenbacker's watch showed 1436 hours, Honolulu time, 21 October 1942.

Rickenbacker had learned to pray at his mother's knee as a young boy. At his suggestion, the men began daily prayer meetings. On the eighth day, after the mid-morning prayer service, Rickenbacker pulled his cap down over his eyes to get some sleep. Suddenly, a sea gull landed on his head. The other men saw it, but no one moved. Inch by inch, Rickenbacker slowly moved his hand towards the hat's brim. With all the strength he could muster, Rickenbacker grabbed for the bird and caught it by its legs before it could escape. They cut it into eight pieces and enjoyed their first meal in more than a week at sea. Using the intestines as bait and items collected from the life rafts as fishing hooks and line, the men caught a sea bass and mackerel. That night, it rained, and the men were able to catch rainwater in their caps. After twenty-four days at sea, a Navy plane finally spotted and rescued the crew.

The psalmist never saw God forsake His own, and God promises in Hebrews 13:5 that He will never leave or forsake us. If He can take care of the fowls of the air, He can take care of our needs as well. "Behold the fowls of the air: for they sow not, neither do they reap, nor gather into barns; yet your heavenly Father feedeth them. Are ye not much better than they?" (Matthew 6:26). If the God who feeds the birds came through for a stranded crew of airmen at sea, don't you think He cares for you as well?

Leave No Man Behind

14 November 1965

So that contrariwise ye ought rather to forgive him, and comfort him, lest perhaps such a one should be swallowed up with overmuch sorrow. **—2 Corinthians 2:7**

The Battle of Ia Drang began on 14 November 1965 when elements of the 1st Battalion, 7th Cavalry Regiment landed US troops at a landing zone called LZ X-Ray. Led by (then) Lieutenant Colonel Harold "Hal" Moore, US troops had no idea they had been inserted into a position only a couple of hundred meters from two North Vietnamese regiments. Outnumbered two to one, fierce fighting ensued for three days before Moore's battalion was finally relieved by elements from the 2nd and 5th Cavalry regiments. When it was all over, Moore had lost seventy-nine men while the North Vietnamese suffered the loss of more than a thousand.

Prior to embarking upon the helicopters that would transport the men of the 7th Cavalry to the battle, Lt. Col. Moore promised his men,

> Let us understand the situation. We are going into battle against a tough and determined enemy. I can't promise you that I will bring you all home alive, but this I swear, before you and almighty God: that when we go into battle, I will be the first one to set foot on the field, and I will be the last to step off. And I will leave no one behind. Dead or alive, we will all come home together. So help me God.

True to his word, Moore ensured every US soldier who stepped off those helicopters on 14 November 1965 returned, dead or alive. He had left no man behind.

A sad but oft-quoted maxim in Christendom is that "Christians eat their own." Countless professing Christians have left the faith because of a fellow believer's poor behavior. Do we seek to judge wayward brothers and sisters in Christ, or do we seek to restore them? Let us emulate Hal Moore's attitude towards his fellow soldiers. Don't leave behind someone you know who struggles to be faithful or has forsaken your local church. Humbly pray for a prodigal today. With God's grace, seek to leave no man behind.

The Whole Picture

15 November 1806

But as it is written, Eye hath not seen, nor ear heard, neither have entered into the heart of man, the things which God hath prepared for them that love him. **—1 Corinthians 2:9**

Zebulon Pike was one of the first military explorers to reach the vast Colorado Territory. Born in 1794, Pike joined the army at only fifteen years of age. In 1806, Lieutenant Pike and a band of fellow soldiers were dispatched on a mission to discover where the Arkansas River began. On 15 November 1806, Pike saw what he described as "a small blue cloud," which in reality was the summit of a mountain with an elevation over fourteen thousand feet high. The summit would later be named Pikes Peak in honor of the famous explorer.

Little could Pike realize that what he was seeing was actually the tip of a huge, magnificent mountain. In like manner, we who have trusted in Christ for salvation see only a glimpse of the wonderful things "God hath prepared for them that love him." The Apostle Paul wrote, "For now we see through a glass, darkly; but then face to face: now I know in part; but then shall I know even as also I am known" (1 Corinthians 13:12). The beauties of eternity are not something we can fully comprehend in our mortal bodies, but one day, we will understand. We will be resurrected and see the beauties of Heaven for all of eternity. The greatest privilege we will be granted, no doubt, will be seeing the Lord Jesus face to face. "Beloved, now are we the sons of God, and it doth not yet appear what we shall be: but we know that, when he shall appear, we shall be like him; for we shall see him as he is" (1 John 3:2).

Do you desire to see the Saviour who died for you? Too often, Christians are distracted with the things of this world—travel, entertainment, sports. Does your heart yearn to see the Lord, or do earthly pursuits call your attention? If a mountain—the creation of God—can so impress us with its majesty, imagine what it will be like to see the whole picture—not just Heaven, but God Himself!

Blame Shifting

16 November 1941

So when they continued asking him, he lifted up himself, and said unto them, He that is without sin among you, let him first cast a stone at her.—**John 8:7**

Dr. Joseph Goebbels was one of the leading cogs in the Nazi war machine. As Minister of Propaganda, Goebbels regularly wrote the lead article for a Nazi weekly called *Das Reich (The Reich)*. On 16 November 1941, Goebbels wrote a seven-page article entitled "The Jews Are Guilty!" In the opening sentences of the article, Goebbels laid total blame for World War II at the feet of what he called "world Jewry." He went on to state that "the Jews wanted war, and now they have it." Despite Hitler's madness, paranoia, and the false flag operation he orchestrated to justify his invasion of Poland on 1 September 1939, Goebbels went to his untimely grave blaming the Jews for the war.

The unsavory tactic of blame shifting which Goebbels exemplified started in the Garden of Eden with Adam and Eve, and continues to this day. When God asked Adam whether he had eaten of the forbidden tree, he blamed "the woman whom thou gavest to be with me" (Genesis 3:12). When the Lord confronted Eve, she claimed "the serpent beguiled me" (Genesis 3:13). Of course, the serpent had no one to blame but himself! But neither Adam nor Eve took their share of responsibility for succumbing to temptation.

Before we call attention to the faults of others, we would be wise to consider our own failures. When the scribes and Pharisees brought Jesus a woman who was "taken in adultery" and tried to trap Jesus into saying she must be stoned, Jesus told them that whichever of them was without sin in his own life could cast the first stone. Of course, Jesus was the only one who actually was "without sin," but He did not stone her either. Rather, He instructed her to "go, and sin no more" (John 8:11). Rather than rushing to judge and condemn, let's hurry to help and restore. Blame shifting is ineffective, but giving mercy while speaking truth encourages holiness (Proverbs 16:6).

"The Desired"

17 November 1755

And I will shake all nations, and the desire of all nations shall come: and I will fill this house with glory, saith the LORD of hosts.—**Haggai 2:7**

Louis Stanislas Xavier was born 17 November 1755 in the Palace of Versailles. Fourth in line to the throne of France, he is better known to historians as King Louis XVIII. During the French Revolution, his brother, King Louis XVI, was deposed and guillotined, and his nephew died in prison. These events effectively made him King of France; but the events of the French Revolution, followed by the reign of Napoleon Bonaparte, forced Louis into exile for twenty-three years. After Napoleon's abdication in 1814, Louis returned to Paris and was nicknamed "The Desired." However, a year later, Napoleon escaped exile on Elba Island, marched on France, and tried to regain power. Napoleon was soundly defeated by Lord Wellington at Waterloo in 1815 and was imprisoned at St. Helena, where he later died. Louis XVIII was restored a second time to the throne in July and reigned in France until his death in 1824.

One can speculate as to how Louis obtained his nickname. It is likely that pro-monarchy French citizens had long awaited the return of a French king and thus referred to him as "desired" upon taking the throne.

As citizens of Heaven, our hearts yearn for Christ's kingdom. Those of us who claim the name of Christ are awaiting His return to rapture His Bride (1 Thessalonians 4:16–18). The Bible tells us that Christ will one day establish His kingdom on Earth (Revelation 20:1–6). Charles Wesley's familiar hymn "Hark! the Herald Angels Sing," in a line reminiscent of Haggai's writing, refers to Christ as the "Desire of Nations" and implores Him to return.

Christ is the only Ruler who has never made a mistake, and never will. Earthly rulers, even at their best, can fail and make wrong decisions. As Christians, we have the perfect King. It's only a matter of time until He arrives, presides for a millennium on Earth, and is forever on His throne in Heaven (Revelation 22:1). Believers are blessed, for Christ is coming soon!

Steadfast Samson

18 November 1916

Greater love hath no man than this, that a man lay down his life for his friends.
—John 15:13

The Great War, or World War I, ushered in the age of industrialized killing on a scale never before seen. Veterans of that conflict, when asked of their worst experience, invariably spoke of the horrors of trench warfare along the Western Front. Many soldiers have relayed how the trenches came alive after sunset. This was the time when wire repair parties were sent out to fix the barbed wire. It was also the time when a wounded man's comrades would try to reach him to either drag him back to his own trench or administer first aid. This proved particularly deadly, as enemy snipers would target soldiers trying to reach their wounded buddies. Instead of killing one man, the enemy might be able to kill three or four who attempted to help a fallen friend.

One of the deadliest battles on the Western Front was the Battle of the Somme which began on 1 July 1916 and officially ended on 18 November 1916. In four and a half months, it claimed the lives of over a million men. In his autobiography, *Good-Bye to All That,* veteran of the Somme, Robert Graves, tells of a soldier named Samson had been shot seventeen times. Samson knew that if he cried out in pain, his fellow soldiers would risk their own lives to attempt a rescue. Selflessly desiring to spare the lives of his friends, Samson jammed his fist into his mouth to keep from crying out in agony. After the battle, Samson's body was discovered with his fist still stuck in his mouth. He had died sometime during the night—alone, but thinking of his friends.

Samson's selflessness—his choice to die alone in no man's land—reminds us of Jesus' statement that there is no greater love than a willing death for one's friends. But Jesus died alone on a cross for *all*—even those who would reject Him. "But God commendeth his love toward us, in that, while we were yet sinners, Christ died for us" (Romans 5:8). Tell someone today of Christ's love and sacrifice for them.

Foolish Pursuits

19 November 1942

But avoid foolish questions, and genealogies, and contentions, and strivings about the law; for they are unprofitable and vain.—**Titus 3:9**

On 19 November 1942, the Soviets launched a massive counterattack known as Operation Uranus during the Battle of Stalingrad. The fighting in Stalingrad proved to be some of the fiercest of the entire war on the Eastern Front and turned the tide against Nazi Germany. During the six-month struggle, the Germans were no match for the brutal, close quarters street fighting that ensued. German soldiers had an aversion to house-to-house fighting, instead preferring the open steppe of Russia. As a result, they took the opportunity to develop one of their many "wonder weapons." In an effort to literally shoot around corners, the Krummlauf was the epitome of an impractical waste of resources. Designed to clamp to the end of an MP-44 rifle, the thirty-degree curved barrel and large mirror allowed soldiers to shoot over obstacles or around the corners of buildings without exposing themselves to enemy fire. The Krummlauf turned out to be a failure because the barrel quickly wore out and it cost the Germans vital resources that could have been used in more practical pursuits.

Some war tactics turn out to be unprofitable. Have you ever caught yourself wasting time on something that has no great value? God's Word cautions Christians against foolish pursuits that will likely lead nowhere. We are to be "redeeming the time, because the days are evil" (Ephesians 5:16). Maybe the television blares for too many hours at your home every day, or long periods of web surfing leave you feeling completely unaccomplished and unproductive. Argumentation is one of the great time wasters as well—usually, both parties walk away still convinced of their own beliefs.

Rather than chasing fruitless goals, seek to purposefully use your time toward things of lasting value. Our lives have limited length. May we be found faithful in how we have used our resources—especially time. We can pray with the psalmist, "So teach us to number our days, that we may apply our hearts unto wisdom" (Psalm 90:12).

Judgment Day

20 November 1945

And I saw the dead, small and great, stand before God; and the books were opened: and another book was opened, which is the book of life: and the dead were judged out of those things which were written in the books, according to their works. —**Revelation 20:12**

On 20 November 1945, the allied nations that had defeated Nazi Germany commenced the notorious Nuremberg Trials. This international military tribunal included trials for allegations of war crimes against twenty-four high-ranking Nazis. Prior to Nuremberg, there had never been a trial quite like this one. The tribunal lasted nearly a year and included over two hundred courtroom proceedings. Lord Justice Geoffrey Lawrence served as presiding judge and—when the trial ended—twelve men were sentenced to death, seven were sent to prison, and three were acquitted.

The Bible warns of a coming judgment day in which the works of all those who have rejected God's Son will be judged. Unlike Nuremberg, the Lord Jesus Christ, the Righteous Judge, will serve as presiding judge. We do not have to wonder about the verdict for unbelievers—the book of Revelation is clear that "whosoever was not found written in the book of life was cast into the lake of fire" (Revelation 20:15). The Nazis who stood trial at Nuremberg had sealed their own fate by the choices they made during the war. Those who stand before the Lord at the Great White Throne Judgment will find their fate already has been determined by their rejection of Jesus Christ while they lived on Earth.

The only way to escape the Lake of Fire is to receive the Lord Jesus Christ as Saviour. "But as many as received him, to them gave he power to become the sons of God, even to them that believe on his name" (John 1:12). Once a person makes the decision to trust Christ alone for salvation, he is safe, secure, and sealed by the Holy Spirit. For them, there is "no condemnation" (Romans 8:1), and there never will be. Are your own sins forgiven? Don't delay your decision, for on Judgment Day, it will be too late.

A Faithful Copy

21 November 1864

And it shall be, when he sitteth upon the throne of his kingdom, that he shall write him a copy of this law in a book out of that which is before the priests the Levites:
—Deuteronomy 17:18

The Gold Star Mothers organization was initially started for mothers who had lost a son or daughter in World War II. Yet, long before the Gold Star Mothers, one mother received a written personal condolence from the President himself. On 21 November 1864 President Abraham Lincoln is reported to have composed a letter to Mrs. Lydia Bixby. The Bixby letter, as it became known, expressed the President's sympathy on the loss of Mrs. Bixby's sons during the American Civil War. A copy of the letter was then published in the *Boston Evening Transcript* newspaper four days later. Even popular culture grabbed the letter. In the 1998 war epic *Saving Private Ryan*, General George C. Marshall's character recites the letter to two of his staff officers, quoting the letter verbatim.

Among historians, there is debate over the authorship of this letter. There are some who suggest that the letter may not have been penned by Lincoln himself, but by his secretary John Hay, as no one has produced the original displaying his handwriting. In actuality, the fact that the original has not been produced is no great obstacle to authenticity since the newspapers published it so quickly after it was written. Most people recognize the sheer volume of reproductions that have agreed over the years as a strong testament to the legitimacy of the letter.

A similar debate, although with far greater consequences, exists over the preservation of the Bible since there are no original manuscripts still in existence for this most sacred book. What people fail to realize is that God promised to preserve His Word (Psalm 12:6–7; Matthew 24:35; Isaiah 40:8). To do so, He used human instruments to make faithful copies of His Word, and those copies are no less the Word of God than if we possessed the original manuscripts. The Lord promised to preserve His Word through every generation, and we can certainly trust that He has done so.

Spousal Support

22 November 1744

Who can find a virtuous woman? for her price is far above rubies.
—Proverbs 31:10

Abigail Smith Adams was born 22 November 1744. She was the second of three daughters born into a preacher's family. In 1764, she married John Adams, who became America's second president. While it would be easy to allow President Adams' fame to overshadow his wife's role in our nation's founding, such thinking would be foolish. Abigail rose to prominence, and her intellect led her to be considered her husband's most trusted advisor, encourager, and confidante. One example of her role as his encourager is an excerpt from a letter she wrote him after the Battle of Bunker Hill, the first two sentences of which are quotes from Scripture:

> The race is not to the swift, nor the battle to the strong; but the God of Israel is he, that giveth strength and power unto His people. Trust in Him at all times, ye people, pour out your hearts before Him; God is a refuge for us.—Charlestown is laid in ashes. The battle began upon our entrenchments upon Bunker's Hill, Saturday morning about three o'clock, and has not ceased yet, and it is now three o'clock Sabbath afternoon. It is expected they will come over the Neck tonight, and a dreadful battle must ensue. Almighty God, cover the heads of our countrymen, and be a shield to our dear friends!

In so many marriages, spouses seek to compete or selfishly tear one another down. But Abigail Adams exemplified the supportive and encouraging spirit described in Proverbs 31.

Have you been blessed by a loving and supportive spouse who follows Christ? Thank God, and thank your spouse. Do you find yourself competing rather than working with your spouse? Ask God to forgive you, and ask your spouse to forgive you as well. Ephesians 5:20–21 gives good advice for every Christian marriage, "Giving thanks always for all things unto God and the Father in the name of our Lord Jesus Christ; Submitting yourselves one to another in the fear of God."

Behold the Fake

23 November 1499

For there shall arise false Christs, and false prophets, and shall shew great signs and wonders; insomuch that, if it were possible, they shall deceive the very elect. —**Matthew 24:24**

During the tumultuous time in British history known as the Wars of the Roses, the House of York vied for the throne against the House of Lancaster. During the Battle of Towton in 1461, Yorkist king Edward IV crushed the Lancastrians. After his death in 1483, his surviving brother, Richard III, seized the throne for himself. As was customary at that time in history, Richard had the surviving sons of his brother imprisoned so they could not assume the throne for themselves. Mysteriously, the boys disappeared and were presumed dead. In 1497, a man named Perkin Warbeck invaded England and claimed he was the rightful heir to the throne, being the lost son of Edward IV. After fleeing battle, Perkin was captured and imprisoned. On 23 November 1499, he was executed as an imposter.

The Lord Jesus spoke of those who would come in His name, falsely claiming to be Christ (Matthew 24:5). Like those deceived by Perkin Warbeck, many will be fooled when the Antichrist arrives on the world stage. Although Christians will have been raptured before the Antichrist's rule, even today, false prophets use "great signs and wonders" to lead many to believe their message. We should not be surprised, for "Satan himself is transformed into an angel of light" (2 Corinthians 11:14).

Those who have placed their faith and trust in the real Christ, God's Son, have the tools to avoid being deceived by an imposter. Speaking of believers, Christ said "a stranger will they not follow" and "my sheep hear my voice" (John 10:5, 27). Stay in His Word. When you hear a preacher or teacher speak something contradictory to it, you will be able to discern between truth and error. Not everyone who claims spirituality is sent of God. "Try the spirits whether they are of God: because many false prophets are gone out into the world" (1 John 4:1).

"Others, Lord"

24 November 1807

And he kneeled down, and cried with a loud voice, Lord, lay not this sin to their charge. And when he had said this, he fell asleep.—**Acts 7:60**

The Iroquois were an alliance of Native American tribes that included the Mohawk. Prior to the American Revolution, the Iroquois tried to remain neutral, but by 1777, Mohawk Chief Thayendanegea, also known as Joseph Brant, had led the Iroquois into an alliance with Britain. Brant's reasoning was the British represented the last defense against land-hungry colonists who would continue to encroach upon the land belonging to the Native Americans. Brant fought the colonists in various battles, the most noteworthy being the Battle of Oriskany. On 24 November 1807, Brant lay dying in his home in Ontario. His reported last words were, "Have pity on the poor Indians. If you have any influence with the great, endeavor to use it for their good."

Brant's dying wish was for his people, not for himself. Stephen, the first Christian martyr, asked God not to charge the crowd with his murder. No doubt, a number of them were Jewish by heritage, just as he was. He had a concern and desire for the welfare of his own people, especially for their salvation.

Our Lord's dying wish was also for others. As the Lord Jesus Christ hung on the cross, He commissioned the Apostle John to care for his mother (John 19:26–27) and He asked His Father to forgive the crowd that consented to His crucifixion (Luke 23:34).

How much of your life and heart is focused on others? An old song says, "Yes, others, Lord, yes, others, Let this my motto be; Help me to live for others, That I may live like Thee." Christ laid down his life for others, yet we sometimes struggle to meet needs directly in front of us. This week, find an extra opportunity to be a blessing to someone else. Write a note of encouragement, lend a listening ear, or give monetary assistance. You are like your Saviour when you selflessly give to others.

Evacuation Day

25 November 1783

And the great dragon was cast out, that old serpent, called the Devil, and Satan, which deceiveth the whole world: he was cast out into the earth, and his angels were cast out with him.—**Revelation 12:9**

For much of the Revolutionary War, New York was under British occupation. On 25 November 1783, General Washington marched his Continental Army across the Harlem River as they watched the British Army officially depart New York City. Known as "Evacuation Day," Britain's departure from New York marked both a symbolic and a literal end to the eight-year struggle for American independence.

Though the Revolutionary War was an immense conflict, a far greater spiritual battle rages today. The Bible tells us in 2 Corinthians 4:4 that Satan is the "god of this world" and has great influence over the world system. He is doing what he can to disrupt the work of God—in particular, by deceiving the world. One day, however, there will be an "evacuation day" as Satan is banished and Jesus takes His rightful position as everlasting Sovereign over this universe.

Meanwhile, we remain in a spiritual battle, and we can find strength by embracing God's promises. If you feel as if you're not making progress, cling to Isaiah 40:30–31: "Even the youths shall faint and be weary, and the young men shall utterly fall: But they that wait upon the Lord shall renew their strength; they shall mount up with wings as eagles; they shall run, and not be weary; and they shall walk, and not faint." When you start to get discouraged, quote 2 Corinthians 12:9: "And he said unto me, My grace is sufficient for thee: for my strength is made perfect in weakness." When burdens weigh you down, remember Matthew 11:28, "Come unto me, all ye that labour and are heavy laden, and I will give you rest."

There is a promise for any situation you face. If nothing else, cling to the truth that one day the devil *will* cease his destruction and will be punished forever in the Lake of Fire (Revelation 20:10). God asks us to be patient until he gets his due and is banished, once and for all.

Battle of Montelimar

26 November 2014

My soul melteth for heaviness: strengthen thou me according unto thy word. **—Psalm 119:28**

On 26 November 2014, I discovered that my great uncle, Norris B. Wells, Jr., was killed in action fighting in World War II. Norris left Columbus, Ohio, at nineteen years of age to answer his country's call to service. He was assigned to L Company in the 143rd Infantry Regiment of the 36th Infantry Division. During the last two weeks of August 1944, his regiment was engaged in hard combat around Montelimar in France. Sometime on 28 August, Norris was killed by an enemy mortar.

Several years ago, my thirst to know more about my great uncle led me to discover a web-based forum devoted to veterans and family members of the 36th Infantry Division. In 2009, I posted his full name, rank, service number, and unit and asked for any information others may have.

Five years later, on 26 November 2014, I received an e-mail from a woman who had seen my post. She shared that her father had been wounded at the Battle of Montelimar. He was still alive and had just been in Montelimar for a commemoration ceremony. While there, he found the old farmhouse that served as an aid station where he had been taken after being wounded in battle. After the ceremony, a granddaughter of the family who owns the farmhouse gave him a Bible which had been sitting in the farmhouse for seventy years. The Bible has the name PFC NORRIS B. WELLS written in the inside flap. A few days after receiving this email, I was able to speak to the woman's mother, still in France, who offered to mail me the Bible, which I still have today.

I wonder sometimes how that Bible ended up in the aid station. Did nineteen-year-old Norris take it there to share the gospel days before he was killed? Did he leave it behind when he died and a wounded buddy found hope through its message while receiving medical care? I will probably never know. But, I do know that God's Word provides strength and that in its pages we find God and the help of His promises.

Thank God for the Lighthouse

27 November 1703

And the light shineth in darkness; and the darkness comprehended it not. **—John 1:5**

Storms are never something we look forward to. On 27 November 1703, a two-week storm that had wrought havoc on much of England and claimed the lives of thousands finally abated. In addition to the widespread destruction on shore, the Eddystone Lighthouse, built in 1698, was completely destroyed. This loss arguably caused the destruction of more than three hundred Royal Navy ships and the deaths of their eight thousand sailors. In what was most likely the result of the hurricane, the loss of the lighthouse prevented ships that had been blown off course from ever reaching safety.

Unlike the Eddystone, we never need worry that the Word of God will cease to light our path or guide us safely to God. We live in a dark world, but, as it has been wisely said, "The darker the night, the brighter the light." The Word of God is needed more today than ever as we see evil proliferated throughout our world at an unprecedented pace. Unsaved people do not understand the Word of God, for the Holy Spirit has not been given to illuminate it to them (1 Corinthians 2:14). If we stop pointing people toward the light, they will continue to grope in darkness.

And for us who know Christ, the "lighthouse" of God's Word can keep us from being blown off course during the storms of life. Jesus told a parable of a foolish man and a wise man. The foolish man built his house on sand, and it was destroyed in a storm. The wise man, however, built his house on a rock. "And the rain descended, and the floods came, and the winds blew, and beat upon that house; and it fell not: for it was founded upon a rock" (Matthew 7:25). Jesus likened this man to one who hears His words and does them.

As the wise man, listen to God's Word. Build your life upon it. When you do, you will find that it provides a sturdy foundation and a light to guide you as you follow Christ.

Out to Sea

28 November 1941

What then shall we say to these things? If God be for us, who can be against us?
—Romans 8:31

Mention the name USS *Enterprise*, and most people will think of the 1960s sci-fi television show with Captain Kirk and Mr. Spock. In reality, the USS *Enterprise* (CV-6) was a Yorktown-class aircraft carrier during World War II. Commissioned in 1938, the massive carrier displaced over 25,000 tons, was more than 800 feet long, and was capable of a top speed of 32 knots. The *Enterprise* was the only one of three US aircraft carriers commissioned before World War II to survive the war. On 28 November 1941, the *Enterprise* set sail for Wake Island with a contingent of twelve F4F-3 fighters on her deck for delivery to the VMF-211 Marine Fighter Squadron. As a result of having been deployed, the *Enterprise* was not present during the surprise Japanese attack on Pearl Harbor just nine days later. In fact, none of the three US Pacific Fleet carriers were present at Pearl Harbor that day—a saving that was tremendously beneficial to the US throughout the war.

Much has been made of the providential hand of God and the fact that the *Enterprise* was "conveniently" out to sea that Sunday morning. The sovereignty of God means that He is in charge of our universe. As you read historical incidents, remember to look for the sovereign hand of God over them. In Isaiah 46:9–10 God declares, "For I am God, and there is none else; I am God, and there is none like me, Declaring the end from the beginning, and from ancient times the things that are not yet done, saying, My counsel shall stand, and I will do all my pleasure."

We don't understand even a fraction of God's purposes for what He allows to occur. And certainly some events are a result of evil choices man makes. But, although history is filled with times when man has disobeyed God and others have suffered the consequences, it also includes times when God graciously spared the loss of resources or people, even as he spared the *Enterprise* decades ago.

Axis Sally

29 November 1900

Wherefore we would have come unto you, even I Paul, once and again; but Satan hindered us.—**1 Thessalonians 2:18**

Mildred Gillars was born on 29 November 1900 in Maine but was raised in Conneaut, Ohio. After studying drama at Ohio Wesleyan University, Gillars moved to Dresden, Germany, in 1934 to study music. In 1940, she took a job as a radio announcer with the German State Radio. Going against US State Department advice, Gillars swore an oath of allegiance to Nazi Germany. In 1942, she began broadcasting propaganda in a show called *Home Sweet Home Hour.*

Gillars was the original "shock-jock" of radio, serving up daily doses of discouragement and dismay in her congenial Midwest tones. She spoke to the American home front with news of US servicemen, identified by name and hometown, who had been wounded and captured or killed in action. A quip from one of her broadcasts spoke about the husbands, sons, or brothers who were, "Perishing, losing their lives. At best, coming back home crippled . . . useless for the rest of their lives. For whom? For Franklin D. Roosevelt and Churchill and their Jewish cohorts." Gillars also crafted her show to discourage US forces serving in Europe. A running theme of her broadcasts was the infidelity of soldiers' wives and sweethearts. Servicemen referred to her as "Axis Sally" because of her obvious loyalty to the Axis cause.

Gillars was tried and charged with ten counts of treason, but the jury convicted her on only one count. She was sentenced to prison for ten to thirty years and given a $10,000 fine. Gillars served her sentence at the Federal Reformatory for Women in Alderson, West Virginia. She was released on parole 10 June 1961.

While Christians try to serve God, there is an enemy who, like Axis Sally, continually attempts to discourage us. When Satan works to tell you that your work or sacrifices for God are worthless or futile, don't believe him. He is only working to undermine your progress for God.

Scraps

30 November 1939

And, behold, a woman in the city, which was a sinner, when she knew that Jesus sat at meat in the Pharisee's house, brought an alabaster box of ointment, And stood at his feet behind him weeping, and began to wash his feet with tears, and did wipe them with the hairs of her head, and kissed his feet, and anointed them with the ointment.—**Luke 7:37–38**

On 30 November 1939, Soviet troops crossed the border and attacked tiny Finland in the "Winter War." The war lasted about one hundred days and cost the lives of around 25,000 people. Over 420,000 Finns lost their homes during the conflict—one of them an elderly peasant woman. But, unlike other Finnish citizens, she was a willing participant.

A detachment of Finnish border guards came upon the woman's home and regretfully informed her that she must prepare to leave her home, possibly for good, with only her personal belongings. The men told her that in the morning they would return and burn her house to the ground to prevent it from being used by the invading Russian soldiers. When the guards returned the following morning, they found her sled parked by her front door piled high with her possessions. As they entered, they were shocked to see that the entire dwelling had been meticulously scrubbed and whitewashed until it sparkled. The woman left behind a note on the door saying that she had gone to borrow something from a neighbor and would return in time to drive the sled away from her home. In the meantime, the note concluded, the soldiers would find some matches, kindling wood, and fuel next to her stove, which should allow them to burn her house quickly and completely. When she returned, the guards asked her why she had gone to so much trouble. Mustering all the dignity she could, the elderly woman looked them in the eye and replied, "When one gives a gift to Finland, one desires it should be like new!"

So often, instead of giving God our best, we give Him the "scraps" of our time, finances, and worship. When we love, we give freely and sacrificially. Our giving to God is really an indication of our love and loyalty to Him.

DECEMBER

War No More

1 December 1959

And he shall judge among many people, and rebuke strong nations afar off; and they shall beat their swords into plowshares, and their spears into pruninghooks: nation shall not lift up a sword against nation, neither shall they learn war any more.—**Micah 4:3**

Throughout mankind's history, there have only been brief periods of relative peace. For example, historians have labeled the years 1945 to the present day as "the long peace" because of the absence of a major war. But that in no way should imply that there is total peace. The Greek Civil War, Korea, Rhodesia and Vietnam are but a few of the many wars that have sprung up during the "long peace."

On 1 December 1959, a coalition of twelve nations, to include America and the Soviet Union, signed the Antarctica Treaty, banning any military activity and weapons testing on that continent. Since that time, there has never been a war of any kind on Antarctica.

The Treaty of Antarctica pales in comparison to the time when the Lord Jesus Christ will rule and reign in the New Jerusalem. Earthly nations have broken many treaties. But, there is coming a day when man will no longer learn war, and peace will be the order of the day because of the Prince of Peace (Isaiah 9:6).

We cannot achieve real world peace until the reign of Christ. But we *can* help others know peace in their own hearts. And the only way to have the peace *of* God in our hearts is to first have peace *with* God through Christ. Romans 5:1 says, "Therefore being justified by faith, we have peace with God through our Lord Jesus Christ." Introduce people to your Saviour. So many know *of* Him, but they do not personally know *Him*.

When we know Christ, we can experience the peace He gives, even in a troubled world. Jesus said, "These things I have spoken unto you, that in me ye might have peace. In the world ye shall have tribulation: but be of good cheer; I have overcome the world" (John 16:33).

No Dominion

2 December 1823

For sin shall not have dominion over you: for ye are not under the law, but under grace.—**Romans 6:14**

As one of our Founding Fathers, James Monroe served in the Continental Army's 3rd Virginia Infantry during the Revolutionary War, helped draft the US Constitution, and founded the Democratic-Republican Party in opposition to the Federalists. During his presidency, Monroe is perhaps best remembered for creating a foreign policy that bears his name—the Monroe Doctrine. The Monroe Doctrine, issued on 2 December 1823, forewarned imperialistic European powers not to interfere in the affairs of the newly independent Latin American states or potential US territories in the Western hemisphere. Following the Industrial Revolution, several European nations began colonizing territories that they felt could enrich their status as world powers. While America did the same, Monroe laid down a staunch warning aimed primarily at Spain and France to keep out of Central and South America. The Monroe Doctrine became a cornerstone of US Foreign policy for several future administrations.

President Monroe was so adamant against allowing any foreign encroachment reaching the Western Hemisphere, he issued a formal declaration. It would benefit Christians if we would issue our own "Monroe Doctrine" against sin. In a sense, *God* has issued a formal declaration against sin in our lives, saying that it is not to "have dominion over you." When we allow sin to encroach upon territory that rightfully belongs to the Lord, we surrender to occupation by the enemy—the world, the flesh, or the devil. "But put ye on the Lord Jesus Christ, and make not provision for the flesh, to fulfil the lusts thereof" (Romans 13:14).

Someone once said, "If you give an inch, the devil will make it a mile." If you miss church the first time, it becomes easier to miss the next time. When you skip time with God in prayer today, it is often even harder to pray tomorrow. When you see yourself slipping, renew your stand against sin. In your life and mine, let's make sure the enemy does not intrude!

No Going Back

3 December 1776

For which of you, intending to build a tower, sitteth not down first, and counteth the cost, whether he have sufficient to finish it?—**Luke 14:28**

On 3 December 1776, General George Washington wrote to John Hancock from his Trenton headquarters that he had successfully transported the majority of his Continental Army's supplies across the Delaware River into Pennsylvania. Later, Washington relayed how he had ordered the confiscation and destruction of all boats along the Delaware to keep the British from pursuing his forces. In doing this, however, Washington also immediately eliminated any chance for retreat among his army.

Washington and his men were so committed that they prevented themselves from turning back. Sometimes Christians, however, hold back from surrendering their all to God. While it is easy to sing "I Surrender All" during an invitation, it takes more effort to live it out. Being a servant of Christ requires dedication and isn't always easy.

I suppose every Christian has considered quitting at one time or another. You may experience times of feeling unappreciated in ministering to others. You may simply grow weary of the spiritual battle in your personal life. Remember, however, that your Saviour never quit on you. Look to Him for fresh strength and renewed hope. "Looking unto Jesus the author and finisher of our faith; who for the joy that was set before him endured the cross" (Hebrews 12:2). He is not just the originator of our faith; He is also the finisher. He Himself finished what He came to do and confirmed this as He cried out on the cross, "It is finished" (John 19:30).

Don't arrange an escape route for yourself. Where there is an escape route, there is often limited commitment. Put away the rationalizations about why God won't use you or why the journey is too hard or why you cannot continue. "And Jesus said unto him, No man, having put his hand to the plough, and looking back, is fit for the kingdom of God" (Luke 9:62). Commit to serve Christ, and never look back.

Mind Your Own Business

4 December 1992

He that passeth by, and meddleth with strife belonging not to him, is like one that taketh a dog by the ears.—**Proverbs 26:17**

During President George H. W. Bush's administration, the nation of Somalia underwent intense civil unrest due to rival factions. On 4 December 1992, President Bush dispatched 28,000 US troops to serve in a humanitarian-only capacity. They were to ensure needed supplies reached the starving Somalis. It was not long, however, until US forces became embroiled in a non-American war. Fifteen months later, President Clinton called off the mission, but not before eighteen American soldiers had died during the Battle of Mogadishu. Excessive involvement is partially to blame for the American lives lost during this Somalian conflict.

The Bible is clear that Christians are not to be busybodies, wandering about interfering in matters that do not concern them. Many churches and friendships have been damaged as a result of people who cannot mind their own business.

Start with your own heart first. The Bible advises us to "speak evil of no man, to be no brawlers, but gentle, shewing all meekness unto all men" (Titus 3:2). "Keep thy tongue from evil, and thy lips from speaking guile" (Psalm 34:13). Do gossip and arrogant criticism of others sneak into your conversations? It can be so subtle and quick that we don't recognize it. If you're not sure, ask your friends to be honest with you about your conversational habits. They'll know!

"Evil speaking" is sometimes hidden under the disguise of a prayer request. When you share prayer requests about others, use discretion. Not everything needs to be shared about another's struggles. "He that keepeth his mouth keepeth his life: but he that openeth wide his lips shall have destruction" (Proverbs 13:3).

If we would follow the advice of 1 Thessalonians 4:11, our relationships will be stronger: "And that ye study to be quiet, and to do your own business, and to work with your own hands."

Never Lost

5 December 1945

If I ascend up into heaven, thou art there: if I make my bed in hell, behold, thou art there.—**Psalm 139:8**

The Bermuda Triangle is one of those topics of discussion that seems to rank alongside Bigfoot and the Lochness Monster. Located in the North Atlantic, travelers have been both frightened and intrigued at the mystery surrounding this ominous body of water that has become associated with—and even blamed for—numerous unexplained disappearances of ships, aircraft, and people. Speculation abounds as to the scientific reasons for the phenomenon. On 5 December 1945, five US Navy Avenger torpedo bombers assigned to Flight 19 deployed from a Naval Air Station in Florida for a routine training operation. Shortly after reaching the airspace over the Triangle, pilots radioed they were experiencing strange instrumentation malfunctions. They never returned and were never found.

The strange Bermuda Triangle leaves many questions unanswered to those of us who hear of these unfortunate incidents. As Christians, sometimes we feel that we are in our own Bermuda Triangle and that God Himself does not see or know where we are. Maybe He doesn't see the valley we are walking through or the trials we are experiencing. We may even be certain He is far from us or that we cannot gain entrance into His presence. Such a conclusion can come, sometimes, because of sin and our own hard-heartedness. Perhaps at other times, it merely reminds us of the imperfections and challenges of fallen humanity.

But, God has promised He will never leave or forsake us (Hebrews 13:5). He is always there. If we have received Christ as Saviour, we are not lost; we have been found (Luke 15:3–6). The psalmist recognized that, wherever he was, God was with Him. If the Holy Spirit has convicted you of sin that is keeping you from fellowship with God, confess it (1 John 1:9). Turn to God's Word, and seek His face in prayer (Hebrews 4:15–16). Most of all, trust Him; believe His promises that He is there. As the great preacher Charles Spurgeon once said, "When you can't trace His hand, trust His heart."

Discouragement Breeds Failure

6 December 1421

For when they went up unto the valley of Eshcol, and saw the land, they discouraged the heart of the children of Israel, that they should not go into the land which the L*ORD had given them.*—**Numbers 32:9**

King Henry VI was born 6 December 1421 and succeeded the English throne at the age of nine months upon the death of his father. Like many medieval European monarchs, his reign was fraught with conflict. One of those conflicts was the long-running Wars of the Roses.

During the Battle of Towton in 1461, Yorkist forces under King Edward IV fought Lancastrian forces led by King Henry VI. As the battle began, the opposing armies formed with a valley between them and the wind blowing from the south into the faces of the Lancastrians. One of the commanders of the Yorkist army exploited this to his advantage and ordered his archers to loose only one volley and then cease. As expected, the Lancastrian archers immediately countered with a volley of their own, but their arrows fell short due to the fierce wind. With limited visibility, the Lancastrians continued to shoot until they exhausted their entire supply of arrows. The Yorkist army then moved forward, picking up Lancastrian arrows as they went and fired back into the Lancaster lines. At some point, the order was given for the Lancastrians to advance, and each side engaged in the brutal close combat so typical of medieval warfare. The turning point of the battle came when a fresh Yorkist division, led by the Duke of Norfolk, arrived and attacked the Lancastrian flank. Unable to hold back the overwhelming opposition, the Lancastrians became discouraged and a rout ensued. Many of King Henry's forces dropped their weapons, removed their helmets and ran for their lives only to be cut down by Yorkist horsemen as they fled.

A discouraged army is never victorious. Similarly, a discouraged Christian will struggle to gain the victory. This is why the bad report of the ten spies of Canaan was so egregious. They could have encouraged Israel to win a victory for God, but they discouraged the people away instead. Look for a discouraged Christian soldier to encourage today.

A Date Which Will Live in Infamy

7 December 1941

And having spoiled principalities and powers, he made a shew of them openly, triumphing over them in it.—**Colossians 2:15**

At 0748 hours, Hawaii time on 7 December 1941, more than 300 Imperial Japanese aircraft, in two waves, suddenly attacked United States forces based at Pearl Harbor, Hawaii. Eight US Navy battleships, all lined up in a tidy row, were damaged. Four were sunk. Other ships suffered damage, as did 180 aircraft. More significantly, however, 2,403 Americans lost their lives during the surprise attack. The following day, US President Franklin D. Roosevelt gave a speech to a Joint Session of the US Congress, describing the attack as "a date which will live in infamy." The dictionary defines *infamy* as "the state of being well known for some bad quality or deed." Indeed, the attack on Pearl Harbor goes down in history as an egregious day that propelled the United States into World War II.

Though this day in history carries a reputation for violence, the day of Christ's crucifixion is distinct for its victory. When the Lord Jesus Christ gave up the ghost on Calvary, He cried out "It is finished" (John 19:30), signifying that He had fully paid for the sins of all mankind, making salvation available to all who will believe (1 Timothy 4:10). To the followers of Jesus, Christ's death on Calvary must have seemed like a day of infamy as they watched His lifeless body being removed from the cross and placed in a tomb. But three days later, as the song writer wrote, "up from the grave He arose, with a mighty triumph o'er His foes!" What seemed like defeat gave way to triumph as the Son of God arose from the dead.

When life becomes heavy, you and I need not be defeated or discouraged. We are living our Christian lives based on the greatest victory that ever took place: the triumph over sin on the cross. Temptations may be hard to bear. Trials may seem overwhelming. But nothing can change Christ's victory for us. When you find yourself overwhelmed with the struggle, remember 1 Corinthians 15:57: "But thanks be to God, which giveth us the victory through our Lord Jesus Christ."

That Wasn't the Plan

8 December 395

The lot is cast into the lap; but the whole disposing thereof is of the Lord. **—Proverbs 16:33**

During the fourth century, China was divided into sixteen kingdoms, each vying for hegemony over the other. On 8 December 395, the north-central province under control of the Yan, launched a punitive expedition against a rival province called the Wei. The Yan leader—Murong Chui—led his forces to Canhe Slope, only to become embroiled in sudden darkness due to a storm. Unbeknownst to Chui, Tuoba Gui had amassed his Wei forces just west of Canhe Slope at dusk the evening before. Gui ensured his men kept silent as they set up positions on the hills surrounding the Yan camp. At sunrise, around 30,000 Wei troops launched a surprise attack on the Yan, which numbered approximately 38,000. Yan forces panicked and died by the thousands as they trampled one another or drowned by jumping in a nearby river. Those who survived were buried alive.

The account of the Battle of Canhe Slope is reminiscent of Gideon's victory over the Midianites. Gideon, already outnumbered, was told by God to thin down his army to three hundred men—and face a force "like grasshoppers for multitude" (Judges 7:12). Yet, God wrought a great victory.

Sometimes in war situations, it can seem like simply a matchup of strategies, and the side with the best strategy emerges victorious. But Proverbs teaches us that the whole "disposing thereof"—the end result of a situation—is in the hands of God. Daniel 2:21 says that God "removeth kings and setteth up kings." David testified, "And all this assembly shall know that the Lord saveth not with sword and spear: for the battle is the Lord's, and he will give you into our hands" (1 Samuel 17:47).

Our plans are simply that—*our plans*. But God commands us to not lean on our own understanding (Proverbs 3:5) when it comes to the issues of life. God never rebukes us for being prepared. But are you preparing along with depending on God, or with merely depending on self?

Faithful Behind the Scenes

9 December 1989

Let nothing be done through strife or vainglory; but in lowliness of mind let each esteem other better than themselves.—**Philippians 2:3**

When the US Navy commissioned the USS *Normandy* on 9 December 1989, they invited dozens of Army veterans of the Normandy invasion, but none from the Beach Battalions. Of all the special units that took part in D-Day, none have been so forgotten as the US Navy Beach Battalions. Due largely to inter-service rivalry and ignorance, history has mostly chosen to ignore these brave men who played such a central role in the success of Operation Overlord on 6 June 1944.

While these sailors served under Army command, the Navy realized that a war in the Pacific would be much more of a naval war than a land fight such as was happening in Europe, so the Navy wanted to dominate the attack against Imperial Japan. The Army, on the other hand, did not want a repeat of World War I, from which the Marines had received a greater share of credit for their part in France than the Army felt appropriate. Because of this, Naval Beach Battalions (NBB) handled all ship-to-shore functions during the D-Day invasion. When Army troops were safely ashore, the NBB returned to their vessels and left. The Naval Beach Battalions safeguarded some 2,955 landing craft that were deployed for the D-Day operation. Although they received little recognition, these brave men have remained humble and content just to have served their country.

It's time for Christians to exemplify faithful service even when, like the Navy Beach Battalions, their labors are not recognized. President Ronald Reagan once remarked, "There is no limit to the amount of good you can do if you don't care who gets the credit." When we don't care who gets the credit, the Lord can do amazing things through us by His Spirit. Esteem others better than yourself—give *others* credit and praise for their good decisions and deeds. If we live as faithful people who desire to glorify God, it won't bother us when our names are not written on plaques or publicly announced. We'll simply rest in knowing we've been faithful to our Lord.

The Sausage War

10 December 1939

And put a knife to thy throat, if thou be a man given to appetite. **—Proverbs 23:2**

The Winter War (1939–1940), also called the Russo-Finnish War, began on 26 November 1939 when Russian planes bombed Helsinki. Four Soviet armies launched an all-out attack against Finland, primarily to gain control over the crucial Karelian Isthmus. The war lasted about four months and was an embarrassment to the Red Army.

One of the stranger events of the war happened on a late December evening. At 2300 hours on the night of 10 December, the Russians erupted from the forest, taking the Finns completely by surprise. The Finns *should* have been annihilated; however, the first area the Soviets overran was a field kitchen. For that entire day, Finnish cooks had been simmering large vats of sausage soup. When the starving Russian soldiers caught a whiff of the soup, the force of the attack suddenly stopped.

Hunger trumped tactical momentum as hundreds of ravenous Russian soldiers dropped their weapons to scarf down the meaty delicacy. Of course, this gave the Finns time to reorganize, and they counterattacked the Russians, killing nearly every man who stopped for a bite to eat. Known as the "Sausage War," this event marked one of the few recorded occurrences of bayonet fighting during the Winter War.

The Russian soldiers' hunger clouded their tactical judgement, which cost them their lives. Something similar happens to our spiritual lives when we live according to the desires of our flesh, rather than being yielded to the control of the Holy Spirit. Romans 8:6 warns, "For to be carnally minded is death; but to be spiritually minded is life and peace." A few verses later, the passage goes on to say, "Therefore, brethren, we are debtors, not to the flesh, to live after the flesh. For if ye live after the flesh, ye shall die: but if ye through the Spirit do mortify the deeds of the body, ye shall live" (verses 12–13). Are you living with reflexive obedience to the desires of your flesh, or are you living with purposeful surrender to the will of God?

A Lost Opportunity

11 December 1936

He that is faithful in that which is least is faithful also in much: and he that is unjust in the least is unjust also in much.—**Luke 16:10**

In the years leading up to the outbreak of World War II, England faced a crisis in leadership. Edward VIII had fallen in love with an American socialite named Wallis Simpson, who was married at the time to a businessman. Intent on marrying Mrs. Simpson, Edward intended to seek his father's council, but King George V died in January 1936. As the next in line for the throne, Edward was proclaimed king. Edward continued his affair with Simpson, and when she divorced her husband in October, Edward moved to marry her, which ignited a major scandal across Great Britain. Once the newspaper headlines broke, King Edward VIII abdicated his position as king on 11 December 1936. His brother, George VI, was suddenly thrust on to the throne as England's new king.

While Edward and Wallis lived out their lives in relative ease and comfort as the Duke and Duchess of Windsor, England and the world never got the chance to see what he *could* have done as England's king.

Are you in your God-given place? God has an express purpose for each one of us. When we disregard His will for our lives and go our own way, we are essentially abdicating our place in His sovereign plan, and we lose opportunities to serve Him. We also miss out on the blessings God would have for us. In Jeremiah 5:25, the prophet told God's backslidden people, "Your iniquities have turned away these things, and your sins have withholden good things from you."

Thankfully, God is a God of second chances (just ask Jonah). We shouldn't live in regret over a past we cannot change, but we should seize the moments in front of us while we can. If you have opportunities to serve God, do it! And when temptation comes knocking, never rationalize that the short-term loss doesn't seem too great. There is a larger picture of God's great purpose for you. Demonstrate your trust in God's plan by following Him and seizing the opportunities to serve that He brings your way.

Missing Out

12 December 627

Then the same day at evening, being the first day of the week, when the doors were shut where the disciples were assembled for fear of the Jews, came Jesus and stood in the midst, and saith unto them, Peace be unto you. . . . But Thomas, one of the twelve, called Didymus, was not with them when Jesus came.
—John 20:19, 24

Flavius Heraclius was Emperor of the Byzantine Empire from AD 610 to 641. The Byzantine Empire began as the Eastern Orthodox off-shoot of the Roman Empire, which disintegrated in the fifth century. Because the Byzantine Empire extended so close to neighboring Asia Minor, the rise of Islam proved a constant threat. During the Byzantine-Sassanid War, Heraclius lost a significant amount of lands to the Sassanids. However, in mid-September 627, he chose to invade the Sassanids to recoup lost territory.

On 12 December 627, Heraclius assembled his forces on a plain just west of the ruins of ancient Nineveh. His opponent, General Rhahzadh, arrayed his Sassanid troops into three companies and attacked. Feigning retreat, Heraclius led his men further into the plains only to order a sudden reverse to the chagrin of the Sassanids. Outnumbered, the Sassanids were defeated, and the Battle of Nineveh resulted in a decisive victory for Heraclius.

This battle could have turned out differently, however. General Rhahzadh had three thousand Persian reinforcements, but they arrived after the battle had ended—too late to make a difference.

One of the missing-out moments of Scripture is that of Thomas not being present with the other disciples on that first Sunday night after Jesus' resurrection when Jesus showed up. Because Thomas was not there, he went through a week of doubt. The next time you are tempted to stay home from church, remember Thomas! Who knows what God may do in your heart or what needed truth He may give you through the service? This is one reason Hebrews 10:25 exhorts us to not forsake the assembling of ourselves together. When we miss church, we miss out on a blessing.

Avalanche!

13 December 1916

But Moses' hands were heavy; and they took a stone, and put it under him, and he sat thereon; and Aaron and Hur stayed up his hands, the one on the one side, and the other on the other side; and his hands were steady until the going down of the sun.—**Exodus 17:12**

Scientists tell us that an avalanche is caused when a stronger layer of packed snow lying on a weaker layer gives way to the pressure, fractures, and slides down a steep slope. On 13 December 1916, hundreds of Austrian soldiers died when their barracks were leveled by an avalanche at the foot of Mount Marmolada in the Italian Alps. Although their camp was located in an area well-placed to fend off enemy attack, it was situated right under a mountain of unstable snow. Though historians are unsure what caused the avalanche, more than 200,000 tons of snow, rock, and ice obliterated the Austrian camp. Most of the bodies were never recovered.

We can experience a spiritual avalanche in our own lives as well. No matter how strong the surface of our Christian walk appears, if we don't have a real and abiding walk with Christ, we will eventually cave to pressure and temptation. And prayer is a tremendous part of strengthening the hidden layer under the surface of our lives. When our prayer life is weak, we become like that underneath, weak layer of snow that can no longer effectively uphold the stronger layer. The result can be a spiritual avalanche.

Before Jesus was crucified, He told Peter, "Simon, Simon, behold, Satan hath desired to have you, that he may sift you as wheat: But I have prayed for thee, that thy faith fail not" (Luke 22:31–32). Peter, however, disregarded Jesus' warning. The night before Jesus was crucified, when Jesus asked Peter to pray, Peter slept instead. Hours later, during Jesus' trial, Peter denied that he even knew Jesus.

Prayer is not only necessary for our own spiritual walk. It is also necessary in our ministry toward others. As Aaron and Hur held up Moses' arms during battle, one of our responsibilities as Christians is to hold up the arms of others—particularly the pastor—through prayer.

Friendly to a Foe

14 December 1862

Put on therefore, as the elect of God, holy and beloved, bowels of mercies, kindness, humbleness of mind, meekness, longsuffering;—**Colossians 3:12**

During the battle of Fredericksburg, the army of Northern Virginia made their stand behind a stone wall in an area called Marye's Heights. The following morning, 14 December 1862, thousands of wounded and helpless men lay on the open field, moaning and begging for relief. Confederate Sergeant Richard Kirkland sought permission from his commanding officer, General Kershaw, to carry water to the suffering enemy soldiers. Fearing Kirkland might be killed, Kershaw nevertheless gave permission.

Kirkland gathered as many canteens as he could carry and climbed over the wall and went into the battlefield. It soon became obvious to both sides what Kirkland was doing, and according to Kershaw, cries for water erupted all over the battlefield from wounded soldiers. Kirkland did not stop until he had helped every wounded soldier—Confederate and Federal. For over an hour, he ministered to his suffering foes as both armies watched in amazement and admiration. No one fired a single shot at him. When he had done all he could, he simply returned to his post and once again took up his place in the ranks.

Nine months later, Kirkland was shot in battle. As his friends tried to carry him out of danger, his last words were, "I'm done for . . . save yourselves and please tell my pa I died right." Today, a statue depicting Kirkland's tenderness stands near the battlefield's visitor center. The men on both sides of the war called him "The Angel of Marye's Heights."

Kindness is a rare trait in our world. And Jesus specifically instructed us to be kind, not just to our friends, but also to our foes. "But I say unto you, Love your enemies, bless them that curse you, do good to them that hate you, and pray for them which despitefully use you, and persecute you" (Matthew 5:44). Does your kindness extend only to those just like you? Or are you also friendly to your foes?

Drip Guns

15 December 1915

Having a form of godliness, but denying the power thereof: from such turn away.
—2 Timothy 3:5

During World War I, in early 1915, the British, French, and a newly-formed unit comprised of Australian and New Zealanders called the ANZACS were involved in a battle to take the Dardanelles Straits. But by mid-October, Allied forces had suffered heavy casualties. On 15 December 1915, ANZAC troops were ordered to evacuate the peninsula.

The problem was that retreating armies tend to incur staggeringly heavy casualties. Therefore the Allies had to come up with a new strategy. The most logical decision would be for some troops to remain behind to cover the Allied withdrawal. This would keep enemy troops in their trenches, allowing a retreat to take place unchallenged. Unfortunately, for the troops left behind, however, survival was unlikely.

This predicament gave two young Australians an idea. Lance Corporal W. C. Scurry and Private A. H. Lawrence rigged several rifles to fire sporadically after the last men left. The soldiers set up two kerosene tins, one above the other. The top one was filled with water, and the empty bottom one was attached to the trigger with a string. Right before evacuating their trenches, they punched small holes in the upper tin so water would trickle into the lower one. Once the lower tin got heavy enough to pull the string, the rifle would fire. These guns became known as "drip guns" and successfully fooled the enemy into believing the Allies were dug in for the long haul. The ruse worked, and eighty thousand men made it to safety.

It can be easy to "look the part" when it comes to the Christian life, yet lack a spiritual foundation. The Apostle Paul warned young Timothy that in the last days, there would be those who had a "form of godliness"—looked the part—yet were not believers. Make sure of your salvation. If there has never been a time in your life when you realized your need for a Saviour, believe on the Lord Jesus Christ. Repent of your sin, call upon the name of the Lord, and ask Him to save you.

Covering Up

16 December 1998

He that covereth his sins shall not prosper: but whoso confesseth and forsaketh them shall have mercy.—**Proverbs 28:13**

On 16 December 1998, President Clinton ordered an air strike on Iraq for their failure to cooperate with United Nations weapons inspectors. The four-day bombing mission, code-named Operation Desert Fox, involved both the United States and Great Britain and destroyed military targets throughout Iraq. Unfortunately for President Clinton, Congress did not fully support his decision and instead accused the president of using the air strikes as a ploy to divert attention away from the impeachment proceedings over his scandalous affair and related perjury.

At one time or another, probably all of us have done or said something to divert attention off our sin in the hopes it would be forgotten. But Proverbs 15:3 tells us, "The eyes of the LORD are in every place, beholding the evil and the good." God does not miss a thing in our lives. It is always better to come clean with the Lord than to fool ourselves into thinking He will not notice we have sinned.

King David tried to cover his sin. Not only did the cover up produce disastrous results in David's family, but it also created havoc in his walk with God. In Psalm 32:3–4, he described the agony of those months before he finally came clean with God: "When I kept silence, my bones waxed old through my roaring all the day long. For day and night thy hand was heavy upon me: my moisture is turned into the drought of summer. Selah."

When we hide our sin, we experience multiplied consequences. When we confess our sin, we experience God's mercy. First John 1:9 tells us that confession is the way to restored fellowship with God: "If we confess our sins, he is faithful and just to forgive us our sins, and to cleanse us from all unrighteousness." The very next chapter opens with this encouragement: "My little children, these things write I unto you, that ye sin not. And if any man sin, we have an advocate with the Father, Jesus Christ the righteous" (1 John 2:1–2). Covering up is never a solution; confession is.

The Malmédy Massacre

17 December 1944

Put on the whole armour of God, that ye may be able to stand against the wiles of the devil.—**Ephesians 6:11**

On 17 December 1944, at a crossroads in the Ardennes Forest in Belgium, German SS soldiers surprised a group of eighty-four American soldiers of the 285th Field Artillery Observation Battalion. The Germans lined the Americans up in a field and ordered them to lay down their arms, which they reluctantly did. Once their weapons were gathered up, Lt. Col. Joachim Peiper of the SS ordered all eighty-four unarmed Americans to be shot. German troops machine-gunned the men in the snow and left them for dead. All eighty-four died, and this event, remembered as one of the worst atrocities of World War II, became known as the Malmédy Massacre. The Malmédy Massacre continues to provoke as much argument today as it did during the subsequent war crimes trial at Dachau in 1946. Most Americans believe it was a premeditated act to murder defenseless men.

When a soldier lays down his weapon, he is defenseless. Our adversary, Satan, waits for these moments when Christians let down their guard so he can attack. We cannot afford to live a single moment without protection. Each day, we must endeavor to arm ourselves with the Lord's armor.

What does the Bible tell us about our spiritual weapons? "(For the weapons of our warfare are not carnal, but mighty through God to the pulling down of strong holds;) Casting down imaginations, and every high thing that exalteth itself against the knowledge of God, and bringing into captivity every thought to the obedience of Christ" (2 Corinthians 10:4–5). Christian, whether or not you can wield a physical weapon, become adept at wielding your spiritual weapon—the Word of God, called the "sword of the spirit" (Ephesians 6:17). When Satan tries to get you to put it down, resist. Satan tempted the Lord Jesus, and Jesus quoted the Word of God in response to temptation (Matthew 4:1–11). If Scripture was Jesus' way of fighting temptation, should your weapon be any different? Memorize God's Word. When the time comes, you'll be ready for battle.

The Real Enemy

18 December 1916

For we wrestle not against flesh and blood, but against principalities, against powers, against the rulers of the darkness of this world, against spiritual wickedness in high places.—**Ephesians 6:12**

The Battle of Verdun is distinct for being the largest and longest-running battle fought on the Western Front during the Great War. The battle took place on the hills north of Verdun-sur-Meuse in northeastern France and ended on 18 December 1916. During the ten-month slaughter, about seventy thousand French and German soldiers died every month.

Two years after the battle ended, the US Marines were sent to the trenches of Verdun for training. While not an active sector, US Marine Private Warren Jackson of Houston, Texas, still recalls it as his baptism by fire.

> One night a patrol of thirty men went down to look over No Man's Land. As the men returned we noticed Corporal Toth was missing. Lieutenant Joe Gargan asked for volunteers to find him. As we crept cautiously towards an isolated blockhouse I saw the body of Toth. He lay on his back, his knees drawn toward his body and on his ashen face and ears were dried splotches of blood. His gas mask was out but held in stiffened hands, as though he had been in the very act of trying to put it on when the poison gas overcame him and he died. There, in No Man's Land, in a country I had never been to before, I viewed the first corpse I ever saw out of a casket. It was at that moment I came to the realization that we were up against a foe that meant to kill every single one of us.

Private Jackson came to realize who he and his fellow Marines were up against. His foes were not his fellow soldiers or his Company Commander. His enemy was the German Army. In a time of upset, it is easy and tempting to take your frustrations out on your spouse or your kids. Turning on others in your life will only waste time. The Bible says our conflicts are not really with our spouses, coworkers, or one another. Our battles are with Satan and his minions. Make sure you're recognizing the real enemy.

The Epidemic of Sin

19 December 1942

But your iniquities have separated between you and your God, and your sins have hid his face from you, that he will not hear.—**Isaiah 59:2**

On 19 December 1942, malaria rates reached 972 reported cases per 1,000 for US troops fighting on the island of Guadalcanal. Hospital admission rates from malaria in Army units alone on Guadalcanal from November 1942 to mid-February 1943 averaged 420 admissions. The disease put nearly 65 percent of soldiers out of action, in contrast to the 25 percent wounded in action. Statistically, malaria was more dangerous than Japanese bullets. When a shipment of Atabrine medication finally reached the affected men on Guadalcanal, the men began to recover. United States forces finally took Guadalcanal in early 1943, thanks in some measure to Atabrine.

Sin is often compared in Scripture to the contagious disease of leprosy. In Bible days, a diagnosis of leprosy was a diagnosis of death—a long, painful, lonely death. And just as there was no human cure for leprosy, there is no human cure for sin. No medicine—physical or spiritual—can take away our sin. This is what makes Jesus' sacrifice for us such good news. Through Jesus, a cure for sin is available. His blood can cleanse *all* our sin. "But God commendeth his love toward us, in that, while we were yet sinners, Christ died for us" (Romans 5:8).

Although the primary comparison between leprosy and sin is the incurable nature of leprosy, there is an additional parallel to be seen in the contagion factor as well. Like a contagious disease, ungodly influences in our lives lead us into sin. This is why Proverbs 1:10 warns, "My son, if sinners entice thee, consent thou not." The Bible is clear about the significant effect that your friend circle can have on your decisions. "Be not deceived: evil communications corrupt good manners" (1 Corinthians 15:33). Are your friends encouraging you to be more like Christ or more like the world? Spending long stretches of time with worldly friends *will* corrupt your spiritual life.

Battered in Bastogne

20 December 1944

But it is good for me to draw near to God: I have put my trust in the Lord GOD, that I may declare all thy works.—**Psalm 73:28**

On 20 December 1944, the Germans had the men of the US 101st Airborne "Screaming Eagles" Division surrounded in the Belgian city of Bastogne. For seven harrowing days, German artillery battered the American positions. When the Screaming Eagles entered the Ardennes forest, they were low on ammunition, without winter clothing, and had hardly any food. The forest conditions were so disorienting, soldiers often wandered into enemy foxholes, thinking they were in their own lines. When the Germans launched artillery attacks, the splinters from pulverized trees caused significant damage to American troops. According to one trooper, only the hope that their own leadership would get to them in time sustained these brave men and allowed them to endure.

Trust and hope are connected when our trust is in someone or something reliable. As long as we believe that God is good, that His promises are true, and that He will act on our behalf, we can have hope through the darkest night. But when our confidence in God's goodness erodes, as it did for Asaph who penned Psalm 73, we begin to lose hope as well. Throughout the psalm, Asaph relays his struggle to trust in God's goodness through life's unfairness. It was only when he spent time in God's presence (verse 17) that perspective returned and he could once again have confident hope in God.

Loneliness can creep into our hearts, especially when we are facing a difficult spiritual battle or a heavy trial. Draw near to God during these times. You can trust Him. "And we know that all things work together for good to them that love God, to them who are the called according to his purpose" (Romans 8:28). Christian, God hasn't forgotten you. He knows you by name. He knows the number of hairs on your head, and not even a sparrow falls to the ground without Him knowing (Matthew 10:29; Luke 12:7). Keep trusting. Keep praying. Keep depending. Keep hoping.

"Old Blood and Guts"

21 December 1945

Study to shew thyself approved unto God, a workman that needeth not to be ashamed, rightly dividing the word of truth.—**2 Timothy 2:15**

At 1800 hours on 21 December 1945, America lost one of its most talented military leaders because of a car accident in Heidelberg, Germany. General George Smith Patton, Jr., was one of history's most colorful and amazing military tacticians. His career began with fighting against Pancho Villa in 1916. Patton so impressed General John J. Pershing that he promoted Patton to the rank of captain. He went on to serve in the newly formed US Tank Corps in 1917. Following the war, he completed his upper level Army commander training and was given command of the US Second Armored Division. During World War II, Patton gained the respect of both friend and foe as he dashed across Europe. Following the Battle of Normandy, Patton exploited German weaknesses with great success, covering the six hundred miles across France, Belgium, Luxembourg, Germany, Austria, and Czechoslovakia.

Despite the nickname "Old Blood and Guts" and a penchant for foul language, Patton read his Bible often and admonished his men to do the same. Porter B. Williamson, a major who served as Patton's aid during the war, once remarked that Patton said to his men, "Read some of the Bible every day. Study those chapters where it talks about the desert of North Africa because we are going to be fighting in that area."

Patton's habit of Bible reading stemmed from his belief of its helpful message. God commands that we study His Word so that we, as approved workmen, do not need to be ashamed. When we diligently study Scripture, we gain insight for life's decisions, have the truths to overcome temptation, can be ready with answers to the questions of skeptics, and—most importantly—grow in our relationship with Jesus Christ. Make time with God a daily priority—never an afterthought or something you may get around to. It's the only book of absolute truth on this Earth. Don't be guilty of neglecting it.

Everyone Needs a Hug

22 December 1941

But as touching brotherly love ye need not that I write unto you: for ye yourselves are taught of God to love one another. And indeed ye do it toward all the brethren which are in all Macedonia: but we beseech you, brethren, that ye increase more and more;—**1 Thessalonians 4:9–10**

On 22 December 1941, Prime Minister Winston Churchill arrived at the White House with the intent of encouraging President Roosevelt and his wife Eleanor in light of America's entry into World War II just days prior. During Churchill's three-week stay, President Roosevelt introduced him to the many Christmas traditions held so dear by the Roosevelts. One of those was the Christmas Eve reading of Charles Dickens' *A Christmas Carol*. To the delight of the children gathered round, Churchill joined with Roosevelt, reciting many of the story lines from memory. After the reading, many retired for the evening while Churchill excused himself to work on a speech he planned to deliver to Congress the day after Christmas.

A short while after Churchill began his work, Roosevelt's personal advisor, Harry Hopkins, and his nine-year old daughter, Diana, knocked on his door. When Churchill realized how nervous little Diana was, he snuffed out his cigar, stretched out his arms, and said to her, "I'm a lonely old father and grandfather on Christmas Eve, and I want a little girl to hug." As Diana scampered into Churchill's lap, the two laughed and giggled until it was time for Harry to tuck her in. That single act of kindness instantly disarmed a little girl of her fears about what her country was facing.

Sometimes in the personal pressures of life or in our efforts to make a difference in the larger needs of society, we miss opportunities to reassure those nearest to us that we care about their concerns as well. Sometimes the simple expressions of a smile or hug communicate more than a thousand words could. The Bible speaks of "brotherly love" as the shared bond between Christians. But, like the siblings in our biological families, so our brothers and sisters in Christ deserve us to express our love for them and willingness to be there in their times of need.

The American Crisis

23 December 1776

Fear none of those things which thou shalt suffer: behold, the devil shall cast some of you into prison, that ye may be tried; and ye shall have tribulation ten days: be thou faithful unto death, and I will give thee a crown of life.—**Revelation 2:10**

The *American Crisis* is a collection of pamphlets written by Thomas Paine during the American Revolutionary War. Each pamphlet was an essay, arguing for independence from England and a self-governing America. General George Washington found the first essay so inspiring that he ordered it read aloud to the Continental Army on 23 December 1776, three days before the Battle of Trenton.

The opening lines to this essay are as famous as almost any piece of literature today: "These are the times that try men's souls. The summer soldier and the sunshine patriot will, in this crisis, shrink from the service of his country; but he that stands it now, deserves the love and thanks of man and woman."

Paine wrote scornfully of "the summer soldier and the sunshine patriot." He was referring to gentlemen soldiers who would volunteer their summers after planting their crops in the spring, only to return home at the time of harvest. Paine knew that if there were not men willing to stay all year long and suffer for the sake of freedom at places like Valley Forge, all would be lost and King George would rule the colonies. There would be no United States of America. The speech had the desired effect as Washington's surprise attack at Trenton on the morning of 26 December routed the Hessians and was a major turning point of the war. Americans today owe much to Washington and those brave soldiers in the Continental Army that sacrificially served—not just when it was easy, but when it was needed.

As soldiers of Christ, we owe it to His cause to be more than "summer soldiers and sunshine patriots." Second Timothy 2:3 instructs, "Thou therefore endure hardness, as a good soldier of Jesus Christ." Anyone can serve the Lord when it's easy and the blessings are obvious. Our real loyalty to Christ and His cause is proved when we must endure hardness.

The Christmas Truce

24 December 1914

If a man say, I love God, and hateth his brother, he is a liar: for he that loveth not his brother whom he hath seen, how can he love God whom he hath not seen? And this commandment have we from him, That he who loveth God love his brother also.—**1 John 4:20–21**

The famous "Christmas truce" was a series of widespread unofficial ceasefires that took place along the Western Front beginning in mid-December 1914. While enemy combatants may have disagreed on politics, customs, and the manner in which to wage warfare, they all agreed on the centrality of Christmas. Through the week leading up to Christmas, parties of German and British soldiers began to exchange seasonal greetings and songs between their trenches. On the morning of 19 December, some German soldiers left their trenches to collect their wounded. Since no official cease-fire had been given, this act was tantamount to suicide, yet the British simply looked on with empathy. Soon, British troops emerged from their own trenches and began to gather their wounded. At one point during this exchange, some Germans beckoned the British over to their trenches to assist them in the burial detail. Over the next few days, the tension was reduced to the point that on Christmas Eve, individual soldiers left their trenches to give gifts to their enemy. On Christmas Day, scores of soldiers from both sides independently ventured into no man's land, where they mingled and exchanged food and souvenirs. Small groups even gathered to play a friendly game of football (soccer) and play musical instruments. The music sparked widespread caroling, and a general feeling of comfort descended upon the scene. Sadly, the killing resumed later on Christmas Day, and this extraordinary event was never repeated.

One of the sad realities of nations at war is men and women taking the lives of others. But sadder still is when Christian people do not show love to those in their circles of direct contact—family, friends, co-workers, neighbors. To love God, we must love those whom He loves, and that is everyone.

God's Love Letter

25 December 1920

The cloke that I left at Troas with Carpus, when thou comest, bring with thee, and the books, but especially the parchments.—**2 Timothy 4:13**

On 25 December 1920, the German newspaper, *Völkischer Beobachter (People's Observer),* began its twenty-four year span as the official public face for the National Socialist German Workers' Party—better known as the Nazi Party. The *Völkischer Beobachter* was a key instrument for propagating the Nazi agenda and any news relating to party activities. In 1921, Adolf Hitler took complete control of the Nazi Party, which gave him full rights to the newspaper. He in turn became the sole arbiter for deciding the Nazi message, which was broadcast daily to its antisemitic audience. The paper's initial circulation was around eight thousand, however, that increased to more than a million readers by 1944. And every one of them was receiving a paper filled with hatred and violence.

In contrast, the Holy Bible contains the singular message of God's plan for the redemption of mankind—a plan that involved a love so great that God Himself came to Earth, clothed Himself in human flesh, and was born in a rough manger in a lowly stable outside an inn.

The Bible is inspired by the Holy Spirit of God and was penned by more than forty authors over a 1,600-year period. Second Peter 1:21 tells us, "For the prophecy came not in old time by the will of man: but holy men of God spake as they were moved by the Holy Ghost."

The Apostle Paul valued God's Word so greatly that, even knowing his martyr's death was just around the corner, he wrote to Timothy from prison and asked him to bring "the books, but especially the parchments." In whatever remaining days Paul had on Earth, he wanted to seek God and study His Word. In a previous letter to Timothy, Paul instructed him to also "give attendance to reading" (1 Timothy 4:13).

This Christmas, spend time reading God's love letter to you. And as you approach a New Year, take some time to evaluate the importance you are placing on God's Word. Could it be more of a priority in the coming year?

Relief at Last

26 December 1944

For our light affliction, which is but for a moment, worketh for us a far more exceeding and eternal weight of glory; While we look not at the things which are seen, but at the things which are not seen: for the things which are seen are temporal; but the things which are not seen are eternal.—**2 Corinthians 4:17–18**

On 16 December 1944, Hitler launched a massive counterattack upon the Western Allies known as the Ardennes Offensive. Most know it today as the Battle of the Bulge. For three weeks, over thirty German divisions attacked battle-weary American soldiers in frigid temperatures along miles of the densely-wooded Ardennes Forest.

One of the more famous anecdotes from this battle involved General George S. Patton's relief of the 101st Airborne Division, who had been valiantly holding the town of Bastogne in Belgium. Several times, German units tried in vain to push the "Screaming Eagles" from the town. When asked to surrender, the acting commander of the 101st, Brigadier General Anthony MacAuliffe replied with one word, "Nuts!"

On 26 December, Patton's 3rd Army entered Bastogne to provide much-needed relief to the embattled paratroopers of the 101st. When asked how they felt at being relieved by General Patton, many paratroopers sarcastically quipped that they had no need to be relieved, because "paratroopers are supposed to be surrounded."

Life is hard. We often struggle beneath the weight of burdens we were never designed to carry. But the Lord Jesus Christ is the burden bearer, and He comforts and cares for us. During seasons of difficulty, what we need is perspective and the assurance that relief is coming. Second Corinthians 4:17–18 gives us both. These verses compare our present suffering to our future and joy, and they remind us that our pain is temporary while our relief will be eternal. Even though we know these truths, sometimes we still get beaten down by the cares of this life. But verse 16 tells us how we can press on: "For which cause we faint not; but though our outward man perish, yet the inward man is renewed day by day."

Apollo 8

27 December 1968

Let not your heart be troubled: ye believe in God, believe also in me. In my Father's house are many mansions: if it were not so, I would have told you. I go to prepare a place for you. And if I go and prepare a place for you, I will come again, and receive you unto myself; that where I am, there ye may be also.—**John 14:1–3**

Apollo 8, the second manned mission of the Apollo program, marked the first time American astronauts would orbit the moon. Astronauts Frank Borman, James Lovell, Jr., and Bill Anders left Cape Canaveral, Florida, on a three-stage Saturn 5 rocket, the first time this type of rocket was used for a launch.

On Christmas Eve, Apollo 8 entered orbit around the moon, the first manned spacecraft to do so. As their command module floated above the lunar surface, the astronauts beamed back images of the moon and Earth and took turns reading from the first chapter of the book of Genesis, closing with a wish for everyone "on the good Earth." After completing ten orbits, Apollo 8 began its journey back to Earth. The crew splashed down in the Pacific on 27 December 1968. While a lunar landing was still seven months away, for the first time, humans from Earth had visited the moon and returned home safely.

More than two thousand years ago, the Lord Jesus Christ visited this planet to atone for the sins of all mankind. As His earthly ministry neared completion, the Lord told His disciples that He must shortly leave them. As they pondered this news, Jesus comforted them with the words of John 14. Notice specifically the promise of verse 3: "I will come again, and receive you unto myself; that where I am, there ye may be also."

Like the crew of Apollo 8, the Lord Jesus will return to this Earth. While the world watched and rejoiced at the crew's safe splash-down in the ocean, not everyone in the world will be watching and rejoicing for the return of the Lord Jesus Christ. But, may those of us who know and love Christ be expectantly "looking for that blessed hope, and the glorious appearing of the great God and our Saviour Jesus Christ" (Titus 2:13).

Building and Battling

28 December 1941

Then I told them of the hand of my God which was good upon me; as also the king's words that he had spoken unto me. And they said, Let us rise up and build. So they strengthened their hands for this good work.—**Nehemiah 2:18**

Before the United States entered World War II, the US Navy realized that fighting in theatres halfway across the globe would present new challenges in logistics and would require vast infrastructure. In 1940, they began a program of building bases using civilian contractors. The problem with this, however, was that international law forbade civilians from resisting enemy military action.

On 28 December 1941, Navy Rear Admiral Ben Moreell requested authority to set up a unique organization, one that would support the construction needs of the Navy and Marines in remote locations but would also be enabled to defend themselves if attacked. Known as the Seabees, the first Naval Construction Battalion deployed from Rhode Island in January and arrived at Bora Bora. These soldiers participated in every major amphibious assault of the war, forever impressing their motto of "Can Do" to a grateful nation.

The need for the Seabees reminds me of the challenges Nehemiah faced in rebuilding the wall of Jerusalem. During Nehemiah's time, walls around cities were crucial to people's protection not only from foreign invaders but also from wild animals. The enemies of Israel tried numerous times to get Nehemiah to quit his work on the wall, but instead, he organized his own "seabees": "For the builders, every one had his sword girded by his side, and so builded. And he that sounded the trumpet was by me" (Nehemiah 4:18).

The Christian life could be described as a life of "building and battling." Christians are responsible to help build God's work while also being prepared to fight the enemy. God desires that His work continue throughout the battles of life. As Christians, we can build His work as long as we have our sword—the Word of God—at the ready.

The Penguin Suit

29 December 1987

Beloved, think it not strange concerning the fiery trial which is to try you, as though some strange thing happened unto you:—**1 Peter 4:12**

On 29 December 1987, Soviet cosmonaut Colonel Yuri Romanenko returned to Earth after 326 days on the Mir space station, surpassing the previous Soviet endurance record by 90 days. Upon medical examination, Colonel Romanenko proved to be in good health, but this had not always been the case in such record-breaking voyages.

Five years earlier, touching down after 211 days in space, two Soviet cosmonauts experienced dizziness, high pulse rates, and heart palpitations. Due to the zero gravity in space, their muscles atrophied from the lack of resistance, which weakened their hearts. To prevent further occurrences, the Soviets designed a vibrant exercise regimen for their cosmonauts. Part of that regimen included wearing the "penguin suit," a running suit laced with elastic bands. Every move made while wearing the suit forced the wearer to exert his strength in order to complete simple motor skills like walking and running. After incorporating the penguin suit, Soviet cosmonauts were better prepared for the rigors of space travel.

Like those Soviet cosmonauts, we encounter resistance in life. Trials and temptations come to us all, and God uses them to strengthen us spiritually. James 1:2–3 says, "My brethren, count it all joy when ye fall into divers temptations; Knowing this, that the trying of your faith worketh patience." The joy, faith, and patience found within the trials and temptations of life far outweigh the work found in resisting them.

Paul reminded the Roman Christians, "For I reckon that the sufferings of this present time are not worthy to be compared with the glory which shall be revealed in us" (Romans 8:18). When we view our Saviour's face in Heaven, everything we have endured here on Earth will pale in comparison. So, next time a trial or temptation comes your way that seems debilitating, remember God's promise of His strength and His presence that will come with the suffering.

Happy Birthday, Mr. Sherman

30 December 2018

But thou, O Lord, art a shield for me; my glory, and the lifter up of mine head.
—Psalm 3:3

Duane Sherman served proudly in the US Navy during World War II. As chief sonarman aboard the USS *Lamson*, Sherman never forgot the day he lost thirty of his shipmates when a Japanese kamikaze crashed into his ship. Sherman was wounded in the attack, earning him the Purple Heart.

On 30 December 2018, Sherman turned ninety-six years of age. Feeling lonely and discouraged thinking of his friends and war buddies who had passed away, he did not want to celebrate. So Sherman's daughter, thinking to encourage her dad, posted to social media asking for her friends' help in wishing her dad a happy birthday. The request went viral, and the response was overwhelming. Sherman received over *fifty thousand* birthday cards from all fifty states and ten countries. Additionally, ten US Navy chiefs from San Diego paid Sherman a visit on his special day.

Do you find yourself discouraged today? Or do you know of someone who is going through a rough patch? Words of encouragement can do much to lift someone's spirits and help them see Jesus in the midst of the tough times.

Sometimes, however, those around us do not or will not understand what we are going through. Such was the case for the psalmist in Psalm 3. In these times, we can always find encouragement in the Lord.

In 1 Samuel 30, David and his men had lost everything, including having their families taken captive. In the midst of this grief, David's men blamed him. Talk about a rough day! The Bible tells us that "David was greatly distressed." Then it says, "But David encouraged himself in the Lord his God" (1 Samuel 30:6). Even when earthly comforts fail and our friends flee from our need, we can turn to God and to His Word to find the encouragement we need. Encourage yourself in the Lord today. He can be the "lifter up of [your] head."

Forgive

31 December 1503

Then came Peter to him, and said, Lord, how oft shall my brother sin against me, and I forgive him? till seven times? Jesus saith unto him, I say not unto thee, Until seven times: but, Until seventy times seven.—**Matthew 18:21–22**

Cesare Borgia was the illegitimate son of Rodrigo Borgia, who became Pope Alexander VI. Cesare's career as a shrewd politician, military leader, and nobleman provided the inspiration for Niccolò Machiavelli's book *The Prince*. Serving as a *condottiero* (military captain of a mercenary company) for King Louis XII, Cesare made many enemies. Two of those enemies, Oliverotto and Vitellozzo, arrived at Senigallia, Italy, on the pretext that Cesare had forgiven them their wrongdoings against him. On 31 December 1503, Cesare greeted the two men cordially, welcoming them into a house and seating them at a table. The men were surprised to see Cesare dressed in full battle armor. Suddenly, Cesare gave the order for their hands to be bound behind their backs, upon which they were both strangled. Known as the Coup of Senigallia in Italian Renaissance history, Cesare showed rival Italian factions that he was not willing to forgive.

The fact that the Apostle Peter asked the Lord Jesus how many times he should forgive someone who had wronged him is indicative that he was hoping the Lord would see his point and acquiesce to Peter's earth-bound outlook. Instead, the Lord gave Peter a heavenly outlook, essentially saying there is no proportional formula that registers how many times we should forgive. Forgiveness, when it is genuine, frees the offended party and allows growth to continue.

Unforgiveness hurts the party who holds it in their heart. Unforgiveness becomes bitterness which stunts our spiritual growth. This is one reason that Ephesians 4:31–32 instructs, "Let all bitterness . . . be put away from you, with all malice: And be ye kind one to another, tenderhearted, forgiving one another, even as God for Christ's sake hath forgiven you."

Has someone sinned against you? Don't carry unforgiveness into the New Year. Forgive as Christ has forgiven you.

How to Know Christ as Your Personal Saviour

There are big questions that haunt all of us. What happens when I die? Where will I spend eternity? The single most important question that you will ever answer is this: "If I were to die today, would I spend eternity in Heaven with God?" Your relationship to Jesus Christ is central to the answer to that question.

The Bible tells us in 1 John 5:13, "These things have I written unto you that believe on the name of the Son of God; that ye may know that ye have eternal life." The simple truth is God wants you to know where you're going!

So, here it is in a nutshell:

Recognize Your Condition

The biggest mistake a person can make when they are lost is to be too prideful to admit it. Yet, to know Christ personally, it has to start with realizing that you are lost in sin. Romans 5:12 teaches us that since Adam and Eve, the first man and woman on Earth, a sin nature has been present in all people. Romans 3:23 says, "For all have sinned, and come short of the glory of God." Sin is any act contrary to God's laws and commandments, and those sins that we have committed separate us from God.

The Bible tells us that sin has a penalty. Romans 6:23 says, "For the wages of sin is death; but the gift of God is eternal life through Jesus Christ our Lord." The "wage" or payment for our sin is spiritual death—eternal separation from God.

Religion and Good Works Are Not the Answer

Religions try to create their own ways to God. Their systems may seem logical, but they cannot bridge the gap created by our sin. Proverbs 14:12 says, "There is a way which seemeth right unto a man, but the end thereof are the ways of death." In other words, our thoughts and ways are not what matter. God's Word, the Bible, provides true answers of grace and forgiveness. In Ephesians 2:8–9 the Bible says, "For by grace are ye saved through faith; and that not of yourselves: it is the gift of God: Not of works, lest any man should boast."

The Good News: Jesus Christ Provides the Way!

Even though we were lost and separated from God, He loved us, and because He is love, God sent His Son to die on the Cross and raise from the dead three days later. John 3:16 explains "For God so loved the world, that he gave his only begotten Son, that whosoever believeth in him should not perish, but have everlasting life." Through the death and resurrection of Jesus, He became the payment for our sin. Now, we do not have to pay for our sin ourselves. By His grace, salvation is provided. In Romans 5:8, the Bible says, "But God commendeth [meaning *proved* or *demonstrated*] his love toward us, in that, while we were yet sinners, Christ died for us."

Believe and Receive Christ

In order to have a relationship with God and an eternal home in Heaven, we must stop trusting ourselves, our works, and our religions, and place our full trust in Jesus Christ alone for the forgiveness of our sin and eternal life. In Romans 10:13 the Bible says, "For whosoever shall call upon the name of the Lord shall be saved." That is a promise directly from God that if you will pray to Him, confess that you are a sinner, ask Him to forgive your sins, and turn to Him alone to be your Saviour; He promises to save you and give you the free gift of eternal life. You can make that decision today by praying from your heart, something like this:

> Dear God, I know that I am separated from you because of sin. I confess that in my sin, I cannot save myself. Right now, I turn to you alone to be my Saviour. I ask you to save me from the penalty of my sin, and I trust you to provide eternal life to me.—Amen

You'll never regret that decision. If you have just trusted Christ, send me an email at bootsontheground@strivingtogether.com to let me know. I would love to hear from you. May God bless you in your new walk of faith.

PRACTICES OF EFFECTIVE CHRISTIANS

The Effective Christian Memorizes Scripture

The following principles for effective Scripture memory are taken from *Homiletics from the Heart,* written by Dr. John Goetsch.

1. **Choose a specific time and a quiet place.**
   What gets scheduled gets accomplished. When memorizing the Word of God, you want to free yourself from all distractions.

2. **Organize by topic.**
   Many people attempt to learn the "Golden Chapters" or whole books of the Bible. While this is a noble attempt, it is not the way the Word of God will be used while teaching or preaching. Choose a topic you would like to study and then memorize every verse that deals with it. The next time you are speaking on that particular subject, your mind will be able to tie these verses together to truly allow you to "preach the Word..."

3. **Work out loud.**
   Even though it may sound odd, your mind memorizes better and faster that which it audibly hears. This is why you should choose a specific time and a quiet place!

4. **Walk while you memorize.**
   Your body has a natural sense of rhythm. This is why we memorize the words of songs so quickly. We will memorize much more quickly (and retain it longer) if we are walking around.

5. **Review, review, review.**
   Repetition is the key to learning. The one who is serious about memorizing Scripture cannot simply keep learning new passages weekly. Rather, he must also make the time to review the previous passages already committed to memory. It becomes readily apparent that memorization will take work, but the rewards are worth it!

6. **Set goals of time.**
If you are not careful, you may ask for disappointment by setting goals of verses per week. The reason why is that some verses are more difficult to learn than others. If you set goals of time spent in memorization, God will honor that.

Verses Remembered by Effective Christians

When you lose sight of His greatness:
Jeremiah 32:17; Jeremiah 33:3; Psalm 147:5; Romans 11:33–36; and 1 Chronicles 29:11–14

When you have needs:
Matthew 6:33; Philippians 4:19; Psalm 37:3; Psalm 37:25; and Deuteronomy 2:7

When you are overwhelmed:
Psalm 55:5; Psalm 55:18; Psalm 107:6–8; and 2 Corinthians 4:16

When problems seem insurmountable:
2 Corinthians 4:15–18; Romans 8:18; Psalm 32:7; Psalm 60:12; Psalm 61:2; and Psalm 62:6–8

When you need purpose:
1 Corinthians 10:31; Ephesians 3:16–21; John 10:10; and Psalm 139:14

When you have stress:
Philippians 4:4–7; Deuteronomy 20:1–4; and Jeremiah 32:27

When you are under pressure:
Psalm 27:1–2; Psalm 27:13–14; Psalm 46:1–2; and 2 Corinthians 12:9–10

When you worry:
Philippians 4:6–7; 1 Peter 5:7; Psalm 55:22; and Psalm 46:10

When you are afraid:
Psalm 56:3; Genesis 15:1; Psalm 27:1; 2 Timothy 1:7; and John 14:27

When you have a big decision to make:
Psalm 32:8; Psalm 143:10; Psalm 40:8; Proverbs 3:5–6; and Psalm 37:3–6

When you are discouraged:

1 Samuel 30:6; Joshua 1:9; Isaiah 41:10; Isaiah 40:26–28; and 2 Corinthians 4:15–16

When you are disheartened:

Joshua 1:5–9; Psalm 73:2; Psalm 73:17; and Psalm 73:24–26

When you are facing opposition:

2 Timothy 3:12; 2 Timothy 2:3; 1 Peter 4:12–13; 1 John 4:4; and Romans 8:31–32

When friends seem to let you down:

2 Timothy 4:16–17; Hebrews 12:2–3; Matthew 28:20; and Deuteronomy 32:27

When you are lonely:

Isaiah 41:10; Hebrews 13:5–6; Acts 18:9–10; and Isaiah 43:2

When you ask if it is worth it:

Matthew 25:21; 1 Corinthians 15:58; Galatians 6:9; and 2 Corinthians 4:17

How to Lead a Person to Christ

Someone once said, "The fruit of a Christian is another Christian." There is a lot of truth in that statement. The Christian leader will influence people to be more soul-conscious. Yet, sometimes a person will be very active in sharing the gospel, but will not see much fruit. It is the responsibility of the Christian leader to train others to not only be available, but effective in their witness. Here are some truths that every soulwinner must remember as he prepares to help another soul spend an eternity with Christ.

1. **A soulwinner should start with the truth of God's love for every individual.**
   John 3:16 is perhaps the most familiar verse in all the New Testament. "*For God so loved the world....*" There are sinners living today who actually believe that God hates them and wants them to go to Hell because of their sin. A sinner will never accept a Saviour who he believes will never love him.

2. **A soulwinner must emphasize the fact that we are all sinners—there are no exceptions.**
   There have been some who understand the "love" of God and feel that He would never send anyone to Hell. These sinners must also understand that the God of "love" is also first, and foremost, holy. All men fall short of the holy standard He has set. As a result of this "falling short," we are condemned to an eternity in Hell. Romans 3:23 includes all men everywhere.

3. **A soulwinner must teach the sinner that his sin carries with it an expensive price tag.**
   According to Romans 6:23, "*the wages of sin is death....*" In Ezekiel 18:20, the Israelites learned that the soul that sinned would die. As a soulwinner, the person you are dealing with has the wrath of God already abiding on him (John 3:36).

4. **A soulwinner should demonstrate the good news that Jesus has already paid this price.**
Not only does Romans 6:23 deal with the penalty of sin, it also deals with the promise of salvation. Romans 5:8 continues with this theme by showing the sinner that Christ died for us while we were yet sinners.

5. **A soulwinner must remember that a sinner must personally accept Christ as Saviour.**
This promise is given in Romans 10:13—"*For whosoever shall call upon the name of the Lord shall be saved.*" A sinner may believe that God loves him, may understand the fact that he is a sinner, and may further understand that Jesus died to pay his sin debt and still be lost. The soulwinner is not after a simple mental assent to a list of subscribed facts. He is looking for a sinner to repent, to confess, and to know the joy of being a Christian.

6. **Ask the sinner, "Is there anything that would hinder you from trusting Christ right now, today, as your Saviour?"**
This question will show the soulwinner if there are still any "obstacles" that must be removed before a sinner trusts Christ. It will also serve as a good transition into drawing the gospel net. After a sinner is saved, the Great Commission is still unfulfilled. We are commanded to go, to win, to baptize, and to teach (disciple). An effective soulwinner will determine to see each aspect of the Great Commission come to fruition with those he leads to Christ.

BIBLE READING SCHEDULES

One-Year Bible Reading Schedule

January

❑	**1**	Gen. 1–3	Matt. 1
❑	**2**	Gen. 4–6	Matt. 2
❑	**3**	Gen. 7–9	Matt. 3
❑	**4**	Gen. 10–12	Matt. 4
❑	**5**	Gen. 13–15	Matt. 5:1–26
❑	**6**	Gen. 16–17	Matt. 5:27–48
❑	**7**	Gen. 18–19	Matt. 6:1–18
❑	**8**	Gen. 20–22	Matt. 6:19–34
❑	**9**	Gen. 23–24	Matt. 7
❑	**10**	Gen. 25–26	Matt. 8:1–17
❑	**11**	Gen. 27–28	Matt. 8:18–34
❑	**12**	Gen. 29–30	Matt. 9:1–17
❑	**13**	Gen. 31–32	Matt. 9:18–38
❑	**14**	Gen. 33–35	Matt. 10:1–20
❑	**15**	Gen. 36–38	Matt. 10:21–42
❑	**16**	Gen. 39–40	Matt. 11
❑	**17**	Gen. 41–42	Matt. 12:1–23
❑	**18**	Gen. 43–45	Matt. 12:24–50
❑	**19**	Gen. 46–48	Matt. 13:1–30
❑	**20**	Gen. 49–50	Matt. 13:31–58
❑	**21**	Ex. 1–3	Matt. 14:1–21
❑	**22**	Ex. 4–6	Matt. 14:22–36
❑	**23**	Ex. 7–8	Matt. 15:1–20
❑	**24**	Ex. 9–11	Matt. 15:21–39
❑	**25**	Ex. 12–13	Matt. 16
❑	**26**	Ex. 14–15	Matt. 17
❑	**27**	Ex. 16–18	Matt. 18:1–20
❑	**28**	Ex. 19–20	Matt. 18:21–35
❑	**29**	Ex. 21–22	Matt. 19
❑	**30**	Ex. 23–24	Matt. 20:1–16
❑	**31**	Ex. 25–26	Matt. 20:17–34

February

❑	**1**	Ex. 27–28	Matt. 21:1–22
❑	**2**	Ex. 29–30	Matt. 21:23–46
❑	**3**	Ex. 31–33	Matt. 22:1–22
❑	**4**	Ex. 34–35	Matt. 22:23–46
❑	**5**	Ex. 36–38	Matt. 23:1–22
❑	**6**	Ex. 39–40	Matt. 23:23–39
❑	**7**	Lev. 1–3	Matt. 24:1–28
❑	**8**	Lev. 4–5	Matt. 24:29–51
❑	**9**	Lev. 6–7	Matt. 25:1–30
❑	**10**	Lev. 8–10	Matt. 25:31–46
❑	**11**	Lev. 11–12	Matt. 26:1–25
❑	**12**	Lev. 13	Matt. 26:26–50
❑	**13**	Lev. 14	Matt. 26:51–75
❑	**14**	Lev. 15–16	Matt. 27:1–26
❑	**15**	Lev. 17–18	Matt. 27:27–50
❑	**16**	Lev. 19–20	Matt. 27:51–66
❑	**17**	Lev. 21–22	Matt. 28
❑	**18**	Lev. 23–24	Mark 1:1–22
❑	**19**	Lev. 25	Mark 1:23–45
❑	**20**	Lev. 26–27	Mark 2
❑	**21**	Num. 1–2	Mark 3:1–19
❑	**22**	Num. 3–4	Mark 3:20–35
❑	**23**	Num. 5–6	Mark 4:1–20
❑	**24**	Num. 7–8	Mark 4:21–41
❑	**25**	Num. 9–11	Mark 5:1–20
❑	**26**	Num. 12–14	Mark 5:21–43
❑	**27**	Num. 15–16	Mark 6:1–29
❑	**28**	Num. 17–19	Mark 6:30–56

March

❑	**1**	Num. 20–22	Mark 7:1–13
❑	**2**	Num. 23–25	Mark 7:14–37
❑	**3**	Num. 26–28	Mark 8
❑	**4**	Num. 29–31	Mark 9:1–29
❑	**5**	Num. 32–34	Mark 9:30–50
❑	**6**	Num. 35–36	Mark 10:1–31
❑	**7**	Deut. 1–3	Mark 10:32–52
❑	**8**	Deut. 4–6	Mark 11:1–18
❑	**9**	Deut. 7–9	Mark 11:19–33
❑	**10**	Deut. 10–12	Mark 12:1–27
❑	**11**	Deut. 13–15	Mark 12:28–44
❑	**12**	Deut. 16–18	Mark 13:1–20
❑	**13**	Deut. 19–21	Mark 13:21–37
❑	**14**	Deut. 22–24	Mark 14:1–26
❑	**15**	Deut. 25–27	Mark 14:27–53
❑	**16**	Deut. 28–29	Mark 14:54–72
❑	**17**	Deut. 30–31	Mark 15:1–25
❑	**18**	Deut. 32–34	Mark 15:26–47
❑	**19**	Josh. 1–3	Mark 16
❑	**20**	Josh. 4–6	Luke 1:1–20
❑	**21**	Josh. 7–9	Luke 1:21–38
❑	**22**	Josh. 10–12	Luke 1:39–56
❑	**23**	Josh. 13–15	Luke 1:57–80
❑	**24**	Josh. 16–18	Luke 2:1–24
❑	**25**	Josh. 19–21	Luke 2:25–52
❑	**26**	Josh. 22–24	Luke 3
❑	**27**	Judges 1–3	Luke 4:1–30
❑	**28**	Judges 4–6	Luke 4:31–44
❑	**29**	Judges 7–8	Luke 5:1–16
❑	**30**	Judges 9–10	Luke 5:17–39
❑	**31**	Judges 11–12	Luke 6:1–26

April

❑	**1**	Judges 13–15	Luke 6:27–49
❑	**2**	Judges 16–18	Luke 7:1–30
❑	**3**	Judges 19–21	Luke 7:31–50
❑	**4**	Ruth 1–4	Luke 8:1–25
❑	**5**	1 Sam. 1–3	Luke 8:26–56
❑	**6**	1 Sam. 4–6	Luke 9:1–17
❑	**7**	1 Sam. 7–9	Luke 9:18–36
❑	**8**	1 Sam. 10–12	Luke 9:37–62
❑	**9**	1 Sam. 13–14	Luke 10:1–24
❑	**10**	1 Sam. 15–16	Luke 10:25–42
❑	**11**	1 Sam. 17–18	Luke 11:1–28
❑	**12**	1 Sam. 19–21	Luke 11:29–54
❑	**13**	1 Sam. 22–24	Luke 12:1–31
❑	**14**	1 Sam. 25–26	Luke 12:32–59
❑	**15**	1 Sam. 27–29	Luke 13:1–22
❑	**16**	1 Sam. 30–31	Luke 13:23–35
❑	**17**	2 Sam. 1–2	Luke 14:1–24
❑	**18**	2 Sam. 3–5	Luke 14:25–35
❑	**19**	2 Sam. 6–8	Luke 15:1–10
❑	**20**	2 Sam. 9–11	Luke 15:11–32
❑	**21**	2 Sam. 12–13	Luke 16
❑	**22**	2 Sam. 14–15	Luke 17:1–19
❑	**23**	2 Sam. 16–18	Luke 17:20–37
❑	**24**	2 Sam. 19–20	Luke 18:1–23
❑	**25**	2 Sam. 21–22	Luke 18:24–43
❑	**26**	2 Sam. 23–24	Luke 19:1–27
❑	**27**	1 Kings 1–2	Luke 19:28–48
❑	**28**	1 Kings 3–5	Luke 20:1–26
❑	**29**	1 Kings 6–7	Luke 20:27–47
❑	**30**	1 Kings 8–9	Luke 21:1–19

May

❑	**1**	1 Kings 10–11	Luke 21:20–38
❑	**2**	1 Kings 12–13	Luke 22:1–30
❑	**3**	1 Kings 14–15	Luke 22:31–46
❑	**4**	1 Kings 16–18	Luke 22:47–71
❑	**5**	1 Kings 19–20	Luke 23:1–25
❑	**6**	1 Kings 21–22	Luke 23:26–56
❑	**7**	2 Kings 1–3	Luke 24:1–35
❑	**8**	2 Kings 4–6	Luke 24:36–53
❑	**9**	2 Kings 7–9	John 1:1–28
❑	**10**	2 Kings 10–12	John 1:29–51
❑	**11**	2 Kings 13–14	John 2
❑	**12**	2 Kings 15–16	John 3:1–18
❑	**13**	2 Kings 17–18	John 3:19–36
❑	**14**	2 Kings 19–21	John 4:1–30
❑	**15**	2 Kings 22–23	John 4:31–54
❑	**16**	2 Kings 24–25	John 5:1–24
❑	**17**	1 Chr. 1–3	John 5:25–47
❑	**18**	1 Chr. 4–6	John 6:1–21
❑	**19**	1 Chr. 7–9	John 6:22–44
❑	**20**	1 Chr. 10–12	John 6:45–71
❑	**21**	1 Chr. 13–15	John 7:1–27
❑	**22**	1 Chr. 16–18	John 7:28–53
❑	**23**	1 Chr. 19–21	John 8:1–27
❑	**24**	1 Chr. 22–24	John 8:28–59
❑	**25**	1 Chr. 25–27	John 9:1–23
❑	**26**	1 Chr. 28–29	John 9:24–41
❑	**27**	2 Chr. 1–3	John 10:1–23
❑	**28**	2 Chr. 4–6	John 10:24–42
❑	**29**	2 Chr. 7–9	John 11:1–29
❑	**30**	2 Chr. 10–12	John 11:30–57
❑	**31**	2 Chr. 13–14	John 12:1–26

June

❑	**1**	2 Chr. 15–16	John 12:27–50
❑	**2**	2 Chr. 17–18	John 13:1–20
❑	**3**	2 Chr. 19–20	John 13:21–38
❑	**4**	2 Chr. 21–22	John 14
❑	**5**	2 Chr. 23–24	John 15
❑	**6**	2 Chr. 25–27	John 16
❑	**7**	2 Chr. 28–29	John 17
❑	**8**	2 Chr. 30–31	John 18:1–18
❑	**9**	2 Chr. 32–33	John 18:19–40
❑	**10**	2 Chr. 34–36	John 19:1–22
❑	**11**	Ezra 1–2	John 19:23–42
❑	**12**	Ezra 3–5	John 20
❑	**13**	Ezra 6–8	John 21
❑	**14**	Ezra 9–10	Acts 1
❑	**15**	Neh. 1–3	Acts 2:1–21
❑	**16**	Neh. 4–6	Acts 2:22–47
❑	**17**	Neh. 7–9	Acts 3
❑	**18**	Neh. 10–11	Acts 4:1–22
❑	**19**	Neh. 12–13	Acts 4:23–37
❑	**20**	Esther 1–2	Acts 5:1–21
❑	**21**	Esther 3–5	Acts 5:22–42
❑	**22**	Esther 6–8	Acts 6
❑	**23**	Esther 9–10	Acts 7:1–21
❑	**24**	Job 1–2	Acts 7:22–43
❑	**25**	Job 3–4	Acts 7:44–60
❑	**26**	Job 5–7	Acts 8:1–25
❑	**27**	Job 8–10	Acts 8:26–40
❑	**28**	Job 11–13	Acts 9:1–21
❑	**29**	Job 14–16	Acts 9:22–43
❑	**30**	Job 17–19	Acts 10:1–23

July

❑	1	Job 20–21	Acts 10:24–48
❑	2	Job 22–24	Acts 11
❑	3	Job 25–27	Acts 12
❑	4	Job 28–29	Acts 13:1–25
❑	5	Job 30–31	Acts 13:26–52
❑	6	Job 32–33	Acts 14
❑	7	Job 34–35	Acts 15:1–21
❑	8	Job 36–37	Acts 15:22–41
❑	9	Job 38–40	Acts 16:1–21
❑	10	Job 41–42	Acts 16:22–40
❑	11	Ps. 1–3	Acts 17:1–15
❑	12	Ps. 4–6	Acts 17:16–34
❑	13	Ps. 7–9	Acts 18
❑	14	Ps. 10–12	Acts 19:1–20
❑	15	Ps. 13–15	Acts 19:21–41
❑	16	Ps. 16–17	Acts 20:1–16
❑	17	Ps. 18–19	Acts 20:17–38
❑	18	Ps. 20–22	Acts 21:1–17
❑	19	Ps. 23–25	Acts 21:18–40
❑	20	Ps. 26–28	Acts 22
❑	21	Ps. 29–30	Acts 23:1–15
❑	22	Ps. 31–32	Acts 23:16–35
❑	23	Ps. 33–34	Acts 24
❑	24	Ps. 35–36	Acts 25
❑	25	Ps. 37–39	Acts 26
❑	26	Ps. 40–42	Acts 27:1–26
❑	27	Ps. 43–45	Acts 27:27–44
❑	28	Ps. 46–48	Acts 28
❑	29	Ps. 49–50	Rom. 1
❑	30	Ps. 51–53	Rom. 2
❑	31	Ps. 54–56	Rom. 3

August

❑	1	Ps. 57–59	Rom. 4
❑	2	Ps. 60–62	Rom. 5
❑	3	Ps. 63–65	Rom. 6
❑	4	Ps. 66–67	Rom. 7
❑	5	Ps. 68–69	Rom. 8:1–21
❑	6	Ps. 70–71	Rom. 8:22–39
❑	7	Ps. 72–73	Rom. 9:1–15
❑	8	Ps. 74–76	Rom. 9:16–33
❑	9	Ps. 77–78	Rom. 10
❑	10	Ps. 79–80	Rom. 11:1–18
❑	11	Ps. 81–83	Rom. 11:19–36
❑	12	Ps. 84–86	Rom. 12
❑	13	Ps. 87–88	Rom. 13
❑	14	Ps. 89–90	Rom. 14
❑	15	Ps. 91–93	Rom. 15:1–13
❑	16	Ps. 94–96	Rom. 15:14–33
❑	17	Ps. 97–99	Rom. 16
❑	18	Ps. 100–102	1 Cor. 1
❑	19	Ps. 103–104	1 Cor. 2
❑	20	Ps. 105–106	1 Cor. 3
❑	21	Ps. 107–109	1 Cor. 4
❑	22	Ps. 110–112	1 Cor. 5
❑	23	Ps. 113–115	1 Cor. 6
❑	24	Ps. 116–118	1 Cor. 7:1–19
❑	25	Ps. 119:1–88	1 Cor. 7:20–40
❑	26	Ps. 119:89–176	1 Cor. 8
❑	27	Ps. 120–122	1 Cor. 9
❑	28	Ps.123–125	1 Cor. 10:1–18
❑	29	Ps. 126–128	1 Cor. 10:19–33
❑	30	Ps. 129–131	1 Cor. 11:1–16
❑	31	Ps. 132–134	1 Cor. 11:17–34

September

❑	1	Ps. 135–136	1 Cor. 12
❑	2	Ps. 137–139	1 Cor. 13
❑	3	Ps. 140–142	1 Cor. 14:1–20
❑	4	Ps. 143–145	1 Cor. 14:21–40
❑	5	Ps. 146–147	1 Cor. 15:1–28
❑	6	Ps. 148–150	1 Cor. 15:29–58
❑	7	Prov. 1–2	1 Cor. 16
❑	8	Prov. 3–5	2 Cor. 1
❑	9	Prov. 6–7	2 Cor. 2
❑	10	Prov. 8–9	2 Cor. 3
❑	11	Prov. 10–12	2 Cor. 4
❑	12	Prov. 13–15	2 Cor. 5
❑	13	Prov. 16–18	2 Cor. 6
❑	14	Prov. 19–21	2 Cor. 7
❑	15	Prov. 22–24	2 Cor. 8
❑	16	Prov. 25–26	2 Cor. 9
❑	17	Prov. 27–29	2 Cor. 10
❑	18	Prov. 30–31	2 Cor. 11:1–15
❑	19	Eccl. 1–3	2 Cor. 11:16–33
❑	20	Eccl. 4–6	2 Cor. 12
❑	21	Eccl. 7–9	2 Cor. 13
❑	22	Eccl. 10–12	Gal. 1
❑	23	Song 1–3	Gal. 2
❑	24	Song 4–5	Gal. 3
❑	25	Song 6–8	Gal. 4
❑	26	Isa. 1–2	Gal. 5
❑	27	Isa. 3–4	Gal. 6
❑	28	Isa. 5–6	Eph. 1
❑	29	Isa. 7–8	Eph. 2
❑	30	Isa. 9–10	Eph. 3

October

❑	1	Isa. 11–13	Eph. 4
❑	2	Isa. 14–16	Eph. 5:1–16
❑	3	Isa. 17–19	Eph. 5:17–33
❑	4	Isa. 20–22	Eph. 6
❑	5	Isa. 23–25	Phil. 1
❑	6	Isa. 26–27	Phil. 2
❑	7	Isa. 28–29	Phil. 3
❑	8	Isa. 30–31	Phil. 4
❑	9	Isa. 32–33	Col. 1
❑	10	Isa. 34–36	Col. 2
❑	11	Isa. 37–38	Col. 3
❑	12	Isa. 39–40	Col. 4
❑	13	Isa. 41–42	1 Thess. 1
❑	14	Isa. 43–44	1 Thess. 2
❑	15	Isa. 45–46	1 Thess. 3
❑	16	Isa. 47–49	1 Thess. 4
❑	17	Isa. 50–52	1 Thess. 5
❑	18	Isa. 53–55	2 Thess. 1
❑	19	Isa. 56–58	2 Thess. 2
❑	20	Isa. 59–61	2 Thess. 3
❑	21	Isa. 62–64	1 Tim. 1
❑	22	Isa. 65–66	1 Tim. 2
❑	23	Jer. 1–2	1 Tim. 3
❑	24	Jer. 3–5	1 Tim. 4
❑	25	Jer. 6–8	1 Tim. 5
❑	26	Jer. 9–11	1 Tim. 6
❑	27	Jer. 12–14	2 Tim. 1
❑	28	Jer. 15–17	2 Tim. 2
❑	29	Jer. 18–19	2 Tim. 3
❑	30	Jer. 20–21	2 Tim. 4
❑	31	Jer. 22–23	Titus 1

November

❑	1	Jer. 24–26	Titus 2
❑	2	Jer. 27–29	Titus 3
❑	3	Jer. 30–31	Philemon
❑	4	Jer. 32–33	Heb. 1
❑	5	Jer. 34–36	Heb. 2
❑	6	Jer. 37–39	Heb. 3
❑	7	Jer. 40–42	Heb. 4
❑	8	Jer. 43–45	Heb. 5
❑	9	Jer. 46–47	Heb. 6
❑	10	Jer. 48–49	Heb. 7
❑	11	Jer. 50	Heb. 8
❑	12	Jer. 51–52	Heb. 9
❑	13	Lam. 1–2	Heb. 10:1–18
❑	14	Lam. 3–5	Heb. 10:19–39
❑	15	Ezek. 1–2	Heb. 11:1–19
❑	16	Ezek. 3–4	Heb. 11:20–40
❑	17	Ezek. 5–7	Heb. 12
❑	18	Ezek. 8–10	Heb. 13
❑	19	Ezek. 11–13	James 1
❑	20	Ezek. 14–15	James 2
❑	21	Ezek. 16–17	James 3
❑	22	Ezek. 18–19	James 4
❑	23	Ezek. 20–21	James 5
❑	24	Ezek. 22–23	1 Peter 1
❑	25	Ezek. 24–26	1 Peter 2
❑	26	Ezek. 27–29	1 Peter 3
❑	27	Ezek. 30–32	1 Peter 4
❑	28	Ezek. 33–34	1 Peter 5
❑	29	Ezek. 35–36	2 Peter 1
❑	30	Ezek. 37–39	2 Peter 2

December

❑	1	Ezek. 40–41	2 Peter 3
❑	2	Ezek. 42–44	1 John 1
❑	3	Ezek. 45–46	1 John 2
❑	4	Ezek. 47–48	1 John 3
❑	5	Dan. 1–2	1 John 4
❑	6	Dan. 3–4	1 John 5
❑	7	Dan. 5–7	2 John
❑	8	Dan. 8–10	3 John
❑	9	Dan. 11–12	Jude
❑	10	Hos. 1–4	Rev. 1
❑	11	Hos. 5–8	Rev. 2
❑	12	Hos. 9–11	Rev. 3
❑	13	Hos. 12–14	Rev. 4
❑	14	Joel	Rev. 5
❑	15	Amos 1–3	Rev. 6
❑	16	Amos 4–6	Rev. 7
❑	17	Amos 7–9	Rev. 8
❑	18	Obad.	Rev. 9
❑	19	Jonah	Rev. 10
❑	20	Micah 1–3	Rev. 11
❑	21	Micah 4–5	Rev. 12
❑	22	Micah 6–7	Rev. 13
❑	23	Nahum	Rev. 14
❑	24	Hab.	Rev. 15
❑	25	Zeph.	Rev. 16
❑	26	Hag.	Rev. 17
❑	27	Zech. 1–4	Rev. 18
❑	28	Zech. 5–8	Rev. 19
❑	29	Zech. 9–12	Rev. 20
❑	30	Zech. 13–14	Rev. 21
❑	31	Mal.	Rev. 22

90-Day Bible Reading Schedule

Day	Start	End	✔	Day	Start	End	✔
1	Genesis 1:1	Genesis 16:16	❑	46	Proverbs 7:1	Proverbs 20:21	❑
2	Genesis 17:1	Genesis 28:19	❑	47	Proverbs 20:22	Ecclesiastes 2:26	❑
3	Genesis 28:20	Genesis 40:11	❑	48	Ecclesiastes 3:1	Song 8:14	❑
4	Genesis 40:12	Genesis 50:26	❑	49	Isaiah 1:1	Isaiah 13:22	❑
5	Exodus 1:1	Exodus 15:18	❑	50	Isaiah 14:1	Isaiah 28:29	❑
6	Exodus 15:19	Exodus 28:43	❑	51	Isaiah 29:1	Isaiah 41:18	❑
7	Exodus 29:1	Exodus 40:38	❑	52	Isaiah 41:19	Isaiah 52:12	❑
8	Leviticus 1:1	Leviticus 14:32	❑	53	Isaiah 52:13	Isaiah 66:18	❑
9	Leviticus 14:33	Leviticus 26:26	❑	54	Isaiah 66:19	Jeremiah 10:13	❑
10	Leviticus 26:27	Numbers 8:14	❑	55	Jeremiah 10:14	Jeremiah 23:8	❑
11	Numbers 8:15	Numbers 21:7	❑	56	Jeremiah 23:9	Jeremiah 33:22	❑
12	Numbers 21:8	Numbers 32:19	❑	57	Jeremiah 33:23	Jeremiah 47:7	❑
13	Numbers 32:20	Deuteronomy 7:26	❑	58	Jeremiah 48:1	Lamentations 1:22	❑
14	Deuteronomy 8:1	Deuteronomy 23:11	❑	59	Lamentations 2:1	Ezekiel 12:20	❑
15	Deuteronomy 23:12	Deuteronomy 34:12	❑	60	Ezekiel 12:21	Ezekiel 23:39	❑
16	Joshua 1:1	Joshua 14:15	❑	61	Ezekiel 23:40	Ezekiel 35:15	❑
17	Joshua 15:1	Judges 3:27	❑	62	Ezekiel 36:1	Ezekiel 47:12	❑
18	Judges 3:28	Judges 15:12	❑	63	Ezekiel 47:13	Daniel 8:27	❑
19	Judges 15:13	1 Samuel 2:29	❑	64	Daniel 9:1	Hosea 13:6	❑
20	1 Samuel 2:30	1 Samuel 15:35	❑	65	Hosea 13:7	Amos 9:10	❑
21	1 Samuel 16:1	1 Samuel 28:19	❑	66	Amos 9:11	Nahum 3:19	❑
22	1 Samuel 28:20	2 Samuel 12:10	❑	67	Habakkuk 1:1	Zechariah 10:12	❑
23	2 Samuel 12:11	2 Samuel 22:18	❑	68	Zechariah 11:1	Matthew 4:25	❑
24	2 Samuel 22:19	1 Kings 7:37	❑	69	Matthew 5:1	Matthew 15:39	❑
25	1 Kings 7:38	1 Kings 16:20	❑	70	Matthew 16:1	Matthew 26:56	❑
26	1 Kings 16:21	2 Kings 4:37	❑	71	Matthew 26:57	Mark 9:13	❑
27	2 Kings 4:38	2 Kings 15:26	❑	72	Mark 9:14	Luke 1:80	❑
28	2 Kings 15:27	2 Kings 25:30	❑	73	Luke 2:1	Luke 9:62	❑
29	1 Chronicles 1:1	1 Chronicles 9:44	❑	74	Luke 10:1	Luke 20:19	❑
30	1 Chronicles 10:1	1 Chronicles 23:32	❑	75	Luke 20:20	John 5:47	❑
31	1 Chronicles 24:1	2 Chronicles 7:10	❑	76	John 6:1	John 15:17	❑
32	2 Chronicles 7:11	2 Chronicles 23:15	❑	77	John 15:18	Acts 6:7	❑
33	2 Chronicles 23:16	2 Chronicles 35:15	❑	78	Acts 6:8	Acts 16:37	❑
34	2 Chronicles 35:16	Ezra 10:44	❑	79	Acts 16:38	Acts 28:16	❑
35	Nehemiah 1:1	Nehemiah 13:14	❑	80	Acts 28:17	Romans 14:23	❑
36	Nehemiah 13:15	Job 7:21	❑	81	Romans 15:1	1 Corinthians 14:40	❑
37	Job 8:1	Job 24:25	❑	82	1 Corinthians 15:1	Galatians 3:25	❑
38	Job 25:1	Job 41:34	❑	83	Galatians 3:26	Colossians 4:18	❑
39	Job 42:1	Psalm 24:10	❑	84	1 Thessalonians 1:1	Philemon 25	❑
40	Psalm 25:1	Psalm 45:14	❑	85	Hebrews 1:1	James 3:12	❑
41	Psalm 45:15	Psalm 69:21	❑	86	James 3:13	3 John 14	❑
42	Psalm 69:22	Psalm 89:13	❑	87	Jude 1	Revelation 17:18	❑
43	Psalm 89:14	Psalm 108:13	❑	88	Revelation 18:1	Revelation 22:21	❑
44	Psalm 109:1	Psalm 134:3	❑	89	Grace Day	Grace Day	❑
45	Psalm 135:1	Proverbs 6:35	❑	90	Grace Day	Grace Day	❑

BIBLIOGRAPHY AND INDEXES

Bibliography

arranged by devotional date for ease of reference

January

1. Fowler, William M. Jr. *Empires at War: the French and Indian War and the Struggle for North America, 1754–1763.* New York: Walker & Company, 2005.
2. Irving, Washington. *Conquest of Granada From the Manuscript of Fray Antonio Ag apida.* New York: A.L. Burt, 1829.
3. Merriman, John. *A History of Modern Europe, Vol. 2: From the French Revolution to the Present.* New York: W. W. Norton & Company, 2009.
4. Keegan, John. *The Second World War.* New York: Penguin, 1989.
5. Catiline's Speech to His Troops before the Battle of Pistoria, January 5, 62 B.C. http://www.strategypage.com/cic/docs/cic177c.asp.
6. Wolf, David C. "To Secure a Convenience: Britain Recognizes China – 1950." *Journal of Contemporary History* 18, no. 2 (1983): 299–326.
7. Weapons and Warfare: History and Hardware of Warfare. Peter the Great 1702–25—Russian Army at War II. https://weaponsandwarfare.com/2018/04/20/peter-the-great-1702-25-russian-army-at-war-ii/.
8. Aldrete, Gregory S. *The Decisive Battles of World History.* Chantilly, VA: The Teaching Company, LLC, 2013.
9. Benjamin, Thomas. *The Atlantic World: Europeans, Africans, Indians and Their Shared History, 1400–1900.* New York: Cambridge University Press, 2009.
10. Davis, William Stearns. Suetonius. "Life of Julius Caesar" in *Readings in Ancient History* (1912).
11. J. Llewellyn et al. "The Ruhr Occupation." *Alpha History.* 2014, https://alphahistory.com/weimarrepublic/ruhr-occupation/.
12. Green, David B. "1493: Jews of Sicily Expelled by Spanish Rulers." https://www.haaretz.com/hewish/.premium-1493-sicillian-jews-expelled-1.5300550.
13. "The First Anglo-Afghan War, 1839–1842." *Military History Monthly*, October 1, 2010, https://www.military-history.org/articles/the-first-anglo-afghan-war-1839-1842.htm.
14. Kamen, Henry. *Philip V of Spain: The King who Reigned Twice.* Yale University Press, 2001.
15. Dahl, Roald. *Charlie and the Chocolate Factory.* New York: Puffin Books, 2007.
    Puleo, Stephen. Dark Tide: *The Great Boston Molasses Flood of 1919.* Boston: Beacon Press, 2004.
16. Siggurdsson. "Teddy Roosevelt Awarded Medal of Honor—103 Years After San Juan Hill." *The American Legion's Burn Pit.* January 16, 2013, www.burnpit.us/2013/01/teddy-roosevelt-awarded-medal-honor-103-years-after-san-juan-hill.
17. "The Great Brinks Robbery of 1950: Not Quite the Perfect Crime." *New England Historical Society* (2020). https://www.newenglandhistoricalsociety.com/great-brinks-robbery-1950-not-quite-perfect-crime/.
18. Harris, Bill. "Year of the B-52: B-52s make historic, nonstop around the world flights." *Air Force Global Strike Command.* March 8, 2012, https://www.afgsc.af.mil/News/Article-Display/Article/454903/year-of-the-b-52-b-52s-make-historic-nonstop-around-the-world-flights/.
19. Crocker, H.W. III. *Robert E. Lee on Leadership: Executive Lessons in Character, Courage, and Vision.* New York: Three Rivers Press, 2000.

20. Fadiman, Clifton and André Bernard, eds. *Barlett's Book of Anecdotes.* New York: Little, Brown and Company, 2000.
21. Library of Congress. "Aitken's Bible Endorsed by Congress." *Religion and the Founding of the American Republic.* http://www.loc.gov/exhibits/religion/rel04.html#obj115.
22. Hanson, Victor D. *Carnage and Culture: Landmark Battles in the Rise to Western Power.* New York: Doubleday Publishing Group, 2002. Kindle.
23. Cole, Wayne S. "The America First Committee." *Journal of the Illinois State Historical Society* 44, no. 4 (1951): 305–322.
    Duffy, James P. *Lindbergh vs. Roosevelt: The Rivalry That Divided America.* Washington DC: Regnery Publishing, 2010.
24. Satterfield, John R. *We Band of Brothers: The Sullivans & World War II.* Parkersburg, IA: Mid-Prairie Books, 1995.
25. "The Cullinan Diamond." *Worthy.com.* June 24, 2019. https://www.worthy.com/blog/knowledge-center/diamonds/cullinan-diamond/.
26. "Not Guilty." *St. Louis Post-Dispatch.* September 6, 1883.
    Saar, Meghan. "The Real Frank James." True West. October 30,2017, truewestmagazine.com/frank-james/.
27. Raines, Howell. "Hostages Hailed at White House; Reagan Vows 'Swift Retribution' for Any New Attack on Diplomats." *New York Times.* January 28, 1981, http://www.nytimes.com/1981/01/28/us/hostages-hailed-white-house-reagan-vows-swift-retribution-for-any-new-attack.html.
28. Challies, Tim. "Hymn Stories: Onward, Christian Soldiers." *Challies.com.* June 9, 2013. Accessed January 14, 2016, http://www.challies.com/articles/hymn-stories-onward-christian-soldiers.
29. History.com Editors. "William McKinley." September 6, 2019, www.history.com/topics/us-presidents/william-mckinley.
30. Ronald Reagan: "Remarks at the Annual Convention of the National Religious Broadcasters," January 30, 1984, https://www.presidency.ucsb.edu/documents/remarks-the-annual-convention-the-national-religious-broadcasters-3.
31. Paperless Archives. "World War II: Eddie Slovik Court Martial and Execution Documents." http://www.paperlessarchives.com/wwii-eddie-slovik-court-martia.html.

February

1. Taylor, Robert A. "Extracting Salt from the Sea." *FHC Forum* 34, no. 1 (2010). https://digital.stpetersburg.usf.edu/cgi/viewcontent.cgi?article=1049&context=forum_magazine .
2. John Augustus Sutter. "New Perspectives on the West." www.pbs.org/weta/thewest/people/s_z/sutter.htm.
3. Meyer, G.J. *A World Undone: The Story of the Great War 1914 to 1918.* New York: Bantam Dell, 2006.
4. The Fred W. Smith National Library for the Study of George Washington at Mount Vernon. "Washington Quotes." *George Washington's Mount Vernon.*https://www.mountvernon.org/library/digitalhistory/quotes/.
5. Associated Press, "Air Force finds no trace of lost nuke," *USA Today*, June 17, 2005, http://usatoday30.usatoday.com/news/nation/2005-06-17-lost-bomb_x.htm.
6. Ferling, John. *Almost a Miracle: The American Victory in the War of Independence.* New York: Oxford University Press, 2007.
7. Biographics. "Josef Mengele Biography: German Schutzstaffel Officer & Physician in Concentration Camps." June 27, 2018 https://biographics.org/josef-mengele-biography-german-schutzstaffel-officer-physician-in-concentration-camps/.

8. Regan, Geoffrey. *Great Military Blunders*. London: Andre Deutsch, 2012. Kindle.
9. "G. I. Joe Biography." *Who2 Biographies*. http://www.who2.com/bio/gi-joe/.
10. News & Information. "A Look Back . . . The Cold War: Strangers On a Bridge." *Central Intelligence Agency*. https://www.cia.gov/news-information/featured-story-archive/strangers-on-a-bridge.html.
11. Schwarz, Frederic D. "1573; Drake Sees the Pacific." *American Heritage* 49, no.1 (February-March 1998) https://www.questia.com/magazine/1G1-20458016/1573-drake-sees-the-pacific.
12. Flantzer, Susan. "King Adolf Frederik of Sweden." *Unofficial Royalty: The Site for Royal News and Discussion*. December 21, 2017, www.unofficialroyalty.com/king-adolf-frederik-of-sweden/.
13. English Monarchs. "William III and Mary II." http://www.englishmonarchs.co.uk/stuart_6.htm.
14. Bowerman, Mary. "Infamous USS Juneau that sank during WWII with five Sullivan brothers aboard discovered in Pacific." USA Today Network. March 20, 2018. https://www.usatoday.com/story/tech/nation-now/2018/03/20/sullivan-brothers-uss-juneau-found-pacific/440821002
"In the Depths of the Sea." I've Just Started Living (1989). *Southern Gospel Journal.*
15. "HMS Ramillies." *Submerged*. https://www.submerged.co.uk/ramillies/
Rodger, N.A.M. *The Wooden World: An Anatomy of the Georgian Navy*. New York: W.W. Norton & Co., 1986.
16. Turnbull, Stephen. *Crusader Castles of the Teutonic Knights, Vol. 2: The Stone Castles of Latvia and Estonia, 1185–1560*. Oxford: Osprey Publishing, 2004.
17. Bridge, Antony. *Suleiman the Magnificent: Scourge of Heaven*. London: Thistle Publishing, 2015.
Setton, Kenneth Meyer. *The Papacy and the Levant, 1204–1571: The Sixteenth Century*. Philadelphia: The American Philosophical Society, 1984.
18. Benjamin, Thomas. *The Atlantic World: Europeans, Africans, Indians and Their SharedHistory, 1400–1900*. New York: Cambridge University Press, 2009.
Hanson, Victor Davis. *Carnage and Culture: Landmark Battles in the Rise of Western Power*. New York: Anchor Books, 2002. Kindle.
19. Lynch, Michael. "The Emancipation of the Russian Serfs, 1861." *History Review* 47, December 2003. https://www.historytoday.com/archive/emancipation-russian-serfs-1861.
20. McFadden, Robert D. "Hiroo Onoda, Soldier Who Hid in Jungle for Decades, Dies at 91." *New York Times*. January 17, 2014, http://www.nytimes.com/2014/01/18/world/asia/hiroo-onoda-imperial-japanese-army-officer-dies-at-91.html?_r=0.
21. Powles, Guy C. *The New Zealanders in Sinai and Palestine: Official History of New Zealand's Effort in the Great War Book 3*. Halstad, MN:Pickle Partners Publishing, 2013.
22. Nuxoll, Elisabeth M. "The Selected Papers of John Jay Digital Edition," ed. *University of Virginia Press, Rotunda*. (2014) https:www.upress.virginia.edu/content/selected-papers-john-jay-digital-edition
Wilson Jr, Vincent. *The Book of the Founding Fathers*. Brookeville, MD: American History Research Associates, 1974.
23. Beyond Today. "In Their Own Words: Great Men and Women Who Highly Respected the Bible." https://www.ucg.org/bible-study-tools/booklets/how-to-understand-the-bible/in-their-own-words-great-men-and-women-who-highly-respected-the-bible
History.com Editors. "John Quincy Adams." https://www.history.com/topics/us-presidents/john-quincy-adams.
24. Burgess, R.W. "The date of the persecution of Christians in the army." *The Journal of Theological Studies* 47, no. 1 (1996). https:www.academia.edu/9134902/_The_Date_of_

the_Persecution_of_Christians_in_the_Army_The_Journal_of_Theological_Studies_NS_47_1996_157-8.

25. Cavendish, Richard. "The Kingdom of Prussia is Founded." *History Today* 51, no. 1 (January 2001) https://www.historytoday.com/archive/kingdom-prussia-founded
Craig, Gordon A. The End of Prussia. *Proceedings of the American Philosophical Society* 124, no. 2 (1980) https://www.jstor.org/stable/986204.
26. Endicott, Charles M. *Account of Leslie's Retreat at the North Bridge in Salem on Sunday, Feb'y 26, 1775.* Salem: Wm. Ives and Geo. W. Pease Printers, 1856.https://archive.org/details/accountoflesliesooendi/page/n7/mode/2up
Harris, Gordon. "Leslie's Retreat, or how the Revolutionary War almost began in Salem." *Historic Ipswich on the Massachusetts North Shore.* February 13, 2019, https://historicipswich.org/2019/02/13/leslies-retreat-or-how-the-relvoluationary-war-almost-began-in-salem
27. "Battle of Ancrum Moor." *Historic Scottish Battles.* http://www.rampantscotland.com/Battles/battle_ancrum.htm
28. Kinard, Jeff. *Weapons and Warfare Artillery: An Illustrated History of Its Impact.* Santa Barbara, CA: ABC-CLIO, 2007.
"The Forgotten Tragedy: The 1844 explosion on the USS Princeton shook the presidency of John Tyler." *The Free-Lance Star,* September 25, 2005.
29. "William Harvey Carney." *American Battlefield Trust.* https://www.battlefields.org/learn/biographies/william-carney.
Massachusetts Adjutant General's Office. Massachusetts Soldiers, Sailors, and Marines in the Civil War. Norwood, MA: Norwood Press, 1931.

March

1. Green, Peter. *Alexander the Great of Macedon, 356–323 B.C.* Berkeley, CA: University of California Press, 1992.
2. Pease, Donald E. *Theodor Geisel : A Portrait of the Man Who Became Dr. Seuss.* Oxford University Press, 2010.
3. Duiker, William J. *Ho Chi Minh.* New York: Hatchette Books, 2012.
History.com Editors. "Ho Chi Minh Trail." (July 28, 2019) https://www.history.com/this-day-in-history/u-s-jets-bomb-ho-chi-minh-trail.
Kocher, Matthew Adam, Thomas B. Pepinsky and Stathis N. Kalyvas. "Aerial Bombing and Counterinsurgency in the Vietnam War." *American Journal of Political Science* 55, no. 2 (April 2011) https://onlinelibrary.wiley.com/doi/abs/10.1111/j.1540-5907.2010.00498x.
4. Hanson, Victor Davis. *Carnage and Culture: Landmark Battles in the Rise of Western Power.* New York: Anchor Books, 2002. Kindle.
VanDevelder, Paul. "1519–Cortez lands in Mexico." *Savages & Scoundrels.* http://savagesandscoundrels.org/flashpoints-conflicts/1519-cortez-lands-in-mexico/.
5. Beech, Hannah. "U.S. Aircraft Carrier Arrives in Vietnam, With a Message for China." *The New York Times,* March 4, 2018, https:www.nytimes.com/2018/03/04/world/asia/carl-vinson-vietnam.html.
6. Blanchard, Raoul. "The Battle of Verdun." *The Atlantic,* June 1917, https://www.theatlantic.com/magazine/archive/1917/06/the-battle-of-verdun/567323/.
7. Miller, Rod. "Britain and the Rhineland Crisis, 7 March 1936: Retreat from Responsibility or Accepting the Inevitable?" *Australian Journal of Politics & History* 33, no. 1 (1987) https://onlinelibrary.wiley.com/doi/abs/10.1111/j.1467-8497.1987.tb00359x
Schuker, Stephen A. "France and the Remilitarization of the Rhineland, 1936." *French Historical Studies* 14, no. 3 (1986) https://www.academia.edu/11963094/France_and_the_Remilitarization_of_the_Rhineland_1936.

Watt, Donald Cameron. "German Plans for the Reoccupation of the Rhineland: A Note." *Journal of Contemporary History* 1, no.4 (1966) https://journals.sagepub.com/doi/10.1177/002200946600100408.

8. Smith, Robert Barr. "Mad Jack" Churchill—A Rare Breed of Warrior." *Warfare History Network.*
9. Battle of Camarón: "These Are Not Men, They Are Devils." *The American Legion's Burn Pit.* April 30, 2013. http://burnpit.legion.org/2013/04/battle-camar%C3%B3n-these-are-not-men-they-are-devils.
10. Gritzner, Maximilian. *Handbuch der Ritter- Und Verdienstorden.* Akademische Druck-U. Verlagsanstalt, 1893.
"The 1914 German Iron Cross." Trenches on the Web. http://www.worldwar1.com/sfgcross.htm.
Williamson, Gordon. *The Iron Cross, A History 1813–1957.* Little Rock: Reddick Enterprises, 1995.
11. Hopkins, William B. *The Pacific War: The Strategy, Politics, and Players That Won the War.* Minneapolis: Zenith Press, 2010.
12. Fitzsimons, Bernard. *Illustrated Encyclopedia of 20th Century Weapons and Warfare,* Volume 7. London: Phoebus, 1978.
Preston, Antony. *The Royal Navy Submarine Service: A Centennial History.* Annapolis, MD: Naval Institute Press, 2001.
13. Bergeron, Arthur W. "War Dogs: The Birth of the K-9 Corps." U. S. Army Military History Institute. March 16, 2016, https://www.army.mil/article/7463/war_dogs_the_birth_of_the_k_9_corps.
Hastings, Deborah. "Chips, a U.S. Army Hero Dog That Served in World War II, Gets Posthumous Medal." *Inside Edition.* January 15, 2018, https:www.insideedition.com/chips-us-army-her-dog-served-world-war-ii-gets-posthumous-medal-39811.
14. Payton, Matt. "Birmingham pub bombings: Who are the Birmingham Six? What happened in the IRA attack? Everything you need to know." *Independent,* June 1, 2016, https://www.independent.co.uk/news/uk/home-news/birmingham-pub-bumbings-1974-ira-who-are-the-birmingham-six-what-happened-in-the-attack-everything-a7059876.html.
15. https://thisdayinusmilhist.wordpress.com/2014/03/15/march-15/.
https://en.wikipedia.org/wiki/Assassination_of_Julius_Caesar.
16. Beidler, Philip. "Calley's Ghost." The Virginia Quarterly Review 79, no.1 (Winter 2003). https://www.questia.com/read/1P3-277002381/calley-s-ghost.
Friedersdorf, Conor. "The Unlearned Lesson of My Lai" The Atlantic, March 16, 2019, https://www.democratichub.com/posts/16367/the-atlantic-the-unlearned-lesson-of-my-lai.
17. Kindelan, Katie. "Purple Heart Sold for $4.99 at Goodwill to Be Returned to Recipient's Family." *ABC News.* March 16, 2016, https://abcnews.go.com/Business/purple-heart-sold-499-goodwill-returned-recipients-family-story?id=37697519.
18. McKie, Robin. "Alexei Leonov, the first man to walk in space."*The Guardian.* May 9, 2015, https://www.theguardian.com/science/2015/may/09/alexei-leonov-first-man-to-walk-in-space-soviet-cosmonaut.
19. "March 19." *This Day in U.S. Military History.* Accessed September 9, 2020, https://thisdayinusmilhist.wordpress.com/2014/03/19/march-19/.
20. Wells, William V. *The Life and Public Services of Samuel Adams, Being a Narrative of His Acts and Opinions, and of His Agency in Producing and Forwarding the American Revolution. With Extracts from His Correspondence, State Papers, and Political Essays.* Vol. II. Boston: Little, Brown, and Co, 1865.
21. Murray, Alan V. *"Mighty against the Enemies of Christ:" The Relic of the True Cross in the Armies of the Kingdom of Jerusalem.* Aldershot: Ashgate, 1998.

"The Relic of the True Cross." *TemplarHistory.com*, June 7, 2020. https://templarhistory.com/the-relic-of-the-true-cross.

22. Herodoian. *History of the Roman Empire since the Death of Marcus Aurelius,* Volume 7. Translated by Edward C. Echols. https://www.livius.org/sources/content/herodian-s-roman-history/.
    Southern, Pat. *The Roman Empire from Severus to Constantine.* New York: Routledge, 2001.
23. "Desmond Doss: The Real Story." *Desmond Doss the Conscientious Objector.* https://desmonddoss.com/bio/bio-real.php.
    Varangis, Nicholas. "Desmond Doss: The Hero of Hacksaw Ridge." *Warfare History Network.* October 12,2016, https://warfarehistorynetwork.com/2017/06/15/desmond-doss-the-hero-of-hacksaw-ridge/.
24. Charlmers, General J.R. "Lieutenant General Nathan Bedford Forrest and His Campaigns." *Southern Historical Society Papers* VII, No. 10 (1879) https://civilwarhome.com/forrestcampaigns.htm.
    Lester, J.C. and D.L. Wilson. *Ku Klux Klan: Its Origin, Growth and Disbandment.* Charleston: Nabu Press, 2011. Kindle.
    Scheer, Holly. "Don't Erase Nathan Bedford Forrest From U.S. History." *The Federalist.* July 9, 2015, http://thefederalist.com/2015/07/09/dont-erase-nathan-bedford-forrest-from-u-s-history/.
    Tures, John A. "General Nathan Bedford Forrest Versus the Ku Klux Klan." *Huffington Post.* July 6, 2015, http://www.huffingtonpost.com/john-a-tures/general-nathan-bedford-fo_b_7734444.html.
25. Górski, Szymon and Ewelina Wilczynska. "How the Hussite Wars changed the medieval battlefield - Jan Žižka's wagons of war." *Medieval Warfare.* 2013.
26. History.com Staff. "McCarthy charges that Owen Lattimore is a Soviet spy." This Day in History. 2009. Accessed March 23, 2016. http://www.history.com/this-day-in-history/mccarthy-charges-that-owen-lattimore-is-a-soviet-spy.
27. Bauman, Richard J. "The Strange Disappearance of Admiral Wilcox." *Naval History Magazine* 32, no. 1 (February 2018). https://www.usni.org/magazines/naval-history-magazine/2018/february/strange-disappearance-admiral-wilcox.
28. "Backgrounder on the Three Mile Island Accident." United States Nuclear Regulatory Commission. (June 2018) https://www.nrc.gov/reading-rm/doc-collections/fact-sheets/3mile-isle.html.
29. Times Leader. "Congress passes Vietnam War Veterans Recognition Act." March 29, 2017, https://www.wearethemighty.com/articles/congress-passes-vietnam-war-veterans-recognition-act.
30. "March 30." *This Day in U.S. Military History.* Accessed September 2, 2020, https://thisdayinusmilhist.wordpress.com/2014/03/30/march-30/.
31. "WWII: The Only Person To Shoot Down A Plane With A Handgun." *World War Wings.* https://worldwarwings.com/wwii-the-only-person-to-shoot-down-a-plane-with-a-handgun/.

April

1. "Honoring Gary Beikirch." *National Medal of Honor Museum.* https://mohmuseum.org/honoring-gary-beikirch/.
2. Gopnik, Adam. "Trial of the Century: Revisiting the Dreyfus Affair." *The New Yorker.* September 21, 2009, https://www.newyorker.com/magazine/2009/09/28/trial-of-the-century.

Zollman, Joellyn. "The Dreyfus Affair: The Espionage Conviction of a French military officer was a watershed event in the history of European anti-Semitism." *My Jewish Learning*. https://www.myjewishlearning.com/article/the-dreyfus-affair/.

3. De Long, Bradford J. and Barry Eichengreen. "The Marshall Plan: History's Most Successful Structural Adjustment Program." *National Bureau of Economic Research*, (November 1991) https://www.nber.org/papers/w3899.
   Glass, Andrew. "Truman Signs Marshall Plan, April 3, 1948." *Politico*. April 2, 2016, https://www.politico.com/story/2016/04/this-day-in-politics-april-3-1948-221464.
4. Hollingham, Richard. V-2: The Nazi Rocket that Launched the Space Age. *BBC*. September 8, 2014, http://www.bbc.com/future/story/20140905-the-nazis-space-age-rocket
   Martin Luther King, Jr. Quotes. https://www.brainyquote.com/quotes/authors/m/martin_luther_king_jr.html.
5. Washington, Booker T. *Up From Slavery*. New York: Doubleday & Company, 1901.
6. "Albert Sidney Johnston." *American Battlefield Trust*. https://www.battlefields.org/learn/biographies/albert-sidney-johnston.
   Woodworth, Steven E. *This Great Struggle: America's Civil War*. Maryland: Rowman & Littlefield, 2011.
7. Karnow, Stanley. *Vietnam: A History*. New York: The Viking Press, 1983.
8. Bradley, Omar N., and Clay Blair. *A General's Life: An Autobiography*. New York: Simon and Schuster, 1983.
   "Omar Nelson Bradley." *The State Historical Society of Missouri: Historic Missourians*. https://historicmissourians.shsmo.org/historicmissourians/name/b/bradley/.
11. "Historian stole nearly 300 dog tags of WWII fallen soldiers from National Archives, authorities say." Fox News, April 11, 2018. http://fox2now.com/2018/04/11/historian-stole-nearly-300-dog-tags-of-wwii-fallen-soldiers-from-national-archives-authorities-say/.
12. Fant Jr., Gene C. *God as Author: A Biblical Approach to Narrative*. Nashville: B & H Academic Publishing Group, 2010.
    Higham, N.J. *The Kingdom of Northumbria AD 350–1100*. Stroud, United Kingdom: Sutton Publishing Ltd., 1993.
13. History.com Staff. "Hail kills English troops." *This Day in History*. November 13, 2009, http://www.history.com/this-day-in-history/hail-kills-english-troops.
14. Farago, Robert. "This Day in Gun History: Titanic Fires White Flares." *Truth About Guns*, April 15, 2010, https://www.thetruthaboutguns.com/this-day-in-gun-history-titanic-fires-white-flares/.
    Ponic, Jason. "The SS Californian: The Ship That Watched Titanic Sink." *Owlcation*, March 4, 2018, https://owlacation.com/humanities/The-SS-Californian-The=Ship-That-Ignored-Titanics-Distress-Calls.
15. Allmand, Christopher. The Hundred Years' War: Cambridge Medieval Textbooks. New York: Cambridge University Press, 1988.
    "Battle of Formigny, (1450)." Weapons and Warfare.November 30, 2019, https://weaponsandwarfare.com/2015/11/30/battle-of-formigny-1450/
    Rickard, J."Battle of Formigny, 15 April 1450." http://www.historyofwar.org/articles/battles_formigny.html.
16. Chambers II, John Whiteclay. "*USO*." *The Oxford Companion to American Military History*. Oxford: Oxford University Press, 2000.
    Gallagher, Pat. "Happy 75th Anniversary USO!" *Huffpost*. February 4, 2017, https://www.huffingtonpost.com/pat-gallagher/uso-anniversary_b_9133132.html.
17. NASA Science. "Apollo 13." NASA Science Solar System Exploration. https://solarsystem.nasa.gov/missions/apollo-13/in-depth.

Smithsonian National Air and Space Museum. "Apollo 13 (AS-508)." https://airandspace.si.edu/explore-and-learn/topics/apollo/apollo-program/landing-missions/apollo13.cfm.
18. Hitt, Angela. "St. Peter's Basilica-Initial Research." *Honors Program in Rome.* July 12, 2004, https://depts.washington.edu/hrome/Authors/amhitt/NecropolisoftheVatican/pub_barticle_view_printable.html.
19. Macintyre, Ben. *Operation Mincemeat: How a Dead Man and a Bizarre Plan Fooled the Nazis and Assured an Allied Victory.* New York: Broadway Books, 2011.
20. Washington, George. *The Papers of George Washington.* Revolutionary War Series, vol. 15. *May–June 1778*l, edited by Edward G. Lengel. Charlottesville: University of Virginia Press, 2006.
21. "April 21, 1861: USS Saratoga captures slave ship." *Civil War Talk.* April 21, 2011, https://civilwartalk.com/threads/april-21-1861-uss-saratoga-captures-slave-ship.23538/.
22. Caferro, William. *John Hawkwood: An English Mercenary in Fourteenth-Century Italy.* Baltimore: John Hopkins University Press, 2006.
23. Downham, Claire. "The Battle of Clontarf in Irish history and legend." *Features* No. 5. (Sept/Oct 2005) https://www.historyireland.com/medieval-history-pre-1500/the-battle-of-clontarf-in-irish-history-and-legend/.
24. History.com Staff. "Union issues conduct code for soldiers." *This Day in History.* November 13, 2009, http://www.history.com/this-day-in-history/union-issues-conduct-code-for-soldiers.
25. History.com Staff. "Andropov writes to U.S. student." *This Day in History.* November 24, 2009, http://www.history.com/this-day-in-history/andropov-writes-to-u-s-student
26. Historynet. "Tuskegee Airmen." http://www.historynet.com/tuskegee-airmen.
27. Kahn, David. *General Grant National Memorial Historical Resource Study.* National Park Service. (January 1980) https://www.nps.gov/gegr/learn/historyculture/index.htm
Marx, Arthur. *Life with Groucho.* New York: Popular Library Edition, 1960.
28. History.com Staff. "Mutiny on the HMS Bounty." *This Day in History.* February 9, 2010, http://www.history.com/this-day-in-history/mutiny-on-the-hms-bounty
29. "About Space Shuttle Discovery." *Smithsonian National Air and Space Museum.* https://airandspace.si.edu/explore-and-learn/topics/discovery/about.cfm.
30. Mantle, J. Gregory. *Beyond Humiliation: The Way of the Cross.* Minneapolis: Bethany House, 1975.
Szczepanski, Kallie. "Mahmud of Ghazni." *ThoughtCo.* July 3, 2019, http://asianhistory.about.com/od/afghanista1/p/Bio-Mahmud-of-Ghazni.htm.

May

1. "Lost Liners: Lusitania." *PBS online.* https://www.pbs.org/lostliners/lusitania.html
Simpson, Colin, *The Lusitania: Finally the Startling Truth about One of the Most Fateful of All Disasters of the Sea.* New York: Little Brown & Co., 1973.
3. Federer, William J. *America's God and Country Encyclopedia of Quotations.* Fairfax, VA: Amerisearch, 2000.
National Park Service. "June 28, 1787: Franklin's Proposal for Prayer." *Independence National Historical Park.* November 15, 2019, https://www.nps.gov/articles/constitutionalconvention-june28.htm.
4. Guttman, Jon. "Exocet Antiship Missile: The Flying Fish that Flummoxes Radar."*Historynet.* http://www.historynet.com/exocet-antiship-missile-the-flying-fish-that-flummoxes-radar.htm.
Dugdale-Pointon, T. "The Falklands War 1982." *History of War.* February 18, 2006, http://www.historyofwar.org/articles/wars_falklands.html.

5. Markley, Bill. "Leader of Destiny: Sitting Bull." *True West.* March 25, 2016, https://truewestmagazine.com/article/leader-of-destiny-sitting-bull/.
6. Keighley, Larry. "Greetings from Camden New Jersey." http://www.dvrbs.com/People/CamdenPeople-LarryKeighley.htm.
Nilsson, Jeff and William L. Worden. "A Captured General Goes Free." *The Saturday Evening Post.* September 2, 2015, https://www.saturdayeveningpost.com/2015/09/wwii-scene-from-the-japanese-surrender/.
7. Runyan, Timothy J. and Jan M. Copes, eds. *To Die Gallantly: The Battle of the Atlantic.* Boulder, CO: Westview Press,1994.
8. Glass, Tom. "Union Wives and Their Generals." *Military Images* 34, no. 2 (2016). https://militaryimages.atavist.com/union-generals-and-their-wives-spring-2016
"Military Spouse Appreciation Day." military.com.
9. "Colonel Blood and the Theft of the Crown Jewels." *English Monarchs.*(2004) http://www.englishmonarchs.co.uk/crown_jewels_2.htm.
Hassan, Jennifer. "Sweden's crown jewel heist isn't history's craziest. Ask the Brits about Colonel Blood." *The Washington Post,* August 1, 2018. https://www.washingtonpost.com/news/retropolis/wp/2018/08/01/swedens-crown-jewel-heist-isnt-historys-craziest-ask-the-brits-about-colonel-blood/.
10. Dupuy, R. Ernest and Trevor N. Dupuy. *The Compact History of the Civil War.* New York: MJF Books, 1960.
Federer, William J. *America's God and Country Encyclopedia of Quotations.* Fairfax, VA: Ameriseach, 2000.
11. Herodotus. *The Histories: Complete.* Robin Waterfield, et al. New York: Oxford University Press, 1998. Kindle.
Day, Thomas G. ed., *The United States Postal Service: An American History 1775–2006.* https://warlca.com/documents/postal%20history_pub100.pdf.
12. Stith, William. *The History of the First Discovery and Settlement of Virginia: Being an Essay Towards a General History of this Colony.* Williamsburg, VA: William Parks, 1747.
13. "John Clem." *American Battlefield Trust.* https://www.battlefields.org/learn/biographies/john-clem.
14. "10 Prophecies Fulfilled in 1948." Watchman Bible Study. http://watchmanbiblestudy.com/articles/1948PropheciesFulfilled.html.
"Creation of Israel, 1948." Office of the Historian. https://history.state.gov/milestones/1945-1952/creation-israel.
15. https://thisdayinusmilhist.wordpress.com/2014/05/15/may-15/.
"Sinking of USS *Guitarro.*" *Naval History and Heritage Command.* October 31, 2017, https://www.history.navy.mil/research/library/online-reading-room/title-list-alphabetically/s/sinking-of-the-uss-guitarro.html.
16. Feuer, Alan and Richard G. Jones. "Thousands Flee New Jersey Wildfire Ignited by Flare From F-16." *The New York Times,* May 16, 2007, https://www.nytimes.com/2007/05/16/nyregion/16fire.html.
Stevens, Citabria and others."New Jersey blaze 70 percent contained." *CNN.com,* May 17, 2007, http://www.cnn.com/2007/US/05/16/wildfires/index.html.
17. Federer, William J. *America's God and Country Encyclopedia of Quotations.* Muscle Shoals, AL: Fame Publishing Company Inc., 1996.
18. Benjamin, Thomas. *The Atlantic World: Europeans, Africans, Indians and Their Shared History, 1400–1900.* New York: Cambridge University Press, 2009.
19. Toro, Nestor A. "The Defeat of the Spanish Armada." *The Reformed Church God* https://rcg.org/youth/articles/1104-tdatsa.html.

History.com edictors. "Spanish Armada." *History.com.* September 6, 2019, https://www.history.com/topics/british-history/spanish-armada.

20. Karnow, Stanley. *Vietnam: A History*. New York: The Viking Press, 1983.
    Willbanks, James H. "Hamburger Hill." *Vietnam* 22, no.1 (2009): 22–31.
21. "Clara Barton." *American Battlefield Trust*. https://www.battlefields.org/learn/biographies/clara-barton.
22. Elton, G.R. *England under the Tudors*. London: Methuen, 1974.
    Haigh, Philip A. *The Military Campaigns of the Wars of the Roses*. Gloucestershire: Allan Sutton Publishing, 1995.
23. Taylor, Alan. "Remembering Dresden: 70 Years After the Fireboming." *The Atlantic*. February 12, 2015, https://www.theatlantic.com/photo/2015/02/remembering-dresden-70-years-after-the-firebombing/385445/.
    "German city partially evacuated after WWII bomb found." *Fox News*. May 23, 2018. http://www.foxnews.com/world/2018/05/23/german-city-partially-evacuated-after-wwii-bomb-found.html.
24. Doherty, Rosa. "Heinrich Himmler's daughter Gudrun Burwitz, unrepentant neo-Nazi, dies aged 88." *The JC Network*. June 29, 2018, https://www.thejc.com/news/world/daughter-nazi-heinrich-himmler-dies-gudrun-burwitz-1.466312.
25. Worden, Blair. *The English Civil Wars: 1640–1660*. London: Weidenfeld & Nicolson, 2009.
26. Henig, Ruth B. *The Origins of the First World War*. 3rd ed. New York: Routledge, 2002.
    Tuchman, Barbara W. *The Guns of August*. New York: Ballantine Books, 2009. Kindle.
27. Keegan, John. *The Second World War*. New York: Penguin, 1989.
    Murray, Williamson and Allan R. Millett. *A War to Be Won: Fighting the Second World War*. Cambridge: Harvard Press, 2000.
28. Blitz, Matt. "The Amazing Jim Thorpe." *Today I Found Out*. October 4, 2013, http://www.todayifoundout.com/index.php/2013/10/jim-thorpe-facts/.
29. The Great Courses. Narrated by Gregory S. Aldrete. *The Decisive Battles of World History*. 2013. Audiobooks.
30. National Aeronautics and Space Administration. "Mariner 9: NSSDCA/COSPAR ID: 1971-051A." NASA Space Science Data Coordinated Archive. https://nssdc.gsfc.nasa.gov/nmc/spacecraft/display.action?id=1971-051A .
31. Cross, Wilbur. *Zeppelins of World War I: The Dramatic Story of Germany's Lethal Airships*. St. Paul: Paragon House, 1956.

June

1. Plutarch. *Plutarch: Lives of the Noble Grecians and Romans*. Oxford, England: Benediction Classics, 2015. Kindle.
   Stokesbury, James L. *A Short History of World War II*. New York: Harper Collins, 1980.
2. "Act of June 2, 1924, . . . which authorized the Secretary of the Interior to issue certificates of citizenship to Indians." *National Archives*. https://www.archives.gov/historical-docs/todays-doc/?dod-date=602.
3. Willets, Gilson. *Inside History of the White House*. North Charleston, SC: CreateSpace Independent Publishing Platform, 2016.
4. CriticalPast. "President Coolidge and Secretary of the Navy Wilbur review a fleet underway." May 11, 2014. YouTube Video, 0:56. https://www.youtube.com/watch?v=cs3SPx-7rFc
5. Eames, Christopher. "Miracle in Six Days: The story of the amazing, documented miracles that led the small nation of Israel to victory 50 years ago." *The Trumpet*, May 24, 2017, https://www.thetrumpet.com/15858-miracles-in-six-days.

Lancaster, D. Thomas. "Miracles of the Six-Day War." *Messiah Magazine*, May 14, 2017, https://ffoz.org/discover/messiah-magazine/miracles-of-the-six-day-war.html.

6. Barbier, Mary. *D-day deception: Operation Fortitude and the Normandy invasion.* Westport, CT: Greenwood Publishing, 2007.
7. Shirer, William L. *The Rise and Fall of the Third Reich: A History of Nazi Germany.* New York: Simon and Shuster, 1960.
8. Thomas, Heather. "The Bones of Thomas Paine." *Library of Congress.* April 2, 2019, https://blogs.loc.gov/headlinesandhearoes/?s=the+bones+of+thomas+paine.
9. Hughes, Linsey. *Russia in the Age of Peter the Great.* New Haven: Yale University Press, 1998.
   Tucker, Spencer C., ed. *500 Great Military Leaders*. Santa Barbara, CA: *ABC-CLIO, LLC*, 2015.
10. "Tolstoy Undercover." *Tolstoy's Ghost Blog.* August 7, 2013,"https://tolstoysays.blogspot.com/2013/08/tolstoy-undercover.html.
11. Reese, Roger R. "Stalin Attacks the Red Army." *MHQ: The Quarterly Journal of Military History.* August, 2014.
12. Robinson, Peter. "Tear Down This Wall:" How Top Advisors Opposed Reagan's Challenge to Gorbachev – But Lost." *Prologue Magazine* 39, No. 2 (2007). https://www.archives.gov/publications/prologue/2007/summer/berlin.html.
13. Webley, Kayla. "TO THE RESCUE: Cher Ami the Pigeon." *Time.* March 21, 2011, http://content.time.com/time/specials/packages/article/0,28804,2059858_2059863_2060209,00.html.
14. "Fight Them on the Beaches, 4 June 1940." *International Churchill Society.* https?wwwinstonchurchill.org/resources/speeches/1940-the-finest-hour-flight-them-on-the-beaches/.
   Smith, Stewart. "Why the U.S. Flag Is Worn Backward on Army Uniforms: Troops have adopted the phrase "assaulting forward." *The Balance Careers*, December 8, 2018, https://www.theblanacecareers.com/why-is-the-u-s-flag-worn-backwards-on-army-uniforms-3357002.
   United States Army Regulation 670-1, *Wear and Appearance of Army Uniforms and Insignia*, paragraph 28-18.
15. Weinstein, Janet. "Berlin Airlift 'Candy Bomber' still dropping sweets from the sky after 70 years." ABCnews, July 25, 2018.
   Tunnell, Michael O. *Candy Bomber: The Story of the Berlin Airlift's "Chocolate Pilot."* Watertown, MA: Charlesbridge, 2010.
16. *The Peacemaker and the Court of Arbitration*. Vol. VIII. New York: Universal Peace Union, 1889.
17. Bennett, W. W. *The Great Revival in the Southern Armies*. Philadelphia: Claxton, Remsen & Haffelfinger, 1877.
18. Creasy, Edward Shepherd. *The Fifteen Decisive Battles of the World: From Marathon to Waterloo.* New York: Oxford University Press, 1915.
19. "Quotable Quote: Ronald Reagan." goodreads.com.
   "Holocaust Memorial Center Hosts 'The Ritchie Boys' Exhibit," *62 CBS News Detroit.* July 23, 2011, https://detroit.cbslocal.com/2011/07/23/holocaust-memorial-center-hosts-the-ritchie-boys-exhibit/.
   Hubred-Golden, Joni. "New Holocaust Center Exhibit Honors Word War II's Ritchie Boys." *Patch.* July 21, 2011, https://patch.com/michigan/farmington-mi/new-holocaust-center-exhibit-honors-world-war-iis-ritchie-boys.

20. McCormick, Jinny. "1898: Spanish at Guam Thought the Attacking USS Charleston Fired Salute Shots & Asked For Gunpowder To Return the Gesture." *War History Online*, June 22, 2016, https://www.warhistoryonline.com/history/uss-charleston-guam-salute.html.
21. Liddell Hart, Sir Basil Henry. *Strategy*. Auckland: Pickle Partners Publishing, 1991.
    Livy. *History of Rome*. Translated by Canon Roberts. Chicago: Acheron Press, 2012. Kindle.
22. Creasy, Sir Edward Shepherd. *The Fifteen Decisive Battles of the World: from Marathon to Waterloo*. New York: Humphrey Milford, 1915. Kindle.
23. Hull, Michael. "George Washington's One-Man Army." *Military History* 23, no. 5 (2006): 24–31.
24. Tucker, Spencer C., ed. *500 Great Military Leaders*. Santa Barbara, CA: ABC-CLIO, LLC, 2015.
    Wawro, Geoffrey. *The Austro-Prussian War: Austria's War with Prussia and Italy in 1866*. New York: Cambridge University Press, 1996.
25. Chief Rain-in-the-Face; Thomas, H. Kent. "The Little Big Horn." *Outdoor Life* 204, (Aug 1999).
    Regan, Geoffrey. *Great Military Blunders*. London: Andre Deutsch, 2012. Kindle.
26. Vinci, John., ed. "Caesar Rodney." *Colonial Hall. com.* http://colonialhall.com/rodney/rodney.php.
27. "Post-traumatic Stress Awareness." *American Psychological Association*. https://www.apa.org/topics/ptsd/ptsd-awareness.
28. Ferling, John. *Almost a Miracle: The American Victory in the War of Independence*. New York: Oxford University Press, 2007. Kindle.

July

1. Asbridge, Thomas. *The First Crusade A New History: The Roots of Conflict Between Christianity and Islam*. London: Oxford, 2004.
   Carey, Brian Todd and Joshua B. Allfree. *Warfare in the Medieval World*. Pen & Sword, 2006.
   Madden, Thomas F. *The Concise History of the Crusades*. Rowman & Littlefield, 2013.
2. History.com Staff. James A. Garfield. *History.com*. June 10, 2019, http://www.history.com/topics/us-presidents/james-a-garfield.
3. Diehl, William. *In Search of Faithfulness: Lessons from the Christian Community*. Oregon: Wipf and Stock, 2001.
   Mondello, Bob. "George M. Cohan, 'The Man Who Created Broadway,' Was An Anthem Machine." *National Public Radio*, December 20, 2018. https://www.npr.org/2018/12/20/677552863/george-m-cohan-the-man-who-created-broadway-american-anthem.
4. Xenophon. *Xenophon in Seven Volumes*, 1 and 2. Cambridge: Harvard University Press, 1971.
6. Shapley, Deborah. *Promise and Power: The Life and Times of Robert McNamara*. Boston: Little Brown & Co., 1993.
   Gregory, Hamilton. *McNamara's Folly: The Use of Low-IQ Troops in the Vietnam War plus the Induction of Unfit Men, Criminals, and Misfits*. Pennsylvania: Infinity, 2015.
7. Mashal, Mujib and Thomas Gibbons-Neff. "'Insider Attack' Kills U.S. Service Member in Afghanistan." *The New York Times*, July 7, 2018.
8. Rickover, Robert. "My Father Remembered." http://www.rickover.com/.

9. Brumwell, Stephen. *White Devil: A True Story of War, Savagery, and Vengeance in Colonial America*. Cambridge: Da Capo Press, 2004. Kindle.
Taylor, Alan. *American Colonies: The Settling of North America*. New York: Penguin Books, 2001).
10. "Marchand and the Race for Fashoda." *Military Sun Helmets.com*. http://www.militarysunhelmets.com/?s=marchand+and+the+race+for+fashoda.
12. Bruce, K.S. "Teddy Roosevelt, Jr.: The Toughest Old Man in WWII." *InsideHook*. July 12, 2017, https://www.insidehook.com/article/history/teddy-roosevelt-jr-toughest-old-man-wwii.
"Edward R. Murrow—See It Now—McCarthy (03-09-1954)." YouTube Video, 2:02. March 30, 2013. https://www.youtube.com/watch?v=OtCGlqA2rrk.
13. Hillenbrand, Laura. *Unbroken: A World War II Story of Survival, Resilience, and Redemption*. New York: Random House, 2010.
Interview with Louis Zamperini by Dr. Lois Ferm on May 16, 1976.
14. History.com Staff. "French revolutionaries storm Bastille." *This Day in History*. http://www.history.com/this-day-in-history/french-revolutionaries-storm-bastille.
15. Maurice, Frederick. "The First and Second Battles of the Marne: A Comparison." *Fortnightly Review* 105, No. 625 (1919).
Mombauer, Annika. "The Battle of the Marne: myths and reality of Germany's "fateful battle." *The Historian* 68 No. 4 (2006).
16. Temperton, James. " 'Now I am become Death, the destroyer of worlds'. The story of Oppenheimer's infamous quote." *Wired*. August 9, 2017, https://www.wired.co.uk/article/manhattan-project-robert-oppenheimer.
17. Badsey, Stephen. *Essential Histories: The Franco-Prussian War* 1870–1871. Oxford, England: Osprey Publishing, 2003.
German General Staff. *The Franco-German War*, 1870–71, *Vol.* 1: *First Part: History of the War to the Downfall of the Empire; From the Outbreak of Hostilities to the Battle of Gravelotte*. Translated by Francis Coningsby Hannam Clarke. London: Clowes & Sons, 1881.
18. Davis, William C. *Battle at Bull Run*. Baton Rouge: Louisiana State University Press, 1977.
"The Skirmish at Blackburn's Ford." *National Park Service*. April 10, 2015, https://www.nps.gov/mana/learn/historyculture/the-skirmish-at-blackburns-ford.htm.
19. "Mary Bickerdyke - A Civil War Hero." *Legends of America*. http://www.legendsofamerica.com/ah-marybickerdyke.html.
Ohio History Central. "Mary Ann Bickerdyke." *Ohio History Connection*. http://ohiohistorycentral.org/w/Mary_Ann_Bickerdyke.
20. Hasic, Albinko. "A Group of German Leaders Tried to Kill Hitler in 1944. Here's Why They Failed." *Time*. July 19, 2019, https://time.com/5629999/operation-valkyrie-july-plot/.
21. McQuaid, Elwood. *Come, Walk With Me: Poems, Devotionals, and Short Walks Among Pleasant People and Places*. New Jersey: The Friends of Israel Gospel Ministry, Inc., 1994.
Scott, Jeffery Warren and Mary Ann Jeffreys. "The Gallery—Fighters of Faith." *Christian History Magazine: Christianity & the Civil War* 33, 1992.
22. Arad, Yitzhak, Yisrael Gutman and Abraham Margaliot. Eds. *The Warsaw Ghetto:Journal Entries on the Eve of Deportation*. Jewish Virtual Library. https://www.jewishvirtuallibrary.org/the-eve-of-deportation-from-the-warsaw-ghetto.
Green, Emma. "The World Is Full of Holocaust Deniers." *The Atlantic*. May 14, 2014, https://www.theatlantic.com/international/archive/2014/05/the-world-is-full-of-holocaust-deniers/370870/.
23. "Constructing, Equipping and Armouring HMS Victory." nelsons-victory.com.

24. "Apollo 11 Mission Overview." *NASA*. https://www.nasa.gov/mission_pages/apollo/missions/apollo11.html.
Kremer, Ken. "Apollo 11 Splashdown 45 Years Ago on July 24, 1969 Concludes 1st Moon Landing Mission." *Universe Today*. July 24, 2014, https://www.universetoday.com/113428/apollo-11-splashdown-45-years-ago-on-july-24-1969-concludes-1st-moon-landing-mission-gallery/.
25. Adams, John A. Battle for Western Europe, Fall 1944: An Operational Assessment. Bloomington: Indiana University Press, 2010. eBook.
Lodieu, Didier. *Dying for Saint-Lô Hedgerow Hell, July 1944*. Philadelphia: Casemate Publishers, 2008.
26. Hopkins, William B. *The Pacific War: The Strategy, Politics, and Players That Won the War*. Minneapolis: Zenith Press, 2010.
Murray, Williamson and Allan R. Millett. *A War to Be Won: Fighting the Second World War*. Cambridge: Harvard Press, 2000.
27. Kawai, Kazuo. "Japan's Response to the Potsdam Declaration." *Pacific Historical Review* 19, no. 4 (1950): 409–14. http://www.jstor.org/stable/3635822.
28. Meyer, G.J. *A World Undone: The Story of the Great War 1914 to 1918*. New York: Bantam Dell, 2006.
29. Skylitzes, John. *Synopsis Historion*. Translated by Paul Stephenson. Cambridge: Cambridge Press, 2010.
Zlatarski, Vasil. *History of Bulgaria in the Middle Ages, Vol. I, Part 2*. Sofia, Bulgaria: Marin Drinov Academic Publishers, 1994.
30. Regan, Geoffrey. *Great Military Blunders: History's Worst Battlefield Decisions from Ancient Times to the Present Day*. London: Andre Deutsch, 1991. Kindle.
31. Rudlin, A. James. "The dark legacy of Henry Ford's anti-Semitism." *The Washington Post*. October 10, 2014, https://www.washingtonpost.com/national/religion/the-dark-legacy-of-henry-fords-anti-semitism-commentary/2014/10/10/c95b7df2-509d-11e4-877c-335b53ffe736_story.html.

August

1. Hopkins, William B. *The Pacific War: The Strategy, Politics, and Players That Won the War*. Minneapolis: Zenith Press, 2010.
Morrison, Samuel Eliot. *The Two Ocean War*. Canada: Little Brown and Company, 1963.
Murray, Williamson and Allan R. Millett. *A War to Be Won: Fighting the Second World War*. Cambridge: Harvard Press, 2000.
2. Gilbert, Martin. *The Somme: Heroism and Horror in the First World War*. New York: Henry Holt and Company, 2006. Kindle.
Plutarch. *Plutarch: Lives of the Noble Grecians and Romans*. Oxford, England: Benediction Classics, 2015. Kindle.
3. Tanner, J.R., C.W. Previte-Orton, and Z.N. Brooke, eds. *The Cambridge Medieval History: Contest of Empire and Papacy*, Vol. V. Cambridge: Cambridge University Press, 1926.
Strategy Page: The News as History. https://www.strategypage.com/default.aspx.
4. United States Holocaust Memorial Museum. https://www.ushmm.org/.
5. Cowan, Mary Morton. *Cyrus Field's Big Dream: The Daring Effort to Lay the First Transatlantic Telegraph Cable*. Pennsylvania: Calkins Creek, 2018.
McNamara, Robert. "Biography of Cyrus Field: Businessman Connected America and Europe" *ThoughtCo*. January 24, 2018, https://www.thoughtco.com/cyrus-field-1773794.
6. Gibson, John Winslow. *Judge Crater, the Missingest Person: How He Disappeared and Why They Couldn't Find Him*. Indianapolis: Dog Ear Publishing, 2010.

Tofel, Richard J. *Vanishing Point: The Disappearance of Judge Crater, and the New York He Left Behind*. Chicago: Ivan R. Dee, 2004.

7. Rosenberg, Jennifer. "The History of the Swastika." *About Education*. July 14, 2015, http://history1900s.about.com/cs/swastika/a/swastikahistory.htm.
8. Bakamson, Collin. "A Mother's Life Preserver." *The National WWII Museum New Orleans*. May 12, 2012, http://www.nww2m.com/2012/05/a-mothers-life-preserver/.
9. Carey, Brian Todd, Joshua B. Allfree and John Cairns. *Warfare in the Ancient World*. Barnsley, South Yorkshire: Pen and Sword Books, 2005.
10. Ferling, John. *Almost a Miracle: The American Victory in the War of Independence*. New York: Oxford University Press, 2007. Kindle.
    History.com Staff. "London learns of American independence." *This Day in History*. http://www.history.com/this-day-in-history/london-learns-of-american-independence.
11. History.com Staff. "Last U.S. ground combat unit departs South Vietnam." *This Day in History*. http://www.history.com/this-day-in-history/last-u-s-ground-combat-unit-departs-south-vietnam.
12. History.com Staff. "Russian sub sinks with 118 onboard." *This Day in History*. http://www.history.com/this-day-in-history/russian-sub-sinks-with-118-onboard.
13. Hess, Earl J. *In the Trenches at Petersburg: Field Fortifications and Confederate Defeat*. Chapel Hill, NC: University of North Carolina Press, 2009.
    History.com Staff. "Deep Bottom Run campaign begins." *This Day in History*. http://www.history.com/this-day-in-history/deep-bottom-run-campaign-begins.
14. Duffy, Michael. "The Battle of Lorraine, 1914." *firstworldwar.com* https://www.firstworldwar.com/battles/lorraine.htm.
    Tuchman, Barbara W. *The Guns of August*. New York: Ballantine Books, 2009. Kindle.
15. McCullough, David. *Truman*. New York: Simon & Schuster, 1992.
    National Archives. Harry S. Truman Library. http://www.trumanlibrary.gov.
16. FAASouza, "August 16 1812: Hull Surrenders Detroit." *1812now Blog*. https://1812now.blogspot.com/2012/08/august-16-1812-hull-surrenders-detroit.html.
    Hannings, Bud. *The War of 1812: A Complete Chronology with Biographies of 63 General Officers*. Jefferson, NC: McFarland & Co., 2012.
17. Murray, Williamson and Allan R. Millett. *A War to Be Won: Fighting the Second World War*. Cambridge: Harvard Press, 2000.
    Williams, Pat and Jim Denney. *Character Carved in Stone: The 12 Core Virtues of West Point That Build Leaders and Produce Success*. Grand Rapids: Revell, 2019.
18. Di Plano Carpini, Friar Giovanni. *The Story of the Mongols Whom We Call the Tartars*. Translated by Erik Hildinger. Boston: Branden Publishing, 1996. Kindle.
    Ratchnevsky, Paul. *Genghis Khan: His Life and Legacy*. Hoboken, NJ: Blackwell Publishing, 1991.
    Turnbull, Stephen. *Essential Histories: Genghis Khan & the Mongol Conquests 1190–1400*. Oxford: Osprey Publishing, 2003.
20. Quintin, Brandon. "The Little Army that Won Big." *HistoryNet*. Autumn, 2018, https://www.historynet.com/little-army-won-big.htm.
21. "Nat Turner." *Biography.com*. https://www.biography.com/activist/nat-turner.
    Woodworth, Steven E. *This Great Struggle: America's Civil War*. Maryland: Rowan & Littlefield, 2011.
22. Guthrie, W. P. "Naval Actions of the Thirty Years War." *The Mariner's Mirror* 87, no. 3 (2001): 262–280. Accessed January 12, 2016. DOI: 10.1080/00253359.2001.10656800
23. Kershaw, Robert. *War Without Garlands: Operation Barbarossa 1941–1942*. Surrey, England: Ian Allan, 2000.

24. Williams, Pat and Jim Denney. *Character Carved in Stone: The 12 Core Virtues of West Point That Build Leaders and Produce Success.* Grand Rapids: Revell, 2019.
"The Secret Payment." *PBS: American Experience.* https://www.pbs.org/wgbh/americanexperience/features/macarthur-secret-payment/
25. Morn, Frank. *The Eye That Never Sleeps: A History of the Pinkerton National Detective Agency.* Bloomington, IN: Indiana University Press, 1982.
Robinson, Charles M. *American Frontier Lawmen 1850–1930.* Oxford: Osprey Publishing, 2005.
26. Meyer, G.J. *A World Undone: The Story of the Great War 1914 to 1918.* New York: Bantam Dell, 2016. Kindle.
27. Finley, James P. *Buffalo Soldiers at Huachuca: The Battle of Ambos Nogales.* Fort Huachuca, AZ: Huachuca Museum Society, 2006.
Parra, Carlos Francisco. "Valientes Nogalenses: The 1918 Battle Between the U.S. and Mexico that Transformed Ambos Nogales." *Journal of Arizona History 51* (Spring 2010).
28. Brinkley, Douglas, "The Man Who Won the War for Us." *American Heritage* 51, no 3. (May/June 2000) https://www.americanheritage.com/man-who-won-war-us.
Herman, Arthur. *Freedom's Forge: How American Business Produced Victory in World War II.* New York: Random House, 2013.
29. Chamberlin, Ray. *Quotes and Quaint Stories of Great Americans.* New York: Larry Harrison, 1993.
30. "Allied Warships: Trout (SS-202)." *Uboat.net.* https://uboat.net/allies/warships/ship/2916.html.
Blair Jr., Clay. *Silent Victory: The U.S. Submarine War against Japan.* Annapolis: Naval Institute Press, 2001.

September

1. Grier, Peter. "The Death of Korean Air Lines Flight 007." *Air Force Magazine.* January 2013. http://www.airforcemag.com/MagazineArchive/Pages/2013/January%202013/0113korean.aspx.
2. Ho Chi Minh, *Selected Works* Vol. 3. Hanoi: Foreign Languages Publishing House, 1960–62.
3. Bennett, William J. and John T.E. Cribb. *The American Patriot's Almanac: Daily Readings on America.* Nashville: Thomas Nelson, 2010.
Glass, Andrew. "American flag flown in battle, Sept. 3, 1777." *Politico.* September 2, 2016. https://www.politico.com/story/2007/09/american-flag-flies-in-battle-sept-3-1777-005563.
4. "Geronimo Surrender Monument." *Atlas Obscura.* https://www.atlasobscura.com/places/geronimo-surrender-monument.
Stilwell, Blake. "This is why people yell 'Geronimo' when jumping from heights." *We Are the Mighty.* August 11, 2017, https://www.wearethemighty.com/articles/this-is-why-people-yell-geronimo-when-jumping-from-heights.
5. "Sam Houston Elected President of Lone Star Republic September 5." *Veteran Energy.* September 5, 2017, https://www.veteranenergy.us/blog/sam-houston-elected-president-lone-star-republic-september-5/.
6. Durkin, Jim. "Little Willie, the world's first tank, turns 100." *Daily Echo.* August 20, 2015, https://www.bournemouthecho.co.uk/news/13618044.little-willie-the-worlds-first-tank-turns-100/.
7. "Learning to Overlook the Flaws." Jentezen Franklin Media Ministries. April 21, 2015. https://www.jentezenfranklin.org/daily-devotions/learning-to-overlook-the-flaws.
8. Smith, Gordon. "United States Navy's Disaster at Point Honda 1923 from his scrapbook." Naval-History.net. Accessed March 18, 2016, https://www.naval-history.net/WW1z07Americas.htm.

10. Ambrose, Stephen E. *The Supreme Commander: The War Years of Dwight D.* Eisenhower. New York: Doubleday, 1970.
11. Dodge, Theodore Ayrault. *Gustavus Adolphus*. Seattle: Tales End Press, 2012. Kindle.
13. MacNaylor, Mitchell. "The Battle of Quebec: The Day France Lost North America." *Military History* 24, no. 6 (2007): 57–61. Accessed February 8, 2016.
14. National Park Service. "Theodore Roosevelt Inaugural National Historic Site." https://www.nps.gov/thri/september14.htm.
15. Orlean, Susan. *Rin Tin Tin: The Life and Legend*. New York: Simon & Schuster Publishing Co., 2012.
"The legend of Rin Tin Tin." *CBS News*. June 4, 2012. https://www.cbsnews.com/news/the-legend-of-rin-tin-tin/.
16. Johnson, Caleb. "Voyage of the *Mayflower*." *MayflowerHistory.com*. http://mayflowerhistory.com/.
17. Simpson, Brooks D. *America's Civil War*. Baldwin City, KS: Harlan Davidson, 1996.
18. Citino, Robert. "The Louisiana Maneuvers." *The National WWII Museum New Orleans*. July 11, 2017, https://www.nationalww2museum.org/war/articles/louisiana-maneuvers.
Gabel, Christopher (1991). *The U.S. Army GHQ Maneuvers of 1941* (PDF). Washington: United States Government Printing Office, 1991.
19. Cole, Rhea. "The Most Remarkable Survivor of The Civil War." *American Civil War Forum*. https://www.americancivilwarforum.com/the-most-remarkable-survivor-of-the-civil-war.-1351.html.
History Buff. "This Civil War vet walked around with a bullet in his face for 31 years." *We Are the Mighty*. March 24, 2016, https://www.wearethemighty.com/articles/this-civil-war-vet-walked-around-with-a-bullet-in-his-face-for-31-years.
20. Nicholson, Helen J. "Defending Jerusalem: Sybil of Jerusalem as a Military Leader." *Medieval Warfare* 9, no. 4 (2019).
21. Given, J. *The Fragmentary History of Priscus: Attila, the Huns and the Roman Empire, ad 430–476*. Merchantville, NJ: Evolution Publishing, 2014.
Tucker, Spencer C., ed. *500 Great Military Leaders*. Santa Barbara, CA: ABC-CLIO, LLC, 2015.
22. Smallwood, Karl. "The Ridiculous Way British Sailors Were Ordered to Stop German U-Boats During WWI." *Today I Found Out: Feed Your Brain*. January 19, 2019. http://www.todayifoundout.com/index.php/2019/01/the-ridiculous-way-british-sailors-were-ordered-to-stop-german-u-boats/.
23. Hickman, Kennedy. "American Revolution: Battle of Flamborough Head." *ThoughtCo*. January 28, 2020, https://www.thoughtco.com/american-revolution-battle-of-flamborough-head-2361166 .
Hiscocks, Richard. "The Battle of Flamborough Head – 23 September 1779." Morethan nelson.com. December 31, 2016, https://morethannelson.com/battle-flamborough-head-23-september-1779/.
24. "Glenn Miller's farewell before joining the US Army (24 Sept 1942)." Jamespower. YouTube video. May 27, 2011. Accessed September 7, 2020. https://www.youtube.com/watch?v=l8v5uRUqdoE.
"Mysteries & Secrets—Glenn Miller." *Skygaze.com*. Accessed September 8, 2020. https://www.skygaze.com/content/mysteries/GlennMiller.shtml
25. Brown, John S. Brig. Gen. "The United States Army in Somalia." *CMH*. Pub 70-81-1. https://history.army.mil/html/books/070/70-81-1/cmhPub_70-81-1.pdf.
26. Hoffman, David. "I Had A Funny Feeling in My Gut." *Washington Post*. February 10, 1999, https://www.washingtonpost.com/wp-srv/inatl/longterm/coldwar/soviet10.htm.
27. Hickman, Kennedy. "World War II: The Liberty Ship Program." ThoughtCo. July 21, 2019. https://www.thoughtco.com/the-liberty-ship-program-2361030.

Maritime Administration." SS Patrick Henry." *MARAD*. https://www.maritime.dot.gov/content/ss-patrick-henry.
28. Ferling, John. *Almost a Miracle: The American Victory in the War of Independence*. New York: Oxford University Press, 2007. Kindle.
29. Stokesbury, James L. *A Short History of World War II*. New York: Harper Collins, 1980.
30. "$1.96 OF $4,966 Boston Tea Party Debt Paid by Oregon County." *Desert Sun* 35, no. 65 (1961) https://cdnc.ucr.edu/?a=d&d=DS19611019.2.38&e=-------en--20--1--txt-txIN--------1.

October

1. Carey, Brian Todd, Joshua B. Allfree, and John Cairns. *Warfare in the Ancient World*. Barnsley, South Yorkshire: Pen and Sword Books, 2005.
   Plutarch. *Plutarch: Lives of the Noble Grecians and Romans*. Oxford, England: Benediction Classics, 2015. Kindle.
2. Jackson, Melanie. "Bagpipes: Weapons of War." January 5, 2015, http://www.melaniejackson.com/bagpipes-weapons-war/.
3. Glass, Andrew. "West Germany, East Germany Reunite." *Politico*. Oct. 3, 1990.
   Murray, Williamson and Allan R. Millett. *A War to Be Won: Fighting the Second World War*. Cambridge: Harvard Press, 2000.
4. Strachan, Hew. *The First World War*. New York: Penguin Books, 2013.
5. "Cuban MIG Lands at Air Force Base in Florida; Pilot Granted Asylum by U.S." *New York Times*, October 6, 1969.
   Urribarres, Ruben and Mike Little. "The Cuban MiGs." *The Latin American Aviation Historical Society*. April 15, 2018, https://www.laahs.com/the-cuban-migs/.
6. Glass, Andrew. "JFK urges Americans to build nuclear bomb shelters, Oct. 6, 1961." *Politico*. October 6, 2017, https://www.politico.com/story/2017/10/06/jfk-urges-americans-to-build-nuclear-bomb-shelters-oct-6-1961-243469.
7. "Prisoner Mutinies." *Memorial and Museum: Auschwitz-Birkenau Former German Nazi Concentration and Extermination Camp*. http://auschwitz.org/en/history/resistance/prisoner-mutinies.
8. "USS Midway: Fleet's Finest Carrier." *USS Midway Rockin' & Rollin.'* http://www.midwaysailor.com/midway1980/rocknroll.html.
9. Prisco, Jacopo. "SR-71 Blackbird: The Cold War spy pane that's still the world's fastest airplane." *CNN Style*. December 19, 2019.
10. Miller, T. Christian. "A History of the Purple Heart." NPR. September 8, 2010, http://www.npr.org/templates/story/story.php?storyId=129711544.
11. Farwell, Byron. *The Great Boer War*. South Yorkshire: Pen & Sword, 2009.
12. Harman, Troy D. "The Great Revival of 1863: The Effects Upon Lee's Army of Northern Virginia." *National Park Service*. http://npshistory.com/series/symposia/gettysburg_seminars/8/essay5.pdf.
    Jones, Reverend J. William. *Christ In The Camp: Religion in the Confederate Army*. Virginia: B.F. Johnson & Company, 1888.
    Shattuck, Gardiner H. "Revivals in the Camp." *Christianity Today*, April 2019. https://www.christianitytoday.com/history/issues/issue-33/revivals-in-camp.html.
    Wagner, Margaret E. and Gary W. Gallagher, eds. *The Library of Congress Civil War Desk Reference*. New York: Simon & Schuster, Inc. 2002.
13. History.com Editors. "Benito Mussolini." *A & E Television Networks*. March 5, 2020, https://www.history.com/topics/world-war-ii/benito-mussolini.
    Keegan, John. *The Second World War*. New York: Penguin, 1989.
    Lyons, Michael J. *World War II: A Short History*. 4th ed. New Jersey: Prentice Hall, 2004.

14. Carey, Brian Todd, Joshua B. Allfree, and John Cairns. *Warfare in the Medieval World*. Great Britain: Pen & Sword, 2006.
15. Bridge, Anthony. *Suleiman the Magnificent: Scourge of Heaven*. London: Thistle, 2015.
Davison, Derek. "Today in European History: The Siege of Vienna ends (1529)." *Foreign Exchanges*. October 15, 2019.
16. Bisson, Terry. "John Brown-150 Years After Harpers Ferry." *Monthly Review* 61, no.5 (2009): 37–39.
Bordewich, Fergus M. "Day of Reckoning." *Smithsonian* 40, no.7 (2009): 62–69.
Cavendish, Richard. "John Brown's raid on Harpers Ferry." *History Today* 59, no.10 (2009): 8.
17. National Constitution Center. "The Pardon of Jefferson Davis and the 14th Amendment." https://constitutioncenter.org/blog/the-pardon-of-jefferson-davis-and-the-14th-amendment.
Woodworth, Steven E. *This Great Struggle: America's Civil War*. Maryland: Rowman & Littlefield, Inc., 2011.
18. Space.com Staff. "The 10 Weirdest Facts About Venus." *Space.com*. June 4, 2012.
Howell, Elizabeth. Venera 13 and the Mission to Reach Venus. *Space.com*. March 25, 2019, https://www.space.com/search?searchTerm=venera+13.
19. Brew, Cowan. "Old Jube's Last Stand." *Civil War Quarterly*. Fall 2015.
20. Latson, Jennifer. "Walt Disney, Ronald Reagan and the Fear of Hollywood Communism." *Time*. October 20, 2014.
Storrs, Landon R. Y. "McCarthyism and the Second Red Scare." *Oxford Research Encyclopedia of American History*. July 2, 2015.
21. Johnson, Ben. "Admiral Lord Nelson." Historic.UK. https://www.historic-uk.com/HistoryUK/HistoryofEngland/Admiral-Lord-Nelson/.
"The Battle of Trafalgar." The Molossian Naval Academy. http://www.molossia.org/milacademy/trafalgar.html.
23. Michelson, Menachem. "Pinchas Tibor Rosenbaum." *Shalom: The European Jewish* Times. Fall 2004, http://www.shalom-magazine.com/Article.php?id=420311.
24. "Eisenhower Offers Support to Ngo Dinh Diem (1954)." *Alpha History*. https://alphahistory.com/vietnamwar/eisenhower-ngo-dinh-diem-1954/.
Vietnam: Economic and Development Strategy Handbook. USA: International Business Publications, 2008.
26. Military.com. "National Day of the Deployed." https://www.military.com/deployment/national-day-deployed.html.
27. Roosevelt, Theodore. *Theodore Roosevelt: An Autobiography*. New York. Macmillan, 1913.
28. Biography.com Editors. Abigail Adams Biography. *Biography*. http://www.biography.com/people/abigail-adams-9175670.
29. Glenn, John and Nick Taylor. *John Glenn: A Memoir*. New York: Bantam Books, 1999.
30. History.com Staff. "Orson Welles's "War of the Worlds" radio play is broadcast." *This Day in History*, October 30,1938, https://www.history.com/this-day-in-history/welles-scares-nation.
31. History.com Editors. "Stalin's body removed from Lenin's tomb." *This Day in History*. October 31, 1961, https://www.history.com/this-day-in-history/stalins-body-removed-from-lenins-tomb.

November

1. Simpson, Brooks D. *America's Civil War*. Illinois, Harlan Davidson, 1996.ac
2. MacDonald, Charles B. *The Battle of the Huertgen Forsest*. University of Pennsylvania Press, 2002.

3. From George Washington to Henry Laurens, 31 January 1778," *Founders Online*, National Archives, accessed September 29, 2019, https://founders.archives.gov/documents/Washington/03-13-02-0348.
4. "Iran Hostage Crisis." *The Cold War Museum*. http://www.coldwar.org/articles/70s/IranHostageCrisis.asp.
5. Robinson, Bruce. The Gunpowder Plot. *BBC*. March 29, 2011, http://www.bbc.co.uk/history/british/civil_war_revolution/gunpowder_robinson_01.shtml.
   Vance, Laurence M. *A Brief History of English Bible Translations*. Vance Publications, 1993.
6. Childress, Diana. *Barefoot Conquistador: Cabeza de Vaca and the Struggle for Native American Rights*. Twenty-First Century Books, 2008.
   "Learning From Cabeza De Vaca." *Texas Beyond History*. December 6, 2014. http://www.texasbeyondhistory.net/cabeza-cooking/encounters.html.
7. Stanton, Doug. *In Harm's Way: The Sinking of the USS Indianapolis and the Extraordinary Story of Its Survivors*. New York: Owl Books, 2003.
8. Schlenoff, Dan. "X-Rays at War, 1915." *Scientific American*. January 30, 2015. http://blogs.scientificamerican.com/anecdotes-from-the-archive/x-rays-at-war-1915/.
9. Gerwarth, Robert. *Hitler's Hangman: The Life of Heydrich*. New Haven: Yale University Press, 2011. Kindle.
   Keegan, John. *The Second World War*. New York: Penguin, 1989.
10. Glass, Andrew. "Bush addresses U.N. in aftermath of terrorist attack: Nov. 10, 2001." *Politico*. https://www.politico.com/story/2016/11/bush-addresses-un-in-aftermath-of-terrorist-attack-nov-10-2001-230946.
11. O'Reilly, Bill and Martin Dugard. *Killing Patton: The Strange Death of World War II's Most Audacious General*. New York: Henry Holt and Company, 2014.
    Tzu, Sun. *The Art of War*. Translated by Lionel Giles. Westminister,England: Musaicum Books. Kindle.
12. Ellis Island History. "Together We Tell the Story." *The Statue of Liberty" – Ellis Island Foundation, Inc.* https://www.libertyellisfoundation.org/ellis-island-history.
13. Sparks, Nancy J., ed. *Reader's Digest True Stories of World War II*. New York: Reader's Digest Accociation, 1980.
14. Guardia, Mike. *Hal Moore: A Soldier Once…And Always*. Oxford: Casemate, 2013.
15. "Zebulon Pike: Explorer." Colorado Virtual Library. https://www.coloradovirtuallibrary.org/digital-colorado/colorado-histories/beginnings/zebulon-pike-explorer/.
16. Goebbels, Joseph. "Die Juden sind schuld!" *Das eherne Herz* (Munich: Zentralverlag der NSDAP, 1943), 85–91.
17. Walton, Geri. "Louis XVI's Sibling: Louis XVIII of France." *Geri Walton Unique histories from the 18th and 19th centuries* Blog. September 16, 2016. https://www.geriwalton.com/louis-xvis-sibling-louis-xviii/.
18. Graves, Robert. *Good-Bye to All That*. New York: Anchor Books, 1957.
19. "Forgotten Weapons: The Nazis' Desperate Attempts to Curve a Bullet." *Popular Mechanics*, July 13, 2016.
    Mizokami, Kyle. "This Gun Can Do the Impossible: Shoot 'Around the Corner'." *The National Interest*. August 25, 2019, https://nationalinterest.org/blog/buzz/gun-can-do-impossible-shoot-around-corner-75976.
20. Mills, Nicolaus. What We Gained and Lost at the Nuremberg Trials. *Daily Beast*. April 13, 2017.
    Yad Vashem: The World Holocaust Remembrance Center. "The Nuremberg Trials." https://www.yadvashem.org/holocaust/about/end-of-war-aftermath/nuremberg-trials.html .

21. Abraham Lincoln Online. "Letter to Mrs. Bixby." http://www.abrahamlincolnonline.org/lincoln/speeches/bixby.htm.
American Gold Star Mothers Inc. "Our History Then and Now…" https://www.goldstarmoms.com/our-history.html.
Burlingame, Michael. "The Trouble with the Bixby Letter." *American Heritage* 50, no. 4 (1999).
22. Adams, Abigail. *Letters of Mrs. Adams, the Wife of John Adams. With an Introductory Memoir by Her Grandson Charles Francis Adams.* Boston: Charles C. Little and James Brown, 1840.
23. Guy, J. *Tudor England.* Oxford University Press, 1990.
Santiuste, David. *Edward IV and The Wars of the Roses.* Barnsley: Pen & Sword Books, 2010.
24. Paxton, James. *Joseph Brant and his world: 18th Century Mohawk Warrior and Statesmen.* Toronto: James Lormier & Company, 2008.
25. Fraunces Tavern Museum. *A Toast to Freedom: New York Celebrates Evacuation Day.* New York : Fraunces Tavern Museum, 1984.
26. Wells, Randy. "A Serviceman's Bible: Hope Found Through an Amazing Discovery." *The Baptist Voice.* Fall, 2015.
27. Defoe, Daniel. *The Storm: A Collection of the most Remarkable Casualties and Disasters which happened in the late Dreadful Tempest, both by Sea and Land.* London: Sawbridge, 1704.
Eddystone Lighthouse History. https://web.archive.org/web/20060502095435/http://www.eddystoneeel.com/LIGHTHOUSE%20HISTORY.htm.
28. Chen, C. Peter. "Enterprise." *World War II Database.* https://ww2db.com/ship_spec.php?ship_id=296.
"Enterprise VII (CV-6) 1938–1956." *Naval History and Heritage Command.* https://www.history.navy.mil/research/histories/ship-histories/danfs/e/enterprise-cv-6-vii.html.
29. Albrecht, Brian. "Ohio-bred Axis Sally's journey from Nazi propagandist to federal pen to Columbus convent." *The Plain Dealer.* May 22, 2011.
30. Trotter, William R. *Frozen Hell: The Russo-Finnish Winter War of 1939–40.* North Carolina: Alonguin Books, 1991.

December

1. Scientific Committee on Antarctic Research. "The Antarctic Treaty System." https://www.scar.org/policy/antarctic-treaty-system/.
Marshall, Jenna. "Nothing unusual about 'the long peace' since WWII." *BioFrontiers Institute.* February 27, 2018, https://www.colorado.edu/biofrontiers/2018/02/26/nothing-unusual-about-long-peace-wwii.
2. Foner, Eric and John A. Garraty. *The Reader's Companion to American History.* Houghton Mifflin Harcourt, 1991.
Office of the Historian. "Biographies of the Secretaries of State: James Monroe (1758–1831)." https://history.state.gov/departmenthistory/people/monroe-james.
3. History.com Editors. "Washington arrives at the banks of the Delaware." *History.* https://www.history.com/this-day-in-history/washington-arrives-at-the-banks-of-the-delaware.
4. Bowden, Mark. "The Legacy of Black Hawk Down." *Smithsonian Magazine*, January 2019.
5. Hemmings, Jay. "The Mysterious Disappearance of US Navy Flight 19." *War History Online.* May 3, 2019, https://www.warhistoryonline.com/history/mysterious-disappearance.html .
National Ocean Service. "What is the Bermuda Triangle?" https://oceanservice.noaa.gov/facts/bermudatri.html.
6. Gravett, Christopher. *Towton 1461.* Great Britain: Osprey, 2003.

7. Morison, Samuel Eliot. The Two-Ocean War: A Short History of the United States Navy in the Second World War. Naval Institute Press, 2007.
8. Guang, Sima., et al. *Comprehensive Mirror in Aid of Governance.* Beijing: Zhonghua Book Company, 2011 ed.
9. Davey, Kenneth C. "Sailors Dressed Like Soldiers." *U.S. 6th Naval Beach Battalion.* http://www.6thbeachbattalion.org/sailors-dressed.html.
"USS Normandy (CG 60)." *Unofficial US Navy Site.* Accessed September 8, 2020, https://www.navysite.de/cg/cg60.html.
10. Trotter, William R. *Frozen Hell: The Russo-Finnish Winter War of 1939–40.* Chapel Hill, NC: Alonguin Books, 1991.
11. Bloch, Michael. *The Duke of Windsor's War.* London; Weidenfeld & Nicolson, 1982.
12. Kaegi, Walter Emil. *Heraclius: Emperor of Byzantium.* Cambridge: Cambridge University Press.
13. Brugnara Y, Brönnimann S, Zamuriano M, Schild J, Rohr C, Segesser DM (2016) "December 1916: Deadly Wartime Weather." *Geographica Bernensia* G91. doi:10.4480/GB2016.G91.01 2003.
14. Carroll, Les. *The Angel of Marye's Heights: Sergeant Richard Kirkland's Extraordinary Deed at Fredericksburg.* Lexington, SC: Palmetto Bookworks, 1994.
15. Strachan, Hew. *The First World War.* New York: Penguin Books, 2013.
16. Glass, Andrew. Clinton Orders Airstrike on Iraq: Dec. 16, 1998." *Politico.* December 16, 2016, https://www.politico.com/story/2016/12/clinton-orders-airstrike-on-iraq-dec-16-1998-232571.
17. Reynolds, Michael. "Massacre At Malmédy During the Battle of the Bulge." *History.net.* June 12, 2006, http://www.historynet.com/massacre-at-malmedy-during-the-battle-of-the-bulge.htm.
18. Jackson, Warren R. *His Time in Hell: A Texas Marine in France.* New York: Presidio Press, 2001.
19. Miller Jr., John. *The War in the Pacific - Guadalcanal: The First Offensive.* Washington, D.C.: Center of Military History United States Army 1949.
20. Bando, Mark. *Vanguard of the Crusade: The 101st Airborne Division in World War II.* Bedford, PA: Aberjona Press, 2003.
21. Williamson, Porter W. *Gen. Patton's Principles for Life and Leadership.* Tucson: Management and Systems Consultants, 1988.
22. Trickey, Erick. "In the Darkest Days of World War II, Winston Churchill's Visit to the White House Brought Hope to Washington." *Smithsonian Magazine.* January 13, 2017, https://www.smithsonianmag.com/history/darkest-days-world-war-ii-winston-churchills-visit-white-house-brought-hope-washington-180961798/.
Wilson, James Mikel. *Churchill and Roosevelt: The Big Sleepover at the White House: Christmas 1941-New Year 1942.* Columbus: Gatekeeper Press, 2015.
23. Ferling, John. *Almost a Miracle:The American Victory in the War of Independence.* New York: Oxford University Press, 2007. Kindle.
24. Weintraub, Stanley. *Silent Night: The Story of the World War I Christmas Truce.* New York: Penguin, 2001.
25. Shirer, William L. *The Rise and Fall of the Third Reich: A History of Nazi Germany. New York.* Simon & Schuster, 1960.
26. Ambrose, Stephen E. Band of Brothers: E Company, 506th Regiment, 101st Airborne from Normandy to Hitler's Eagle's Nest. New York: Simon & Schuster, 2001.
Keegan, John. The Second World War. New York: Penguin, 1989.

27. "Apollo 8: Christmas at the Moon." *NASA*. December 23, 2019, http://www.nasa.gov/topics/history/features/apollo_8.html.
Howell, Elizabeth. "Apollo 8: First Around the Moon." *Space.com*. September 18, 2018, http://www.space.com/17362-apollo-8.html.
28. Seabee Museum and Memorial Park: Rhode Island. "Seabee History World War II." https://www.seabeesmuseum.com/seabee-history.
29. Keller, T.S. and A.M. Strauss. "Bone Loss and Human Adaptation to Lunar Gravity. "2nd Conference on Lunar Bases and Space Activities. April 5–7, 1998, http://adsabs.harvard.edu/full/1992lbsa.conf.569K.
Whalen, Robert T., Dennis R. Carter and Charles R. Steele. "Analysis of U.S. and Soviet Efforts to Maintain Muscle and Bone Mass with Exercise during Prolonged Bedrest and Spaceflight." Research Gate. (1989).
30. McDonald, Scott. "World War II Veteran Receives 50,000 Cards for His 96th Birthday." Newsweek. January 3, 2019, https://www.newsweek.com/world-war-ii-veteran-receives-50000-cards-his-96th-birthday-1277771.
Taylor, Eryn. "World War II veteran receives 50,000 cards to celebrate 96th birthday." *Channel 3 News*. https://wreg.com/2019/01/02/world-war-ii-veteran-receives-50000-cards-to-celebrate-96th-birthday/.
31. Bradford, Sarah. *Lucrezia Borgia: Life, Love, and Death in Renaissance Italy*. New York: Penguin Books, 2004.

Title Index

January

February

March

April

May

June

July

August

September

October

November

December

Scripture Index

Mark

Luke

John

Acts

Romans

1 Corinthians

2 Corinthians

Galatians

Ephesians

Philippians

Colossians

1 Thessalonians

2 Thessalonians

1 Timothy

2 Timothy

Titus

Hebrews

About the Author

Born on Marine Corps Air Station (MCAS) Cherry Point, North Carolina, on 21 February 1965, Randy has had a life that began with service to country. After his father's enlistment in 1967, the family eventually moved to Zanesville, Ohio, where he met his wife Denise and resided until he enlisted in the United States Air Force on 5 July 1983.

In 1997, the Air Force brought Randy and his family to Edwards Air Force Base, California, where they joined Lancaster Baptist Church and have been actively involved in its ministries since.

Randy retired from the Air Force as a Master Sergeant after having served honorably for twenty-five years. He serves as a deacon at Lancaster Baptist Church and has led the Navigators veterans and military adult Bible study class since July of 2000. He earned a Bachelor's degree in Military History from the American Military University and a Master's degree in History from Liberty University. Since 2014, he has taught in the History Department at West Coast Baptist College. He is a living historian who reenacts World War I and World War II events. His academic associations have included the Historical Studies Honor Society, the American Historical Association, the Society for Military History, the California Historical Group, and the Great War Historical Society.

Randy and his wife Denise have been married for thirty-six years and have two sons and three grandchildren.

BOOKS WE THINK YOU WILL LOVE . . .

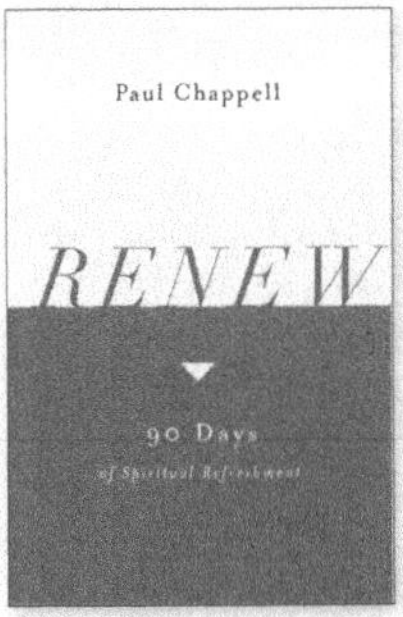

Renew by Paul Chappell

90 Days of Spiritual Refreshment

This ninety-day devotional guide will encourage you to seek God's face and renew your heart in His Word. Each devotion includes a Scripture passage and provides an encouraging or admonishing truth regarding your walk with the Lord.

Time Out for Parents by Paul Chappell

90 Days of Biblical Encouragement

The ninety devotions in this book are written to encourage parents to seek God's wisdom as they raise their children for Him. At the close of each devotion is a single actionable thought given as "Today's Parenting Principle."

Revival Today

by John Goetsch and Nathan Birt

365 Challenging Devotions from Revival History

Each devotion in this book is written to encourage you that revival is still possible today. Each daily reading describes an event or individual from the past that God has used to bring revival.

STRIVINGTOGETHER.COM

ALSO AVAILABLE AS EBOOKS